THE WEEKLY WAR

THE WEEKLY WAR

Newsmagazines and Vietnam

James Landers

University of Missouri Press   Columbia and London

Copyright © 2004 by
The Curators of the University of Missouri
University of Missouri Press, Columbia, Missouri 65201
Printed and bound in the United States of America
All rights reserved
5 4 3 2 1   08 07 06 05 04

Library of Congress Cataloging-in-Publication Data

Landers, James, 1947–
   The weekly war : newsmagazines and Vietnam / James Landers.
       p.   cm.
   Includes bibliographical references and index.
   ISBN 0-8262-1534-3 (alk. paper)
   1. Newsweek. 2. Time. 3. U.S. news & world report.
 4. Vietnamese Conflict, 1961–1975—Press coverage—United
States. 5. Press coverage—United States. I. Title.
   DS559.46.L36 2004
   070.4'499597043—dc22
                                                            2004004790

♾ This paper meets the requirements of the
American National Standard for Permanence of Paper
for Printed Library Materials, Z39.48, 1984.

Designer: Kristie Lee
Typesetter: Crane Composition, Inc.
Printer and binder: The Maple-Vail Book Manufacturing Group
Typefaces: Adobe Garamond and Britannic

Some of the material in chapter 5 first appeared in *American Journalism,* Summer 2002, under the title "Specter of Stalemate: Vietnam War Perspectives in *Newsweek, Time,* and *U.S. News & World Report,* 1965–1973," and is used by permission.

**To journalists who esteem news as a principle,
not a product**

Contents

Introduction 1

1. Cold War: Commitment and Competition 6

2. War Stories 50

3. Americans at War: Heroism and Horror 74

4. American Ways of War: Firepower and Futility 117

5. Determination, Doubt, Despair 157

6. The War at Home: Debate and Dissent 199

7. "Our" Vietnamese and the "Other" 225

8. Perspectives 271

Sources 279

Index 295

THE WEEKLY WAR

Introduction

The news media occupy a prominent place in the history of the Vietnam War. According to the lore of America's lost war, news coverage from Vietnam had a decisive impact on public opinion and national policy. Because journalists reported the war free from military censorship, they described death and destruction on the battlefield, expressed serious criticisms of military strategy and tactics, cited corruption and incompetence among the southern Vietnamese ally, and exposed terrible problems with discipline and morale among American troops. Although factors other than news coverage from Vietnam certainly weighed heavily on the public mind—most notably the American death toll and the indefinite length of the war—a perception has persisted that the cumulative effect of bad news so dismayed and discouraged Americans that it weakened their resolve to continue, which compelled a military withdrawal without victory. During the war, the news media incurred the resentment and wrath of presidents, policymakers, and the military for undermining a righteous cause. After the war, myth and misinformation distorted the actual amount of vividly descriptive and critical reports presented by the news media, particularly television.

Vietnam became "the living-room war" while Americans fought it. The phrase, from a 1966 *New Yorker* column by Michael J. Arlen, promptly entered the lexicon because it aptly associated television with combat imagery conveyed directly to American homes, an unprecedented phenomenon. Speculation immediately arose about the extent to which television imagery from Vietnam contributed to public disillusionment and eroded support. Network news programs indeed brought some terrible scenes into American homes, but postwar public memory erroneously remembered a nightly horror on the television screen when instead nightmarish visions were rare. Understandably, the combination of a popular phrase and a common misperception abetted an obsession with television coverage of the Vietnam War, thereby underrating the wartime role played by the other prominent source for national news, the weekly newsmagazines: *Newsweek, Time,* and *U.S. News & World Report.*

The national news system during the Vietnam War essentially consisted of three television networks and three weekly newsmagazines. News programs on ABC, CBS, and NBC attracted fifty-one million viewers on any given night, of whom about half watched at least three programs each week. *Newsweek, Time,* and *U.S. News & World Report* reached thirty-eight million readers a week, most of whom turned first to the national and international news sections. No other source of general news with national distribution came close to those numbers. Radio news programs attracted nine million listeners daily, and the national edition of the *New York Times* sold about eighty thousand copies of the Sunday edition outside its home metropolitan area. The Associated Press and United Press International funneled war news to the nation's 1,750 daily newspapers, which qualified both news services as national sources of information, but the placement and length of a story from AP or UPI varied tremendously from newspaper to newspaper because space fluctuated every day and local items often took priority over reports from Vietnam—for example, a story that ran for twenty paragraphs on the front page of the *Grand Rapids Press* could run six paragraphs on an inside page of the same day's *Baltimore Sun.* In terms of total recipients and national scope, the network television news programs and newsmagazines were the primary providers of information on the war.

Newsweek, Time, and *U.S. News & World Report* delivered information on the Vietnam War to millions of Americans from March 1965 through January 1973, the period of formal military intervention. Newsmagazine articles from Vietnam contained dramatic narratives of combat, interpretive judgments of events, and commentary on military methods, war policy, and the Vietnamese. The newsmagazines also reported the intense political debate on the war and the actions of antiwar protestors. By freely blending opinion with reportage, each newsmagazine conveyed a particular perspective on the war. At various points in the war, especially from early 1966 until mid-1967 and from late 1968 until early 1972, the newsmagazines offered contradictory assessments of military progress and the prospect for success in

Introduction

Vietnam. The specific effect of the newsmagazines on public discourse on the Vietnam War cannot be determined, but the prominence and purpose of *Newsweek, Time,* and *U.S. News & World Report* in the national news system of the era must be recognized.

Of course, the difference between television and the newsmagazines was significant in many ways. Producers of network news programs relied on film segments, and later video, that showed action or drama. However, the nature of the Vietnam War was such that camera crews spent most of their hours filming generic footage of troops getting on and off helicopters, artillery firing at unseen targets far away, warplanes dropping bombs in the distance, and infantrymen walking on patrol. Several scholars have established that few film segments on ABC, CBS, or NBC depicted actual combat or casualties, ranging from about 3 percent to 6 percent of all war segments shown, depending on how the scenes are categorized.[1] Despite their rarity, such scenes obviously made an impression on viewers and made for exciting footage in postwar documentaries, which fed the myth of television's impact on the public. Documentary programs on the Discovery Channel, History Channel, and Public Broadcasting System have created an impressionistic portrayal of the Vietnam War unlike the typical segments shown on network television news programs at the time. For their part, the newsmagazines occasionally published extremely graphic descriptions of death and injury on the battlefield, and the vivid details illustrated the horrors of war.

Television news programs also required words to accompany the images. With correspondents in Vietnam busy providing descriptive voice-overs to accompany generic footage, the nightly segments on the war often had newscasters simply relay information from the daily news summary provided by AP or UPI, which newspapers also published. Also, because news programs operated on a daily basis, the network producers emphasized immediacy rather than context. The idea that network news programs presented an adversarial viewpoint or otherwise consistently challenged government policy is not supported by the evidence. Scholars have established that war policy rarely was analyzed or criticized on ABC, CBS, or NBC.[2] Television relied on sights and sounds.

---

1. Lawrence W. Lichty, Daniel C. Hallin, William M. Hammond, and Clarence R. Wyatt have all examined or commented on the scarcity of graphic television coverage.
2. George Arthur Bailey, William M. Hammond, Chester J. Pach, Jr., and Michael Mandelbaum have determined that television provided little interpretive material.

Unlike the television networks, the newsmagazines worked on weekly deadlines. The lack of timeliness compelled *Newsweek, Time,* and *U.S. News & World Report* to emphasize a summary and synthesis of the previous week's events and to determine the significance of those events. Television and newspapers mostly offered episodic coverage of the Vietnam War. Newsmagazines provided analysis. None of the newsmagazines pretended to be objective, which was the buzzword for newspapers of the era. *Newsweek, Time,* and *U.S. News & World Report* practiced point-of-view journalism. Each publication aimed its ideology at like-minded readers. People who disliked a newsmagazine's attitude or tone had the option of choosing another, a factor that editors of newsmagazines fully realized. Precisely because public opinion about the war shifted as the years passed, the newsmagazines, too, especially *Time,* altered their tone.

The passage of years has not diminished the importance of examining the news media coverage of the Vietnam War. Government actions and public attitudes have since reflected the experiences of Vietnam. When the United States sent troops to Saudi Arabia to fight Iraq in the Persian Gulf War of 1990–1991, the Defense Department restricted access by journalists to troops and combat zones and imposed censorship, which a clear majority of Americans supported. Military escort officers, nicknamed "minders," accompanied journalists everywhere during the Gulf War, unlike in Vietnam where unaccompanied journalists hitched rides aboard helicopters and walked patrol with the troops. Military commanders for the Gulf War, many of them veterans of Vietnam, regarded the news media with suspicion and hostility, no doubt based on their memory of criticism and negative portrayals from twenty years before. Curiously, the military did an about-face during the Iraq war of 2003 when it reversed the policy of restricted access and direct supervision of journalists. Instead, the military "embedded" journalists with combat units. Modern technology permitted the transmission of news reports without interference by military overseers. Perhaps, at last, planners in the Pentagon realized the real lessons of military-media relationships during the Vietnam War: research has indicated that the news media remained generally uncritical toward military operations in Vietnam until autumn 1967, then adopted a more critical tone in the aftermath of the Tet 1968 offensive by the communists; also, news reports positively portrayed American troops until late 1969, when disclosure of the My Lai massacre led to more frequent reports of misconduct, drug abuse, and poor morale. The newsmagazines conformed to this pattern. In some important ways, though, they deviated from other news media: *Newsweek, Time,* and *U.S. News & World Report* had become critical and skeptical toward war policy by mid-1967, preceding by several months similar attitudes expressed on network news programs and on the editorial pages of most metropolitan newspapers.

This book examines the journalistic performance of *Newsweek, Time,* and *U.S. News & World Report* during the Vietnam War. To ascertain whether differences existed among the three newsmagazines in coverage of the war and to determine any shifts in editorial tone during the eight years of formal American military intervention, the examination included reading nearly nine hundred newsmagazine articles pertaining to warfare in Vietnam, war policy decisions, congressional debate, and dissent by antiwar activists. A review of numerous pertinent archives at the Lyndon Baines Johnson Library in Austin, Texas, and the Richard M. Nixon Presidential Materials Project in College Park, Maryland, documented the attention paid to the newsmagazines by presidential aides and policymakers, while memos and reports detailed attempts by the White House to influence their coverage. Lastly, interviews with newsmagazine correspondents and editors responsible for wartime coverage provided insight into the procedures and processes that shaped the articles seen by millions of Americans.

Newsweek, Time, and *U.S. News & World Report* created a niche in the media marketplace by supplying information that complemented and supplemented network television news programs and newspapers. Millions of Americans subscribed to these newsmagazines throughout the Vietnam era because they wanted more depth than television offered and more perspective than newspapers provided. The people who subscribed came from the upper tier of the population in education, income, and political involvement. They considered *Newsweek, Time,* and *U.S. News & World Report* worth reading. And presidents and their policymakers considered the newsmagazines worth monitoring and manipulating. The editors and correspondents of the newsmagazines were journalists, but they regarded themselves as observers whose job was to provide insight and perspective on the war, not to merely report what happened. The psychological ebb and flow of the American experience in Vietnam, from confidence to wariness to despair, appeared in the pages of *Newsweek, Time,* and *U.S. News & World Report.*

1

Cold War

Commitment and Competition

> Despite all its excruciating difficulties, the Vietnamese struggle is absolutely inescapable for the U.S. in the mid-60s—and in that sense, it is the right war in the right place at the right time.
> —*Time* commentary, May 14, 1965

> The War No One Wants—Or Can End
> —*Newsweek* headline, August 9, 1965

> What It Will Take to Win in Vietnam
> —*U.S. News & World Report* headline, September 6, 1965

They were all newsmagazines, but the news about the Vietnam War in *Newsweek, Time,* and *U.S. News & World Report* often differed in emphasis and tone. Ideology and economic competition in the media marketplace shaped the selection and presentation of war news. Differences in perspective emerged, sometimes slight but sometimes sharp, on the pages of the weekly newsmagazines. These differences matched the ideology of each newsmagazine and presumably appealed to the majority of each magazine's readers: *Time,* the largest newsmagazine, presented a mainstream conservative viewpoint; *Newsweek,* a distant second, presented a mainstream liberal outlook; *U.S. News & World Report,* with one-half the readership of *Time* and two-thirds that of *Newsweek,* manifested an ultraconservative attitude. Although

Cold War

conservatives, liberals, and ultraconservatives generally embraced the anticommunist doctrine of the era and endorsed the purpose of war in Vietnam, significant disagreement gradually developed over military methods and policy.

Newsmagazine articles published during the first years of formal military intervention starting in March 1965—whether an assessment of military progress in Vietnam, an evaluation of military strategy and tactics, an analysis of war policy, or an examination of the effects of dissent and antiwar demonstrations—tended to reflect the particular political alignments of *Newsweek, Time,* and *U.S. News & World Report* and to affirm the presumed preferences of their readers, which newsstand sales and subscription renewals either confirmed or refuted.[1] *Newsweek*'s liberal perspective appeared in articles that criticized the purpose of aerial bombardment of northern Vietnam, doubted the effectiveness of large-scale military operations in southern Vietnam, focused on the inability or unwillingness of the southern army to fight, and mentioned concern for civilians killed and wounded by artillery and warplanes long before the other newsmagazines paid attention. *Time*'s conservative perspective was on display in articles that expressed certainty in the ultimate triumph of American ideology, technology, and weaponry, urged public patience and determination for a long-term struggle, and treated with contempt or disdain prominent congressional critics of war policy and all antiwar activists. *U.S. News & World Report*'s ultraconservative perspective showed in articles that advocated rapid intensification of military operations in southern Vietnam and into Laos and Cambodia, argued for unrestricted bombardment of the north despite the risk of confrontation with China, repeatedly referred to dissatisfaction among military commanders with restraints imposed by the White House, and portrayed antiwar activists as unpatriotic and subversive.

Editorial differences among the newsmagazines extended beyond Vietnam. *Time*'s conservative slant favored Republicans and their political platform, promoted militant anticommunism, and preferred middlebrow and middle-

---

1. A market study commissioned by Time Inc. in February 1971 indicated that half of all subscribers agreed with *Time*'s presentation of the news, one-third neither agreed nor disagreed, and one-sixth disagreed (Lieberman Research Inc., "How *Time* Subscribers Feel about *Time* Magazine," courtesy of Time Inc. corporate archives). In "Content and Meaning: What's It All About?" Doris A. Graber concludes that journalists write for readers whose ideological and informational preferences are presumed.

class cultural tastes. *Time*, in fact, had become so closely identified with Republicans that it irritated some of its readers. A widely used history of magazines refers to the "solid conservative Republicanism" of Henry Luce, *Time*'s founder, and the bedrock conservative ideology of *U.S. News & World Report*. *Newsweek*'s liberalism lamented poverty and racism, considered lifestyle issues important to society, and paid attention to developments in movies, music, and television programs—a recognition that popular culture mattered to many of its readers, especially those in their twenties and thirties. *Newsweek* had made a sudden shift to a liberal position beginning after its purchase in 1961 by the *Washington Post*, itself a liberal newspaper; the purpose of the shift was to make *Newsweek* an alternative to *Time*. *U.S. News & World Report*'s ultraconservative mindset promoted policies favorable to business over labor, preferred to rely on comments from militant anticommunists in Congress and private organizations, and perceived communism as a monolithic adversary directed by the Soviet Union. Osborn Elliott, former *Newsweek* editor-in-chief, has described the editor-publisher of *U.S. News & World Report* as "highly conservative," and an authoritative book on magazine history describes its appeal to conservatives less affluent and less educated than *Time* readers.[2]

Readers of all three newsmagazines initially received optimistic appraisals of military progress. But almost a year after the first combat troops deployed to Vietnam, *U.S. News & World Report* began to seriously doubt the prospect for victory because it believed that restraints imposed by the White House had hampered military commanders, and *Newsweek* became critical and skeptical of military methods because progress on the battlefield seemed negligible. Not until summer 1967 did *Time* also decide that the war seemed destined for stalemate. Still, despite the span that elapsed until all three newsmagazines concurred that the war was not going well, the pessimism seen in *Newsweek*, *Time*, and *U.S. News & World Report* appeared months ahead of similar concerns published by major newspapers

---

2. Osborn Elliott, *The World of Oz*, 31; John Tebbel and Mary Ellen Zuckerman, *The Magazine in America, 1741–1990*, 171–74. For *Time* as a mainstream conservative periodical, see James L. Baughman, *Henry R. Luce and the Rise of the American News Media*, 173–74, 188–89, and W. A. Swanberg, *Luce and His Empire*, 384; for *Time*'s overt editorializing, see Herbert I. Schiller, *The Mind Managers*, 119–20. For *Newsweek*'s shift from politically moderate to liberal, see Elliott, *World of Oz*, 31–35, 89–91, and Katherine Graham, *Personal History*, 281–83, 386.

and heard on network television news programs, which became most pronounced during the Tet 1968 offensive by the communists. Antiwar activists and critics of war policy in Congress received harsh treatment in *Time* and *U.S. News & World Report* but more sympathetic portrayals in *Newsweek;* by the time of the national moratorium in late 1969, *Time* and *U.S. News & World Report* had eased up on the dissenters. However, throughout the entire war the newsmagazines depicted the Vietnamese ally and enemy in derogatory and stereotypical terms—the southern ally with contempt and condescension, the communist enemy with hateful descriptions. Articles in all three magazines portrayed the brutality, savagery, and horror of warfare. *Time,* more than the others, spared few details concerning the damage done to humans by artillery, bullets, and napalm. Despite the danger, hardship, and ultimate futility of the war in Vietnam, American combatants did their duty bravely and nobly, according to hundreds of newsmagazine articles. Negative imagery of American troops evading combat, using drugs, or mistreating Vietnamese civilians rarely appeared prior to the disclosure of the My Lai massacre in late 1969, and only occasionally afterward.

From March 1965 through January 1973 the three newsmagazines ran nearly nine hundred articles pertaining to military operations, war policy, the Vietnamese ally and enemy, congressional dissent, and antiwar demonstrations. *Newsweek* put the war on the cover of forty-one editions, and *Time* made it the cover story of thirty-eight editions. (*U.S. News & World Report* lacked a single-topic cover until summer 1972; instead, it ran a stack of headlines on its cover, which did not assign priority to any single event or issue.) Cover stories typically occupied eight to ten pages. When not a cover story, articles about the war usually occupied at least the equivalent of a full page of text in the standard format of three columns, or nearly a thousand words. The newsmagazines provided nearly constant, frequently dramatic, and occasionally graphic coverage of combat in Vietnam from summer 1965 until autumn 1969, the period when American casualties were heaviest and the commitment of troops in-country peaked at 540,000; five of every six editions carried articles on the war during this span. The last year of the war received much less attention from the newsmagazines, except for coverage associated with military activity, because editors sensed that the public had tired of the war and its consequences.

To provide almost continuous coverage from spring 1965 through summer

1971, by which time the withdrawal of American troops had reduced in-country personnel significantly, newsmagazine correspondents in Vietnam and Washington, D.C., cultivated and maintained sources within the military, among policymakers, and at the White House. Some articles pleased presidents and policymakers, but most articles displeased them. Memoranda and other material from presidential archives document efforts to influence and manipulate coverage by the newsmagazines. In addition, correspondents who reported from Vietnam dealt with the internal politics and pressures inherent in news organizations, and editors who handled the text in New York coped with the demands of space limitations and deadlines.

The newsmagazines did not compete directly against newspapers or network television news programs. Rather, they complemented or supplemented information that their readers obtained elsewhere. Newsmagazines had developed a niche by emphasizing the summary and synthesis of news, and had deliberately created an interpretive style to differentiate their journalism from newspapers. Articles blended traditional journalism—a report of an event or issue—with editorial commentary, a unique stylistic hybrid. Articles laden with descriptive details relied on so-called stance words—adjectives, adverbs, verbs—to impart judgment and evince tone: a "scruffy" antiwar demonstrator; a "rock-jawed" infantry commander; a "whining" congressional critic; a "sly" communist leader; an "indolent" villager; infantrymen "spoiling for a fight." Each magazine constructed point-of-view articles that indicated to readers the right and wrong of actions, decisions, and policies. "The newsmagazines compete with other news media partly by taking stands," concludes Herbert J. Gans, a sociologist who studied newsroom procedures at *Newsweek* and *Time* during the 1970s. Douglass Cater, a journalism scholar, observed in 1959 that newsmagazines "disguise [their] opinions with a synthetic news treatment" and "show no restraint in reshaping" information from correspondents "to suit certain preconceived and sometimes highly partisan notions." Cater lamented that "what comes out is often a deliberately doctored narrative, the more sinister because it is subtle." Peter Braestrup, a war correspondent who later analyzed news coverage of the Tet 1968 offensive, described newsmagazine journalism as follows: "The tendency of the writer and his editors, in the face of space limitations, was to avoid ambiguities and complexities, to fashion a clear story-line with a beginning, middle, and snappy close. Facts and 'color' were selected which supported the thesis in hand." George E. Christian, who was President Johnson's press secretary for three years, concurs: "They sniped a lot. They had their favored sources and their own agendas."³

Because newsmagazines had discarded all pretense to objectivity and separation of opinion from news, commentary came to be stated as fact. Frank Luther Mott, the dean of journalism historians, writes that *Time* had become a "journal of opinion" rather than a newsmagazine. A 1962 poll of two hundred news correspondents in Washington by the *Columbia Journalism Review* assigned *Time* the least credibility among the newsmagazines. The hybrid style of interpretive journalism practiced by *Newsweek, Time,* and *U.S. News & World Report* made it extremely difficult for proponents of the interpretive format to persuade newspaper editors to adopt it in response to the rise of television news. Most newspaper editors agreed in principle that interpretive journalism was a good idea, but they resisted the actual practice of it for a variety of reasons, not the least of which was the poor example set by the newsmagazines. Norman Isaacs, an editor of several major metropolitan newspapers of the era, warned other editors that the "opinionated style" of *Time* antagonized readers. Isaacs blamed newsmagazine journalism for tainting newspapers in a guilt-by-association in the public mind.⁴ The *Bulletin of the American Society of Newspaper Editors,* the official publication of ASNE, reflected the intense debate about perceptions of interpretive journalism throughout the 1960s and into the 1970s. The *Bulletin* contained numerous articles and summaries of panel discussions that expressed the reluctance of newspaper editors to adopt interpretive journalism.

Although many newspaper editors envied the freedom *Time* editors had to shape a directed summary of an event or issue, they were wary of the obvious selection of quotes and information to fit a preconceived theme. "The sad aspect of the situation is that the news [a] magazine purveyed to its mass audience should have developed more rather than less responsible standards

---

3. Herbert Gans, *Deciding What's News: A Study of CBS Evening News, NBC Nightly News, Newsweek and Time,* 197; Douglass Cater, *The Fourth Branch of Government,* 102–4; Peter Braestrup, *Big Story: How the American Press and Television Reported and Interpreted the Crisis of Tet 1968 in Vietnam and Washington,* 40; author interview with George E. Christian. For a discussion of the reliance on stance words to impart journalistic judgments, see Lisbeth Lipari, "Journalistic Authority: Textual Strategies of Legitimation."

4. Frank Luther Mott, *Sketches of Magazines, 1905–1930,* 308; Swanberg, *Luce and His Empire,* 444; Norman Isaacs, "The New Credibility Gap—Readers vs. the Press," 2. For a discussion of the construction of news with the intent to influence, see William A. Gamson, "News as Framing."

of journalism," commented Cater in *The Fourth Branch of Government*. The newsmagazines' use of complimentary or pejorative adjectives, adverbs, and nouns to describe newsmakers and the abundance of quotes from anonymous or unidentified sources who neatly criticized or praised the people or policies being reported on violated the standards of objective reporting that most newspaper editors believed they practiced. Interpretive journalism also failed to find a home on network television news programs. Time constraints and a need for visual scenes worked against the inclusion of analysis and perspective on ABC, CBS, and NBC. "The network anchormen, in their daily summaries of the war, read short stories of events without much interpretation, certainly without challenging, adversary interpretation," concluded George Arthur Bailey, a media scholar.[5]

Despite the reluctance of other news media to accept interpretive journalism, the newsmagazines found their approach popular with many Americans. A marketing study commissioned by *Time* in 1971 determined that most of its readers recognized the point-of-view journalism in the magazine: 58 percent perceived that "*Time* takes a position on controversial issues," while 35 percent believed it covered issues "neutrally." Because the Vietnam War years encompassed a newsy era of cultural transformation, political conflict, racial unrest, and social turmoil, all three newsmagazines attracted hundreds of thousands of new subscribers—approximately seven of every eight newsmagazine copies sold were to subscribers. Also, the national population increased steadily as the first baby boomers became adults by the late 1960s and the formation of new households accelerated, rising by 21 percent during the 1965–1973 period. The newsmagazines gained circulation rapidly. Newsstand sales and subscriptions totaled an aggregate 6,420,000 copies weekly in 1965 and 9,460,000 copies weekly in 1973, a net gain of 47 percent.[6]

Newsweek, which targeted a younger readership with coverage of cultural and social issues, experienced the greatest percentage growth, from 1.8 million copies weekly in 1965 to 2.9 million copies weekly in 1973, a 61 percent difference. *Time* distributed 3.2 million copies a week in 1965 and 4.6

---

5. Cater, *Fourth Branch*, 104; George Arthur Bailey, "Interpretive Reporting of the Vietnam War by Anchormen."

6. Lieberman Research, "How *Time* Subscribers Feel about *Time* Magazine"; Association of National Advertisers, *Magazine Circulation and Rate Trends, 1940–1974*; U.S. Bureau of the Census and *Statistical Abstract of the United States* data for relevant years. *Newsweek* did not respond to requests for archival material and subscription data.

million copies a week in 1973, a 44 percent difference. *U.S. News & World Report* sold 1.4 million copies each week in 1965 and 2 million each week in 1973, a 43 percent difference.[7] Obviously, the newsmagazines fulfilled an informational need for millions of Americans, including many younger adults of the era. (For historical perspective, twenty-five years later *Time* had a circulation of 4.1 million copies, which was a half-million copies less; *Newsweek* had 3.2 million, which was an increase of one-tenth; and *U.S. News & World Report* had 2 million, which was the same—although the national population had increased by nearly half from 1973 to 1998. Put another way, together the newsmagazines had reached an average of almost one-sixth of the nation's households during the Vietnam War while reaching only one-ninth of households twenty-five years later.)

The period of peak circulation growth for *Newsweek* during the war years occurred from 1966 through 1969 when the amount of copies printed each week increased consecutively each year by 119,000 (6.5 percent), 160,000 (8 percent), 179,000 (9 percent), and 220,000 (10 percent); circulation increases for other war years ranged from 4 to 6 percent. Similar data for *Time*'s peak years, also from 1966 through 1969, were 187,000 (6 percent), 241,000 (7 percent), 224,000 (6.5 percent), and 216,000 (5.5 percent); increases in other war years varied from 3 to 4 percent. *U.S. News & World Report* experienced exceptional growth in 1966 and 1968 when it added 87,000 copies (6 percent) and 118,000 copies (8 percent), respectively; other war years showed gains of 2 to 5 percent.[8] Certainly, the occurrence of major news events not connected to the war and the seemingly swift changes in culture and society abetted the surge in newsmagazine circulation.

More readers meant more advertising. Newsmagazines thrived economically during the Vietnam era. The number of pages in weekly editions moved upward, although each magazine allocated a different proportion of pages for news and ads. *Newsweek* typically gave news pages 45 percent to 55 percent of the total, *Time* gave the news 40 percent to 50 percent of total space, and *U.S. News & World Report* often gave the news 60 percent of total pages. In terms of actual page growth, *Newsweek* led the three newsmagazines with an average edition of 92 pages in 1965 and 102 pages in 1973; the ten-page increase usually allowed editors to fill four or five more pages with news each

---

7. Association of National Advertisers, *Magazine Circulation and Rate Trends, 1940–1974*.
8. Ibid.

week. *Time* began the period with an average edition of 96 pages and ended with 104 pages; this brought readers four additional pages of news. *U.S. News & World Report* had average editions of 86 pages and 94 pages, respectively; its news expanded by six pages weekly. The newsmagazines lived up to their designation from 1965 to 1973—news was the dominant content, with so-called "soft" news given little space: of *Newsweek*'s average of fifty-two news pages each week, only eleven pages went to articles on art, celebrities, movies, music, sports, and lifestyles; of *Time*'s forty-eight pages of news, about fourteen went to similar items; of *U.S. News & World Report*'s average of fifty-four pages for news, none went to soft news, unless it involved some legal or moral controversy regarding movies, music, or television.

The newsmagazines spent much of the additional dollars from advertisers on new technology to further appeal to readers and to become more efficient. Color photographs and ink brightened considerably more pages in the 1970s. Cover-story articles regularly filled lengthy sections with colorful pictures, while color ribbons of type, known as banners, adorned the first pages of numerous departments. What readers did not notice were improvements to systems for transmitting copy from numerous bureaus in the United States, Europe, and Asia. *Time* established its own telex system, operational during the Vietnam War, which allowed instantaneous communication between the newsroom in New York City and the domestic and international bureaus. *Newsweek* leased transmission rights on the Reuters News Service telex system, which connected international bureaus to New York City via relay stations in London and Tokyo. *U.S. News & World Report* paid a fee for an international telex system until the late 1960s when it arranged a direct line from Vietnam to its Washington newsroom. The telex represented a tremendous time-saving benefit over the combination courier-and-teletype system used by newsmagazine correspondents during the Korean War, a method that often took two days to deliver files to stateside newsrooms. The telex not only sped the delivery of files from correspondents but enabled correspondents to see edited versions of articles prior to publication, which helped eliminate some inaccurate information.[9]

The readership of *Newsweek, Time,* and *U.S. News & World Report* during

---

9. Descriptions of the copy filing process are from author interviews with Nicholas Horrock, former *Newsweek* correspondent; Burton Y. Pines and Rudolph Rauch III, former *Time* correspondents; and Stanley W. Cloud, former *Time* bureau chief.

the Vietnam War was affluent and educated: 44 percent had graduated college or university, compared to 10 percent of the general population; another 24 percent had attended college or university, compared to 13 percent of the general population. Other data placed the percentage of college-educated newsmagazine readers at 54 percent, with college-educated network news watchers at 28 percent; in terms of income, 56 percent of newsmagazine readers ranked in the upper-fifth category, compared to 32 percent of the network news audience. Newsmagazine readers included the nation's business and political leaders during the Vietnam era, according to a study by the Columbia University Bureau of Applied Social Research. Among corporate executives, the three newsmagazines placed in the top five periodicals most frequently read, along with *Business Week* and *Fortune;* among members of Congress, the newsmagazines went to two-thirds of the senators and representatives surveyed; among media executives, *Newsweek* and *Time* ranked first and third, respectively, with the *New York Times Magazine* second. Newsmagazines performed a valuable function within the news media, especially for editors of small and medium-sized newspapers in rural areas of the country. William J. Cook, a former *Newsweek* correspondent in Vietnam with newspaper experience in the Pacific Northwest, recalls that few editors subscribed to the *New York Times* during the early 1960s but almost every editor he knew read either *Newsweek* or *Time* each week. "Lots of newspaper editors read the newsmagazines for political guidance," says Cook. "Say you're sitting there in a newsroom in Salem, Oregon, and all you have is the AP or United Press copy to go on. The newsmagazines gave you so much more background and insight."[10]

Newsmagazines mattered to presidents and policymakers, too. White House aides monitored newsmagazine coverage, marking or summarizing articles for presidential attention and a possible response relayed through an aide or advisor. Articles from *Newsweek, Time,* and *U.S. News & World Report* warranted rebuttals—and, rarely, praise. Documents at the Lyndon Baines Johnson Library show that the president personally directed responses to occasional articles and sometimes met with a correspondent to influence coverage.

10. Carol H. Weiss, "What America's Leaders Read"; author interview with William J. Cook. Readership education and income data are from Lieberman Research, "A Study of Consumer Attitudes toward *Time* Magazine and Other News Media," February 1971 (courtesy of Time Inc. corporate archives); John P. Robinson, "World Affairs Information and Mass Media Exposure"; and Gans, *Deciding What's News.*

Johnson and his aides also communicated directly with the newsmagazines' top editors and D.C. bureau chiefs by telephone, mail, or a summons to the White House. Documents from the Richard M. Nixon Presidential Materials Project note that the presidential news summaries included newsmagazine articles and that chief of staff H. R. Haldeman instructed others to respond to coverage.[11]

Newsmagazine correspondents had priority access to policymakers, especially during the Johnson administration. "Newsmagazines were great in a way," says Stanley W. Cloud, former *Time* bureau chief in Saigon. "They guaranteed access to sources." Correspondents also met with people in power in other nations, a privilege accorded them because of the newsmagazines' international distribution to the economic and political elite. "There was no better way to learn about a country than to be a *Time* correspondent," says Burton Y. Pines, who reported from Germany and Vietnam. "We were treated with phenomenal deference wherever we went." Such perquisites attracted journalists of a higher caliber than worked at newspapers of the era. A national study of journalists conducted during 1971 found that 89 percent of newsmagazine correspondents had college degrees, compared to 63 percent of newspaper reporters. Of the newsmagazine correspondents with college degrees, 40 percent had graduated from upper-tier universities and one-third had a master's degree. *Newsweek, Time,* and *U.S. News & World Report* offered better money, too. "They paid well," Cloud says. Newsmagazine correspondents of the era typically earned $15,000 to $20,000 a year (equivalent to $90,000 to $120,000 in 2003), which was about twice the salary of Associated Press reporters and one-fourth higher than reporters for metropolitan newspapers.[12]

Domestically, newsmagazines ranked in importance with network news programs, the *New York Times,* and the *Washington Post* among policymakers and politicians, including President Johnson. Capital reporters considered the newsmagazines part of the "inner ring" of news organizations because of

---

11. Christian interview; author interview with George Reedy, former presidential press secretary; author interview with Walt W. Rostow, former national security advisor.

12. Cloud and Pines interviews; 1971 study cited in David H. Weaver and G. Cleveland Wilhoit, *The American Journalist in the 1990s: U.S. News People at the End of an Era,* 35; Stephen Hess, *The Washington Reporters,* 45, 116–17 (Hess identifies "upper-tier" as Ivy League and a select group of major state universities); John Hohenberg, *Between Two Worlds: Policy, Press, and Public Opinion in Asian-American Relations,* 42–43.

their nationwide distribution and influential readership, which attached to them, Johnson believed, the status of "opinion makers." George Reedy, who was Johnson's press secretary, believes newsmagazines appealed to a certain type of person: "Television went for the gut, the newsweeklies went for the mind. They were for people who thought about things, intellectuals of a sort."[13]

Perhaps few newsmagazine readers qualified as intellectuals, but many were information seekers whose opinions carried weight, particularly in smaller communities—precisely the places where international news received scant space in newspapers in the decade prior to the Vietnam War. "*Time* was most important to a subset of Americans living in smaller cities and towns without access to larger metropolitan dailies with more ambitious news agendas," states James L. Baughman, a historian who examined editorial policies and practices at Time-Life, Inc. "[*Time*] readers often served as 'opinion leaders' of those within their social strata who lacked the time or energy to follow national and world events." Baughman identifies readers of Luce publications as residing usually in smaller cities and towns, but the newsmagazines also appealed to residents of metropolitan areas. The number of copies distributed in the nation's twelve largest cities during the Vietnam era was favorably disproportionate to the population: approximately 39 percent of total newsmagazine circulation went to the dozen cities that had 29 percent of the national population. Evidently, people in places like Boston, Chicago, Los Angeles, New York City, and Philadelphia wanted information from the newsmagazines as much as readers in Dayton, Portland, and Topeka. A study commissioned by the Time-Life corporation in the early 1970s indicated that *Time* readers subscribed because the magazine gave them essential information about international and national events and issues. The favorite sections of the magazine were the national and world sections.[14]

13. President Johnson: Melvin Small, *Covering Dissent: The Media and the Anti–Vietnam War Movement,* 28; "inner ring": Hess, *Washington Reporters,* 24; "opinion makers": George Christian, *The President Steps Down: A Personal Memoir of the Transfer of Power,* 186; Reedy interview.

14. Baughman, *Henry R. Luce,* 170–71; Audit Bureau of Circulations data, 1965–1971; Lieberman Research, "A Study of Consumer Attitudes toward *Time* Magazine and Other News Media," July 1973 (courtesy of Time Inc. corporate archives). Bernard C. Cohen, *The Press and Foreign Policy,* cites a 1960 study of international news published in the *Milwaukee Journal, Chicago Tribune, New York Times,* and two daily newspapers in Madison, Wisconsin.

Commitment

Time's stalwart declaration for "the right war in the right place at the right time" appeared two months after American combat troops deployed to Danang. Its ardent endorsement pleased the White House. "You should know that Time Magazine is in thorough accord with your current foreign policy . . . in Viet Nam," an aide informed President Johnson. A *Time* article several months later told readers why southern Vietnam must be saved: "Were Hanoi to conquer the South and unify it under a Communist regime, Cambodia and Laos would tumble immediately." *Time* not only proclaimed support for an anticommunist crusade in Vietnam, it had also expressed basic Cold War tenets: specifically that a communist superpower, the People's Republic of China, dictated policy for a minor communist nation, the Democratic Republic of Vietnam, and that a communist triumph in southern Vietnam would result in eventual subversion of adjacent nations, also known as the "domino theory." The strategic significance of Southeast Asia, not just southern Vietnam, persuaded three successive administrations from 1954 to 1965 that the United States must actively support anticommunist governments in Saigon. American military equipment, much of it surplus materiel, went to the Republic of Vietnam, and military personnel trained the southern army.[15]

The newsmagazines uncritically presented anticommunist ideology as the guiding principle of American foreign policy from the beginning of the Cold War era in the late 1940s through the early years of military intervention in Vietnam. *Time, Newsweek,* and *U.S. News & World Report* conformed to the pattern seen on network television news programs and in most newspapers. The national news media reflected a consensus among policymakers and politicians during the Cold War that accepted a pragmatic approach for coping with the threat of communism. Noncommunist governments, whether they were autocratic or democratic or despotic, automatically received eco-

---

Hohenberg, *Between Two Worlds,* examines international news coverage in six metropolitan daily newspapers during summer 1964. Both authors determined that metropolitan newspapers generally and nonmetropolitan newspapers particularly provided an insignificant amount of international news to readers.

15. Jack Valenti to President Johnson, memo, May 12, 1965, *Time* name file, box 131, White House central files, Lyndon Baines Johnson Library; "The Guardians at the Gate," *Time,* January 7, 1966, p. 13; Russell H. Fifield, *Americans in Southeast Asia: The Roots of Commitment,* 251–56.

nomic aid and military equipment if they promoted the policy interests of the United States. Although pragmatism occasionally caused moral qualms about aligning the United States with repressive regimes, the consensus held. "The world view of the Cold War dominated American thinking about international affairs so totally during these years that it became not merely dangerous but virtually impossible for most Americans to question or to step outside it," writes Daniel C. Hallin, a political scientist. "Journalists were no exception."[16]

Formation of Cold War policy from the late 1940s to the mid-1950s occurred during an almost continuous stretch of civil wars, rebellions, and revolutions in Europe and Asia initiated by communists and/or nationalists. When a noncommunist government survived, usually with American materiel and money, or when noncommunists ascended to power, the United States often arranged a formal military alliance pledging an American response to an internal or external enemy. A series of military alliances erected a security barrier to block communism. Cold War policy relied on this containment strategy. Although containment intended originally to stop the spread of communism in Europe, it soon extended to Asia. The United States fought a war in Korea from June 1950 to July 1953 to thwart a communist invasion, which the Soviet Union supplied and which China later reinforced with hundreds of thousands of soldiers. Then ensued military alliances with Japan, the Philippines, Taiwan, and Thailand. A doctrinaire anticommunist ideology evolved. With few exceptions during the first twenty years of the Cold War, American policymakers regarded nationalist activities in colonial territories and opposition to noncommunist governments, whether authoritarian or democratic, as the work of communist agents or sympathizers rather than reflections of genuine indigenous political protest.[17]

American policymakers and politicians functioned within a Cold War consensus, which the news media reinforced. The development of these viewpoints in government, the news media, and American society during the early Cold War era resulted from cultural influences and historical factors, including American exceptionalism, expansionist ideology, Eurocentric values,

---

16. Schiller, *Mind Managers*, 119–20; Daniel C. Hallin, *The "Uncensored War": The Media and Vietnam*, 49–50.

17. Allen J. Levine, *The United States and the Struggle for Southeast Asia, 1945–1975*, 81; Henry J. Kenny, *The American Role in Vietnam and East Asia: Between Two Revolutions*, 9–15; William Appleman Williams, *The Tragedy of American Diplomacy*, 198.

racial attitudes, modernity theory, and democratic idealism. The notion that the American Way was superior to every other way had permeated academe, government, media, and society. Journalists dutifully reported a simplistic version of complicated cultural, economic, and social turmoil in Europe and Asia by often identifying communism as the root cause of conflict. To monthly magazines, weekly newsmagazines, daily newspapers, and nightly news programs, civil strife in most other nations became a battle with the Red menace of communism. Herbert J. Gans writes: "Civil wars with Communist participation have rarely been called civil wars either by public officials or journalists. Most often, they have been seen as instances in the Cold War." Alternative opinions that might have questioned such portrayals seldom reached consumers of mainstream news media. Journalists relied almost exclusively on government sources of information and on scholars or specialists who agreed with national policy. Dissenting opinions rarely appeared in print. *Time* certainly fit this mold. According to one of Luce's biographers, the magazine insisted "that Communism was a monolithic world conspiracy, and that Communism anywhere was therefore an enemy." The Cold War consensus also embraced the idea that other countries should emulate the obviously superior American Way, which involved capitalism, democracy, and individualism. *Newsweek, Time,* and *U.S. News & World Report* informed readers that reluctance or refusal by noncommunist governments to adopt American principles indefinitely delayed, or doomed, victory over communism.[18]

After the end of World War II concern about communism initially centered on Europe. Soon enough, however, attention switched to Asia. "Now the Pacific has become an Anglo-Saxon lake," Gen. Douglas MacArthur told the *New York Times* in March 1949. The general's remark, and its racial connotation, suggested suzerainty of the Pacific Ocean from the shores of North America to Asia. Not too long after MacArthur issued his pronouncement about American dominance in the Pacific, Chinese and Koreans demonstrated that Asia lay beyond American control. Communists in China led by Mao Zedong triumphed over an American-supported regime in October 1949, ending a lengthy civil war and ruining American postwar plans. U.S.

18. Gans, *Deciding What's News,* 202; Nancy E. Bernhard, "Clearer than Truth: Public Affairs Television and the State Department's Domestic Information Campaigns, 1947–1952"; Swanberg, *Luce and His Empire,* 337; Kenneth J. Bindas, "The Strains of Commitment: American Periodical Press and South Vietnam, 1955–1960."

policymakers had planned for China to serve as a bulwark against the Soviet Union in Asia, and the American military intended to have several major ports and airfields on the Asian mainland. The loss of China to a communist revolution haunted policymakers and presidents during the 1950s and 1960s, and each president afterward wished to avoid blame for the loss of another nation to communism. Then the Korean War resulted in a truce that reestablished the postwar partition at the 38th parallel, which had divided the communist north from the noncommunist south. The nations of Indochina—Cambodia, Laos, and Vietnam—suddenly had political significance.[19]

Policymakers and presidents promoted economic development and military alliances in Asia. The doctrine embodied a belief that the political economy of the United States offered the best hope for everyone. This certainty of purpose inspired influential Americans during World War II to adopt the philosophy of globalism, a belief that the United States should assert itself in the international arena to advance democratic ideals and economic progress. Their faith in the American Way seemed justified considering the cycle of warfare that had swept through Europe, the militarism of Japan prior to its defeat in 1945, and the social revolutions occurring in former European colonial territories in Africa and Asia. Globalism appealed to progressive thinkers. *Time* enthusiastically promoted globalism, and persistently urged abandonment of isolationist attitudes.[20]

Because the United States had risen, by circumstance and default, to economic and military preeminence during World War II, policymakers searched for short- and long-term strategies to stop communism. Short-term approaches involved military alliances, agricultural and economic aid, and weaponry. President Harry S. Truman formulated a doctrine to provide aid automatically to nations facing external communist pressure and to those dealing with internal insurrections led by communists. The Truman Doctrine applied first to Greece, then Turkey, but then served to commit U.S. troops in Korea and to supply surplus military equipment to French colonialists fighting insurgents in Indochina. Truman's proclamation signaled a new direction for the United States in the international arena. The Monroe Doctrine now

19. MacArthur quoted in Mark Selden, "Okinawa and American Security Imperialism," 280; Gary R. Hess, *The United States' Emergence as a Southeast Asian Power, 1940–1950*, 340–41; Fifield, *Americans in Southeast Asia*, 130–31.
20. Thomas J. McCormick, *America's Half-Century: United States Foreign Policy in the Cold War*, 48–50; Baughman, *Henry R. Luce*, 142.

extended beyond the Americas to the rest of the world if combating communism required it. Long-term economic, political, and social programs conceived for postcolonial nations and other agrarian nations evolved during the 1950s. "A truly amazing conceptual arsenal—theories of economic phases, social types, traditional societies, systems transfers, pacification, social mobilization, and so on—was deployed throughout the world," commented philosopher Edward W. Said. "Universities and think tanks received huge government subsidies to pursue these ideas, many of which commanded the attention of strategic planners and policy experts in (or close to) the United States government."[21]

What resulted was modernity theory, or modernization. Modernity theorists responded to historical developments during the decade after World War II. The United States became an economic and military superpower, communism emerged as a worldwide movement, and the European colonial empires crumbled. Capitalism competed against communism for the newly independent nations. Modernization offered tremendous opportunities because all of the former colonies relied on agricultural commerce. According to the theory, all societies moved from an agrarian to an industrial stage, a movement representing economic, political, and social progress. This transformation took generations to complete. Along the way, a middle class appeared, which gradually exercised real political influence. Modernization also meant economic development to some policymakers, so the two terms often were interchanged.[22]

Strictly speaking, however, modernity encompassed economic, political, and social development. "Modernity," writes sociologist Timothy W. Luke, "means gaining rational control of the physical and social environment, building a liberal democratic state, participating in the world culture, and joining the scientific revolution." With the world divided into nations aligned with the United States, called the Free World, and those aligned with the Soviet Union, called the Communist World, dozens of newly independent nations constituted a Third World of nonaligned countries, a category especially promising for modernization. By creating wealth for a substantial

21. McCormick, *America's Half-Century,* 75; Edward W. Said, *Culture and Imperialism,* 290.
22. Alvin Y. So, *Social Change and Development: Modernization, Dependency, and World-System Theories,* 17–19; David E. Apter, *Rethinking Development: Modernization, Dependency, and Postmodern Politics,* 16–18; Peter L. Berger, Brigitte Berger, and Hansfried Kellner, *The Homeless Mind: Modernization and Consciousness,* 3–9.

segment of a society, modernization would make communism an unlikely alternative. "Western capitalism was an integral part of the dominant developmental theory that emerged after 1945," comments historian Edward H. Berman. Optimism abounded regarding the ultimate outcome. Each new nation, it was thought, would generate a sense of common purpose, replacing a society fragmented by ethnic and tribal loyalties.[23]

Newsweek, Time, and *U.S. News & World Report* reported on nation-building concepts, economic development programs, and political reform efforts in Vietnam all through the war. The articles conveyed the message that Vietnam must adopt the plans recommended by their American advisors to create a society resistant to communism. "The U.S. is supporting several big development projects," *Time* wrote. "One such program that [President] Johnson has in mind: a TVA-type system for the vast Mekong River basin." *Newsweek* focused on democratic development. "The Vietnamese still need to be convinced that democracy is on the way," the magazine commented. "For if the deserving people of Vietnam were finally convinced of the feasibility of democracy by their own small successes, South Vietnam might finally became a real country."[24]

Whatever name it went by, modernity entered academe and influenced government policy. Scholars in sociology, political science, and economics participated in determining its effects and planning its application. Walt W. Rostow, an economic historian at the Massachusetts Institute of Technology and later the national security advisor to President Johnson, wrote a classic conceptual work that likened development in the Third World to an airplane taking off, building momentum with each transformative phase from an agrarian society to industrial society. Rostow also connected democratic idealism to economic development. Democracy would appeal more to Third World citizens than communism, he argued, because capitalism created a society of material comfort and personal wealth compared with the restrictive consumer choices of a centrally planned economy. Economic development formed the long-range component of containment strategy. Short-term planning relied on military strength to dissuade the Soviet Union and China

---

23. Timothy W. Luke, *Social Theory and Modernity,* 212; Edward H. Berman, *The Influence of the Carnegie, Ford, and Rockefeller Foundations on American Foreign Policy: The Ideology of Philanthropy,* 123; Michael H. Hunt, *Ideology and U.S. Foreign Policy,* 160.

24. "War of Words & Deeds," *Time,* April 2, 1965, p. 19; "Vietnam: Correcting the Crucial Error," *Newsweek,* September 12, 1966, pp. 48–49.

from venturing too far with sponsorship of communist insurgents and to confront insurgents whenever feasible. When the nations of the Third World had capitalist economies, their citizens would have immunity against communism. Scholars at upper-tier universities received government or foundation grants, signed on as consultants to private and public agencies, and worked as advisors to policymakers and presidents. During the 1950s, the Rockefeller Foundation gave $250,000 to Columbia University and the Carnegie Corporation awarded $740,000 to Harvard University to establish programs for the study of world regions. Georgetown University, Massachusetts Institute of Technology, Princeton University, Stanford University, and the University of California at Berkeley also received substantial sums to finance regional studies scholarship. Many scholars eagerly hoped to demonstrate the validity of their theorems.[25]

College students who were enrolled in social sciences courses early in the Cold War heard and read about socioeconomic programs designed specifically for Third World societies and learned a contemporary version of the traditional concept of the American sense of mission. Students enrolled in the humanities studied history and literature from a Eurocentric and Anglo-Saxon ethnocentric perspective, a "theoretical mapping and charting of territory" that placed the European or American scholar or writer in the role of an observer who defined and described other cultures and societies.[26] Students also had opportunities to take courses in the new curriculum of international studies, a specialty subsidized by private foundations and government money. Attendance at an upper-tier university assisted the cultural and ideological cultivation of future corporate executives, diplomats, government officials, journalists, policymakers, and politicians.

Modernization theory was all the rage from the 1950s until the 1970s. Policymakers in the White House and State Department coordinated with specialists who created programs for noncommunist Asian nations. Aid and advisors went to the Republic of Korea, the Philippines, and Thailand to promote industrialization—which had varying degrees of success—and the development of commercial agriculture. Vietnam never received the full treat-

25. So, *Social Change and Development*, 29–31; Michael H. Hunt, *Lyndon Johnson's War: America's Cold War Crusade in Vietnam, 1945–1968*, 57, 159–64; Berman, *Influence of the Carnegie, Ford, and Rockefeller Foundations*, 119–20.
26. For a discussion of Eurocentrism in college studies of literature, see Said, *Culture and Imperialism*, 58–59.

ment because of wartime conditions, however. The concepts of modernization were passed along to the public by journalists who relied on sources in government to explain the big picture. Articles in *Newsweek, Time,* and *U.S. News & World Report* positively, but not altogether uncritically, relayed the vision of modernization as a strategy to stop communism.

Competition

The interpretive journalism practiced by *Newsweek, Time,* and *U.S. News & World Report* during the Vietnam War emerged from economic, political, and social factors shaping the development of American magazines since the 1880s. Beginning in the late nineteenth century, the first modern magazines appeared. These magazines shared certain characteristics: an emphasis on timely subjects of interest and importance, which superseded fiction in the pages of most monthly and weekly periodicals; dependence on advertisements as the major revenue source, which relegated revenue from subscriptions and single-copy sales to subordinate status; and direct competition in the national marketplace for readers, which necessitated editorial differentiation. The weekly newsmagazines formed a subset of modern magazines, reflecting universal characteristics while also displaying unique traits.

The initial transformation of the magazine industry occurred rapidly from the 1880s to World War I. After domination for years by limited-circulation literary periodicals, journals of opinion, and women's publications edited for genteel readers, the industry spawned magazines edited for popular tastes. Dozens of new national magazines appeared, including *American, Arena, Century, Collier's, Cosmopolitan, Everybody's, Forum, Good Housekeeping, Ladies Home Journal, Literary Digest, McCall's, McClure's, Munsey's Weekly, National Geographic, New Republic, Public Opinion, Outlook, Popular Science,* and *World's Work*. Some of these magazines contained nothing but journalistic articles on contemporary subjects. Others survived by reducing literary material to accommodate timely articles. Others abandoned literary material almost altogether to publish pieces on politics, science, and social issues, retaining but a few pages of poetry and space for serial fiction.[27] Most

---

27. For pertinent scholarship in this area, see James Playsted Wood, *Magazines in the United States;* Frank Luther Mott, *Sketches of Magazines, 1885–1905,* and *Sketches of Magazines, 1905–1930;* Theodore Peterson, *Magazines in the Twentieth Century;* John Tebbel, *The American Magazine: A Compact History;* Theodore P. Greene, *America's Heroes: The*

published monthly, others weekly. *Newsweek, Time,* and *U.S. News & World Report* trace their heritage to these monthly and weekly periodicals that concentrated on current events and issues.

Some journalism historians refer to the 1890s as the Magazine Revolution: the decade of mass production, nationwide distribution, and abundant advertising. At the start of the 1890s, only four magazines had a circulation exceeding 100,000 copies; at the end of the decade, twenty magazines had a circulation exceeding that number. Yet it would be simplistic to state that a revolution began in the 1890s. Rather, a magazine evolution continued from the 1880s. A new generation of editors and publishers, and some editor-publisher entrepreneurs, entered the magazine industry during the final two decades of the nineteenth century. "Their magazines possessed qualities that better newspapers prized—lively stories and articles, illustrations and eye-catching formats, timeliness in topics covered, and low prices," writes historian John Milton Cooper, Jr.[28]

Demographic and economic synergy benefited magazines as the new breed sensed and responded to tremendous changes in American society. First, national population soared from 50.1 million in 1880 to 91.9 million in 1910, an 84 percent increase—and more people meant potentially more readers. Second, a major shift in the national economy during 1870–1900 placed employment in the industrial sector ahead of agricultural employment; also, a one-third increase in managerial-proprietor, professional-technical, and other white-collar jobs occurred during the final two decades of the century to amount to 10.1 percent of the workforce in 1900 and to 11.3 percent in 1910, creating a sizable middle class that could afford magazines. Third, because of industrialization the population clustered in cities: 46 percent of Americans lived in communities of 2,500 or more in 1910 compared to 26 percent in 1880, and cities, naturally, became bigger, with the number of cities having ten thousand or more residents listed at 598 in

---

Changing Models of Success in American Magazines; Harold S. Wilson, McClure's Magazine *and the Muckrakers;* Arthur John, *The Best Years of the* Century: *Richard Watson Gilder,* Scribner's Monthly *and the* Century Magazine, *1870–1909;* Christopher Wilson, "The Rhetoric of Consumption: Mass-Market Magazines and the Demise of the Gentle Reader, 1880–1920"; Tebbel and Zuckerman, *The Magazine in America;* Matthew Schneirov, *The Dream of a New Social Order: Popular Magazines in America, 1893–1914.*

28. John Milton Cooper, Jr., *Walter Hines Page: The Southerner as American, 1855–1918,* 92.

1910 compared to 224 in 1880. The movement to cities in the late nineteenth century was "the largest rural-to-urban shift of population in American history," one economist states.[29] Urbanization made distribution easier and faster. Fourth, a virtual flood of consumer products streamed from manufacturers to distributors and retailers, and national brands needed magazines to advertise mass-produced wares: apparel, candy, canned vegetables and meat, cereal, rolled-film cameras, patent medicines, shoes, soaps, and soups. National advertising expenditures leapt from almost $50 million in 1870 to $542 million by 1900. Fifth, postal rates permitted inexpensive delivery of periodicals across the nation. Between 1879 and 1885, Congress lowered second-class postage from three cents a pound to one cent. As magazines filled with advertisements, amounting to dozens of pages in each edition, their bulk grew but not their delivery cost. At one point, the Post Office was spending eight cents to handle each periodical mailed for a penny. Subscribers paid artificially low rates to receive magazines that prospered on advertising revenue and benefited from a generous government subsidy. Aggregate circulation for the twenty largest monthly magazines soared from 600,000 copies in 1885 to 5,500,000 copies in 1905. "With advertising-filled periodicals blanketing the nation, second-class mailings grew twenty times faster than population in the four decades after 1880," an economic historian writes. Lastly, literacy expanded the pool of readers. In 1870, only five out of nine school-age children (age 5 to 17) attended classes, but by 1910 three out of four did.[30]

Technology advanced rapidly, too, contributing to mass publication of periodicals with photographs, color illustrations, and attractive typography. Acid-base engraving improved the quality of photographic reproduction, and magazines replaced artful and expensive woodcut illustrations, which cost $300 apiece, with photographs that cost $35 each. Color ink and better paper lent the magazines a classier appearance than newspapers, adding to their

---

29. Eric E. Lampard, "Urbanization," 1048. Population data from Stuart Bruchey, *Enterprise: The Dynamic Economy of a Free People*, 263–64, and Robert Higgs, *The Transformation of the American Economy, 1865–1914: An Essay in Interpretation*, 59. Employment and occupational data from Robert Margo, "The Labor Market in the Nineteenth Century," and U.S. Bureau of the Census, *Occupational Trends in the United States, 1900–1950*.

30. Richard S. Tedlow, "Advertising and Public Relations"; Richard B. Kielbowicz, "Postal Subsidies for the Press and the Business of Mass Culture, 1880–1920," 458; Harold G. Vatter, *The Drive to Industrial Maturity: The U.S. Economy, 1860–1914*, 304.

appeal. Steam-power rotary presses allowed timely and efficient publication of tens of thousands of copies. The low-priced, mass-circulation magazine became a new force in journalism.[31]

If a person wanted more information about the nation, sought a broader perspective than the local newspaper provided, or desired to become a member of the national community of informed citizens, a monthly general-interest magazine served the purpose. Magazines were "the only medium that reached a national audience on a regular basis and, second, they did not claim to represent a particular subculture, political party, or interest group, ideology or constituency," according to sociologist Matthew Schneirov.[32] Many magazines flourished from the 1880s to World War I, and three of these represented the spectrum of quality general-interest periodicals that influenced later generations of journalists: *Century, Cosmopolitan,* and *McClure's*. Each reached a readership of middle-class Americans that advertisers of brand merchandise wanted, and each had a separate editorial identity, which economic necessity dictated.

Century, a literary monthly, separated from ownership by a book publisher in 1881. Though reluctant to compete with livelier, more current magazines, editor Richard Watson Gilder revised the format in reaction to competition beginning in the early 1890s, gradually adding more nonfiction articles and paring fiction and poetry over the years until the magazine achieved a rough parity between journalistic and literary material. Before its transformation into a journalism-literary magazine, *Century*'s readership consisted predominantly of older, liberal Republicans, characterized by journalism historian Theodore P. Greene as "high-minded, educated, principled, professional and mercantile gentlemen of old families who looked with considerable distaste upon the political corruption and unscrupled industrial competition of the Gilded Age." At the beginning of the 1890s, *Century* had a circulation of 198,000 copies; by 1900, circulation had declined to 150,000 copies, and a few years later it dropped to 125,000 copies. The magazine regarded itself as a genteel publication compelled to offer its upper-middle-class and educated readership articles on contemporary subjects. Because it straddled the journalism-literature line, *Century* eventually alienated its older readers while failing to attract enough newer readers to survive, and

---

31. Peterson, *Magazines in the Twentieth Century,* 5–7; Mott, *Magazines, 1885–1905,* 4–8.
32. Schneirov, *Dream of a New Social Order,* 4.

it slowly faded away, merging with *Forum* in 1930 and ceasing publication altogether in 1940.[33] *Century* represented the reluctance of literary magazines to respond to a succession of contemporary trends.

Cosmopolitan reinvented itself in 1889 under the guidance of John Brisben Walker, who bought the literary periodical at a bankruptcy auction when it had twenty thousand subscribers. Walker enthusiastically embraced journalistic articles, publishing timely pieces on educational, political, and social issues in the United States. *Cosmopolitan* ran fine woodcuts to illustrate its nonfiction articles, then adopted photography as the 1890s progressed. Fiction and poetry received far fewer pages by 1900. Circulation rose from 75,000 copies in 1891 to 350,000 copies in 1900. Walker espoused a utopian socialist philosophy occasionally, and the magazine regularly featured articles on the technology of the day. He sold *Cosmopolitan* to William Randolph Hearst in 1905, and the magazine published muckraking articles for several years. It changed formats again when muckraking lost popularity among readers and advertisers, reducing its nonfiction material to give more space to mainstream fiction just before World War I.[34] *Cosmopolitan* represented magazines that changed with the times by radically revising formats whenever necessary.

McClure's started in June 1893 with the purpose of publishing series and "articles of timely interest, which included the newest book, the latest important political event, the most recent discovery or invention," according to journalism historian Harold S. Wilson. *McClure's* initially presented laudatory profiles of industrialists, entrepreneurs, and other financially successful people. Medical technology and science also received much attention, with fiction occupying a minor number of pages. *McClure's* attained a circulation of 369,000 by 1900. Historians generally regard its January 1903 edition—with articles on Standard Oil, machine politics in Minneapolis, and labor racketeering—as the premiere of muckraking journalism in American magazines. *McClure's* did not realize much profit from muckraking, however, and abandoned its exposés several years later. Unable to find a successful format,

---

33. Greene, *America's Heroes*, 71–72; circulation figures from *Ayer Directory of Newspapers*, 1891–1900, and John, *Best Years of the Century*, 233; Alan Nourie and Barbara Nourie, *American Mass-Market Magazines*.

34. Greene, *America's Heroes*; Schneirov, *Dream of a New Social Order*; Mott, *Magazines, 1885–1905*, 482; Nourie and Nourie, *American Mass-Market Magazines*. Circulation figures from *Ayer Directory*.

it slipped into oblivion, ending publication in 1929.[35] *McClure's* is representative of magazines that willingly tried various formats but failed to sustain circulation.

The economic factors that expanded the middle class also produced a political movement during the early 1900s. Municipal reform campaigns and social betterment efforts later became identified with the Progressives, essentially a middle-class movement. "Magazines stood near the center of the burgeoning national reform mood known as progressivism, which grew after the turn of the century," according to Cooper. The urban middle class transformed the social landscape. Home ownership averaged 23 percent in cities of 100,000 or more, which was more than triple the figure of thirty years earlier.[36] As more middle-class citizens owned property or otherwise had a vested or altruistic interest in a better society, they supported efficiency in municipal government, elimination of graft and corruption, public health regulations, and more control over the giant corporations that dominated essential sectors of the economy. Newspapers in many cities had for years exposed municipal corruption involving utility franchises, trolley contracts, and other services. Many magazines joined the journalistic endeavor to make the nation a better place for their middle-class readers. Articles promoted the idea of cities managed by professional administrators, state agencies empowered to regulate industry for reasons of public health and workplace safety, and public employees selected on the basis of merit rather than political connections.[37]

But readers were fickle, and magazines endured cycles of prosperity and penury. When readers deserted a magazine, advertisers did too. Experimentation with editorial formats marked this era, as well as successive eras. Soon after *McClure's* started the investigative journalism trend in 1903, a slew of magazines competed for readers by presenting exposés on life insurance companies, investment scams, church ownership of tenements, patent medicine ingredients, contaminated food products, political corruption, price-fixing, and predatory practices by financiers and industrialists. *American, Arena, Collier's, Cosmopolitan, Everybody's, Forum, Public Opinion,* and *World's Work* were

---

35. Wilson, McClure's Magazine *and the Muckrakers,* 104ff.; Nourie and Nourie, *American Mass-Market Magazines.* Circulation figures from *Ayer Directory.*
36. Cooper, *Walter Hines Page,* 219; Alan Trachtenberg, *The Incorporation of America: Culture and Society in the Gilded Age,* 128.
37. Schneirov, *Dream of a New Social Order,* 259.

among the notable periodicals engaged in muckraking. Circulation soared for some magazines from 1903 to 1907: *American* reached 300,000 copies; *Collier's* attained 568,000; *Everybody's* leveled off at 750,000 copies.[38] Still, muckraking brought little profit. Advertising rates often lagged behind circulation growth, placing financial pressure on magazines that expanded too quickly, and readers tired of a steady stream of investigative articles, some of which seemed not particularly relevant or significant. President Theodore Roosevelt, a reformer and leader of progressivism, reacted to a muckraking series on corrupt U.S. senators by chastising the magazines for their frenzied attempts to expose wrongdoing, which Roosevelt believed caused more harm than good by destroying public faith in government. His derisive designation "muckraker" gave investigative journalism its legendary nickname.[39] By the start of World War I, muckraking had disappeared from most magazines.

Other magazines offered serious commentary along with news. A distinguishing feature of these magazines was the absence of fiction, a radical experiment for the era. *Forum,* although never a major magazine, began monthly publication in 1886, presenting opinion essays on important contemporary subjects and articles on political, economic, and social issues. *Literary Digest,* a weekly first produced in 1890, provided a roundup of newspaper articles on specific subjects, summaries of selected articles of a timely nature, and articles that blended original reporting with edited material from other publications. *Public Opinion,* a weekly that first appeared in 1886, reprinted dozens of news items arranged by topic. *World's Work,* a monthly, began in 1900 and featured an opening news summary now typical to weekly journals of opinion. However, according to Cooper, editor Walter Hines Page preferred to publish commentary on the news rather than direct advocacy: "Such postures of blatant commendation without formally

38. Walter M. Brasch, *Forerunners of Revolution: Muckrakers and the American Social Conscience,* 40–64. For a discussion of experimentation with editorial formats, see A. J. van Zuilen, *The Life Cycle of Magazines: A Historical Study of the Decline and Fall of the General Interest Mass Audience Magazine in the United States during the Period 1946–1972.* For the subjects of muckraking exposés, see Nourie and Nourie, *American Mass-Market Magazines,* 115–18; Schneirov, *Dream of a New Social Order,* 205–6; and Mott in *Magazines, 1885–1905,* 651.

39. Ellen F. Fitzpatrick, ed., *Muckraking: Three Landmark Articles,* 112–14; Robert C. Hilderbrand, *Power and the People: Executive Management of Public Opinion in Foreign Affairs, 1897–1921.*

endorsing parties and candidates sustained the impression in readers' minds that *World's Work* was viewing events just the way they would if they were better informed. Page had developed the basic device of the twentieth-century newsmagazine."[40]

Collier's, with a circulation of 490,000 copies, and *Outlook,* with a circulation of 125,000, exemplified the standard for political reportage and commentary by weekly general-interest magazines in the early 1900s. *Collier's* and *Outlook* focused on presidential candidates, commented on the platforms of the political parties, and identified various issues as significant for the nation. The consistent attention paid to presidential politics demonstrated an editorial transformation that had brought news coverage to the forefront of magazine journalism during the twentieth century's first dozen years. *Collier's* and *Outlook* also symbolized the journalistic evolution spawned by the tremendous cultural and social changes in the 1890s and early 1900s. Prior to the emphasis by *Collier's* and *Outlook* on original reporting, weekly magazines had offered readers a compendium of editorials and articles from newspapers across the country, supplemented by interpretive and opinionated commentary on events and issues. Original reportage of events was infrequent, and usually consisted of commissioned pieces written by prominent politicians, ex-cabinet members, or college professors. The editors at *Collier's* and *Outlook,* however, decided that timely reports from correspondents at the scene of an event were essential if their magazines were to succeed in the marketplace. "They took many of their ideas from daily journalism or the Sunday supplements," one historian observes.[41]

By the 1920s, *Literary Digest* dominated the weekly magazines devoted to current events and commentary. Other magazines with timely commentary and essays existed, but they were journals of opinion with limited circulation that wrote for like-minded citizens rather than the mainstream. *Common Sense, Dial, Nation, New Republic,* and *Survey* were the quality journals of opinion. With the exception of *Literary Digest,* magazines apparently had little regard for news as a commodity. *Collier's,* always a cyclically noteworthy magazine, had resorted to boosting its fiction component to rebuild circula-

---

40. Cooper, *Walter Hines Page,* 91–101, 178–80; Mott, *Magazines, 1885–1905,* 57–64, 570–72, 650–51; Nourie and Nourie, *American Mass-Market Magazines,* 126–28; Cooper, *Walter Hines Page,* 178–79.

41. Tebbel and Zuckerman, *The Magazine in America,* 66, 76, 109–10; Richard Hofstadter, *The Age of Reform,* 192.

tion. "None better exemplified the drabness of the early 1920s magazines than the weekly *Literary Digest*," Baughman notes. The magazine distributed an estimated 900,000 copies a week, "[y]et it lacked a personality," he states. "Staff members summarized but rarely judged events, relying instead on extensive quotations from American and overseas newspapers."[42] Two young journalists, Henry R. Luce and Briton Hadden, believed an opportunity existed for a newsmagazine with a livelier format than *Literary Digest*.

Influential intellectuals and social philosophers believed the time ripe for journalists to bring comprehension, order, and substance to news. John Dewey saw potential benefit from a rational approach: "Presentation is fundamentally important, and presentation is a question of art." Dewey knew that academic journals would not appeal to most citizens. Still, he argued, information on substantive ideas and issues should be available. Sociologist Robert E. Park points out the myopia of journalism: "News, as a form of knowledge, is not primarily concerned either with the past or with the future but rather with the present—what has been described by psychologists as 'the specious present.' News . . . as the publishers of the commercial press know, is a very perishable commodity."[43] Although aware of the competitive pressures affecting journalism in the 1920s, academicians and intellectuals promoted a philosophy for journalists based on rationality and public duty.

Luce and Hadden brought forth *Time* in 1923. The "news-magazine" arranged articles by departments, as did *Literary Digest* and *Public Opinion*. It also applied an ideological perspective, presenting what its founders considered a responsible viewpoint that exalted individualism, political pragmatism, and economic progress. Articles contained derogatory and laudatory descriptions that clearly passed judgment on ideas and people. Luce advocated analysis rather than partisanship. "Luce insisted that *Time* have a point-of-view," Baughman observes. "*Time* would not deny the correctness or banality of one side or another." *Time*'s lively style attracted attention; Luce and Hadden had found a formula for journalistic success. "It was as if they understood that a salable commodity lay between the hyped-up sensationalism

---

42. Tebbel and Zuckerman, *The Magazine in America*, 203–8; Peterson, *Magazines in the Twentieth Century*, 132–39; Nourie and Nourie, *American Mass-Market Magazines*, 53–58; Tebbel, *The American Magazine*, 157–59; Baughman, *Henry R. Luce*, 31.

43. Daniel J. Czitrom, *Media and the American Mind: From Morse to McLuhan*, 105–6; John Dewey, *The Public and Its Problems*, 183; Robert E. Park, "News as a Form of Knowledge," 40.

of the tabloids and the pallid paragraphs of the news agencies," writes media scholar Herbert I. Schiller. *Time* resurrected the narrative that had made nineteenth-century newspapers exciting to read. "The event was, at one level, the hard news story—the accurate, factual information; at another level, it was the 'plot' or part of a plot around which drama was woven to create the thrill that would make people want to read and therefore buy the newspaper," writes Hazel Dicken-Garcia.[44]

Hadden died in 1929, and over the years Luce let *Time*'s point of view become more partisan, with Republicans the preferred political party. No single event or issue caused this alignment, but certainly the triumph of communism in China in 1949 loomed large. Luce, born in China in 1898 to Presbyterian missionary parents, employed *Time* and *Life* magazines to plead the case for tremendous amounts of military aid to the Nationalist government led by Chiang Kai-shek. President Harry S. Truman, a Democrat, and his advisors considered Chiang's regime corrupt, inept, and doomed to defeat. The communists led by Mao Zedong controlled most of the countryside in China by 1947, leaving the Nationalists in control of coastal cities and several inland cities on major rivers accessible from the coast. Truman refused to ask Congress for additional aid to the Nationalists. Some congressional Republicans agreed with Luce that the Nationalists should receive an infusion of weaponry and equipment. Congress eventually appropriated money to supply the Nationalists, although Truman rejected arguments for direction intervention. The experience in China made Luce eager to avert a similar situation in Vietnam. "Luce himself consistently supported America's involvement," Baughman states. "To the end [he died in 1967] he remained confident that the United States could prevent the fall of the South.... Luce had concluded that the nation had to make a stand in Southeast Asia, regardless of the cost. Vietnam had symbolic value."[45]

Naturally, the early success of *Time* spawned imitators. *News-Week*—it soon changed its name to *Newsweek*—and *U.S. News* both appeared in February 1933. *News-Week*'s prospectus declared it would not engage in *Time*-style journalism, which it derided as flippant, inaccurate, and superficial. "It had no distinctive writing style and no particular approach to the news ex-

44. Baughman, *Henry R. Luce,* 27–29; Schiller, *Mind Managers,* 120; Hazel Dicken-Garcia, *Journalistic Standards in Nineteenth-Century America,* 89–90. For a discussion of the return to a narrative style, see Baughman, *Henry R. Luce,* 44–46.
45. Baughman, *Henry R. Luce,* 9–11, 156–57, 187–89.

cept to digest it, yet it was cast in roughly the same format as *Time,* with the same kind of departmentalization," states one history of magazines.[46] *U.S. News* decided to aim its format at archconservatives. *Time*'s stylistic flair kept it far ahead of competitors in readership, which solidified its top position among advertisers. Its dominance wore down *Literary Digest,* which had suffered public ridicule after a 1936 presidential poll debacle. The magazine's poll predicted victory for Alf Landon, the Republican candidate, over Franklin D. Roosevelt, the Democrat seeking a second term. But the nationwide sample had been polled by telephone, and during the Depression-era 1930s few blue-collar families or other low-income households could afford phones. Roosevelt easily won reelection. *Time* bought the subscription list of the fallen *Literary Digest* in 1938. *Newsweek* remained a stolid competitor, avoiding the paeans and putdowns for which the senior newsmagazine had a reputation. *U.S. News,* which merged with *World Report* in 1948, held on to its archconservative readership by interpreting the news within that context. All three newsmagazines attempted to forecast the direction of events and issues; their weekly schedules required a forward-looking theme because the news already was dated when it was published. Projection of the news stretched the boundaries of interpretive journalism as the newsmagazines weighted their articles with information that supported their themes.[47]

Throughout the 1940s and 1950s, the newsmagazines established norms for journalistic practices that further separated them from newspapers, which had adopted objectivity as the norm for news. Objectivity had gained acceptance among newspapers because it supposedly removed bias from the news. News articles met the standard of objectivity by presenting "both sides" of a story, offering information on events and issues from observers, participants, and official sources, without overt commentary. Only columnists and the review-of-the-news sections in Sunday editions expressed opinions or otherwise interpreted information to provide necessary perspective. (Sunday news-review sections rarely judged the merit of information contained in news articles, but instead explained the underlying political or social factors.) Simply by segregating editorial opinion from the news, newspapers pretended that bias did not affect their presentations. "In this view, objectivity was not an ideal but a mystification," writes Michael Schudson, a

46. Tebbel and Zuckerman, *The Magazine in America,* 172–73.
47. Ibid., 171–74.

sociologist who examines journalistic practices. Mott believed that *Time* initially strayed beyond journalistic norms in the 1940s: "[W]hile keeping up its adjectival attacks, *Time* launched more and more frequently into full-scale editorializing."[48]

Time's steady circulation growth into the 1960s persuaded *Newsweek* and *U.S. News & World Report* that readers accepted interpretive journalism that appealed to their own ideological viewpoints. All three newsmagazines concocted "cleverly fictional" representations of events and individuals, according to W. A. Swanberg, a Luce biographer. But the Cold War era witnessed an increasingly doctrinaire anticommunism in the pages of *Time*. By the early 1960s, when ideological conflict between capitalism and communism affected American political discourse on an assortment of domestic and international issues, *Time* slanted articles to fit its worldview—and presumably that of its millions of faithful readers. "There was no publication in the world of such size and influence which was regarded by the innocent as a purveyor of news and yet which succeeded in being an instrument of propaganda," Swanberg comments. Mott, too, believed *Time* had forsaken all fundamental journalistic norms concerning news. "By the 1960's *Time* had become, in the main, a collection of editorial articles, filled with information about news events and situations, and emphasizing vivid narrative and description," he wrote. "Thus *Time* had become not only a newsmagazine but also definitely a journal of opinion."[49]

At the start of the Vietnam War, heightened competition among the newsmagazines for readers transformed *Newsweek* to a greater degree than *U.S. News & World Report*. As a marginally profitable newsmagazine with a limited future, *Newsweek* went up for sale in 1961. Purchased by the owners of the *Washington Post*, the magazine purposely distanced itself from *Time*'s mainstream conservative viewpoint by inching toward a more liberal, yet mainstream, identity.[50] The transformation made economic sense because *Time*, although immensely popular, managed to aggravate many readers. An internal memo to Luce from a marketing executive blamed *Time*'s tone for a minor drop in readership after years of continuous growth. At the same time, *Newsweek* and *U.S. News & World Report* had gained readers. "If the

---

48. Michael Schudson, *Discovering the News: A Social History of American Newspapers*, 162–63 (see also 144–55); Mott, *Magazines, 1905–1930*, 314–15.

49. Swanberg, *Luce and His Empire*, 384; Mott, *Magazines, 1905–1930*, 316.

50. Graham, *Personal History*, 276–80; Gans, *Deciding What's News*, 197–98.

news were to be reported in an overtly political or ideological manner," writes journalism scholar John Soloski, "the market would be ripe for competition from news organizations that held opposing political or ideological points of view."[51] *Time* recovered, and readership for each newsmagazine increased substantially during the Vietnam War.

Newsmagazines during the 1965–1973 period reflected a heritage attributable to the birth of modern magazines from the 1880s to World War I. They concentrated on covering timely events and issues. They offered editorial formats appealing to society's mainstream. They served Americans who traditionally considered magazines a worthwhile medium: in 1919, 62.6 percent of households in the upper-fifth income category subscribed to magazines, compared to 46.5 percent of all households; in 1960, 83.8 percent of upper-income households subscribed to magazines, compared to 62 percent of all households; and in 1972, 64.3 percent of upper-income households subscribed to magazines, compared to 44.6 percent of all households.[52] The interpretive journalism practiced by *Newsweek, Time,* and *U.S. News & World Report* during the Vietnam War derived from a generation of magazines produced for affluent, educated, and mainstream Americans. For several decades, the newsmagazines had served a readership that was responsive to their editorial formats, but competition meant a continual challenge to maintain circulation.

Vietnam and the United States

Nationalists and communists in the French territory of Indochina rebelled against colonial rule in summer 1945. The Vietnamese shared governance with France in Tonkin, the northern province, under a compromise arrangement until November 1946 when French warships shelled Haiphong and colonial troops expelled the Vietminh, a political-military coalition commanded by communists. France lost despite $2.6 billion in materiel, money, and weaponry from the United States (approximately $21 billion in 2003 dollars), which amounted to 78 percent of the cost of battling the insurgents. Congress readily agreed to furnish the aid because the United States

---

51. Swanberg, *Luce and His Empire*, 399; John Soloski, "News Reporting and Professionalism: Some Constraints on the Reporting of the News."
52. Carl F. Kaestle and others, *Literacy in the United States: Readers and Reading since 1880*, table 5.4.

wanted to ease the financial burden on France, which then could play a vital role in the European anticommunist alliance.[53] The rebellion failed, but an eight-year insurgency produced a communist victory in the north. In summer 1954, an international conference arranged the partition of Vietnam at the 17th parallel. The Democratic Republic of Vietnam, governed by communists, occupied the northern section; the Republic of Vietnam, governed by noncommunists, occupied the southern section.

Aid to the newly created southern republic began at once, with U.S. Navy ships transporting 300,000 of an estimated 900,000 northerners who moved south of the 17th parallel prior to the closing of the partition in summer 1955. Food, temporary housing, and construction material for permanent homes for these refugees, approximately two-thirds of whom were Catholics, was paid for by the United States. American engineers supervised construction of bridges, roads, and port facilities built with U.S. money, while consultants explored ways to diversify Vietnam's agrarian economy and scholars studied cultural and social systems. An innovative commercial import program subsidized the cost of foreign merchandise so ordinary Vietnamese could buy fashionable clothes, motorcycles, radios, tools, and sundry items. Idealism motivated many of the Americans assigned to Vietnam. They genuinely hoped that economic progress would result in broader political participation among the Vietnamese and that social reforms would improve conditions. The grand plan was to build a nation in the south from a society consisting of isolated rural villages, where five of every six Vietnamese lived, numerous ethnic groups, and an urban populace disdainful of its country cousins. During the first decade of its existence, the Republic of Vietnam received $1.5 billion in aid from the United States, making it one of the top half-dozen recipient nations in the world. Catholic politicians, including Sen. John F. Kennedy of Massachusetts, eased the process for obtaining aid, and Catholics in the United States contributed additional tens of millions of dollars.[54]

---

53. George C. Herring, *America's Longest War: The United States and Vietnam, 1950–1975*, 11–17, 192. For more on the relationship between France's crucial role in the European alliance and U.S. aid for its Indochina war, see Fifield, *Americans in Southeast Asia*, 182–88. Gary R. Hess also discusses the paramount concern that American policymakers had for European security and their desire to ease France's financial burden in Indochina (*United States' Emergence*, 208, 321).

54. Herring, *America's Longest War*, 43–44; Frances Fitzgerald, *Fire in the Lake: The Vietnamese and the Americans in Vietnam*, 499–500 passim. For more on the social factors affecting nation-building in Vietnam, see Levine, *Struggle for Southeast Asia*, 82–89; for relocation

Vietnam symbolized the so-called domino theory. President Dwight D. Eisenhower borrowed the term from British strategists who considered a communist nation anywhere a threat to its neighbors because it would function as a center for subversion. In April 1954, the president likened the possible fall of Indochina to the first in a "row of dominoes" in Southeast Asia, and the news media popularized the term. By the 1960s, it seemed axiomatic that a communist triumph in any nation in Africa, Asia, and Central or South America would topple adjacent nations. Eisenhower reportedly emphasized the domino theory in Southeast Asia when he briefed President-elect Kennedy on foreign policy in January 1961, but applied it to Laos, where a civil war raged, rather than to Vietnam.[55]

To give the southern government in Saigon time to create a modern economy with minimal interference from communist guerrillas, the United States sent hundreds of U.S. Army advisors to Vietnam starting in 1956 to train officers and soldiers. According to the plan, the Vietnamese army soon would be able to protect cities, establish outposts in strategic rural areas, and hunt communist guerrillas. With a strong army and a strong economy, Vietnam would be secure. This optimism was not misplaced, because American assistance to Greece from 1948 to 1949 and to the Philippines from 1948 to 1954 had contributed to the defeat of communist insurrections.[56]

Newsweek, Time, and *U.S. News & World Report* matter-of-factly reported developments in southern Vietnam early on. Articles informed readers about the assortment of programs originated by the United States, the advisory effort to strengthen the army, and the chaotic social conditions hindering the grand plan. The magazines never questioned the premise that the United States should assist and subsidize the wholesale restructuring of Vietnamese society.[57]

The situation in southern Vietnam steadily deteriorated. Communist

---

efforts and economic development plans, see Michael Maclear, *The Ten Thousand Day War: Vietnam, 1945–1975,* 50–53, 145–46; for relocation aid and the importance of influential Catholics in the United States, see George McT. Kahin, *Intervention: How America Became Involved in Vietnam,* 75–77, 78–80.

55. Herring, *America's Longest War,* 12–13; Levine, *Struggle for Southeast Asia,* 12, 35–36. Maclear quotes a Kennedy aide concerning Eisenhower's statement, although some historians have wondered if Eisenhower actually believed the domino theory (*Ten Thousand Day War,* 58–59).

56. Kahin, *Intervention,* 69–70; Levine, *Struggle for Southeast Asia,* 53–58.

57. Bindas, "Strains of Commitment," 69.

guerrillas accelerated their attacks in 1959 and 1960. The Army of the Republic of Vietnam rarely ventured far from the cities as the guerrillas controlled ever larger areas. The newsmagazines and the rest of the American news media found much to criticize and question concerning the government in Saigon, and by implication reasons to doubt American methods, but not American purpose.[58] Ngo Dinh Diem, president of southern Vietnam, proved to be more independent than Americans had anticipated. Diem and the officials who directed government departments altered or rejected proposals for democratic principles, economic liberalization, and social reforms that the United States considered essential to nation-building. Diem also limited redistribution of land owned by French colonials to the northern Catholics who had moved south in 1954 and 1955, thereby alienating millions of resident tenant farmers who continued to pay exorbitant rent to absentee landlords.[59]

News articles in the American mainstream media ignored these complex issues. Instead, crisis journalism thrived from 1955 to 1961. Journalists paid attention to religious sectarian warfare, corruption, thievery from aid programs, government suppression of opponents, and public protests against Diem. The few journalists intermittently assigned to Saigon by the AP, United Press International, Reuters, and Agence France-Presse had no difficulty getting their stories about these dramatic events into print. Newspapers relying on this sporadic coverage published stories that treated each episode discretely, rarely connecting the underlying social factors to the flare-ups. Journalists from the newsmagazines, *New York Times,* and other major newspapers arrived from Hong Kong and Tokyo, stayed a week or two until the crisis ended, then departed. Contract journalists, known as stringers, filed information on demand, although demand was not great most of the time. Newsmagazine articles and newspaper stories described Diem's autocratic style, his nepotism, the friction between the majority Buddhist population and the predominantly Catholic government, the Vietcong's dominance in the countryside, and the poor performance of Vietnam's army. Riots and other evidence of serious instability in southern Vietnam could not be ignored by journalists. News coverage portrayed the political and social prob-

58. Herring, *America's Longest War,* 57–65; Levine, *Struggle for Southeast Asia,* 83–85, 88; Bindas, "Strains of Commitment," 63–67.
59. Herring, *America's Longest War,* 48–49, 53–57, 84–85; Maclear, *Ten Thousand Day War,* 54–55; Kahin, *Intervention,* 78–80, 94–95.

lems that interfered with the effort to defeat the communist insurgency. Despite the acceptance of the necessity for American involvement in Vietnam, journalists told the story of a government unable and unwilling to meet the demands of many of its citizens.[60] Several years later, in the midst of a war fought by Americans, journalists would report similar circumstances that interfered with military progress.

The newsmagazines and weekly journals also offered favorable portraits of Diem. According to many articles, Diem had no choice but to quell dissent because such turmoil unwittingly aided the communist insurgents. Other articles explained Diem's nepotism by pointing out that he could rely on few people outside his own family. *Time* called Diem "the tough miracle man" and *Newsweek* joined in praise of his anticommunism and determination to modernize Vietnam. Readers were reminded that Diem and the Vietnamese people needed several years to learn self-governance and adapt to new ways.[61] *Time*, however, distorted events and issues affecting Vietnam much more than other newsmagazines. *Time*'s editors wanted readers to believe in Diem. The managing editor personally rewrote information from his correspondents to make the situation in Vietnam appear better than it was. The inept performance of the southern army, evidence of Vietcong encroachment in populated areas, and other portents of disaster were minimized or omitted by *Time*.[62]

The number of in-country American military advisors swelled to several thousand in 1962. Stateside editors sensed that Vietnam was becoming a bigger story. Newsmagazine correspondents spent longer periods in Vietnam, rotating in and out from Hong Kong. Crisis coverage still dominated, but more crises continued to occur, so the AP, UPI, and *New York Times* opened Saigon bureaus that year. Buddhist monks continued to protest inequitable treatment of the majority population, and a series of self-immolations in the streets of Saigon horrified many Americans who saw the burning bonzes in newsmagazine and newspaper photographs and in film segments on television. Vietcong attacks increased in intensity and severity. The

60. Bindas, "Strains of Commitment," 64–68; Hohenberg, *Between Two Worlds,* 42–43, 82, 146–47, 416–17; Clarence R. Wyatt, *Paper Soldiers: The American Press and the Vietnam War,* 49.
61. Herring, *America's Longest War,* 66; Kahin, *Intervention,* 95–97; Wyatt, *Paper Soldiers,* 63–64.
62. Baughman, *Henry R. Luce,* 186–87.

Vietnamese army restricted its operations to the perimeters of major cities, with infrequent forays into the countryside. Vietcong cadres controlled the Mekong Delta within forty miles of Saigon at night, collected a rice tax to feed its troops, and often ambushed army patrols in daylight. Half of the south's population lived in the delta, and most of its rice was grown there. Journalists reported these developments. Some journalists worked with the embassy and senior military advisors to emphasize army victories whenever possible, transforming minor skirmishes into major battles. Other journalists ventured outside Saigon to meet junior advisors whose criticisms about the Vietnamese army, particularly its officer corps, displeased American generals and embassy officials in-country and stateside. Friction increased between journalists and the senior American commanders and government representatives. Privately and publicly, policymakers and presidential advisors castigated journalists for negative reporting.[63]

Tension also affected relationships between editors in New York City and journalists in Saigon, especially by 1963. Some journalists in Saigon recognized the discrepancy that existed between the official statements of the U.S. embassy and the commander of American military advisors and the reality of the situation. Officially, the Army of the Republic of Vietnam was improving, the communist guerrillas were losing ground, rural hamlets were secure from attack, and highways were safe to travel. But journalists who got out of Saigon to do their reporting knew from personal observation and from interviews with plainspoken military advisors that quite the opposite was true. Articles written by these journalists often contradicted what their stateside colleagues had written based on interviews with officials at the Pentagon, State Department, and White House, where optimism prevailed. Although not all journalists in Saigon during the early 1960s regarded embassy officials and military commanders as their adversaries, enough treated them that way to worry their editors, who feared that consistently confrontational reporting from Vietnam might anger policymakers and sources, who would shut off access to information.[64] Also, the procedure at newsmagazines and wire services involved blending information from different sources, which occasionally produced problems. If editors received information from jour-

63. Kahin, *Intervention*, 142; Levine, *Struggle for Southeast Asia*, 82. For more on the different journalistic practices of reporters, see William Prochnau, *Once upon a Distant War*, 231–82.
64. Gans, *Deciding What's News*, 117.

nalists in Saigon that had a negative emphasis and information from journalists in Washington that had a positive emphasis, they tended to delete or downplay the information from Saigon. Editors based their decisions on two factors: first, the experienced journalists assigned to the White House, State Department, and Defense Department had received those coveted assignments based on their performance and conformance to the norms of the organization; second, news sources in Washington had more credibility and veracity than news sources in Saigon by virtue of their higher rank in government, which conferred greater legitimacy in the minds of editors.[65]

A notable incident involving friction between editors and reporters occurred in January 1963. Vietcong guerrillas and Vietnamese army soldiers fought a battle near Ap Bac in the Mekong Delta. The army outnumbered the guerrillas ten to one, but incompetent army leadership and poor discipline among the soldiers resulted in heavy casualties. Several hundred guerrillas easily evaded capture. A few alert journalists learned of the battle, accurately reconstructed events, and quoted an American military advisor who criticized the southern army. However, editors in New York City with AP, UPI, and *Time* rewrote the information from their Saigon journalists to emphasize statements by senior American advisors that Ap Bac was an army victory. "After Ap Bac, correspondents, convinced that the Mission [embassy and military advisory command] was lying to them, relied on their own sources—in fact, withdrew into their own community," comments military scholar Douglas Kinnard.[66]

No example better demonstrated tension between editors and journalists than the public furor between *Time* managing editor Otto Fuerbringer and *Time* correspondent Charles Mohr in summer 1963. Mohr, though accustomed to *Time*'s editorial system, had written a withering profile of a Diem family member prominent in the government. Fuerbringer supervised the rewrite, which made the person seem eccentric and purposeful rather than

---

65. S. Holly Stocking and Paget H. Gross conclude that experience and responsibility made journalists less ideological (*How Do Journalists Think? A Proposal for the Study of Cognitive Bias in Newsmaking*, 23–25). For an examination of organizational factors affecting the editorial process, see Michael Schudson, "The Sociology of News Production." For a discussion of the journalistic preference to present dominant ideology, see Gans, *Deciding What's News*, 203, and George A. Donohue, Phillip J. Tichenor, and Clarice N. Olien, "A Guard Dog Perspective on the Role of Media."

66. Stanley Karnow, *Vietnam: A History*, 259–62; Douglas Kinnard, *The War Managers*, 126–27.

venal and arrogant. Mohr sent a scathing letter to Fuerbringer, which angered him and other senior editors. The letter motivated Fuerbringer to publish a nearly full-page denunciation of Saigon correspondents that included this judgment: "To Saigon's Western press corps, President Ngo Dinh Diem is stubborn and stupid, dominated by his brother and sister-in-law.... The Saigon-based press corps is so confident of its own convictions that any other version of the Viet Nam story is quickly dismissed as the fancy of a bemused observer." Mohr resigned. Richard M. Clurman, chief of correspondents for Time-Life, persuaded Mohr to rescind his resignation upon publication of a second article in *Time* to rebut the first. (In the meantime, another Mohr article on the apparently hopeless military situation in the countryside also was rewritten in an optimistic tone.)[67]

Clurman had made his offer in good faith. Fuerbringer, however, had other plans. *Time* editor Ed Magnuson got the assignment to write the rebuttal. "In the wake of the first flap and Charlie Mohr's resignation, [a senior editor] explained that Otto Fuerbringer, the managing editor, wanted to say it all again—only better and with more specifics," Magnuson remembers. "He wanted to make the case that the emotional involvement and antimilitary bias of the reporters was not only unprofessional as the magazine had claimed, but had led to serious reporters' mistakes, which the first story had not cited." Clurman traveled to Saigon to talk with reporters. A copy of his telex to publisher Henry R. Luce, Time-Life editor Hedley Donovan, and Fuerbringer contains marginalia from the managing editor at points where Clurman defended the accuracy of reporting from Saigon: "Sad!" "All wrong." Clurman now argued against a second article on the correspondents: "[I] now strongly believe on the basis of elaborate first-hand knowledge that our press story was out of kilter in such delicately unremediable ways that its next to impossible right now to run a story in print setting the matter straight." Fuerbringer nevertheless decided to continue. Five rewritten versions of the second article were prepared. *Time* did not retract its original criticism. The second article ran longer than the first, but no specific examples of inaccurate reporting were presented. The only concession to Mohr was a parenthetical comment in one sentence: "What they reported about the course of the war was seriously questioned in Washington; what they

---

67. Prochnau, *Distant War*, 355–58, 425–29; "The View from Saigon," *Time*, September 20, 1963, p. 62; Baughman, *Henry R. Luce*, 186–87.

wrote about the deterioration of the Diem government (not sufficiently emphasized in the *Time* story) was correct."⁶⁸ Mohr resigned permanently and joined the *New York Times*.

While in Saigon to handle the Mohr mess, Clurman interviewed Diem at the presidential palace. Vietnamese officials knew where power resided in the American press and they invariably treated visiting columnists and influential journalists to interviews with Diem. A telex from Clurman to Time-Life in New York City contained notes from the interview and ended with a message for Luce: "President Diem asked me to convey to you and CBL [Clare Boothe Luce] his personal regards and respects."⁶⁹ It was *Time*'s last formal interview with the president.

The situation in Vietnam promptly worsened. Vietnamese army officers murdered Diem in a coup on November 1, 1963. Actions by the Kennedy administration, including suspension of economic aid and an indication to army generals that a coup would meet with American approval, contributed to the overthrow. An extended period of coups, military juntas, and other temporary regimes effectively made the army the government in Vietnam. American military aid assumed greater importance, and the number of in-country advisors totaled 16,000 at the start of 1964. Americans patrolled with Vietnamese army units, directed artillery fire during tactical operations, flew helicopters ferrying Vietnamese soldiers into combat, and occasionally piloted aircraft on bombing missions against Vietcong targets in the central highlands, Mekong Delta, and I Corps, the northernmost military region of southern Vietnam adjacent to the demilitarized zone at the 17th parallel. But the Vietcong continued to expand their territory, and infantry battalions from northern Vietnam infiltrated into the south to attack and intimidate the southern army.

The increase in military activity brought more media attention. Because some journalists in Saigon insisted on reporting negative news when American officials wanted only positive news, the U.S. government decided to attempt to influence the interpretations of events the stateside public received.

---

68. Author interview with Ed Magnuson; Clurman to Luce, Donovan, and Fuerbringer, telex, October 3, 1963 (courtesy of Ed Magnuson); article drafts and revisions, *Time* files copies 83, 124, 156, 211, 236, October 3–4, 1963 (courtesy of Ed Magnuson); "The Saigon Story," *Time,* October 11, 1963, p. 55.

69. Clurman to Luce, Donovan, and Fuerbringer, telex, October 1, 1963 (courtesy of Ed Magnuson).

Consumers of news may not have known about the crucial role editors played in shaping articles in newsmagazines and newspapers, but policymakers knew. Beginning in 1964, the Department of Defense appropriated $50,000 a year to transport columnists and editors from the United States to Vietnam, provide them with military uniforms, fly them around the country in helicopters, and escort them on guided two-week tours. The cost for each journalist amounted to almost $1,000 (the equivalent sum in 2003 would be $5,700 per journalist). The Defense Department named the program Operation Maximum Candor.[70] Barry Zorthian, the public affairs coordinator for the embassy and military, encouraged influential journalists to visit, in an attempt to counter the pessimistic reporting from Saigon. Zorthian disliked the absolute distrust that many in-country journalists had for American officials. "Theirs was a questioning, a skeptical, a challenging, if you will, generation of journalists," Zorthian said. Editors from newspapers in smaller cities received trips, too; the Defense Department hoped they would edit AP and UPI stories more carefully after personally seeing progress in Vietnam. Few editors had any experience covering a war, much less a guerrilla war. They were led on tours by military officers who took them to fortified villages and to camps where American advisors demonstrated weaponry to them. Most flew home from Vietnam impressed by what they had seen.[71]

As the situation in southern Vietnam deteriorated, American policymakers approved positioning U.S. Navy warships in the Gulf of Tonkin closer to the coast but still in international waters; the warships shielded patrol boats of southern Vietnam's navy that shelled ports and harbors above the 17th parallel. These details were not revealed to journalists.[72] Torpedo boats from the Democratic Republic of Vietnam responded on August 2, 1964, with a daylight attack on a U.S. Navy destroyer. No damage to the Navy ship occurred, but one torpedo boat took a hit from the Navy destroyer and sank while the other two sped away with minor damage. Another destroyer arrived in the area the next day. On the night of August 4, torpedo boats may or may not have fired torpedoes at one of the Navy destroyers; official reports initially indicated that wakes from torpedoes were observed and sailors

70. Wyatt, *Paper Soldiers*, 80–97, 158; Hohenberg, *Between Two Worlds*, 43; George C. Herring, *LBJ and Vietnam: A Different Kind of War*, 126–28.
71. Barry Zorthian oral history, tape 3, no. 6, transcript, LBJ Library. Leon V. Sigal, *Reporters and Officials: The Organization and Politics of Newsmaking*, 54.
72. Herring, *America's Longest War*, 86–87, 102–5; Maclear, *Ten Thousand Day War*, 92–94, 100–2.

had seen gunfire, but reports filed a few hours later cast doubt on whether an attack actually happened, because it had been a proverbial dark and stormy night with poor visibility. President Johnson ordered immediate retaliatory aerial bombardment of northern ports. Administration officials and the military released selective details about the latter attack, focusing on the verified presence of the north's torpedo boats near the U.S. Navy destroyers. News reports did not question the official version, which minimized the confusion about specific details.

Magnuson wrote the *Time* cover story on the Gulf of Tonkin incident. "It's a brisk narrative on events described in such specific detail that it rings true," he remembers. "Later revelations would suggest that we should have been more skeptical. That may be correct, but we had no reason to believe that the president and so many military officials at so many levels would develop such intricate lies—if that is what they were." Johnson also asked Congress for permission to deploy troops in Southeast Asia wherever communists threatened noncommunist governments and to take whatever measures were necessary to protect American troops in the Republic of Vietnam. Congress quickly approved the Southeast Asia Resolution, popularly called the Gulf of Tonkin Resolution.[73]

American combat troops were not sent for several months. Military advisors continued to advise and participate in combat. Less pretense was employed to hide their fighting role. No aerial bombardment sorties were sent north after August 1964. However, American aircraft intensified attacks against Vietcong bastions in remote areas and regularly provided support for Vietnamese army units. Eventually, Vietcong leaders decided to launch assaults on the airfields and on barracks where American personnel stayed. Two assaults in February 1965 killed thirty-two Americans. Johnson ordered a series of aerial bombardment raids against northern military installations. Then, following advice from the military's Joint Chiefs of Staff, Johnson ordered continuous bombardment of northern Vietnam. Operation Rolling Thunder began March 2, 1965, and would last three years. To protect the aircraft, pilots, mechanics, and support personnel, the first contingent of American combat troops arrived within a week.[74]

Years of policy decisions and public discourse influenced by news-media

73. Magnuson interview; Maclear, *Ten Thousand Day War*, 111–15; Levine, *Struggle for Southeast Asia*, 100–102.

74. Maclear, *Ten Thousand Day War*, 125–33; Shelby L. Stanton, *The Rise and Fall of an American Army: U.S. Ground Forces in Vietnam, 1965–1973*, 18–21.

presentations had prepared the ideological groundwork for formal intervention in Vietnam. Truman had pledged American assistance to noncommunists around the world, and then had obligated the nation to a three-year war in Korea and support for colonialists in Indochina. Eisenhower had evoked the specter of falling dominoes in the Third World and dispatched American military advisors and planners to transform Vietnam into a nation modeled on American standards. Kennedy had upped the ante by promising an activist anticommunist approach, and then pressured the Vietnamese to reform their economic, political, and social systems. Johnson had embarked on a confrontational course and provoked northern and southern communists to attack Americans in Vietnam. Like the rest of the news media, *Newsweek*, *Time*, and *U.S. News & World Report* had defined these policy decisions and American actions within an anticommunist schemata that assigned primary importance to communist agitation in nations troubled by political instability rather than to economic and social conditions. For years the newsmagazines relayed the viewpoints of their sources to a solidly middle- and upper-middle-class readership predisposed to anticommunist ideology. Their sources—policymakers and politicians—reflected the dominant precepts of the Cold War consensus.[75]

Newsweek, *Time*, and *U.S. News & World Report* had properly informed their readers about the occurrences in southern Vietnam prior to March 1965. But they had not properly explained the cultural and social circumstances causing those occurrences. Vietnam was home to numerous ethnic groups, including Chinese and Khmers, and many tribal people resided in the mountains, including Montagnards and Hmong. The country's recent colonial past had divided the social elite into a minority of ardent nationalists and a majority of passive nationalists, a division which made it difficult to form an effective government. The military's officer corps depended on bribery and graft to supplement its income, and its generals were chosen for command based on political factors rather than martial knowledge.

The explanations offered by *Newsweek*, *Time*, and *U.S. News & World Report* influenced public discourse on a war that killed 58,000 Americans and possibly a million Vietnamese, Hmong, Khmer, and Laotians. The con-

---

75. For an examination of the relationship between media attentiveness to policy issues and public opinion on those issues, see Benjamin I. Page and Robert Y. Shapiro, *The Rational Public: Fifty Years of Trends in Americans' Policy Preferences*, 224–28. For a description of middle-class hostility toward communism, see Baughman, *Henry R. Luce*, 170–71.

sciously opinionative style crafted by the newsmagazines sent impressions to a readership of affluent, educated, and influential citizens on an issue of paramount national importance. With a unique journalistic liberty to interpret events and issues, the newsmagazines had confined their presentations to parameters set by anticommunism and ethnocentrism. Vietnam would not be the right war in the right place.

2

War Stories

In his role as Saigon bureau chief and correspondent for *Time,* Stanley W. Cloud concentrated on the broader aspects of Vietnam policy rather than the drama of combat. His primary responsibilities included maintaining contacts with U.S. embassy personnel and the ambassador, senior officers at American military headquarters, and government ministers of the Vietnamese ally. To develop articles based on information obtained from these sources, Cloud visited military outposts, provincial capitals, and operational zones for firsthand observations that provided the details for an effective story. Late in 1971, Cloud, who regularly monitored military action reports available from the headquarters staff, noticed unusual activity in the border region with Laos to the north. "I had discovered all sorts of weird little patterns," Cloud says. "For instance, that they [the People's Army of Vietnam] were shelling areas with an intensity unknown before. I spent weeks interviewing military people and analyzing the activity, and reached the conclusion that they were about to launch a major offensive the following year." Cloud decided to assess the capability of the Army of the Republic of Vietnam (ARVN), which had primary responsibility for infantry operations after the withdrawal by the United States of most Army and Marine Corps combat units. Cloud sent a memo to *Time* editors in New York explaining his theory, and requested permission to develop a lengthy article. His editors approved the idea because it would offer an update on Vietnamization, the American program to improve ARVN.

Cloud traveled around the country to observe ARVN operations. From his extended period of research, he learned about serious problems affecting ARVN. He saw the inefficiency and ineptitude of ARVN while accompanying units on a few military operations. Infantry battalions never reached their staging areas on time, commanders failed to coordinate action among battalions in the field, and ARVN hesitated to venture into territory where the Vietcong and People's Army roamed. Cloud heard from American military advisors about corruption within the officer corps and poor morale among ARVN soldiers. If the People's Army launched a coordinated offensive, ARVN probably would perform poorly. Upon returning to Saigon from his up-country legwork, Cloud contacted Military Assistance Command officers, who confirmed his conclusions, and one officer recommended an appointment with Gen. Creighton W. Abrams, the commander. "I interviewed General Abrams, off the record, of course, who expressed grave doubts about the Vietnamese ability to withstand a major attack," Cloud says. "So the story was scheduled and written."[1]

Cloud soon received a telex copy of the final draft prior to publication, and he disliked it. "There at the end was a paragraph saying, completely unattributed, 'Despite all this, the South Vietnamese army is improving and has a good chance of surviving'—a very upbeat, positive ending," Cloud remembers. "It ran exactly counter to virtually all the reporting." Cloud sent a telex to New York asking for deletion or revision of the last paragraph. The editor responded that a correspondent in Washington had filed the contrary conclusion on ARVN based on information from a source in the State Department, a source the editor insisted was authoritative. It seemed odd to Cloud that the positive judgment on ARVN came from the State Department, not from a source at the Defense Department, which would be the logical place for a military viewpoint. Later, Cloud learned that the *Time* editor, himself a former correspondent in Vietnam, considered the original version of the article too negative and personally believed that ARVN had improved, no matter what Cloud's sources said. The article appeared in *Time* with the add-on paragraph. "We lost," Cloud says. "Except for the upbeat ending, it was a good story."[2]

The actual text that Cloud found objectionable stated: "But for the moment, U.S. military men in Saigon and Washington remain reasonably sure that the new Vietnamized war machine can accomplish its mission: to give the Saigon regime a 'reasonable chance' of survival when American troops go

1. Cloud interview.
2. Ibid.

home."[3] Seven weeks after the article appeared, the People's Army began its Easter Offensive, and most ARVN units in the border provinces collapsed and fled, abandoning the key provincial capital of Quang Tri without a fight. The United States halted the offensive in this area with intense aerial bombardment that disrupted the People's Army supply system, destroyed many artillery and tanks, and killed thousands of soldiers. ARVN soldiers nearer Saigon fought capably, and endured a siege at An Loc.

Cloud experienced the frustration of all newsmagazine correspondents of the era, whether filing their material from Saigon or Washington. "Group journalism was an acquired taste," he says. Correspondents and editors for *Newsweek, Time,* and *U.S. News & World Report* practiced a unique form of journalism during the Vietnam War that differed significantly from newspapers in several ways. A typical newsmagazine article contained information from multiple correspondents, each responsible for a specific coverage area, or beat; a typical newspaper story was the effort of a sole reporter who might interview sources from different areas of responsibility or expertise. A newsmagazine correspondent worked independently of others, usually unaware of interviews done by colleagues; a newspaper reporter always was notified if another reporter could contribute information for a story. A newsmagazine article presented only a small fraction of all the information gathered by correspondents, and the decision to omit the majority of material was made by at least two editors; a newspaper reporter often self-edited for length if the space available for the story was known beforehand, and only one editor normally cut text to make the story fit. A newsmagazine article usually was written by an associate editor, and the correspondents' words rarely survived the editing process intact; a newspaper reporter's writing sometimes was restructured by an editor and smoothed by a copy editor, but the original text influenced the typeset version. Lastly, a newsmagazine article typically offered commentary that imparted a judgment or established a theme; a newspaper story almost always strove for balance and impartiality, unless labeled as news analysis. "Newsmagazines have the advantage of having a little time to think," Cloud says. "If done properly, to take reports from various places and combine them, not in a blender way but in a scholarly way, to construct an account of what happened. The advantage is that you could do in a relatively little space what newspapers require much space to do, and you could

---

3. "Vietnamization: Is It Working?" *Time,* February 7, 1972, p. 36.

do it in a way that doesn't confuse the readers, unlike newspapers, which may have two or three stories that contradict one another." These unique methods for the production of news constituted an editorial process called directed synthesis. Originally devised by *Time* and adopted with modifications by *Newsweek* and *U.S. News & World Report,* directed synthesis involved framing information to guide a reader toward a perception of an event or issue preferred by the newsmagazine.[4]

Although the weekly publication schedule of the newsmagazines offered certain advantages in Vietnam, correspondents and editors faced a real challenge to sustain the interest of readers, many of whom watched the mostly generic film footage of warfare shown by television news programs and read the daily war summaries in their hometown newspapers. Storytelling was essential. "They [the correspondents] did their job by getting every possible detail, and I did my job by creating a compelling tale," says Ed Magnuson, who wrote several *Time* cover stories on the Vietnam War while an associate editor with the national section. Magnuson and the other associate editors wrote their weekly articles after sifting through an incredible volume of material from correspondents. They selected the dramatic, descriptive details that gave a sense of realism, found the colorful and meaningful quotes that added a human dimension, and crafted a tightly written story that summarized a week of war. *Newsweek* used a similar system in which correspondents filed copious amounts of text for editors to winnow, but *U.S. News & World Report* basically let its correspondents write their own pieces, much like newspaper reporters who usually worked on their own. The standards of newsmagazine journalism allowed certain liberties with storytelling that newspapers of the era did not tolerate, namely the omission of direct attribution for sources of information. By eliminating attribution, newsmagazines offered seemingly eyewitness accounts from correspondents. "Attribution wasn't essential to the piece," Magnuson says.[5]

Although their distinct characteristics separated newsmagazines from newspapers of the era, the newsmagazines shared certain fundamental traits of

---

4. Author interviews with Cloud, Cook, Horrock, and James N. Wallace, all of whom were newspaper reporters prior to joining the newsmagazines; Gans, *Deciding What's News,* 89–90, 136; Baughman, *Henry R. Luce,* 6–7, 60; Robert M. Entman, "Framing: Toward Clarification of a Fractured Paradigm."

5. Author interviews with Magnuson, Cloud, Rauch, Cook, Horrock, Wallace, and Jason McManus.

journalism with newspapers and television news programs. Upon assignment to a beat, correspondents devoted their efforts to identifying people who had information that was newsworthy, which meant information that met the criteria for publication. Correspondents developed a routine of contacting these sources on a regular basis, either by telephone or personal visits. The longer a correspondent was on a beat, the more likely it was that sources would yield results. Correspondents also bartered for information with sources in one place by exchanging information from sources in another place, a transaction dependent on the relevance and value of their network of sources. This barter transaction met the needs of both the sources, who for bureaucratic purposes wanted to know the gossip and activities of rival agencies or departments, and of correspondents, who for journalistic purposes sought to gather potentially newsworthy material. Ultimately, correspondents, and journalists generally, were dependent on their sources for information. This empowered those sources to construct the news by selectively revealing material for consideration by journalists.[6]

The organizational structure at newsmagazines conformed to the pattern at other news organizations, which placed journalists at sites where newsworthy information could be obtained efficiently from sources deemed authoritative: government agencies and departments, Congress, the White House, capital cities of certain nations.[7] Sources and journalists negotiated over information—the source to present a particular viewpoint and the journalist to obtain sufficient material to serve the perceived interests of readers or viewers. As noted, journalists selected information for newsworthiness, a standard based on common journalistic criteria and the interests of readers or viewers. Finally, journalists structured newsworthy information to attract and sustain attention. At every level of the process, values based on cultural, professional, and organizational norms affected the actions of journalists and their sources.[8] The newsmagazines, however, because of competition and editorial identity, practiced an overt point-of-view journalism.

6. Roy E. Carter, Jr., "Newspaper 'Gatekeepers' and the Sources of News"; Mark Fishman, *Manufacturing the News;* Robert Drechsel, *News Making in the Trial Courts;* Sigal, *Reporters and Officials;* Gaye Tuchman, *Making News: A Study in the Construction of Reality.*

7. Daniel C. Hallin, "Cartography, Community, and the Cold War," 111–12; Edward S. Herman and Noam Chomsky, *Manufacturing Consent: The Political Economy of the Mass Media,* 22–23; Sigal, *Reporters and Officials,* 4; Teun A. Van Dijk, *News as Discourse,* 7–8.

8. For an examination of the power of sources to set the news agenda, see Donohue, Tichenor, and Olien, "Guard Dog Perspective," 120–21; Leon V. Sigal, "Sources Make the

Getting in the Book

The process of publication—or, in the jargon of correspondents, "getting in the book"—began each week on Wednesday or Thursday and finished on Friday. The actual workweek began on Sunday or Monday in Saigon and on Monday in New York and Washington, but Wednesday and Thursday were the days when correspondents in the various bureaus sent "takes" to the central newsrooms. Final takes arrived at the newsrooms for *Newsweek* and *Time* in New York on Friday and at the *U.S. News & World Report* newsroom in Washington on Thursday, because its publisher wanted the newsmagazine delivered a day ahead of the competition. (The time difference between New York and Saigon meant that correspondents could file late Friday night from Vietnam, and on Saturday morning if absolutely necessary.) A take sent by telex consisted of four or five pages of text, which a correspondent typed at the console of a teletype machine. Each keyboard stroke punched a hole in a paper tape; when the correspondent had finished typing, he fed the perforated tape through a sprocket for high-speed transmission to the newsroom. The weekly volume for a correspondent ranged from a dozen typewritten pages to twenty or more, the equivalent of 3,000 to 6,000 words. "The correspondents at *Time* were trained to do a 'dump,'" explains Jason McManus, a senior editor at *Time* during the Vietnam era and later editor-in-chief of Time-Life magazines. "I mean, they just handed you their notebooks. The theory was [that] something they think is unimportant might be a real nugget of gold." The week's takes constituted a correspondent's "file" and provided descriptive details, quotes from sources, personal observations, and data for an article. The number of takes filed by correspondents varied according to the level of activity in Vietnam or their own story development schedule. Depending on the military and political events relevant to Vietnam during the week, correspondents in Saigon and at the White House, Defense Department, State Department, and Congress might ship files to the newsroom. From a set of files totaling 10,000 to 20,000 words, a published

---

News," 29; and Stocking and Gross, *How Do Journalists Think?* 13–17. For more on narrative presentations, storytelling, and the construction of reality, see Baughman, *Henry R. Luce*, 44–46; S. Elizabeth Bird and Robert W. Dardenne, "Myth, Chronicle, and Story: Explaining the Narrative Qualities of News," 78–81; and Schudson, "Sociology of News Production," 20. For more on newsworthiness and common criteria, see Stocking and Gross, *How Do Journalists Think?* 39, 46–50, 64–65, and Gans, *Deciding What's News*, 41–52.

article of three or four columns of text, amounting to 1,300 to 1,700 words, might result. Therefore, no correspondent expected to read in print most of the information arduously gathered during the week. Magnuson, who wrote more than a hundred cover stories during his years at *Time* and hundreds more inside-page articles for various sections, recalls the difficulty of the process: "The toughest decisions I had as a writer were what to leave out, not what to put in. I could understand how hard a correspondent may have worked to dig up a bit of detail, but if it did not neatly fit the narrative or the scope of the story, it had to go."[9]

The purpose and importance of an article determined the amount of effort expended by correspondents and editors. A subject deemed worthy of single-column treatment did not require exceptional effort. Editors discussed story ideas on Monday and made preliminary judgments on length. The number of lines assigned to an article signified its importance: 75 lines equaled one column and 165 lines a full page, minus space for a headline and a subheadline or two. McManus, who was *Time*'s World editor from 1968 to 1969 and then Nation editor through the end of the war, provides an example of the procedure: "If a bureau received notice—'World [section] scheduling seventy-liner on PX products in Saigon commissary, by Wednesday be sure you give us examples of luxury goods available and what they cost'—right away, the bureau would know not to bust their butt for a seventy-liner."[10]

The length of newsmagazine articles also varied according to the period of the war and by their designation. When an article on the war warranted designation as a cover story, it could reach 5,000 words, or almost twelve columns of text in a standard three-column page format.[11] Other war-related articles were considerably shorter. During spring and summer 1965, when few incidents of combat occurred and the newsmagazines had yet to send additional correspondents to Vietnam, *Newsweek* and *Time* generally published articles amounting to 900 to 1,100 words, or the equivalent of three columns of text; *U.S. News & World Report* articles had 700 to 1,000 words.

9. Cloud, Cook, Horrock, Pines, Rauch, Wallace, and McManus interviews.
10. McManus interview.
11. Length of articles was determined by calculating columns of text for each to the nearest one-fourth, then multiplying by 430 words per column. A newsmagazine column measured ten inches and contained seventy-five lines of type, with each line averaging six words; after deducting lines for subheads, the average number of words per column was computed.

From autumn 1965 through summer 1968, *Newsweek* articles averaged 1,600 words, or nearly five columns of text; *Time* articles averaged 1,900 words; and *U.S. News & World Report* articles averaged 1,200 words. From late 1968 onward, war-related articles appeared less frequently, but contained as much text. *Newsweek* and *Time* articles had comparable lengths during the latter years, averaging about 1,600 words, while *U.S. News & World Report* averaged 1,100 words. (For comparative purposes, a page of double-spaced typewritten text with standard margins has about 280 words.) The actual amount of space allocated to Vietnam articles by each newsmagazine was amazingly similar, however, despite the different word totals. Publication design factors accounted for the similarity. *Newsweek*, more often than *Time*, ran two- and three-column photographs in the upper third of an introductory page, which meant its articles frequently equaled *Time*'s in total space although with less text. *U.S. News & World Report* ran multiple-line headlines, presented more charts, maps, and graphs, and relied on typographical devices such as insets or block quotes, all of which extended its shorter articles.

The organizational system at each newsmagazine influenced the production of news. The magazines had some similar organizational factors. A hierarchy of assignments existed, with senior correspondents at the bureau in Washington and junior correspondents in Saigon. Most of the correspondents assigned to Saigon had been at their magazines four years or less. Editors often decided in favor of senior correspondents when a dispute arose over contradictory information from different sources. Correspondents sent their files to a specific section of the magazine, which meant the Saigon bureau filed to the editor of the international section and the Washington bureau filed to the editor of the national section. The senior editor of the section in which the article would appear had responsibility for reviewing the material; the managing editor saw all articles prior to publication and had final editing authority. The actual writing was done by associate editors for the specific sections. An associate editor read every correspondent's file for the intended article, coordinated research and fact-checking by editorial assistants, and wrote the article. The senior editor for the section looked at the article, ordered revisions and reductions in text, sometimes directed the associate editor to insert material from the files that had been omitted, and then approved the subsequent version. If the managing editor also wanted changes, the article would again be rewritten. "The changes in copy were rarely sharp," Magnuson says. "Adjectives were changed or dropped. It was usually fairly subtle and nuanced, nothing that could be factually challenged." Editors did their jobs without consulting the correspondents in Vietnam, mainly due to the communication system. "We didn't have a phone connection at the [*Newsweek* Saigon] bureau to make or get international calls," says William J. Cook. "Even by telex there wasn't much back-and-forth [with editors]. They were trying to get the magazine out."[12]

Notably different organizational factors existed at the newsmagazines, however, relating to editor-correspondent relationships and editorial authority. Former *Newsweek* correspondents describe an atmosphere of cooperation. "Newsmagazine reporters at that time were just anonymous fact-gatherers contributing to unsigned stories," Cook explains. "*Newsweek*'s editors were good enough that this system worked very well. It required a lot of trust between fieldworkers and those at the home office." The editor-correspondent relationship benefited from the management practice at *Newsweek* that gave considerable authority to a senior editor, who generally decided the final content of an article. The *Newsweek* system also featured a "readback" process. Bureau correspondents received a last draft of an article to review, could suggest revisions, and could appeal to the managing editor if their suggestions were rejected, which happened infrequently. "They listened to us," says Nicholas Horrock, another former *Newsweek* correspondent. "I argued some things out of the readbacks." Correspondents also felt their opinions mattered when editors handled contradictory information from different bureaus. Most often, a compromise settled the matter, with at least a reference to a contradictory perspective included in the published version. "They [editors] weren't about to slant or hype a story by ignoring facts that didn't fit their view," Cook says. Osborn Elliott, editor-in-chief of *Newsweek* from 1961 to 1976, described the atmosphere in the newsroom. "Week in, week out the Saigon bureau would report a generally downbeat view of events in the field," he wrote. "Week in, week out the Washington bureau—understandably reflecting the views of the administration more closely—would weigh in with more optimistic reports. It was up to the editor in New York to try to strike a balance—and since we tended to be less in sympathy with the war, there were frequent fights with Washington."[13] *Newsweek* correspondents had

---

12. Baughman, *Henry R. Luce,* 41; Hedley Donovan oral history transcript, Columbia University, 162; Elliott, *World of Oz,* 100–101; Gans, *Deciding What's News,* 91–92; Cloud, Horrock, Pines, Rauch, Wallace, Magnuson, and Cook interviews.

13. Cook interview; Gans, *Deciding What's News,* 100; Horrock interview; Elliott, *World of Oz,* 100–101.

confidence in their editors. Horrock says, "We had no horror stories comparable to *Time*."

Former *Time* staffers recall a major transformation in editor-correspondent relationships during the late 1960s. The autocratic managerial methods of Otto Fuerbringer, managing editor from 1960 to 1968, had angered and frustrated many correspondents. "It was known in those days as the 'weekly surprise,'" Cloud says. "You had no idea how your files would end up." The displeasure of correspondents finally compelled Fuerbringer to modify his methods somewhat, and in 1967 correspondents started receiving prepublication drafts of the articles based on their files. Correspondents had sought this review, called "comments-and-corrections," for a long time. Magnuson remembers that Fuerbringer and some of his senior editors preferred to exclude correspondents from reviewing articles for the sake of efficiency. "It slowed the closing process considerably," Magnuson says, explaining that correspondents would interfere with the final writing of an article by seeking changes in the text. Henry A. Grunwald, who replaced Fuerbringer in May 1968, believed otherwise. Grunwald required correspondents to review articles prior to publication. "Reporters always received copies of edited stories, and the story could not be closed for publication until each correspondent who worked on it sent in what we called c-and-c's [comments-and-corrections]," Magnuson says. On occasion, correspondents reacted angrily to a draft that omitted their information in favor of contradictory material from another bureau. "Sometimes 'rockets' were fired," says former *Time* correspondent Burton Y. Pines, using the jargon for a strongly worded protest sent by telex.[14]

Time, however, differed from *Newsweek* because senior editors felt no obligation to revise the text unless a correspondent had marked a factual error or misquote. "As a result, you would not be pleased with what was published," Cloud says. Rudolph Rauch III, who reported from Vietnam in 1971 and 1972, appreciated the comments-and-corrections policy. "They would send the final version back before it went in the book," Rauch says. "If we found something outrageous, we could change it and send it back. The gross misrepresentation that might have occurred previously just was not going on when I was there." Grunwald was less autocratic than Fuerbringer, but he still monitored the crafting of articles in the international and national sections. Hedley Donovan, the editor-in-chief at Time-Life

---

14. Cloud interview; Gans, *Deciding What's News,* 100; Magnuson and Pines interviews.

during the Vietnam War, stated bluntly, "The managing editor of *Time* has great scope as to how he chooses to treat that story." Magnuson agrees: "The general notion that managing editors would sit down with lower editors or writers and outline stories in any specifics is simply wrong," he said. "Fuerbringer might order up a story on a rare day and Grunwald softened our tone, but they let the news guide them. Files would come to us, we would read them, items would be marked, the writing would begin, then the editing."[15]

U.S. News & World Report, a distant third among the newsmagazines in readership and revenue from advertising, lacked the resources of its competitors. It had fewer correspondents and fewer editors. The major organizational difference pertained to the preparation of articles for publication. "We reported and wrote our own stories," says James N. Wallace, who reported from Vietnam for *U.S. News & World Report.* "Every once in a while, the Washington office would insert some material in your copy from the White House person or Pentagon."[16] Wallace usually built his articles on information from two or three sources in Vietnam, unless it was a combat piece and he talked to combatants, while *Newsweek* and *Time* articles routinely included information from several sources in Vietnam and Washington. Another difference at *U.S. News & World Report* involved editors. Their function closely resembled that of newspaper editors—primarily reviewing text for clarity and structure, then cutting text for reasons of space—and did not entail settling disputes over contradictory material filed by different bureaus.

All three newsmagazines relied on their correspondents for ideas. "Their attitude was that the guys in the field knew more than the editors in the office," Horrock says. Not every idea was accepted, although correspondents for each newsmagazine estimated that at least five of every six articles they developed had originated from the bureau. Pines, of *Time,* appreciated the autonomy: "We would gather Monday at the bureau, let New York know what we had in mind, and by Tuesday we would learn what story had been scheduled." Cloud and McManus cite the role played by the bureau chief. "I coordinated assignments and made assignments," Cloud says. "Correspondents worked on their own, but someone—me—had to make efficient use of their time." McManus likens the bureau chief to a supervisor. "Bureau chiefs managed the story ideas. The bureau chief presided over a story con-

---

15. Cloud and Rauch interviews; Donovan oral history, 160–66; Magnuson interview.
16. Wallace interview.

ference, and he decided what the bureau could manage," he says. "He had limited resources, and couldn't do every story willy-nilly."[17]

Correspondents enjoyed a high degree of trust from editors, too. Of all articles on the war published by *Newsweek, Time,* and *U.S. News & World Report,* 93 percent presented conclusions, judgments, or quotations from unidentified or anonymous sources. Although editors occasionally removed the identification of a source for reasons of space, the usual circumstance was that correspondents did not name their sources unless it was essential to the narrative. This enabled the newsmagazines to analyze the effect of policy decisions, assess the military situation, describe an incident or situation, evaluate strategy and tactics, and interpret the significance of political developments without attribution. At one level, the absence of attribution was an expedient device that offered detail and perspective to readers without adding unnecessary verification; at another level, however, it was a convenient way to insert commentary. Articles on combat regularly featured colorful descriptions obtained from participants, but the newsmagazines often let the narrative flow uninterrupted by attribution. At other times, a quotation from a combatant merely identified someone as "a pilot," "the sergeant," "the gunner," or "a rifleman." Cook explains the practice: "More often than not, putting 'an officer' was a helluva lot quicker than to say the name." Quicker, and shorter. "Space was at a premium," *Time*'s Cloud says. "If you fully identified a person with name, rank, hometown, unit, all of that, you would take up two or three lines. What we put in [the file] was 'name available on request,' if an editor wanted to have it." *Newsweek* had a similar process. "A lot of times the names were in the original file," Cook says. "They would be taken out just for space, to make the story move faster."[18]

Of more significance, newsmagazine articles passed along from anonymous sources negative conclusions, judgments, and quotes on war policy, military methods, and political developments. These examples typify the style in which substantive criticisms and doubts were expressed: from *Newsweek,* "a high-ranking U.S. adviser," "a senior U.S. adviser," "a top Pentagon official," "one top U.S. commander," "one Pentagon general," "one U.S. intelligence expert," "a senior U.S. officer"; from *Time,* "one American general," "experts in Saigon," "a senior officer in Saigon," "one top-ranking U.S. officer,"

---

17. Horrock, Pines, Cloud, and McManus interviews.
18. Cook and Cloud interviews.

"a high-ranking U.S. general"; from *U.S. News & World Report,* "an American officer in Saigon," "a ranking officer," "a Pentagon officer."[19] The absence of names protected the identity of sources in military headquarters, the embassy in Saigon, and commanders of military units in the field. "Careers were at stake," Horrock says. Cloud, for example, obtained crucial comments from General Abrams concerning ARVN in an off-the-record interview, a stipulation necessitated by the fact that Abrams was dubious about the capability of the southern ally's army. The factions within the military that dueled over strategy and tactics advanced their arguments through off-the-record or background-only interviews with correspondents and other journalists. "MACV [military headquarters in Saigon] had factions," Wallace says. "There was a Westmoreland faction and an Abrams faction." The former faction favored conventional warfare, the latter small-unit warfare. In other cases, generals and colonels, embassy staff, and military advisors simply vented their frustrations to journalists. "If you went to see Barry Zorthian [deputy ambassador for public affairs], you couldn't say Zorthian said it," Cook says. "You could say 'U.S. officials said.' That was the rule. And the rule is you never burn a source until you have to."[20]

However, deception occurred concerning unidentified sources. Robert Sam Anson, a *Time* correspondent in Vietnam in 1969 and 1970, has described how *Time* published his commentary on the invasion of Cambodia without informing readers that he was the source. According to Anson, whose antiwar attitude created tension within the Saigon bureau, editors approved very few of his story ideas because they clashed with *Time*'s viewpoint. But when Anson happened to be in Cambodia on assignment at the time of the 1970 invasion, he said, his commentary on the success and failure of specific military operations and the destruction and death in the countryside made it into *Time,* attributed to a "military observer." Pines, who worked with Anson in the Saigon bureau, disputes this account. "We

---

19. *Newsweek:* "A New Ball Game?" May 3, 1965, pp. 53–54; "Strictly Military," August 16, 1965, p. 30; "The Air War: Less Than a Success," August 29, 1966, p. 21; "An Election, a Barrier and Talk of Peace," September 18, 1967, p. 28; "The Tet Offensive: How They Did It," March 11, 1968, p. 65. *Time:* "The Bloody Hills," June 11, 1965, p. 34; "A New Kind of War," October 22, 1965, p. 28; "And Now, Civil War," May 27, 1966, p. 27; "Inoffensive Tet," March 16, 1970, p. 29. *U.S. News & World Report:* "Reds Don't Talk Peace—What's Holding Them Up?" November 8, 1965, p. 44; "Stalled War: Now What?" July 17, 1967, p. 25; "'The Coin Has Flipped Over to Our Side,'" November 27, 1967, p. 50.

20. Horrock, Wallace, and Cook interviews.

had so much from so many people out in the field, we blended it all together," says Pines, himself a correspondent for the Cambodia invasion. "We had a mechanism called an internal byline for quoting ourselves, and we did [it] when it was warranted, for drama and color." Rauch remembers another procedure. "We would talk to the bureau chief, and he would make sure we had reasonably good sources, that these weren't people we had just cooked up," he explains.[21]

Saigon

Correspondents assigned to Vietnam by *Newsweek* and *Time* divided their coverage into military and nonmilitary beats. The military beat included Military Assistance Command headquarters in Saigon and sources with corps, division, and brigade headquarters throughout southern Vietnam; when bureaus were fully staffed, one correspondent focused on headquarters in Saigon and nearby military units while another had responsibility for up-country Army and Marine Corps operations. Nonmilitary coverage was subdivided into two beats: the U.S. embassy and Central Intelligence Agency station chief were usually assigned to the newsmagazine's bureau chief, and the second beat included other U.S. government departments and the southern Vietnam government and military.

For a newsmagazine correspondent, an assignment to Vietnam involved a routine similar to anywhere else—except for the danger and the exposure to the effects of war. Typically, a correspondent spent four to five days of the week in Saigon and two to three days out in the field; during an atypical week, a correspondent stayed in Saigon only two to three days while spending the other days covering a major tactical operation for immediate publication or developing a story idea for later publication. Late in the war when combat involving American troops had become infrequent, correspondents spent longer periods away from the Saigon bureau to develop articles on the Vietnamese military and conditions in the countryside. *Newsweek* correspondents usually spent Monday through Wednesday away from Saigon; *Time* correspondents spent Tuesday through Thursday outside the city, except for the correspondent designated to cover combat operations, who often was gone Sunday through Tuesday or Wednesday. *U.S. News & World Report*

---

21. Robert Sam Anson, *War News: A Young Reporter in Indochina*, 33, 39, 41–42, 68–71; Pines and Rauch interviews.

correspondents were out of the bureau from Monday through Wednesday. Events on the battlefield often disrupted the weekly routine.[22]

The workday of a newsmagazine correspondent in Saigon began at nine or nine thirty with arrival at the bureau and ended at six or six thirty with dinner and drinks at a hotel chosen by colleagues. "We could sip martinis served outside at a rooftop bar by a waiter in a tux—and see machine-gun tracers off in the distance," Cook says. *Newsweek* rented a spacious hotel suite in central Saigon for a bureau. *Newsweek* correspondents typed their reports, making copies with carbon paper, then sat at a telex machine to keyboard the information for transmission to Tokyo and a relay to New York; the magazine initially shared a telex line with *Stars & Stripes,* a newspaper for military personnel, but later shared a line with the Reuters news service. *Time* leased a villa as a residence for its correspondents and rented a three-room suite in a downtown hotel for a bureau; later in the war, when fewer correspondents were in-country, it leased a three-room suite in a hotel. Its bureau had a darkroom for *Life* photographers, a secretarial staff, and a Time-Life telex line. *U.S. News & World Report* had a small office with two desks in a downtown business building. Its correspondents filed on a common telex line, which often meant delays, until the magazine got its own line in late 1968.

Between the start and finish of each workday in Saigon, correspondents arranged interviews with Military Assistance Command officers, U.S. embassy officials responsible for economic and political programs, CIA analysts, and military public affairs officers, who in turn would arrange other interviews for the correspondents with unit commanders or schedule visits to brigades and divisions in various areas of the country. Correspondents followed customary patterns for journalists. They asked their sources about military and political activities, traded gossip, received tips on potential developments, and pieced together assortments of items about which to ask their sources for details. Correspondents wasted much of their workday in Saigon waiting to interview people and attempting to contact sources. They devoted most of their time to talking with Americans.

Newsweek and *Time* had similar beat systems for their correspondents. One or two correspondents covered combat, one covered policy and programs, and the bureau chief covered the upper levels of the Military Assis-

---

22. Cloud, Cook, Horrock, Pines, Rauch, and Wallace interviews are the source of information in this and the next several paragraphs.

tance Command, U.S. embassy, and Republic of Vietnam government. The combat correspondents provided the weekly drama around which most newsmagazine articles revolved, and these correspondents had sources at the middle level of the Military Assistance Command to broaden coverage from the basic battlefield events. The policy-program correspondents monitored economic, political, and social conditions in Vietnam, and these correspondents had sources at the embassy and among CIA analysts. "Frank Snepp was one of our sources," Horrock says, mentioning a CIA analyst. "Of course, he would give you the impression that what he was telling you was hush-hush, but he was getting the agency's point across," Horrock says.[23] The bureau chiefs supplied assessments of the overall military situation and the operation of the southern government. *U.S. News & World Report* lacked the personnel of its competitors, so its two correspondents divided their time between combat coverage and the other aspects of reporting the war.

At the end of a workday in Saigon, newsmagazine correspondents gathered for dinner and drinks. Many a night at the veranda bar of the Continental Palace Hotel or the rooftop bar at the Caravelle Hotel lasted from sunset until the midnight curfew—but not on Thursdays because that was the deadline for transmitting files to New York, which almost always kept correspondents in the bureaus until the curfew. The correspondents talked and drank with their peers from the newspapers, television, and news services, but they exchanged information only with newsmagazine colleagues. "We checked each other's notes, in a sense, so we could tell if we were getting some line of bull they [the American sources] hoped you'd swallow," Pines says. Horrock recalls, "You compared notes and saw if you should develop some angle." Although an inadvertent comment sometimes revealed details from a conversation with a source, correspondents carefully refrained from letting their competitors know what they were working on.

But the legend of those nightlong sessions tells a different tale. According to some military commanders, policymakers, and critics of wartime coverage, the barroom chitchat created copycat journalism. The legend has it that journalists conspired to report the war negatively by sharing details about every military misstep, every incidence of civilian casualties, and every criticism of military strategy and official policy. At the bars, rumors became facts,

23. Snepp later wrote an exposé, *Decent Interval*, on American decisions during the collapse of the south in spring 1975. He was sued successfully by the federal government for violating his CIA contract, which prohibited unauthorized disclosure of information, and he forfeited payments received for the book.

which then became the basis for news coverage that essentially reported the same information. "Part of the problem was the correspondent corps in Saigon," said Walt W. Rostow. Thirty years after his last policy decision in the Johnson administration, Rostow still resented the Saigon press corps: "They wrote only for each other, and they got their stories at the Caravelle bar." Pines laughs at the remark. "The Caravelle was rather luxurious," he remembers. "It would have been more correct to say the Continental, the great veranda there." On the substantive issue of journalistic conspiracy, Pines says: "There were too many reporters who never got out of Saigon, and they soaked up what the reporters up-country talked about." Cook also dismisses the legend of the Caravelle bar. "That's just bullshit," he says. "Some people were lazy and wrote their stories without doing the actual reporting. But not the *New York Times* or the magazines, and certainly it wasn't true of the television reporters." Cook believes some of the suspicion about the Saigon press corps might have originated from the camaraderie and common bond among a core group. "Virtually every civil rights reporter from the South ended up in Vietnam," Cook says. "In Saigon, we all spent one drunken evening singing freedom songs, because we all knew the words."[24]

A corollary to the legend, and a criticism founded on a journalistic trait, is that journalists in Saigon sought acceptance from their peers, which caused them to go along with the negative view of the war. "It was inevitable, in the circumstances, that they came to write, in the first instance, for each other," argues Robert Elegant, a former journalist who reported the Vietnam War. "After each other, correspondents wrote to win the approbation of their editors, who controlled their professional lives and who were closely linked with the intellectual community at home." None of the journalists interviewed for this book disputed that a primary goal was to have information from their files appear in the pages of their newsmagazines. But each one believes their files reflected the war they witnessed. "I wanted to tell people what I was seeing, and what my point of view was," Rauch says. Newsmagazine correspondents considered a personal viewpoint permissible, even mandatory. "We were observers, not note-takers," Cloud says. "It was our job to look and listen and decide what made the most sense."[25]

24. Rostow, Pines, and Cook interviews. For discussions of the alleged unity among Saigon correspondents concerning coverage of the war, see Martin F. Herz, *The Vietnam War in Retrospect*, 36, and William C. Westmoreland, *A Soldier Reports*, 419.

25. Robert Elegant, "How to Lose a War: Reflections of a Foreign Correspondent," 74; Rauch and Cloud interviews.

Washington, D.C.

Presidential assistants and policymakers in the White House realized full well that senior correspondents in Washington and editors in newsrooms outranked correspondents in Saigon. "Our best chance was to reach the reporters in Washington and the editors to counter what the Saigon correspondents were saying," Rostow said. President Johnson met personally with *Newsweek, Time,* and *U.S. News & World Report* correspondents thirty-eight times from April 1965 through March 1968 to discuss Vietnam. "Johnson wanted their support and approval," says George Reedy, the presidential press secretary in 1965 and later a political advisor. "Of course, he wanted everybody's approval. I was skeptical about their impact." Johnson considered journalists crucial to the formation of public opinion and political support. "The press virtually lived with him," a presidential profile states. "He had reporters in for private, off-the-record conversations, one-on-one and in small groups, nearly every week he was in the White House." President Nixon, whose relationship with journalists was the opposite of Johnson's, met four times from December 1969 through January 1972 with newsmagazine editors or correspondents to discuss Vietnam. "I believe this would be advantageous in maintaining their perspective," Herbert G. Klein, the presidential communications director, advised.[26]

Johnson and Nixon monitored newsmagazine coverage. Johnson read the newsmagazines himself, receiving advance copies on Sunday, a day before newsstands and subscribers. "They went straight to his desk," Reedy says. "I marked things he should read." Johnson's obsession with news coverage forced his press secretaries to devote many hours to reading the newsmagazines and major newspapers. "He was just such a news junkie," remembers George Christian, one of Reedy's successors. "He paid too much attention to the news." Nixon read a summary of newsmagazine articles included in a general wrap-up. Aides suggested responses or rebuttals and offered strategies to influence coverage.[27] Johnson and his assistants also

---

26. Rostow interview; president's appointment file and diary backup, LBJ Library; Reedy interview; Kenneth W. Thompson, ed., *The Johnson Presidency,* vol. 5, *Portraits of American Presidents,* 119–20, 121; White House special files, staff member and office files, Klein, boxes 3–6, and memorandum for the president, December 5, 1969, Klein, box 3, Nixon Presidential Materials Project.

27. Tom Johnson to Marvin Watson, memorandum regarding distribution of newsmagazines to the president and White House staff, September 30, 1966, White House central files, *Newsweek* name file, box 95, LBJ Library; Reedy and Christian interviews; White

attempted to monitor the contacts of White House personnel with journalists. The press secretary received daily reports from presidential assistants concerning conversations, or the absence of same, with journalists. "I have not personally seen nor talked with any member of the press today," Robert W. Komer, an assistant and later the pacification program coordinator, informed the office. A daily checklist with thirty-eight names, including Rostow and other senior assistants, circulated for verification of contacts with journalists. Presidential staff needed occasional reminders. "During the past two weeks there has been a slacking off of memoranda reporting press contacts," Rostow informed people on the list. "This is a reminder that memoranda for the record should be made of all press contacts, telephone calls, office calls, and social encounters which involve discussions of substance."[28]

Presidential assistants also tried to generate favorable articles about Vietnam policy. Five of Johnson's presidential policy assistants—Joseph Califano, Douglass Cater, Robert Kintner, Harry McPherson, and Rostow—met to plan a strategy. The "purpose was to establish a weekly meeting to develop items for columnists," Kintner told the president, mentioning Hugh Sidey of *Time* and Charles Roberts of *Newsweek*. Several weeks later, Kintner wrote to Christian, "Per our talk, I will now await word from you on how you want to work out our weekly contacts with *Newsweek* and *Time*." Kintner also responded to a directive from Johnson to push for better coverage. "This refers to your asking me to set up such a meeting to get items from your principal assistants for planting with *Time, Newsweek,* etc," Kintner wrote.[29]

Presidents also courted the support of newsmagazine editors. Cater, a Johnson policy assistant, had lunch with a *Newsweek* editor for such a purpose. "Shall we meet at the Sans Souci?" Cater asked. Numerous memos, notes, and conversations occurred between Johnson administration assis-

---

House central files, staff member and office files, annotated news summary, Patrick J. Buchanan, box 2, Nixon Project.

28. Robert W. Komer to Bill Moyers (press secretary to President Johnson), memorandum, July 28, 1966, White House central files, Komer name file, box 3, LBJ Library; Tom Johnson to the president, memorandum, June 8, 1967, president's appointment file and diary backup, box 68, LBJ Library; Walt Rostow to all staff officers, memorandum, August 9, 1967, national security files, Vietnam country file, box 7, LBJ Library.

29. Robert E. Kintner to the president, January 18, 1967; Kintner to George Christian, March 1, 1967; and Kintner to the president, January 12, 1967, all personal notes in White House central files, *Newsweek* name file, box 95, LBJ Library.

tants and newsmagazine editors.[30] Johnson never took support for granted. "The Editor of *Time,* Otto Fuerbringer, would like to come in to see you," a memo informed the president. "He simply wants to get a reading of your mind, particularly on Viet Nam. As you know, *Time* has been magnificent in support of your Viet Nam policies in the last eight months." Johnson met with Fuerbringer. He also encouraged editors to visit Vietnam. "General [Harold] Johnson wants to take Hedley Donovan of Time-Life with him to Vietnam," another memo noted. "General Johnson wants the President's approval on this." A check mark on the memo indicates that approval was given.[31] During the Nixon administration, an assistant arranged with *U.S. News & World Report* for publication of an article on Vietnam policy. "They are enthusiastic about the idea," the memo stated. A presidential luncheon with *Newsweek* editors offered the prospect for better coverage. "I believe this would be advantageous in maintaining their perspective," a presidential assistant told Nixon.[32]

Presidential efforts to influence coverage apparently had little effect, at least after summer 1967. *Newsweek*'s rather tepid enthusiasm for military intervention in Vietnam had waned by spring 1967, then disappeared altogether a year later. *Time* shifted from ardent supporter to neutral observer by autumn 1967, then became a vociferous critic of Nixon policy. *U.S. News & World Report* remained steadfast regarding intervention throughout the war, although it blamed indecision by Johnson for failure to win. The paper trail left by presidential assistants offers a skewed version of relationships with newsmagazine correspondents and editors. Many documents are self-serving, self-promoting messages intended to impress Johnson and Nixon with the efforts being made on their behalf. Whether these efforts ever accomplished

---

30. Douglass Cater to James M. Cannon, letter, December 19, 1966, White House central files, *Newsweek* name file, box 95, LBJ Library; documents in White House central files, name files for Christian, Kintner, Komer, Moyers, *Newsweek, Time,* and Rostow, listing contacts between officials and editors, 1965–1968, LBJ Library.

31. Bill Moyers to the president, memorandum, March 15, 1966, White House central files, *Time* name file, box 131, LBJ Library; George Christian to the president, memorandum, September 6, 1967, White House central files, Donovan name file, box 234, LBJ Library.

32. Herbert G. Klein to H. R. Haldeman, memorandum, January 14, 1972, White House special files, White House action memoranda, box 6, Nixon Project; Klein to the president, memorandum, December 5, 1969, White House special files, staff member and office files, Klein, box 3, Nixon Project.

anything concrete cannot be discerned in the newsmagazine articles of the period or from interviews with six correspondents who reported from Vietnam, none of whom was aware of any pressure from editors to change the tone of their files. Correspondents assigned to the White House had played the game for a long time, so they were not easily manipulated. *Newsweek*'s Charles Roberts described an episode with Johnson: "He put his arm on my shoulder and said, 'You know, Chuck, I feel a lot better toward you than I do towards Kay Graham, or *Newsweek,* or the *Washington Post.*' And I think this was probably a true statement, that he felt maybe that I was a better personal friend than any of those, than Kay or either of those institutions, but it was another example of that trying to court and woo. He was trying to separate me from my publication and—it seems to me—make me a personal ally of his, even if *Newsweek* wasn't."[33]

New York

The process of publishing newsmagazine articles started on Monday. The effort at each newsmagazine's bureaus and newsroom involved many men, most of them correspondents or editors, and women, most of them editorial assistants or researchers. *Time* employed 228 people to report, research, and write the news: 89 correspondents, 72 editors, and 67 editorial assistant/researchers. *Newsweek* had 194 news personnel: 74 correspondents, 74 editors, and 46 editorial assistant/researchers. *U.S. News & World Report* had 109 news employees: 53 correspondents, 37 editors, and 19 editorial assistant/researchers. (The number of news personnel at each magazine varied between 1965 and 1973; an average was computed for the period.)

Some variation of schedules existed, but most editors at newsmagazines began their workweek at 10 a.m. Monday. The managing editor met with senior editors of specific sections to discuss story ideas submitted by correspondents from the bureaus and at the central newsrooms, the home to correspondents for sections devoted to arts and entertainment, law, religion, and business. This story conference generally lasted until noon. The managing editor designated articles for immediate development, assigned others for long-term consideration, and rejected some. Telex messages went to the bureaus to notify correspondents about the decisions, and to coordinate the effort of several bureaus on a single article if necessary. Editorial assistant/

---

33. Charles Roberts oral history, 1:44, LBJ Library.

researchers at *Newsweek* and *Time* received instructions on gathering material for editors.[34]

Beginning on Tuesday morning, senior editors conferred with associate editors, who then talked with editorial assistant/researchers to obtain background material for writing articles. Some of this was available later Tuesday. Senior editors and associate editors read all the material. Editors marked items of interest, ordered photocopies, and familiarized themselves with the subject. To take an example of the process, when Buddhist monks and militants rebelled in southern Vietnam during early 1966, editors needed books and articles on Buddhism to understand its philosophy and practices; they also reviewed academic journals and magazine articles to become familiar with Buddhist sects in Vietnam, the political disputes between the Catholic leadership of the government and the Buddhists, and the biographies of the monks; and correspondents in bureaus elsewhere in Asia provided files on the relationship between Buddhist sects and governments in other nations. By midafternoon Wednesday, files from correspondents would begin arriving by telex. Wednesday was the last day of the week that editors went home by six o'clock.

The arrival of more files in the central newsrooms from correspondents on Thursday lengthened the workday for editors and editorial assistant/researchers, a category staffed predominantly by women who served in the multifaceted role of coordinators of information gathering, reference librarians, and fact-checkers. For senior editors and associate editors, the task of reading thousands of words from correspondents required the entire day and night. Senior editors walked into the central newsrooms Thursday morning at ten or eleven o'clock and walked out an hour or two before dawn Friday; associate editors ended their work by nine or ten o'clock Thursday night. Friday was "the day from hell," according to Magnuson, the day for writing, rewriting, and more rewriting. Associate editors stayed until six o'clock Saturday morning if they wrote a cover story or a major article for the international or national section. Some editors chose to quit at midnight and return at dawn Saturday to finish. Senior editors remained at their desks until the text went to press. "Often you were put up at a hotel late in the week because you knew you wouldn't be going home if you lived in the suburbs," McManus says. This schedule applied during so-called normal weeks. A

---

34. Horrock, McManus, and Magnuson interviews.

major incident or event in Vietnam or a dramatic antiwar protest in the United States threw the schedule into chaos. As journalists, most editors enjoyed the challenge. "All the best senior editors in the hard-news sections, like Nation and World, loved nothing better than throwing everything out they started on Monday and starting over on closing day [Saturday]," McManus says. "That's what they called 'bounce.' We were always ready to make a change. That was the vitality of the magazine."[35]

The willingness to rip apart a week's worth of labor on the last day demonstrated the intense competition among the newsmagazines. On a less dramatic level, this competitive attitude shaped the presentation of information provided to millions of readers. Within the confines of the newsroom, senior editors at each magazine determined the tone, or viewpoint, that certain articles on the Vietnam War would evince. Senior editors had the final authority to omit material, assign material prominent placement, and approve commentary on a military operation or policy decision. They based their decisions upon the dominant ideology at the newsmagazine, the opinions of news sources, and an expectation of the reaction by readers. This process was not secretive. Everyone in the newsroom and bureaus understood it.

Newsweek, Time, and *U.S. News & World Report* operated in the realm of the marketplace, where presidential persuasion and pressure might have mattered to editors personally but not professionally. By mid-1967, *Newsweek*'s editors and publisher believed that a progressive political tone and skepticism about the Vietnam War had helped increase readership, making it the "hot" magazine for national advertisers. *Newsweek* correspondents and editors considered themselves more attuned to younger adults who questioned, if not rejected, the attitudes of middle-aged and elderly Americans.[36] Conversely, *Time* executives recognized that its pro-intervention tone and Cold War ideology had alienated a segment of its readership, and they noticed that *Newsweek* was gaining new readers at a higher percentage rate than *Time*.[37] *U.S. News & World Report* did not modify its ultraconservative tone

---

35. Magnuson and McManus interviews.

36. Cook and Horrock both believe that *Newsweek*'s coverage of civil rights activities during the early and mid-1960s plus its skepticism about Vietnam made it popular among young soldiers (Cook and Horrock interviews). For more on Newsweek's competitive edge, see Elliott, *World of Oz,* 31, 89–90, and Graham, *Personal History,* 281–83, 386.

37. The effect of *Time*'s doctrinaire tone and the changes made in editorial policy are discussed in James L. Baughman, "The Transformation of *Time* Magazine: From Opinion Leader

because it had created a niche by appealing to a readership with that perspective. But by the end of the war, blatant ideological expressions by *Newsweek* and *Time* had vanished for economic reasons. "Ideologists are not wanted by the news media, for most journalists believe ideology to be an obstacle to story selection and production," Herbert J. Gans wrote in his study of *Newsweek* and *Time*. "Such news might attract other ideologists, but they constitute only a tiny part of the audience."[38]

Institutional and organizational characteristics determined the production of news at *Newsweek, Time,* and *U.S. News & World Report*. These characteristics established the routines for gathering information, certified the sources of information, set the criteria for newsworthiness, and shaped the construction of newsmagazine articles. Correspondents in Saigon functioned under exceedingly difficult conditions, while correspondents in Washington coped with the peculiar nature of reporting from the nation's center of political power. Correspondents and editors operated within the standards associated with journalism generally and newsmagazines specifically. Their presentation of the Vietnam War varied in context but not in form.

---

to Supporting Player"; Baughman, *Henry R. Luce*, 193–94; Hedley Donovan, *Right Places, Right Times,* 321; and Henry Grunwald, *One Man's America: A Journalist's Search for the Heart of His Country,* 358–59.

38. Gans, *Deciding What's News,* 190–93.

3

Americans at War
Heroism and Horror

Newsweek, Time, and *U.S. News & World Report* had certain advantages in covering the Vietnam War. Warfare in Vietnam involved hundreds of infantry patrols going into the countryside every day but few encounters with the enemy, many major military operations in remote areas but few decisive battles. These circumstances favored the newsmagazines, whose weekly publication schedule enabled correspondents to search for combat, travel to the scene, interview participants, and return to write dramatic descriptions of the battlefield. By contrast, the typical scarcity of daily combat and the distance from Saigon to the usual scenes of military action effectively kept television reporters and camera crews from filming the sights and sounds of war for the nightly news programs on ABC, CBS, and NBC. "The trouble is, Vietnam isn't a fast-breaking news event most of the time," observed Michael J. Arlen, whose columns for the *New Yorker* perceptively described wartime television coverage. *Newsweek, Time,* and *U.S. News & World Report* relied on vivid vignettes and eyewitness observations to enliven articles that otherwise explained the overall military situation, political developments, and policy decisions. For the newsmagazines, a single combat vignette conveyed a sense of a week's worth of warfare in Vietnam. "This was really the newsmagazine war," says Nicholas Horrock, a *Newsweek* correspondent in Vietnam for sixteen months. "It may have been a television war back in the States, but not in Vietnam."[1]

Correspondents for the newsmagazines worked an odd schedule to obtain

---

1. Michael J. Arlen, *Living-Room War,* 105–6; Horrock interview.

war stories. They did routine legwork during regular office hours a day or two each week to talk with sources at military headquarters in Saigon, and then on a moment's notice went on round-the-clock forays into the countryside to witness combat or interview combatants. For the most part, correspondents worked independently, simply informing the bureau chief about their plans and leaving word when they had to rush to a combat site. Upon their return to Saigon, they reviewed their notes and wrote text for transmission to newsrooms in New York. "Correspondents submitted files and editors in New York wrote the stories, picking and choosing what they wanted to use," says William J. Cook, a *Newsweek* correspondent in Vietnam in 1965 and 1966. On rare occasions, the bureau chief or stateside editors assigned correspondents to file information on a specific topic, but otherwise the correspondents decided what was newsworthy. "My work was largely dictated by events," Cook says. "I covered what was happening. Editors expected correspondents to generate ideas and act on them." Correspondents' decisions, however, mattered little to the editors if newsworthy developments in the United States, Europe, or elsewhere in Asia warranted priority treatment, in which case articles from Vietnam were trimmed severely or eliminated altogether, especially later in the war when editors believed most readers had lost interest. Rudolph Rauch III, a *Time* correspondent in Vietnam for fifteen months, explains: "They [editors] welcomed the suggestions, and they would often approve our suggestions and then would not run the story because they didn't have space. That was one of the frustrations."[2] Correspondents had much autonomy but little authority.

Editors at *Newsweek, Time,* and *U.S. News & World Report* were keenly aware that they had to compete with television, to offer more than the images of war that flickered on television screens in living rooms across America. Images mattered, and the network programs relied on generic scenes of warfare for a backdrop while anchormen read summaries of the day's events in Vietnam. By the start of the American military buildup in Vietnam in the mid-1960s, many popular magazines in the United States had lost a tremendous amount of advertising dollars to television because the huge audiences for prime-time programs attracted national advertisers. *Collier's,* a popular weekly, had died in 1957 despite a readership in the millions. The *Saturday Evening Post* was reeling. *Look* and *Life* would cease publication by the early

---

2. Cook and Rauch interviews.

1970s. Although the newsmagazines served a niche that most major advertisers continued to find desirable, primarily because of the affluence and age characteristics of the readership, editors recognized that news on television posed a potential threat, despite the limitations that camera crews faced in filming combat. *Newsweek* and *Time* particularly made every effort to provide vivid word portraits on the war in Vietnam, convinced it might give them an edge over television. Descriptive writing—called "color"—was considered essential. "The editors wanted soldier stories," says Horrock.[3]

Combat coverage of Americans at war in Vietnam became the primary focus for *Newsweek, Time,* and *U.S. News & World Report* soon after the first combat troops deployed to Da Nang in March 1965. "Whatever the official line," *Newsweek* wrote, "the Americans are no longer 'advisers' in Vietnam but out-and-out warriors." The newsmagazines gradually relegated ARVN to only occasional mention. Government officials in Washington were displeased that journalists virtually ignored Vietnamese participation in the war. "The fact that the Vietnamese are doing the bulk of the fighting and suffering the largest number of casualties gets scant attention," a State Department memorandum reported. By early 1966, when the United States had assumed the primary combat role in southern Vietnam, newsmagazine articles barely referred to ARVN. This remained unchanged for nearly five years, until the withdrawal of U.S. troops had reduced the American death toll to an average of forty a week. Of nearly six hundred articles on warfare published by the newsmagazines, only 22 percent reported action involving ARVN. Herbert J. Gans identified the rationale for this imbalance: "Once American troops arrived, Vietnam was classified as domestic news, a decision that made the resulting reality and value judgments almost mandatory."[4]

Just as the Pentagon placed troops and materiel into the Vietnam pipeline from 1965 to 1968, so the newsmagazines bolstered their Saigon bureaus. American troops in-country totaled 184,000 in December 1965, 268,000 in June 1966, 449,000 in June 1967, and peaked at 540,000 in October 1968.

---

3. George Arthur Bailey, "The Vietnam War According to Chet, David, Walter, Harry, Peter, Bob, Howard, and Frank: A Content Analysis of Journalistic Performance by the Network Television Evening News Anchormen, 1965–1970," 153–54, 372–79; McManus, Magnuson, and Horrock interviews.

4. "Marines and a Message," *Newsweek,* March 22, 1965, p. 38; State Department to Bill Moyers, memorandum, August 13, 1965, national security files, Vietnam country file, box 197, LBJ Library; Gans, *Deciding What's News,* 202.

Newsweek, which had opened a one-person Saigon bureau in December 1963, sent a second correspondent in March 1965, increased the bureau temporarily to four correspondents from October 1965 to March 1966, maintained a three-person bureau until April 1970 (with a fourth correspondent brought in from Bangkok when necessary), and ended the war with two in-country correspondents. *Time,* which had relied on pairs of correspondents from its Hong Kong bureau to cover the war on rotation, had a three-person Saigon bureau by June 1966; a fourth correspondent joined the bureau in November, and a fifth arrived by December 1967. From April 1968 to October 1969, *Time* had four in-country correspondents, and it finished the war with three. *U.S. News & World Report* created a one-person Saigon bureau in August 1965, assigned a second correspondent in June 1966—although that person occasionally would leave for weeks to develop articles elsewhere in Southeast Asia—and had one permanent correspondent from May 1971 onward; consequently, it had far fewer articles with combat vignettes than its competitors.[5]

Intense coverage ensued with the arrival of more Americans at bases and camps along the coast, in the central highlands, in the Mekong Delta at the southern end, and in the mountains of I Corps at the northern end where a demilitarized zone separated the Republic of Vietnam from the Democratic Republic of Vietnam. Based on an annualized cycle of fifty-two editions, the newsmagazines offered nearly continuous coverage of warfare beginning in mid-1965: *Time,* an average of forty-one editions with combat information from Vietnam until autumn 1969; *Newsweek,* an average of thirty-eight editions with combat information until late 1968; *U.S. News & World Report,* an average of thirty-one editions with combat information until autumn 1968. During one stretch of the war starting in June 1965, *Newsweek* had articles on Vietnam in forty-three of forty-four editions and *Time* had similar articles in fifty-seven of sixty-two editions.

The newsmagazines delivered information about Americans at war pertaining to combat, the conduct of military personnel, and military operations. Though they differed in their attitudes about the way the war was fought, they uniformly presented American combatants as noble warriors.

---

5. Newsmagazine staff directories from March 1965 through January 1973 listed bureaus and their correspondents, and interviews with correspondents provided details about additional correspondents temporarily assigned to Saigon.

Coverage emphasized camaraderie, determination, honor, and valor, an emphasis prevalent from the beginning of the war to its end. Positive imagery rarely resulted in idealized versions of battle or falsely heroic tales, however. Instead, articles depicted American combatants doing their duty and doing their best to survive against a formidable enemy. In a war that had less purpose the longer it continued, the image of combatants conformed to the myth of the American soldier.[6] Almost no negative imagery appeared prior to 1970. Only twenty-six articles on warfare, or 4.5 percent of the total, contained information on atrocity accusations, mistreatment of civilians, racial discord, discipline and morale problems, or drug abuse. Nineteen of those negative portrayals appeared after November 1969, when disclosure of the My Lai massacre—an atrocity committed by an American infantry platoon—resulted in somewhat more candid portrayals of American troops in Vietnam.

While the newsmagazines usually avoided reporting that Americans were anything other than noble warriors, articles never attempted to disguise the brutal nature of the war. Combat imagery conjured up horrific scenes from the start. The newsmagazines reported in words what television often dared not show, describing the mutilation of combatants by bullets and explosives, the agony of the injured on the battlefield, and the savagery of guerrilla warfare.

Combat and Combatants

Combat coverage evolved during summer 1965. For several months, newsmagazine correspondents wrote about new troops arriving in Vietnam, preparing fortifications, becoming familiar with the terrain, and readying themselves for battle. Army and Marine Corps units had skirmished with Vietcong squads on the perimeters of the coastal enclaves at Da Nang, Nha Trang, and Cam Ranh Bay, and military operations had established a deep defensive perimeter around Bien Hoa, the major inland airfield near Saigon. Gradually, infantry patrols extended several miles into the countryside. Newsmagazine correspondents had no daily deadline to worry about, and they regularly visited military units in the field. "Those guys were sure they would win," says *Newsweek*'s Cook. "Their attitude, their toughness impressed me." *U.S. News & World Report* also was impressed. Reviewing a series of battles between Americans and Vietcong, the magazine concluded: "Here in Viet-

6. Bird and Dardenne, "Myth, Chronicle, and Story," 70–71.

nam, the record of the American fighting man is becoming something to marvel at. Morale is found to be high. Officer leadership is judged excellent. All units seem to want to fight—and they all have a driving will to win."[7]

Journalists for newspapers and television networks reported few of these combat incidents from May through July because several factors limited their coverage. First, the coastal enclaves were far from Saigon; journalists usually visited the enclaves only to write about newly arriving combat units and to develop stories about construction of camps, port facilities, and storage depots. Second, the sporadic skirmishes resulted in small numbers of American casualties; these journalists focused instead on stories concerning American policy in Vietnam and the steadily deteriorating situation in the countryside where Vietcong control grew throughout the summer. Third, the Johnson administration and Gen. William C. Westmoreland, commander-in-chief of the Military Assistance Command in Saigon, purposely misled the news media and public about plans for American troops to take the war into the countryside; journalists were not informed that patrols were moving beyond the enclave perimeters. (In June, however, *Time* observed that troops appeared to be preparing for a more direct role. "Evidence was mounting that the U.S. will soon commit its own foot soldiers to battle," the magazine stated in an article about Army and Marine units "probing ever deeper into Red-held territory.")[8] Fourth, most journalists had not created their own source networks yet and received few helpful tips from military personnel. Fifth, many journalists preferred staying in Saigon to going on patrol with the troops; danger, discomfort, and the pressure to produce stories for their stateside editors dissuaded them from leaving Saigon for the time necessary to cover combat in Vietnam. According to historian Clarence R. Wyatt, many journalists went on patrol only once or twice during their assignment to Vietnam. Finally, journalists who spent several days on a military operation that resulted in no contact

---

7. Cook interview; "Fighting Gets Tougher—So Does American GI," *U.S. News & World Report,* December 13, 1965, p. 40.

8. "The Bloody Hills," *Time,* June 11, 1965, pp. 34–35. For a discussion of Johnson administration and Westmoreland efforts to minimize initial combat actions, see *The Pentagon Papers: The Defense Department History of United States Decision Making on Vietnam* (the Senator Gravel edition), 4:461–64, 604. For more on official deception regarding a more active American combat role beginning in May and June 1965, see Hallin, *"Uncensored War,"* 97–100; William M. Hammond, *The Military and the Media, 1962–1968: The U.S. Army in Vietnam,* 152–53; and Maclear, *Ten Thousand Day War,* 125–33.

with the enemy had, in effect, wasted their time; their editors expected news, if not every day at least most days.⁹

Combat intensified during late summer, and the newsmagazines poured forth laudatory articles. "A new generation of Americans tasted major combat last week and passed the test," *Time* noted in August 1965. Several months later, the magazine reiterated its adulation: "With courage and a cool professionalism that surprised friend and foe, U.S. troops stood fast and firm in South Viet Nam." *Time* maintained its boosterism into spring 1967: "With the increase in the U.S. troop levels—which last week reached 427,000—more Americans are ranging through the countryside than ever before, spoiling for a fight." *Newsweek* offered a forthright tribute, without excessive praise: "This is not a stridently hard-boiled army (though some individuals in it are); it is tough, it is trained to fight and it fights exceedingly well—but it does its fighting with the quiet, laconic, can-do doggedness of professionals. They are mostly spare, astringent men. They are out to kill the enemy, but they don't especially hate him. They have no profane or hate-laden epithets for him." *U.S. News & World Report* boasted, "The elite of American fighting forces is here on the ground now."[10]

U.S. News & World Report alerted its readers that a larger commitment lay ahead: "The possibility that war may have to escalate until it involves many American divisions and relentless bombing of North Vietnam cannot be ruled out." This statement appeared in early July 1965, two weeks before the Johnson administration announced that 125,000 additional combat troops would be sent to Vietnam.[11] Combat increased considerably from July 1965 onward. Army and Marine Corps battalions forayed into Vietcong bastions far from the secure enclaves. *Time* and *Newsweek* were optimistic after the first major battle that summer between troops and guerrilla main-force units

---

9. Wyatt, *Paper Soldiers*, 138–39.

10. " 'Big Joe No. 1,' " *Time*, August 20, 1965, p. 24; "The Guardians at the Gate," *Time*, January 7, 1966, p. 15; "Pulling Together," *Time*, March 31, 1967, p. 18; "Americans at War," *Newsweek*, August 1, 1966, p. 28; "Tide Turning in Vietnam War?" *U.S. News & World Report*, September 27, 1965, p. 35.

11. "What It Would Take to Turn the Tide in Vietnam," *U.S. News & World Report*, July 12, 1965, pp. 46–48. Johnson's announcement on July 28, 1965, that combat troop strength would double by the end of the year did not make public the possibility that up to 430,000 troops would be needed in Vietnam by the end of 1966. Troop deployment decisions are discussed in Larry Berman, *Lyndon Johnson's War: The Road to Stalemate in Vietnam*, 9; Maclear, *Ten Thousand Day War*, 139–53; and Fifield, *Americans in Southeast Asia*, 288–91.

on the Van Tuong Peninsula near Chu Lai. "Smashed with the Viet Cong was the myth that the Red foe is invincible in the tangled underbrush of his homeland; smashed also was the myth that the U.S. can't fight on land in Asia," *Time* declared, referring obliquely to the disastrous Korean War experience. *Newsweek* cited the 560 guerrillas killed on the peninsula, ten times the number of dead Marines. "And the results proved, as U.S. military men had long predicted, that, in a slugging match, U.S. regulars have a big edge over even the toughest guerrillas," the article stated. *Newsweek* also mentioned the incredible effort required to wage war in the countryside. A siege of an Army camp near the Cambodia border in the central highlands brought two brigades to the rescue. "This presumably marked a victory of sorts, yet in order to relieve a single, relatively small garrison, the U.S. and South Vietnamese armies had been obliged to tie up thousands of their best fighting men for days," *Newsweek* wrote. "And at the end of the week, as well as anyone could tell, the Viet Cong were still somewhere in the jungle country around Duc Co." *Time* preferred to concentrate on American combat performance rather than the prospect that a meaningful result often was not evident. "U.S. troops were soon besting the Viet Cong in fire fights from Chu Lai to An Khe," the magazine wrote. A summary in *Time* concluded, "In the waning months of 1965, they helped finally to stem the tide that had run so long with the Reds." *U.S. News & World Report* informed readers that "Americans do not intend to get sucked into a trap baited by guerrillas who are skilled in ambushes and jungle warfare."[12]

Late summer marked the beginning of search-and-destroy and search-and-sweep operations. These major tactical maneuvers involved two or more battalions at a time, with each battalion placing eight to nine hundred infantrymen in the field. Troops were driven in trucks or flown in helicopters many miles from their camps to remote valleys, coastal plains, and dense forests, where they spent weeks searching for Vietcong supply bunkers, fortifications, and the staging areas where guerrillas gathered for coordinated attacks. American infantrymen also occasionally battled with the People's Army of Vietnam, regular infantry units from the communist northern nation that had moved south beginning in autumn 1965 to augment Vietcong guerrillas.

12. "The Face of Victory," *Time*, August 27, 1965, pp. 18–19; "The Relief of Duc Co," *Newsweek*, August 23, 1965, pp. 28–29; "A New Kind of War," *Time*, October 22, 1965, p. 30; "The Guardians at the Gate," *Time*, January 7, 1966, p. 13; "What It Would Take to Turn the Tide in Vietnam," *U.S. News & World Report*, July 12, 1965, p. 47.

An increasing number of search-and-destroy/sweep operations and the prospect of combat against northern soldiers made it apparent to journalists that large-unit operations offered opportunities for dramatic stories. Newsmagazines acted accordingly by assigning correspondents to closely monitor these operations. Cook arrived in Saigon in October 1965, the third man in the *Newsweek* bureau. His assignment was to cover combat while the other two correspondents covered the military buildup, policy issues, and government programs in Vietnam. *Time* also divided coverage among its correspondents, giving priority to combat coverage. *U.S. News & World Report,* with its one- and occasionally two-person bureau, often lacked the firsthand observations that characterized *Newsweek* and *Time* combat coverage. "Sometimes I would have to settle for a phoner [telephone interview] with a company commander or a battalion commander after they were back in camp," says James Wallace, a *U.S. News & World Report* correspondent in Vietnam for nearly five years. "It took a lot of effort to get good combat stories."[13]

Newsmagazine editors demanded the drama of combat from correspondents, who eagerly complied. "Fighting, that's what wars are about," says Cook. "When I went there, the focus was combat." "We were waiting for some disaster to happen," remembers Rauch. "When it did, we went." The newsmagazines also covered efforts by the United States to initiate economic, political, and social reforms in southern Vietnam and to transform the southern army into an effective, reliable organization. But editors believed that readers paid more attention to an article if a combat narrative preceded the other material. Correspondents often provided you-are-there narratives for a "top," or introduction, to articles on other war-related topics. This editorial format prevailed during nearly eight years of formal military intervention. Of all newsmagazine articles pertaining to the war published from mid-March 1965 through January 1973, 76 percent contained information on warfare. Combat coverage was quite intense from summer 1965 until autumn 1969, the period of most operational activity by American troops, when 89 percent of all newsmagazine articles included information on warfare. By comparison, 52 percent of segments shown by television news programs dealt with military action from summer 1965 through summer 1968.[14]

13. Cook, Pines, and Wallace interviews.
14. Cook and Rauch interviews; Hallin, *"Uncensored War,"* 112; Michael Mandelbaum, "Vietnam: The Television War," 159; Chester J. Pach, Jr., "The Vietnam War on the Network Nightly News," 94.

To reproduce the drama of combat considered essential to articles on the war, newsmagazine correspondents in Saigon followed a routine familiar to most journalists everywhere—except for being shot at and shelled. The job of covering a beat hardly varied whether at the Pentagon in Washington, the capitol in Madison, Wisconsin, or military headquarters in Saigon. For the military beat in Vietnam, a correspondent cultivated sources at headquarters in Saigon and among brigade and division staff officers with Army and Marine Corps units. All journalists in Vietnam, or at least the Americans, also relied on assistance from public affairs officers (PAOs) assigned to headquarters and operational units up-country. Cook developed a source network to alert him when a major military operation had begun or serious combat had occurred. He used a direct-line telephone from headquarters in Saigon to speak with public affairs officers for brigades and divisions throughout Vietnam. "I'd make my calls to PAOs and see if anything hot was happening," Cook says. "Some PAOs were really good and knew what was going on in the field, so I usually got something worth filing by going there. Others had no idea, and I wasted my time." Based on conversations with these officers, Cook decided whether to travel to the operational area of a brigade or division to develop a combat article. "I went to battles when I could get to them on time," he says.[15]

The decision to visit an up-country site was no small matter. Travel in Vietnam took many hours, even though the military provided space-available transportation on airplanes, helicopters, and trucks. "Many of my trips began at four in the morning," remembers Wallace. Correspondents in Saigon traveled on Air Force cargo planes to airfields in the general vicinity of the Army or Marine unit being visited. Sometimes two or three different flights were required to reach the closest airfield. Rauch describes the process: "You'd go out to Tan Son Nhut [the Saigon airport], catch a C-130 going somewhere close to where you wanted to go, in the direction of where you were going, to Da Nang or Phu Bai. Then you would see what you could rustle up."[16] The goal was to find a helicopter or truck headed for brigade or division headquarters. From there, correspondents could ride aboard another helicopter or hike with a patrol to reach a combat area. Correspondents could spend an entire day traveling, and sometimes had to wait overnight at

---

15. Cook interview.
16. Wallace and Rauch interviews.

an airfield or a command center before going into the field because helicopters and trucks did not journey into the countryside after dark. After all this, they had to consider how many days remained until the deadline for filing copy. If it was early in the week, they could accompany infantrymen in the field for a day or two on the chance that combat would occur; if no combat resulted, they could find troops nearby to interview who recently had fought. If it was late in the week, they could ask the public affairs officer to identify a battalion that most recently had been in combat, and interviews could be conducted in the field. The return trip to Saigon repeated the time-consuming travel process.[17]

Assistance and cooperation from the American military was a necessity for newsmagazine correspondents and other journalists in Vietnam. Travel in the southern countryside was almost totally dependent on the military for safety reasons until late 1969, and then during the last year of the war when the communists regained control of many rural sectors. The Republic of Vietnam covered a sizable area. To reach a site in the provinces near the demilitarized zone with northern Vietnam involved traveling four hundred miles from Saigon, to visit the central highlands was two hundred and fifty miles, and to get to a unit in the Mekong Delta was a journey of one hundred miles south of Saigon. Prior to leaving Saigon, journalists phoned their official sources—courtesy of the military, much of the time. The military telephone system, though undeniably inferior to the telephone network in the United States, at least allowed intelligible communication, unlike the notoriously static-ridden and government-monitored domestic telephone system in southern Vietnam.

The ability to hop a ride on an Air Force cargo aircraft, an Army helicopter, or a Marine Corps truck derived from a journalist's official accreditation. Without a laminated identification card issued by American military headquarters in Saigon, a journalist had no privileges. Receiving accreditation was not difficult. Journalists with newsmagazines, newspapers, news services, and television networks presented their credentials to the press office at military headquarters, then soon received an identification card and a set of guidelines listing violations of military security that would result in loss of accreditation. Anyone could claim to be a journalist—a person only needed a statement on the business letterhead of any news organization that

---

17. Cook, Horrock, Pines, and Rauch interviews.

he or she intended to send material for publication.[18] As a result, dozens of freelance journalists wandered around Vietnam during the war or stayed within the safer confines of Saigon. All accredited journalists received the courtesy rank of officer and the authority to travel aboard cargo airplanes, helicopters, trucks, and jeeps if space was available, which it usually was. If they desired, they also could eat in military mess halls and stay in barracks, bunkers, hootches, and tents reserved for officers.

The military's press office in Saigon scheduled daily briefings for journalists. Nicknamed "the five o'clock follies" by journalists, these sessions offered a summary of military action for the day and an update on major tactical operations. Reporters with AP and UPI regularly attended the briefings, as did reporters with the major newspapers. Newsmagazine correspondents rarely went. The usual practice was to send a stringer, or local freelance person, who then would leave notes with the bureau chief.[19] Summary material from the briefings occasionally was used for statistical purposes in newsmagazine articles.

Although military security regulations prohibited journalists from receiving advance notice of major tactical operations, correspondents learned from their sources when something big was about to happen. "PAOs let me know to be ready," Cook says. "They'd say, 'You should talk to me tomorrow' or some such, and I'd sure-as-hell give them a call." Upon receiving confirmation that a major operation had begun, correspondents hurriedly joined the troops in the field. Sometimes these search-and-destroy/sweep missions resulted in scattered skirmishes with Vietcong or People's Army squads, and correspondents scurried from one battalion to another to interview troops. Sometimes correspondents heard gunfire nearby and managed to talk with soldiers immediately following combat. "We tried hard to be where the fighting was," says Burton Pines, "but you just never knew. We wound up talking to the grunts who had taken fire, and we got enough material to make a good yarn." Sometimes, the correspondents themselves took fire. "That was when the editors barely touched my copy," Cook says. "They liked letting everyone who read the magazine know their guy was in the thick of things." In that pre-byline era, newsmagazines rewarded a correspondent who had experienced combat with an internal byline—mentioning the

---

18. For more about accreditation, see Braestrup, *Big Story,* 9–11.
19. Cloud, Cook, Horrock, and Pines interviews.

correspondent's name in the text of the article—a reward Cook received for his enterprise during the siege of Plei Me in November 1965. Cook had joined an ARVN relief column headed for Plei Me, witnessed an ambush, and rode a helicopter into the camp while fighting continued—a *Newsweek* exclusive. "My editors were very pleased," Cook says, "as was I."[20]

Newsmagazine correspondents competed fiercely for exclusive stories. For the most part, correspondents relied on their own source networks to alert them to potentially newsworthy military operations. They filed copy based on action in different parts of the country, which meant that in a given week the readers of *Newsweek* could learn about a firefight in the central highlands, *Time* readers could learn about a skirmish in the Mekong Delta, and *U.S. News & World Report* readers could learn about an ambush on a coastal highway. This pattern of combat coverage differentiated the newsmagazines from newspapers and television network news programs, which lacked the staff to search the countryside for newsworthy information and relied more on military briefers in Saigon for ideas.[21] Correspondents from *Newsweek, Time,* and *U.S. News & World Report* occasionally found themselves covering the same tactical operation, especially during 1966 and 1967 when large-unit warfare became the dominant operational method. They shared airplane flights and helicopter or truck rides to brigade or division headquarters, but from that point on they went their separate ways. "If there was a *Time* guy on the same story," Cook says, "you both saved yourselves a lot of trouble by hitching a ride to reach the same place. Then you kept your distance. You worked your own story." Pines, of *Time,* recalls one episode that demonstrated competitiveness: "I went with a *Newsweek* person to this village where some captured enemy documents were being loaded up. The battalion commander was very proud of the haul, and he gave me a stack for the two of us to look at. I politely asked him to give *Newsweek* its own stack."[22]

Newsmagazine correspondents enjoyed stature among the troops. Unlike the people at the Pentagon, White House, Congress, and among the political and social elite in Washington who were impelled by the cachet of the *New York Times* to bestow access to the centers of power upon its reporters, most ordinary GIs and officers considered the nation's foremost daily to be

20. Cook and Pines interviews; "How Plei Me Survived," *Newsweek,* November 8, 1965, pp. 43–44.
21. Elegant, "How to Lose a War," 79–82; Wyatt, *Paper Soldiers,* 142–43.
22. Horrock, Wallace, Cook, and Pines interviews.

just another newspaper. *Newsweek* and *Time,* however, were famous national magazines that could be bought at the nearest military store, and troops in Vietnam regarded a visit by a newsmagazine correspondent as something special. "Magazines were passed around and seen by almost everyone," says Horrock. "You'd be out in the field and they'd have us [*Newsweek*] stuck in their packs. They sold us and *Time* in the PXs." Newsmagazine correspondents often received preferential treatment from military personnel. Pines understood why: "They put us in a class above the newspapers because magazines were glamorous to them, and they were probably thinking they had a chance to be in *Time* and the people back home would see it."[23]

The stature that newsmagazine correspondents had in Vietnam paid off in access to combat areas. Whether through interviews with combatants or the personal observation of correspondents, the newsmagazines produced intensely descriptive combat imagery from Vietnam. "In taking Hill 1338, the U.S. troops of the Fourth Infantry had to climb and struggle up a steep, 'lung-busting' incline covered over by jungle growth and defended by a determined enemy," *Newsweek* wrote. "But up they went, fighting all the way." *Newsweek* also noted a peculiar ritual. "Quickly, the men of Alpha Company stripped the dead enemy soldiers of their gear—star-buckled belts, knives and AK-47 assault rifles," the magazine reported. "Then they placed 'Big Red One' shoulder patches on each dead face before leaving the battlefield for the trip back to camp." *Time* provided details about an action involving the 101st Airborne Division: "Young troopers took reckless chances to fetch more bullets and grenades. A draftee and former high-school athlete from Detroit pitched grenades with deadly accuracy at an enemy now less than 30 yds. away. . . . [Another soldier] clubbed down one surprised Viet Cong with his rifle butt." Another article emphasized the horror of combat. "But the flamethrowers proved to be perfect targets—one man was incinerated by a hit on his own canister—and once again relentless fire from the enemy bunkers drove the Americans backward," *Time* wrote. "The North Vietnamese had abandoned Hill 875 during the night, taking many of their dead with them. The summit was a grisly desolation of charred and splintered trees, burned-out machine guns and blackened fragments of bodies."[24]

23. Horrock and Pines interviews.
24. "The Battle of Dak To," *Newsweek,* November 27, 1967, p. 44; "A Small Contribution," *Newsweek,* October 14, 1968, p. 55; "Gathering Intensity," *Time,* March 31, 1967, p. 36; "Will to Win," *Time,* December 1, 1967, pp. 24–27.

Newsmagazine articles portrayed in words what their pages dared not depict in photographs. Most articles contained photographs of Americans at war—on patrol in swamps and jungles, firing weapons, digging foxholes, stacking artillery shells—but only 9 percent of articles in *Newsweek* and 6 percent in *Time* showed American dead or wounded.[25] Instead, the prose painted horrific images. "The V.C. pulled back and zeroed in their mortars on the ridge line," *Time* reported. "The first incoming round landed precisely on a marine's head, blowing him to pieces." American warplanes dropped napalm bombs on the enemy, and "turned the Viet Cong into charcoal sticks," the article stated. *Time* presented an awful account from a combatant who survived a harrowing night on the battlefield. "He was so close to the Reds that when they decapitated a wounded American trooper, blood squirted all over him." Another article mentioned an ambush of a convoy by the Vietcong. "[A] driver tried to squeeze out an escape hatch, but a bullet hit him between the eyes," *Time* wrote. *Newsweek* published a two-page article on the Ia Drang battle, the first major encounter with the People's Army from the north, which killed 240 Americans and an estimated 1,500 communists. Hundreds of corpses lay on the battlefield when a correspondent arrived. "At another spot a dead U.S. sergeant still clutched the bayonet he had buried in an enemy soldier with his last ounce of strength," *Newsweek* wrote. "Then, as the foul smell of death mingled with the odor of cordite, sweat and vegetation, the ants and flies began to crawl over the dead, adding to the bitterness of the Americans still alive." *Newsweek* quoted a paratrooper whose platoon had encountered the Vietcong: "'Next thing I knew the guy beside me had been hit right above the left eye. It almost tore his head off and killed him instantly.'" *U.S. News & World Report* informed readers about the war's savagery: "American troops fighting North Vietnamese regulars in the central highlands have seen their wounded comrades dragged into the brush by their captors and executed."[26]

Such graphic detail about American combat casualties in World War II al-

---

25. Oscar Patterson III, "Television's Living Room War in Print: Vietnam in the News Magazines," 401–3.

26. "'Big Joe No. 1,'" *Time*, August 20, 1965, pp. 24–25; "The Face of Victory," *Time*, August 27, 1965, pp. 18–19; "Humor, Horror & Heroism," *Time*, November 26, 1965, p. 32; "Fury at Ia Drang: Now the Regulars," *Newsweek*, November 29, 1965, pp. 22–23; "GIs Pour In—And the War Looks Up," *Newsweek*, October 4, 1965, p. 38; "Fighting Gets Tougher—So Does American GI," *U.S. News & World Report*, December 13, 1965, p. 40.

most never appeared in newsmagazines and newspapers. Self-censorship and military censorship prevented graphic imagery from being published. News organizations were told by the Office of War Information in the immediate aftermath of the Pearl Harbor attack not to publish photographs that might demoralize the American public, and scenes of the devastation to the U.S. Navy fleet in Hawaii were not shown. (Later in the war, news organizations were urged to be more realistic because the public needed to be aware of the sacrifices that GIs were making and to understand the need for civilians to accept food rationing and to increase productivity at work.) News organizations hesitated to publish stories that would disturb people. Although magazines and newspapers ran some photographs of combat casualty scenes, none revealed explicit or graphic details of American dead or wounded. The first photograph of American corpses did not appear until early 1943, and the image was of a few unidentifiable troops on a smooth sand beach. Journalists of that era wrote about the war's hardships and the emotional toll on combatants, but descriptions of death and injury to Americans omitted the reality of dismemberment and mutilation. Newsmagazines and newspapers typically left it to their readers to imagine the details. "To tell much more was to risk shock, anger, rejection, not to mention censorship," explains James Tobin, a journalism historian. "As for realistic accounts of wounds and suffering, that was the last thing reporters thought anyone wanted." Other scholars refer to World War II journalists reporting a sanitized version of war's physical trauma.[27]

Vietnam War coverage certainly displayed more realism, but the degree of explicitness depended on the news medium. Television news programs, despite the popular perception, infrequently showed graphic scenes. Scholars have reviewed transcripts of network news programs (which summarize film segments) to establish that television imagery rarely disturbed viewers with gruesome scenes. An examination of all news reports on the war broadcast by ABC, CBS, and NBC from summer 1965 through summer 1970 determined that only 3 percent of all film segments from Vietnam showed "heavy

---

27. James Tobin, *Ernie Pyle's War: America's Eyewitness to World War II*, 139–41, 243. Phillip Knightley, *The First Casualty: From the Crimea to Vietnam, the War Correspondent as Hero, Propagandist, and Myth Maker*, discusses general reportage during World War II. Susan D. Moeller, *Shooting War: Photography and the American Experience of Combat*, and George H. Roeder, Jr., *The Censored War: American Visual Experience during World War Two*, examine photographic depictions of World War II as representative of news coverage.

battle," defined as scenes with gunfire, incoming artillery or mortar rounds, and dead or wounded combatants visible. In numeric terms, this means that only 76 of 2,300 news reports contained graphic imagery during the five-year period. A random sample of news programs from August 1968 through August 1973 also found few graphic scenes, ranging from 2.9 percent to 4.2 percent of all Vietnam segments shown.[28]

Newsweek and *Time* routinely described combat with unprecedented candor; *U.S. News & World Report* more selectively reported graphic details, almost always restricting such descriptions to enemy atrocities committed against American casualties on the battlefield. A 1968 *Newsweek* article on a Marine Corps medical center at Da Nang provides an example of the powerful imagery that the newsmagazines published on Vietnam:

> Another of the men had been shot through the neck, and apparently the bullet had snapped his vocal cords.
>
> One was a Negro, wide awake on a stretcher, calmly answering questions. He didn't realize that his left leg had been torn off just below the knee—or that his right foot was hanging only by tendons and flesh. A doctor nodded to a corpsman standing at the foot of the stretcher. Quickly, the corpsman picked up a pair of surgical scissors and started to cut the mangled foot away from the ankle. . . . The amputation was finished in seconds and another corpsman carried away the bone and flesh still packed inside the bloody combat boot.
>
> There was pain in the face of every Marine who was conscious. But not one of them cried out.
>
> Methodically, the corpsmen went about the job of washing the bloodstains from the concrete floor and getting the place ready for the next load.[29]

Two interrelated factors allowed these explicit descriptions to appear during the Vietnam War. First, no censorship existed; second, technology afforded direct contact between combat correspondents and editors. The lack of censorship was a result of both political and practical considerations. The Republic of Vietnam was a sovereign nation, and its government had the authority to establish censorship of wartime news coverage, but American military commanders and embassy officials understood that censorship by the

---

28. Lawrence W. Lichty, "Comments on the Influence of Television on Public Opinion," 158–59; Oscar W. Patterson, "An Analysis of Television Coverage of the Vietnam War," 401–3.

29. "One Step Forward," *Newsweek*, March 25, 1968, pp. 40–41.

Vietnamese undoubtedly would be heavy-handed and problematic. Another factor weighing against censorship was the presence of many journalists from other nations. American officials decided the Vietnamese lacked the sophistication necessary to handle the delicate matter of censorship. On a practical basis, censorship simply would not work because any journalist could take an airplane from Saigon and arrive within a few hours at Bangkok, Hong Kong, Manila, or Tokyo to transmit information to the United States for publication or broadcast. American military commanders had considered imposing censorship the first summer of intervention but quickly recognized the impossibility of controlling the flow of information from Vietnam. Instead of accepting formal censorship, journalists agreed that in return for accreditation and the privileges it gave them, including free transportation in-country from the military and access to American troops, they would not reveal any information that might jeopardize operational security or endanger personnel.[30] The second factor allowing for explicit descriptions was that communications technology available to journalists in Vietnam freed them from reliance on the military for sending their information to the United States. Journalists sent copy via telex systems that connected Saigon by undersea cable with Manila and Tokyo and from there to the United States.

Journalists in Europe and the Pacific during World War II reported under the dual restrictions of formal censorship and dependence on the military communication and transportation systems to deliver their information stateside from sites thousands of miles away. Journalists in Korea practiced self-censorship for the first five months of the Korean War, and had to personally travel to Tokyo or rely on a military courier to take information there for transmission by radioteletype to the United States. The U.S. military imposed censorship after a series of disastrous setbacks in November and December 1950. At first, officers in Korea censored information for review by officers in Tokyo; however, officers in Tokyo defined military security differently from their counterparts in Korea, and often chose to delete information of a political rather than military nature. After formal censorship began, military officers reviewed all information before allowing it to be transmitted.[31]

---

30. Wyatt, *Paper Soldiers*, 159–64; Hammond, *The Military and the Media, 1962–1968*, 138, 160–61, discussed these censorship issues.

31. Clay Blair, *The Forgotten War: America in Korea, 1950–1953*, 640–41, 741. For more on censorship in Korea, see Knightley, *First Casualty*, 337–45. Jack A. Gottschalk, "Consistent with Security: A History of American Military Press Censorship," examines censorship in Korea and the rationale for no censorship in Vietnam.

The absence of censorship in Vietnam meant that newsmagazine correspondents did not have to worry about the military deleting information deemed sensitive or negative. Numerous newsmagazine articles informed readers that American troops had experienced defeat on the battlefield when an ambush or surprise assault overwhelmed a platoon, company, or battalion. "So sudden was the attack that the Air Cav defenses were quickly overrun," *Time* wrote, describing a Vietcong raid on an American camp. "While some of the enemy worked at destroying the howitzers, others ran from bunker to bunker, tossing in grenades and shooting survivors." Modern machinery did not guarantee battlefield superiority. "When the helicopters first set down in the tiny, vulnerable clearing, Viet Cong scouts in nearby trees detonated heavy charges of explosives, blowing up three of the choppers," *Time* reported. "Then the earth erupted all through the U.S. positions, as some 650 mortar shells rained down." *Time* recounted the experience of paratroopers whose attack ended in disaster with two dozen of twenty-eight helicopters shot down or damaged. "The 101st promptly ringed the Viet Cong on three sides of the valley," the article stated. "Trouble was, the dried-up quilt of rice paddies was hard by the V.C. camp. So the Screaming Eagles got the hot welcome of a Viet Cong battalion." Another operation also ended badly for Americans. "The Communists had let the Marines advance into their very midst," *Time* reported. "Popping out of spider holes and bunkers everywhere, they opened up a murderous crossfire. Those Marines caught out in the open were cut to pieces by small-arms fire, grenades and mortars." *Newsweek*, using an analogy familiar to readers who remembered the fight against Japan twenty years earlier, described a fanatical enemy: "Once again the VC erupted out of the rubber trees and charged banzai-style across a wide airstrip runway." Americans often incurred casualties without seeing a guerrilla. "As the GI's scrambled for cover in the jungle lining the road, crude grenades strung in the trees were jerked down on top of them," wrote *Newsweek* about an ambush that resulted in a 50 percent casualty rate for one infantry company. Another ambush involving Marines resulted in ninety-five dead and two hundred wounded. "It had been, all told, a bitter defeat," *Newsweek* stated.[32]

32. "Flak from Hanoi," *Time,* January 6, 1967, p. 15; "Gathering Intensity," *Time,* March 31, 1967, p. 36; "A Buzz Saw & A Bunker," *Time,* October 1, 1965, pp. 38–39; "Arrow of Death," *Time,* May 12, 1967, pp. 24–26; "Slaughter at Loc Ninh," *Newsweek,* November 13, 1967, p. 44; "One Kind of Routine," *Newsweek,* December 20, 1965, p. 34; "Ambush at Con Thien," *Newsweek,* July 17, 1967, p. 45.

Most newsmagazine articles provided an accurate portrait of combat in Vietnam. Ambushes accounted for one of every nine Americans killed and wounded during the war.[33] Of more importance, eight of every nine combat actions were initiated by the People's Army or Vietcong. American troops usually never knew where the guerrillas were or when they would attack. Camouflage hid guerrilla bunkers, camps, and trenches from view until the Americans got within range. *Time* and *Newsweek*, by devoting entire articles to ambushes and surprise attacks, informed readers that American troops could not control the time and place of battle. *U.S. News & World Report* limited its combat coverage to large-unit operations.

Vietcong guerrillas and People's Army soldiers were not the only enemy of Americans in Vietnam. Climate, disease, and terrain challenged the troops. "Virtually all the newsmen paid tribute in their dispatches to the performance and morale of the enlisted men in the field under conditions of extreme heat, dust and other physical hardship," observes Francis Donald Faulkner, a journalism scholar.[34] Newsmagazine articles let readers know about the conditions and hardships confronting military personnel. A *Newsweek* correspondent accompanied the 173rd Airborne Brigade on a four-day sweep northwest of Saigon. "Then into the jungle," the correspondent wrote. "It was slippery going, pushing Indian file, through the bamboo thickets. Mud sucked at our boots. Leeches bit into our legs. As we crossed the occasional stream, the men cursed, trying to keep their weapons dry. But mostly they were silent, straining under their heavy loads of mortar shells—four to a man—plus their personal gear." American troops were not ill-equipped for guerrilla warfare but instead were too well equipped, a circumstance that *Newsweek* repeatedly mentioned. "The Viet Cong guerrillas slip through the jungles as lightly burdened as possible, but the Marines' heavy combat gear puts them through extreme exertions," the newsmagazine reported. A later article discussed the skirmish-and-search method of fighting, a situation aggravated by tropical heat. "The Viet Cong quickly withdrew," *Newsweek* wrote, "leaving the paratroopers to sweat it out in their heavy armored vests." Despite these daunting conditions, *Newsweek* assured readers, "U.S. troops not only proved that they could operate effectively for long stretches of time in the heat, mud and malaria of the jungles—but that they could

---

33. Maclear, *Ten Thousand Day War*, 160–61.
34. Francis Donald Faulkner, "Bao Chi: The American News Media in Vietnam, 1960–1975," 130.

win." *Time* summarized the noncombat dangers. "There were leeches and lice, poisonous vipers and venereal diseases, dengue, and a virulent strain of malaria that has defied preventives and resists cure," an article stated. "Temperatures hit 130 degrees on the sandy beaches, 20 degrees in the mountains." Readers learned about life for Americans in remote outposts. "Because water is scarce, they shave only every other day and can seldom wash," *Time* reported. "They live in crude, sandbagged underground bunkers where often the only light comes from an improvised candle with a rag as a wick."[35]

These conditions and hardships affected all Americans, regardless of color. Because the Vietnam War occurred concurrently with a period of political activism for civil rights and several summers of destructive and violent riots in many African American communities, the issue of race had social significance. *Newsweek* and *Time,* in strikingly different ways, intermittently referred to the all-American character of the war. Their articles, however, implied that combatants were white unless otherwise noted. The newsmagazines routinely attached racial identification only to African Americans; thus, a passage about the combat performance of John Jones of Denver would mention only his name and hometown if he were white, while a passage about John Jones of Indianapolis would preface or follow his name with "Negro" or, beginning in 1969, "black" if he were African American. Their names alone were evidently considered sufficient identification for Hispanics. For the duration of the war, the newsmagazines obviously intended to include African Americans and Hispanics in their coverage and sought to remind readers that combatants of all colors fought in Vietnam, in the nation's first war with full racial integration.

Each newsmagazine handled racial identification in its own way. *Newsweek* mentioned African Americans and Hispanics incidentally in combat coverage, reinforcing the idea that combat was a racially integrated affair. Several articles citing the heroism of combatants included references to African Americans and Hispanics. A *Newsweek* article on medics featured "a Negro from North Carolina" who was awarded the Medal of Honor and a private first class named Eliseo Cruz—a conscientious objector, like many medics in Vietnam. A full-page article on an ambush near Con Thien con-

35. " 'The Mission Is to Kill,' " *Newsweek,* May 10, 1965, p. 49; "Vietnam: The New War," *Newsweek,* July 5, 1965, p. 34; "Strictly Military," *Newsweek,* August 16, 1965, p. 32; "The American Way of War," *Newsweek,* December 5, 1966, p. 50; "The Guardians at the Gate," *Time,* January 7, 1966, p. 20; "Thunder from a Distant Hill," *Time,* October 6, 1967, p. 22.

tained three paragraphs describing the bravery of a Marine who kept fighting despite his injuries. "Cpl. Margarito Garza was wounded three times before he died," *Newsweek* reported. A lengthy article on the rigors of infantry duty contained several quotes from a Marine corporal whose race was not specified until the third page, where it was revealed by the corporal himself: "Back in Marine Cpl. Robert Lee Cotton's bunker, the hour is late. Cotton is still talking about the war, himself, what he wants to do when he gets home (he wants to go to college because 'as a Negro, I know I'm at the ass end of 193 million people as far as making a living goes')."[36] Until late in the war when racial tension among military personnel became newsworthy, *Newsweek* handled racial identification more subtly than *Time*. A cover story by *Time* on African Americans in Vietnam exhibited its different approach:

> The American Negro is winning—indeed has won—a black badge of courage that his nation must forever honor.
> More than anything, the performance of the Negro G.I. under fire reaffirms the success—and diversity—of the American experiment. . . . He may fight to prove his manhood—perhaps as a corrective to the matriarchal dominance of the Negro ghetto back home—or to save Viet Nam for a government in Saigon about which he himself is cynical. Mostly, though, he fights for the dignity of the Negro, to shatter the stereotypes of racial inferiority, to win the judgment of noncoms and officers of whatever color.
> Unlike Negroes in previous wars, the Viet Nam breed is well disciplined. . . . Many of the best Negro warriors are former civil rights demonstrators, men who marched on lunch counters and Washington itself to win equal rights for their race. Not surprisingly, Negroes pull a considerably higher combat death rate than whites.[37]

Neither of the other two newsmagazines published a cover story devoted to African Americans in Vietnam during the war, although racial relations received intermittent attention.

Time's cover story, and other references to the racial diversity of combatants, pleased the Johnson administration, which created programs designed to improve education and devised laws to reduce employment discrimination

---

36. *Newsweek:* "When They Call, Go!" August 7, 1967, p. 37; "Ambush at Con Thien," July 17, 1967, p. 45; "Americans at War," August 1, 1966, pp. 28–32.

37. "Democracy in the Foxhole," *Time,* May 26, 1967, pp. 15–19.

for African Americans. A few weeks after the May 1967 cover story appeared, its principal correspondent, Wallace Terry, requested an interview with President Johnson to discuss another cover story, this one on Thurgood Marshall, the recently appointed first African American on the U.S. Supreme Court. The request, promptly approved, carried a notation from a presidential aide: "Based on my conversation with him today, he [Terry] seems to be very pro-Johnson, pro-administration, and agrees with our policy in Vietnam." During the interview, Terry, an African American, told the president that African American soldiers in Vietnam supported the war. Terry also assured Johnson that African American soldiers disdained militant activists such as Stokely Carmichael, the leader of a national organization. Johnson spoke to Terry about the administration's appointments of African Americans to important federal government positions, and the president "said he was proud of the Negro fighting man in Vietnam."[38]

As the *Time* cover story mentioned, African Americans suffered significantly higher casualties than whites. Until summer 1966, when the Army and Marine Corps responded to public and congressional pressure to reduce the casualty rate, 24 percent of those killed and wounded in action were African Americans, who comprised 12 percent of the national population; by summer 1968, the African American casualty rate was down to 13 percent.[39] *U.S. News & World Report* also cited the disproportionate casualty rate among African Americans in Vietnam. Unlike *Time,* which suggested that African Americans volunteered for infantry units to demonstrate their patriotism, *U.S. News & World Report* informed its readers that the Army and Marine Corps placed African Americans in combat units primarily because many lacked the education required for noncombat specialties, such as clerical and mechanical work. What none of the newsmagazines noted was the disproportionate number of low-income and rural whites who also served in combat units.[40]

The all-American military force in Vietnam was led by poster-perfect commanders. General Westmoreland was, according to *Newsweek,* "the per-

---

38. Tom Johnson to Jim Jones, memorandum, June 14, 1967, White House central files, *Time* name file, box 131, LBJ Library; Terry interview, summary of notes, June 15, 1967, office files, George Christian, box 1, LBJ Library.

39. Lawrence M. Baskir and William A. Strauss, "The Draft and Who Escaped It," 461.

40. "How Negro Americans Perform in Vietnam," *U.S. News & World Report,* August 15, 1966, p. 63; Levine, *Struggle for Southeast Asia,* 113–14.

fect Hollywood model of a general" who worked long hours at headquarters in Saigon, visited Army units throughout the country, and sometimes personally greeted troops on arrival in Vietnam. His successor as commander in Vietnam, Gen. Creighton W. Abrams, was a "hell-for-leather tank commander" whose energetic personality galvanized subordinates, *Newsweek* stated. Brigade and division commanders, according to *Newsweek*, were "pragmatic, hard-nosed officers capable of improvising in the best American military tradition." *Time* selected Westmoreland as its Man of the Year for 1965, allocating half of an eight-page war summary to a biography of the general. The magazine portrayed commanders as aggressive, no-nonsense men. A "rock-jawed veteran of World War II and Korea" commanded one brigade, *Time* wrote, while battle-hardened sergeants steadied young troops in encounters with the enemy.[41]

What the newsmagazines failed to report was the high turnover in the officer corps. Platoon, company, battalion, brigade, and divisional commanders rotated duty between combat units and headquarters positions. The average command tenure for senior officers in the field was seven months, and for junior officers just six months. Casualty rates among lieutenants obviously affected the turnover at the platoon level, but the higher up the chain of command the more careerism played a part, with officers seeking to command a combat unit merely to have it in their personnel files. This turnover would contribute to the discipline problems that afflicted the military in Vietnam from 1968 to 1972.[42] None of the newsmagazines developed this aspect, however.

American troops themselves were professional, too, the newsmagazines reported. "As the war goes on, the number of draftees fighting in Vietnam may rise, but at present they amount to fewer than 25 per cent of the total (a much lower figure than in earlier wars)," *Newsweek* wrote in summer 1966. A year later, the magazine reported, "In Vietnam, about 60 per cent of the enlisted men, 30 per cent of the officers and nearly all the senior noncoms are career soldiers." *Time* also noted the professional character of the combat units. "The new First Team [First Air Cavalry Division] is still 70% 'regular

---

41. "Vietnam: The New War," *Newsweek*, July 5, 1965, p. 32; "The American Way of War," *Newsweek*, December 5, 1966, p. 50; "The Guardians at the Gate," *Time*, January 7, 1966, pp. 13–21; "Bigger & Uglier," *Time*, July 9, 1965, p. 20; "Charge of the Air Cav," *Time*, September 23, 1966, p. 32.

42. Kinnard, *War Managers*, 109–15.

Army'—career soldiers rather than draftees—and thus manages to retain a solid base of experience among junior officers and sergeants," the magazine reported in September 1966. These articles accurately summarized the qualities of combatants during the first two years of intervention.[43] Cook remembers the esprit de corps among the early arrivals, such as the First Infantry, First Air Cavalry, and Ninth Infantry Divisions, and 173rd Airborne Brigade. "These guys were really impressive," he says. "Those first outfits were just sensational, and very, very well-equipped."[44]

Sometimes, however, the all-American troops behaved in an un-American way. "The Marines have begun to kill prisoners," *Time* reported in summer 1965, "embittered perhaps by a recent incident." The article recounted the capture of two wounded Vietcong by a Marine platoon, which took them to a Navy hospital for treatment; after extensive surgery and a recovery period, the Vietcong were transferred to ARVN soldiers, who "took them up in a helicopter and pushed them out of the hatch." *Time* offered this explanation of the incident as a rationalization for Marines executing prisoners. Two years later, the magazine covered the court-martial of an American who murdered a Vietcong prisoner. *Time* consistently prefaced its reports of such incidents with references to Vietcong and People's Army atrocities against Vietnamese civilians and battlefield executions of American combatants. Accounts of Americans mutilating guerrilla corpses—cutting off ears and fingers for trophies—also were reported. *Newsweek* described American troops negatively in this regard on two occasions. The battle for Hué in March 1968 ended "in a weeklong binge of looting" by Marines who carried clothing and merchandise from the rubble of shops. A correspondent accompanying troops during the invasion of Cambodia in May 1970 witnessed a similar sight: "[A]s the Americans passed the smashed and burned-out shops, they helped themselves to whatever loot they could get their hands on."[45] This sort of negative imagery about American troops did not appear during World War II. American troops sometimes executed German and Japanese prisoners and looted

---

43. "Americans at War," *Newsweek*, August 1, 1966, pp. 28–32; "A Nation at Odds," *Newsweek*, July 10, 1967, pp. 45–46; "Charge of the Air Cav," *Time*, September 23, 1966, pp. 31–32. For comparison, see Stanton, *American Army*, 25–27.

44. Cook interview.

45. "Status & Strategy," *Time*, August 6, 1965, pp. 28–30; "Taking Stock," *Time*, July 14, 1967, p. 38; "The Death of Hué," *Newsweek*, March 11, 1968, p. 60; *Newsweek*, May 11, 1970, pp. 26–28.

shops in European cities, but those incidents were not published, either because military censors deleted the information or because correspondents self-censored their text.[46]

Throughout autumn 1967 and into winter, however, the newsmagazines maintained the heroic imagery associated with American troops, but combat coverage suggested that the commitment and dedication of soldiers served no tangible purpose. *Newsweek* sent a correspondent to Dak To, where Americans suffered 600 casualties, including 158 dead, in November 1967. A dramatic and explicit description portrayed the "almost incredible valor" of the Americans. Intense enemy gunfire prevented medical evacuation helicopters from landing to carry out the wounded, and men lay in pain for two days. *Newsweek* wrote, "When the 'friendly' air and artillery support comes in, many of the U.S. soldiers lie in their shallow holes and bury their faces in the earth, refusing to raise their heads even when attacked by sharp-biting black ants." Finally, on the fifth day of combat, the soldiers reached the top of Hill 875, which sat astride the terminus of a trail network from Laos. The article ended with the correspondent in a helicopter, viewing "ridge after ridge stretching off into hazy distance as far as the eye could reach"—each one a potential hilltop to be conquered. *Time* remarked that Dak To displayed "the grim measure of determination" of the American military to remove guerrillas from the area. The article also observed that the nearby border with Cambodia and Laos allowed the guerrillas to withdraw to sanctuary, which would permit them to reinforce their units and return again.[47] These and other observations on the seemingly endless nature of the war were common in the newsmagazines in late 1967.

Newsmagazine articles about combat settled into a pattern from midsummer 1967 until February 1968. With the exception of stories on major battles similar to Dak To, of which several occurred between July and December 1967, combat coverage served mainly to introduce interpretive evaluations of the overall military situation. *Time* adopted a more reflective tone at this stage of the war. A six-page article in October 1967 on the status of the war devoted about half of the text to the lengthy siege at Con Thien, a Marine outpost near the demilitarized zone. Life under constant barrage

---

46. Knightley, *First Casualty,* 422–41; Tobin, *Ernie Pyle's War,* 139–42.
47. "Thanksgiving at Dak To," *Newsweek,* December 4, 1967, pp. 24–28; "Will to Win," *Time,* December 1, 1967, pp. 24–27.

from enemy artillery was the focus, and the story of a garrison mired in mud presented a bleak picture of warfare in Vietnam. "Con Thien dramatized all the cumulative frustrations of the painful war," *Time* stated. The magazine had become less convinced that victory was possible. Hedley Donovan, the successor to Luce as editor-in-chief of all Time-Life publications, had let *Time* editors know that the newsmagazine should be more neutral, less ardent in its tone.[48]

This shift toward providing more perspective on the conduct and status of the war distinguished *Newsweek, Time,* and *U.S. News & World Report* from television network news programs, which continued to rely on combat coverage.[49] Increasingly costly warfare, which saw the deaths of two hundred to three hundred Americans a week, had produced congressional debate challenging the Johnson administration's policy and had caused some measure of public dissent. The newsmagazines responded by intermittently assessing the situation in Vietnam: the degree of control and security in the countryside, infiltration rates of reinforcements and supplies from northern Vietnam, effects of aerial bombardment on northern Vietnam, and the capability of the guerrillas to sustain military operations. Newsmagazine correspondents interviewed combatants and commanders, reviewed documents from the Department of Defense, and received private briefings from Johnson administration policymakers. This information took priority over combat coverage.

Then came the Tet 1968 offensive. Beginning on January 31, the Vietcong and People's Army attacked dozens of cities and most military installations in southern Vietnam. For several weeks, urban warfare devastated Saigon and Hué. Combat imagery formed the backdrop to newsmagazine articles primarily focused on the military and political significance of the enemy onslaught, widely perceived to be a serious setback for American policy after three years of formal intervention.

Combat continued long after Tet 1968. More combat deaths—22,950—occurred from February 1968 to May 1969 than during the first three years of intervention, when 15,700 Americans died.[50] Ironically, the newsmagazines and other news media gradually relegated battlefield events to sec-

---

48. "Thunder from a Distant Hill," *Time,* October 6, 1967, pp. 21–26.
49. Hallin terms television's style "guts-and-glory" reporting (*"Uncensored War,"* 166).
50. Department of Defense, *Combat Casualty Reports, Vietnamese Conflict, 1961–1975;* Ronald H. Spector, *After Tet: The Bloodiest Year in Vietnam,* 25.

ondary status during the period of heaviest casualties. Because the United States sought a political settlement to end the war, military action was deemed less important, and with military action a secondary factor the whole war slowly faded from newsmagazine pages. The frequency of articles from Vietnam began to diminish at a different time at each newsmagazine. *U.S. News & World Report* decreased its coverage beginning in summer 1968. *Newsweek* lessened its coverage starting in late 1968. *Time* reduced its coverage somewhat beginning in autumn 1969 and considerably cut coverage by mid-1970. Robert Sam Anson remembers being warned about diminished interest among editors at the time of his arrival in Saigon in 1969. "The war's winding down and American casualties are way off," a *Time* colleague told Anson. "You're going to have to fight to get into the magazine." Pines, also a *Time* correspondent in Vietnam after Tet 1968, sensed that the public assumed the war could not be won. "The country had, by and large, written off Vietnam and our coverage reflected that."[51]

Combat coverage during the post-Tet period often expressed a sense of purposelessness. "Perhaps, as U.S. spokesmen claimed, this constituted another military victory over the enemy," *Newsweek* observed about a fierce battle near Saigon in May 1968. The magazine also referred to a lengthy tactical operation that captured tons of enemy ammunition, food, and supplies, a victory by the standards of 1965–1966, but the article concluded with the observation that "the enemy would be back in the remote fog-shrouded valley within weeks." Of a village where People's Army soldiers had retreated after fighting destroyed a Catholic church and laid waste to many homes, *Newsweek* wrote, "It was a scene of total wretchedness." *U.S. News & World Report* commented that troops on patrol seemed dispirited. "At this level, the U.S. effort in Vietnam is talked about openly and frankly as a lost cause," the magazine reported.[52]

Newsmagazine coverage of the battle for Ap Bia, a mountain bastion, in late May 1969 forcefully demonstrated the new mood. This three-day standoff between paratroopers and a People's Army battalion resulted in eighty-five American dead and three hundred wounded. The American combatants gave the name Hamburger Hill to the mountain because they said their

51. Anson, *War News,* 26; Pines interview.
52. "Shattered Symbol," *Newsweek,* May 27, 1968, pp. 30–31; "The Mini-Offensive," *Newsweek,* March 10, 1969, pp. 48–50; "The War Without a Goal: Mood of Americans in Vietnam," *U.S. News & World Report,* June 24, 1968, p. 31.

commanders had fed them into a meat grinder. A *Newsweek* article reviewed the carnage and casualties and commented: "By military standards, the troops of the 101st Division had not only done their job. They had done it heroically.... It was a memorable military achievement and yet the question could not be repressed: Was it worth it?" *Newsweek* also questioned the tactics: "Could not the defenders [People's Army] have been smashed with far fewer U.S. casualties by a series of B-52 raids?" *Time* was more sympathetic to the military. An article explained the rationale for the attack at Ap Bia, which occupied a key position on a valley. Also, *Time* stated, the military had orders to maintain pressure on the guerrillas while peace negotiations continued, in order to drive the guerrillas out of southern provinces before a settlement was signed. The magazine did observe, however, that "the war and domestic reaction to it have gone far beyond purely military considerations now, and the battle of Ap Bia raises the question of whether or not the U.S. should try to scale down the fighting by rescinding the maximum-pressure order."[53]

Time also alerted readers to a different attitude among the troops on Hamburger Hill. "After so many costly failures to gain Ap Bia's summit, some U.S. soldiers were dispirited," *Time* noted, in sharp contrast to its portrayal earlier in the war of Americans who were "spoiling for a fight." Significantly, too, *Time*'s article on Hamburger Hill revealed an incident among the troops that would become known as combat refusal. The magazine quoted a paratrooper saying that his unit had decided not to attack a third time because so many men had already died. But the unit eventually returned to battle. "One company commander stilled growing discontent among his men by telling them that 'We are soldiers, and we have to do our job,'" *Time* reported.[54] None of the newsmagazines explored whether this combat refusal incident was isolated or a sign of deeper discontent among combat units. Within a few months, though, they would focus attention on this issue.

Congress reacted strongly to the casualties at Hamburger Hill. Senators criticized the Nixon administration for not ordering General Abrams to avoid such costly battles. *Newsweek* and *Time* interpreted the aftermath in different

---

53. "Woe to the Victors," *Newsweek,* June 2, 1969, pp. 42–44; "The Battle for Hamburger Hill," *Time,* May 30, 1969, pp. 27–28.

54. "The Battle for Hamburger Hill," *Time,* May 30, 1969, pp. 27–28.

ways. "With as little publicity as possible, U.S. paratroopers evacuated Ap Bia Mountain," *Newsweek* reported. "And their leave-taking last week was eloquent testimony that 'Hamburger Hill'—as the mountain was dubbed by the GI's who conquered it—had never been regarded by the U.S. as a piece of real estate worth keeping." *Time* wrote: "So dearly won in American lives the week before, Ap Bia Mountain was abandoned last week by troopers of the 101st Airborne Division. Their aim, as always in the long war, had been not to seize ground but to disperse or destroy their enemies."[55] While *Newsweek* emphasized the apparent purposelessness of the battle, *Time* reminded readers that territory was not an objective in this war.

Americans and Vietnamese

The anger, fear, and frustration felt by Americans in Vietnam sometimes extended beyond the battlefield, touching the people of southern Vietnam, some of whom were victims of cruelty and misconduct. Horrible incidents happened during the war, culminating in the massacre at My Lai of dozens of villagers by an American infantry platoon. The massacre stunned the American public. Many Americans' perceptions of the relationship between American troops and the Vietnamese were influenced by the newsmagazines, and their incomprehension of the tragedy was understandable because *Newsweek, Time,* and *U.S. News & World Report* had provided scant warning. From summer 1965 through autumn 1969, newsmagazine articles presented a traditional portrait of generous, kindly American troops assisting civilians in a war-torn country, an image consistent with magazine and newspaper articles from World War II and the Korean War. Although the articles accurately reported the actions of most American troops, the attitude and behavior of many in-country military personnel exhibited hostility and racism.[56] "Young men from the small towns of America, the GIs who came to Vietnam found themselves in a place halfway round the earth among people with whom they could make no human contact," scholar Frances Fitzgerald concludes. "Like an Orwellian army, they knew everything about military tactics, but nothing about where they were or who the enemy was. And they found themselves not attacking fixed positions but walking through the jungle

55. "A Question of Casualties," *Newsweek,* June 9, 1969, 45. *Time,* June 6, 1969, 22.
56. See, for example, Michael Herr, *Dispatches;* Levine, *Struggle for Southeast Asia,* 114; Maclear, *Ten Thousand Day War,* 132; Spector, *After Tet,* 198–202, 207–21.

or through villages among small yellow people, as strange and exposed among them as if they were Martians."[57]

Newsweek, Time, and *U.S. News & World Report* published reassuring articles about American troops building schools, digging wells, constructing medical clinics, repairing bridges, and distributing schoolbooks. These so-called civic action projects were supposed to demonstrate to Vietnamese that Americans and the Republic of Vietnam government meant to improve their quality of life. "This is the part of my job I like best," an infantry officer told *Newsweek* for an article about troops at a village project. Another article described a special program in rural villages. "Nearby, U.S. Army medical teams bathed babies with running sores in a surgical-soap solution and applied stethoscopes to the concave chests of the old men while a veterinarian examined some ailing water buffalo," *Newsweek* reported. "Later on, an American movie ('The Wyoming Kid') was shown, and nearly every child in the village won a prize in a toy lottery. Clothing was handed out free." *Time* referred to a civilian assistance program operated by Marines, who built a two-room school and rebuilt two bridges in a village. The Marines received "the affection of the local people" as well as intelligence about Vietcong cadres from villagers, *Time* reported.[58]

But the anger and frustration arising from a guerrilla war could not be ignored altogether. *Time* quoted a wrathful sergeant: "We try to help these goddam people and you know what they do? They send in their kids to steal our grenades and ammunition and use them to kill us. The hell with them!" *Newsweek* readers learned about the stress of counterinsurgency warfare on U.S. troops: "Other marines bring in some blindfolded Viet Cong suspects. A small child who follows is screaming, bereft and terrified, trying to get to one of the blindfolded prisoners, presumably his father or brother. 'Sometimes,' says [a captain] with a grimace of distaste, 'this makes you feel just a little inhuman.'" A 1966 *Time* subhead, "Too Many Gooks," introduced part of an article that incorrectly informed readers that the word was American slang for the enemy.[59] Actually, many troops called all Vietnamese gooks.

57. Fitzgerald, *Fire in the Lake,* 494–95.
58. "The Relief of Duc Co," *Newsweek,* August 23, 1965, p. 29; "How Goes Pacification?" *Newsweek,* September 19, 1966, p. 58; "'Big Joe No. 1,'" *Time,* August 20, 1965, pp. 24–25.
59. "The Guardians at the Gate," *Time,* January 7, 1966, p. 19; "Americans at War," *Newsweek,* August 1, 1966, pp. 31–33; "Fresh from the North," *Time,* December 2, 1966, p. 37.

Fitzgerald, whose history of Vietnam won a Pulitzer Prize, states that Americans regarded Vietnam as a "nation of gooks." *Newsweek* told its readers in September 1966 that "gooks" was a common pejorative, while *Time* did not clarify its reference until October 1969 and *U.S. News & World Report* did not mention the pejorative at all until two months after that.[60] The tension, distrust, and occasional hostility between Americans and their Vietnamese allies rarely found its way onto newsmagazine pages, although journalists realized it existed. *Time* devoted a four-column article to American-Vietnamese tension in autumn 1969, telling readers that the in-country presence of a half-million foreign troops had produced hatred and hostility. "[The Vietnamese] accuse the Americans of practicing a kind of cultural defoliation in Viet Nam," *Time* noted. "G.I.s in the field frequently find it impossible to distinguish between 'bad' and 'good' Vietnamese; as a result, they often callously mistreat all of them." *U.S. News & World Report* waited until later in the year to deal with the subject. "It is not uncommon to see an American show his contempt for what he regards as an incompetent, lazy Vietnamese. In many cases, it is simply a case of a bully behaving badly," an article stated. "The relationship between U.S. troops and the Vietnamese people has gone through a change for the worse." *Newsweek* pinpointed the cause of tension during summer 1970 in an article concerning beatings and harassment of American troops. "To many Vietnamese, moreover, the Americans seem simply a new set of colonial masters—subtle and indirect colonizers but colonizers for all that," *Newsweek* declared.[61]

The first indication in the newsmagazines about American misconduct toward civilians appeared in July 1967. In an article about the court-martial of a Marine for murdering a Vietcong prisoner, *Time* reported the courts-martial months earlier of another Marine and four Army soldiers for separate crimes of murder and rape. Considering that nearly three hundred American troops faced courts-martial or other disciplinary action for brutality and mistreatment toward Vietcong prisoners and Vietnamese civilians

---

60. Fitzgerald, *Fire in the Lake*, 494–95; "Vietnam: Correcting the Crucial Error," *Newsweek*, September 12, 1966, p. 48; "South Viet Nam: Rising Resentment of the U.S.," *Time*, October 24, 1969, p. 28; "Massacre Trial—Shift in War?" *U.S. News & World Report*, December 15, 1969, p. 25.

61. "South Viet Nam: Rising Resentment of the U.S.," *Time*, October 24, 1969, pp. 28–29; "Massacre Trial—Shift in War?" *U.S. News & World Report*, December 15, 1969, p. 25; "The Hated Americans," *Newsweek*, August 17, 1970, p. 43.

from 1965 to 1971, the lack of attention to the topic by newsmagazines is noteworthy.[62] Defense Department documents reveal that the military considered misconduct by American troops a serious matter. Weekly reports monitored incidents involving assault, drunkenness, rape, and vandalism. Knowledge of criminal behavior by Americans circulated among embassy officials, Military Assistance Command staff, and the troops themselves. "Incidents cited included wanton shootings, rape, crop damage, arrest and detention of civilians for no disclosed cause," stated a formal report in autumn 1967 on the behavior of American personnel in rural provinces near Saigon.[63] Correspondents for *Newsweek, Time,* and *U.S. News & World Report* heard rumors and knew about the official documentation, but none believed that more than a small number of Americans behaved criminally toward the Vietnamese. "War is nasty and soldiers are nasty," says Horrock. "Some don't know when to stop being nasty. We just never had the notion a lot of our grunts [infantrymen] murdered and raped and committed crimes. If we had, we'd have written it."[64]

Newsmagazine correspondents and other mainstream journalists reacted slowly and with disbelief to the disclosure in autumn 1969 that an infantry platoon of the Americal Division had committed a massacre of villagers at My Lai in March 1968. The Army itself had provided a news release to the Associated Press outlining criminal charges filed against an infantry lieutenant for the murder of "an unspecified number of civilians in Vietnam," and the AP had sent a brief item to its hundreds of newspaper clients. Nobody bothered to follow up except for Seymour Hersh of Dispatch News Service, a small, independent operation in Washington. Several weeks later, Hersh's story appeared in a few dozen newspapers. Anson remembers a telex message to *Time's* Saigon bureau from the New York office asking for information to confirm details about the massacre. One of his colleagues called sources at military headquarters in Saigon, who denied a massacre had occurred. When photographs taken by an Army photojournalist showed up in newspapers, which suddenly began to pay attention to the incident, *Time*

---

62. "Taking Stock," *Time,* July 14, 1967, p. 38; Guenter Lewy, "The Question of American War Guilt," 366.

63. Provincial attitudes, U.S. mission reports, periodic, national security files, Vietnam country file, box 98, LBJ Library; U.S. Mission Report, November 19–25, 1967, national security files, Vietnam country file, box 98, 59F, LBJ Library.

64. Horrock interview.

editors in New York ordered the Saigon bureau to send someone to My Lai immediately.[65]

Commentary on the My Lai massacre in *Newsweek* and *Time* expressed outrage. Each magazine placed the atrocity in a social or political context. "The stark realization that, in at least one instance, American fighting men had betrayed the nation's principles and besmirched its honor could scarcely fail to unsettle even some of the members of Mr. Nixon's silent majority," *Newsweek* wrote, referring to the president's term for Americans who supported his war policy. The next edition of *Newsweek* belatedly recognized that other war crimes had preceded My Lai: "The massacre presumably was not the first atrocity in Vietnam, although it was doubtless the largest." *Time* declared, "Men in American uniforms slaughtered the civilians of My Lai, and in so doing humiliated the U.S. and called in question the U.S. mission in Viet Nam in a way that all the antiwar protesters could never have done." The magazine also compared the massacre, which it considered an isolated case, to the Vietcong's terrorism. "For shocked Americans, what happened at My Lai seems an awful aberration," *Time* stated. "For the Communists in Viet Nam, the murder of civilians is routine, purposeful policy." *U.S. News & World Report* avoided condemning the troops, and its commentary also mentioned the terror inflicted on villagers by the Vietcong.[66]

Disintegration and Departure

A truly symbolic turning point in the Vietnam War occurred during summer 1969 when a contingent of American infantrymen headed home. President Richard M. Nixon, who had taken office in January, announced a phased withdrawal of the military, a process dependent on improvements in ARVN capability to handle tactical operations. A battalion of the Ninth Infantry Division was the first combat unit to withdraw since formal intervention had started fifty-three months earlier. *Newsweek* reported the departure ceremony, using a quotation to indicate its perspective on the war. "Other GIs wondered whether they had done the right thing fighting in Vietnam,"

---

65. Anson, *War News,* 48–49.
66. "The Killings at Song My," *Newsweek,* December 1, 1969, p. 11; "Song My: A U.S. Atrocity?" *Newsweek,* December 8, 1969, pp. 33–35; "My Lai: An American Tragedy," *Time,* December 5, 1969, pp. 23–25, 29; "Massacre Trial—Shift in War?" *U.S. News & World Report,* December 15, 1969, pp. 25–27.

the article stated, quoting a soldier who said, "I can truthfully say I just can't see any good reason for any Americans to have died here."[67]

The redirection in national policy actually had begun in spring 1968 when President Johnson decided not to seek reelection in the wake of the Tet 1968 offensive and when peace negotiations between the Democratic Republic of Vietnam and the United States opened in Paris. Yet American troops were expected to continue fighting. With three full years of inconclusive warfare behind them and the prospect for a compromise settlement likely, American troops wondered why they should continue to risk their lives. This attitude became more widespread after the Nixon administration announced the phased withdrawal of troops beginning in summer 1969. Americans in Vietnam were expected to uphold the national honor rather than secure victory. Nobody knew when peace would come.[68] An Army and Marine Corps predominantly staffed by first-term enlistees and led by career officers and sergeants during 1965–1967 had become mixed with more draftees and hurriedly trained junior officers by 1968, and by 1969 was mostly composed of draftees led by inexperienced sergeants and junior officers of dubious qualifications. Military conscription affected lower- and middle-class youths, but most draftees sent to Vietnam were from the rural and urban poor and a majority of those assigned to infantry units were school dropouts or low scorers on aptitude tests. Put another way, the combatants of 1965–1967 consisted mostly of men who had chosen, for a variety of reasons, to be in the military, while the combatants of 1968 and afterward consisted mostly of men who had not chosen to be in the military and definitely had not wanted to go to war.[69]

The newsmagazines had not prepared their readers for the military's transformation. The articles published from 1965 to 1967 described dutiful troops led by able officers and veteran sergeants, but no articles until summer 1969 focused on the increase in draftees and depletion in qualified officers and sergeants. Military discipline and morale became a public issue in September 1969 when the newsmagazines wrote about the first fully reported combat refusal by American troops. A company from the 196th Light Infantry Brigade refused to advance within range of a People's Army position to re-

---

67. "Beginning of the End?" *Newsweek*, August 18, 1969, p. 42.
68. Maclear, *Ten Thousand Day War*, 276–79.
69. Stanton, *American Army*, 293–94, 364–65.

trieve eight bodies from an American helicopter downed by enemy gunfire in the Song Chang Valley. *Newsweek* carefully explained the situation, telling readers that soldiers did not want to endanger themselves to bring back corpses and that an inexperienced lieutenant had not exerted authority. "The Alpha Company incident, then, was caused by a combination of extraordinary circumstances and a failure of leadership," the article stated. *Newsweek* also placed the incident within the context of society generally. "As in no other modern U.S. war, there is a malaise among the troops in Vietnam," the magazine stated. "Hatred for the war runs deep, especially among the younger draftees. As more and more younger soldiers arrive from the U.S., the antiwar spirit mounts." *Newsweek* returned to this theme in early 1970. "Only in a handful of instances have U.S. units temporarily refused to go into action," an article stated. "Nevertheless, there are signs that a malaise, catalyzed in part by the antiwar conviction of the educated draftees, may be spreading in different forms to other U.S. troops in Vietnam." *Time* offered its own explanation for the combat refusal. "At the present stage of the war, the Song Chang incident seemed symptomatic of U.S. fatigue with the continuing bloodshed," the magazine commented. And, to reassure readers, *Time* stated, "It is doubtful that such incidents are more common in Viet Nam than they have been in other wars."[70] Both newsmagazines, then, considered the combat refusal an aberration. The U.S. Senate Armed Services Committee revealed in 1971 that the military had convicted 361 soldiers for combat refusal and mutiny during 1968–1970, a period when in-country troop strength decreased from 540,000 to 330,000. Most soldiers convicted of combat refusal and mutiny acted singly or in small groups. Incidents involving an entire platoon or company rarely happened.[71] Still, the futility of the war, loss of pride, lack of empathy and respect for the southern Vietnamese, and fear of dying for no reason severely affected all combat units.[72]

As more troops went home, those who remained became angry and resentful. *Newsweek* quoted an unidentified soldier at the siege of Ben Het: "It's fine to let the ARVN do the fighting—but I'm still here." A lengthy article alluded to the technique of search-and-evade that soldiers had adopted.

---

70. "Beginning of the End?" *Newsweek*, September 8, 1969, pp. 17–18; "A New GI: For Pot and Peace," *Newsweek*, February 2, 1970, pp. 24–28; "Incident in Song Chang Valley," *Time*, September 5, 1969, pp. 22–23.
71. Maclear, *Ten Thousand Day War*, 271.
72. Spector, *After Tet*, 61–63.

When a patrol was out of sight of its firebase, soldiers would find a place to wait until it was time to return. "In many more cases, young officers and noncoms have simply failed to carry out their orders," *Newsweek* wrote. *Time* and *Newsweek* also reported an incident involving soldiers assigned to the Twelfth Cavalry Regiment who refused to go on a defensive patrol near their artillery base. "Combat refusals by U.S. soldiers have become a common occurrence in South Vietnam," *Newsweek* observed. "For an increasing number of GI's, there is a feeling of being forgotten men. . . . [M]ore and more U.S. soldiers serving in Vietnam are understandably concerned that they may be among the last to die in a war everybody else considers over."[73] *Time* told readers in January 1971, "The simple fact is that it is hard to exhort soldiers to fight a war that even the Pentagon wants to write off as fast as possible." *U.S. News & World Report* characterized combat refusals as isolated incidents. "High-ranking officers claim not to be worried over an occasional refusal of U.S. soldiers to fight," the magazine wrote. Then the article reminded readers, "Americans are still dying in Vietnam and more will do so even though they are engaged primarily in what senior officers term 'defensive' duties—such as patrolling and guarding [bases]."[74]

Combat refusals were only one aspect of the psychological and sociological turmoil afflicting military personnel in Vietnam. Prior to 1970, despite the fact that sources with command headquarters in Saigon and operational units in the field might have made the real situation known to correspondents if asked, the newsmagazines treated incidents involving racial animosity, disciplinary offenses, and drug usage as discrete occurrences rather than as symptomatic of attitudinal and behavioral patterns.[75] The all-American military had disintegrated slowly since the Johnson administration announced its intention to reach a negotiated settlement in spring 1968. One military historian writes that by 1970 the U.S. Army "was unraveling like the war around it, and morale and discipline were steadily deteriorating."[76]

---

73. "Mutual Education," *Newsweek*, July 7, 1969, pp. 21–22; "The Troubled U.S. Army in Vietnam," *Newsweek*, January 11, 1971, pp. 29–37; "A Question of Protection," *Time*, October 25, 1971, p. 38; "Soldiers Who Refuse to Die," *Newsweek*, October 25, 1971, pp. 67–68.

74. "The War within the War," *Time*, January 25, 1971, p. 35; "As Vietnam Gets Set for Faster Pullout," *U.S. News & World Report*, November 15, 1971, pp. 45–46.

75. Maclear, *Ten Thousand Day War*, 279.

76. Stanton, *American Army*, 348–49.

Three newsmagazine correspondents who reported from Vietnam between Tet 1968 and 1970—Horrock of *Newsweek,* Pines of *Time,* and Wallace of *U.S. News & World Report*—dispute this conclusion, however. These correspondents say some military units with poor leadership did have serious disciplinary and morale problems, but that other units with strong officers maintained orderliness, if not aggressiveness. "You weren't seeing it as clearly as you could later on, because it was happening all around you, slowly, and you would just kind of notice how different the atmosphere or way of doing things was from before," Horrock says. "*Newsweek* was liberal, so we were looking for those kinds of stories, things that demonstrated the effects of the war." Stanley Cloud, the Saigon bureau chief for *Time* in 1971–1972, attributes newsmagazine articles concerning drug usage, racial discord, and discipline problems to journalists searching for newsworthy events. "There was no fighting in Vietnam early in 1972, for that matter most of 1971," Cloud says. "That was why you had all those stories in *Time* especially, and *Newsweek* too, for that matter, about soldiers and drugs, because there were no other stories, at least from the American perspective."[77]

However, distinctly nonmilitary attitudes and behavior had developed among American troops several years earlier, and some journalists knew it. Michael Herr, a correspondent for *Esquire,* visited Army and Marine Corps units during 1967 and early 1968. Perhaps it was because Herr stayed with units for several days at a time and observed them during combat and noncombat situations, but his surreal vision of Americans at war painted an entirely different portrait than that seen in *Newsweek, Time,* and *U.S. News & World Report.* Herr described disillusioned, disoriented, and disturbed young men whose fatalism and cynicism should have startled, if not worried, any visitor.[78] None of the other mainstream media presented such revealing psychological profiles. *Esquire* certainly gave Herr more room to write than any newsmagazine correspondent had, but the newsmagazines never caught the sheer strangeness of it all. By concentrating on combat coverage, newsmagazine correspondents missed opportunities to inform their readers about the toll that conditions and circumstances of war had taken on men who were living an ordinary life until they received draft notices and were sent to Vietnam.

77. Horrock and Cloud interviews.
78. Michael Herr, "Hell Sucks," *Esquire,* August 1968, pp. 66–69, 109–10.

Although quite tardy, an eight-page *Newsweek* article, "The Troubled U.S. Army in Vietnam," appeared in January 1971 and informed readers about racial discord, heroin addiction, and "fragging"—the use by troops of grenades against officers and sergeants to intimidate or kill. *Newsweek* had first reported extensive marijuana use among U.S. troops in November 1967 in a one-column article.[79] The topic did not receive in-depth attention from the newsmagazines until a spate of articles appeared during 1970 and 1971: eight articles primarily about drug usage among troops in Vietnam appeared in *Newsweek, Time,* and *U.S. News & World Report* from January 1970 through May 1971, compared to two articles on the subject from 1967 to 1969. "Marijuana—The Other Enemy in Vietnam" declared a headline in a January 1970 edition of *U.S. News & World Report,* while "A New GI: For Pot and Peace" ran atop a *Newsweek* article a few weeks later.[80] Both newsmagazines connected the predominantly young U.S. troops to their cohorts in the United States, carefully explaining that marijuana smoking did not represent incipient mutiny or insubordination. *U.S. News & World Report* reported in April 1970 that perhaps 60 percent to 80 percent of U.S. troops smoked marijuana, basing the estimate on a congressional inquiry. *Time* highlighted the heroin problem among troops twice during spring 1971, and attributed the deaths of thirty-three Americans at an artillery firebase in April 1971 to carelessness, laxity, and marijuana-induced torpor.[81]

The military itself documented significantly increased drug abuse beginning in 1968. Random testing of troops for the presence of narcotic-based chemicals in blood and urine indicated that 8.9 percent of Army and 9.1 percent of Marine Corps personnel in Vietnam had smoked marijuana in 1968 while 23.7 percent of Army and 29.8 percent of Marine Corps personnel did so in 1970. Similar testing for heroin and opium indicated that 7.6 percent of Army and 9.6 percent of Marine Corps personnel had used either of the narcotics in 1971, percentages that represented a tenfold increase

79. "The Troubled U.S. Army in Vietnam," *Newsweek,* January 11, 1971, pp. 29–37; "Mary Jane in Action," *Newsweek,* November 6, 1967, p. 40.
80. "Marijuana—The Other Enemy in Vietnam," *U.S. News & World Report,* January 26, 1970, pp. 68–69; "A New GI: For Pot and Peace," *Newsweek,* February 2, 1970, pp. 24–25.
81. "Fresh Disclosures on Drugs and GI's," *U.S. News & World Report,* April 6, 1970, pp. 32–33; "Indochina: Nixon's Strategy of Withdrawal," *Time,* March 1, 1971, pp. 19–20; "Another Sort of H-Bomb," *Time,* April 19, 1971, pp. 21–22; "The Wound Reopened," *Time,* April 12, 1971, p. 26.

from 1969. Some military medical officers estimated that 31 percent of all troops departing Vietnam during 1969 had smoked marijuana a dozen or more days each month and that 17 percent had used opium or marijuana cigarettes laced with opium, so-called Thai sticks. During 1970, very high-grade heroin became available in Vietnam. Commanders of infantry, artillery, and supply units in Vietnam regarded drug abuse as a serious problem by 1971.[82]

The final years of American military intervention in Vietnam witnessed a sad spectacle. In 1971, combat injuries sent fewer than 5,000 American troops to hospitals while drug abuse necessitated medical treatment for 20,500 troops. The newsmagazines likened drug usage among in-country troops to a similar pattern among young adults in the United States that had begun during the mid-1960s.[83]

Military discipline deteriorated, too. Attacks against officers and sergeants occurred more often beginning in 1969. The newsmagazines did not report these developments in detail until congressional inquiries publicized the incidents in 1971. Congress heard testimony from Department of Defense officials that 730 fragging incidents, which killed 83 officers, occurred from 1969 to 1971.[84] Under these circumstances, newsmagazine correspondents shifted their attention to problems among U.S. troops. Horrock, of *Newsweek,* recalls a night on patrol in 1971. "I went with an infantry unit, was with them, and night came," he says. "They gave me a choice of where I wanted to be. I could be with the senior NCOs and officers or the enlisted men. They didn't want you crossing back and forth. They were afraid. They had set up their own security. They were afraid of their own men, not all of them but some of them." *U.S. News & World Report* also told its readers about the breakdown. "The point has been reached where officers and sergeants sometimes hesitate to issue an order—out of apprehension that the troops may not obey and will cause trouble," an article reported. *Time* summarized the worsening situation: "Along with drugs, insubordination and

---

82. Hammond, *The Military and the Media, 1962–1968,* 187; Spector, *After Tet,* 272–73, 275–78.

83. Maclear, *Ten Thousand Day War,* 280–81; "Mary Jane in Action," *Newsweek,* November 6, 1967, p. 40; "Marijuana—The Other Enemy in Vietnam," *U.S. News & World Report,* January 26, 1970, pp. 68–69.

84. William M. Hammond, *The Military and the Media, 1968–1973: The U.S. Army in Vietnam,* 174–88; Maclear, *Ten Thousand Day War,* 271.

racial tension in the barracks, fragging is part of a mosaic of disintegrating discipline in Viet Nam that is disturbing the highest echelons of the Pentagon."[85]

All three newsmagazines reported the murder of a white officer by two African American soldiers in January 1971, and each used the incident to explore more deeply the subject of racial tension among American troops. *Time* used it to introduce a two-page article on the "mosaic of disintegrating discipline" among troops in Vietnam. The article described a military divided by hostility, and occasional violence, between African Americans and whites. *Newsweek* provided a detailed account of the confrontation to illustrate the social divide between an almost all-white officer corps and the multiracial units they commanded. *U.S. News & World Report* devoted three pages to the effects on military units in Vietnam of militancy among African Americans and racial hostility.[86] These articles signaled a willingness to write about the reality of racial discord in Vietnam. Previous articles on the all-American military in 1966–1967 had briefly noted the discord affecting African Americans and whites. "Despite the foxhole comradeship of most G.I.s in Viet Nam," *Time* wrote, "the war is not all interracial amity: vicious racist graffiti from both sides mar the walls of latrines in Saigon; white and Negroes slug it out on occasion along the night-town streets of Tu Do and in 'Soulsville,' the Negro's self-imposed ghetto of joy along Saigon's waterfront." *U.S. News & World Report* reported, "Negroes and whites practice a voluntary separation when off-duty." Open confrontations between African Americans and whites began during winter 1968. Army commanders reported twenty "serious incidents" of a racial nature in Vietnam from January to September 1969, but the newsmagazines did not deal with the discord for months afterward.[87]

Although a few articles published in 1966 and 1967 alluded to tension and off-duty separation in connection with African Americans and whites,

---

85. Horrock interview; "As Fighting Slows Down in Vietnam: Breakdown in GI Discipline," *U.S. News & World Report,* June 7, 1971, pp. 16–17; "The War within the War," *Time,* January 25, 1971, pp. 34–35.

86. "The War within the War," *Time,* January 25, 1971, pp. 34–35; "Shootout at Quang Tri," *Newsweek,* January 25, 1971, p. 49; "Sagging Morale in Vietnam," *U.S. News & World Report,* January 25, 1971, pp. 30–33.

87. "Democracy in the Foxhole," *Time,* May 26, 1967, p. 16; "How Negro Americans Perform in Vietnam," *U.S. News & World Report,* August 15, 1966, 63; Hammond, *The Military and the Media, 1962–1968,* 175–77; Spector, *After Tet,* 246–58.

the widening racial divide among military personnel in Vietnam, which reflected the terrible turmoil in the United States during the summers of 1967–1969, went mostly without comment in the newsmagazines. Finally, *Newsweek* published articles in February and June 1970 that dealt at length with the issue. The magazine commented that "discontent is also growing among black troops, who arrive in Vietnam already radicalized by racial tensions at home." *Newsweek* later mentioned the lack of African American officers in the Army and Marine Corps, and connected racial animosity with militancy among stateside African American organizations.[88] *Time* devoted a full-page article to Soul Alley, a racially separate area in Saigon. Whites, even military police, did not enter the area because of hostility. But it had become a haven for others. "Soul Alley is home for somewhere between 300 and 500 black AWOLs and deserters," *Time* reported. The magazine also referred to harassment by white officers and sergeants of younger African Americans for their fuller hairstyle, called an Afro, and casual wearing of uniforms, which violated military regulations stipulating buttoned pockets and no adornment other than insignia. African Americans wore peace symbols, as did many white soldiers, but they also wore symbols associated with militant African American organizations.[89]

Phased withdrawal finally ended the American combat role in August 1972. A boxed *Newsweek* sidebar, beneath the headline "The Last Battalion," described the last patrol by the last infantry company of the last American infantry battalion in the Republic of Vietnam: "240 men of the Third Battalion, 21st Infantry, happily scrambled aboard their helicopters and flew off to Danang on the first leg of the long journey back to 'the world.' "[90] The departure of the last combat troops assured the virtual disappearance of military-related articles from *Newsweek, Time,* and *U.S. News & World Report* during the final five months of the Vietnam War, although approximately 43,000 Americans remained in-country, including pilots, mechanics, technicians, logistics personnel, and security police. When military-related articles appeared, the focus was on Air Force and Navy fighter-bomber attacks against targets in northern Vietnam and Laos and

---

88. "A New GI: For Pot and Peace," *Newsweek,* February 2, 1970, pp. 24–28; "How Sad to Be a Cambodian," *Newsweek,* June 29, 1970, pp. 48–50. Maclear notes that only 2 percent of the officer corps were African American (*Ten Thousand Day War*).

89. "Soul Alley," *Time,* December 14, 1970, p. 40.

90. "Back to the Big Muddy," *Newsweek,* August 21, 1972, p. 20.

the two-week assault by B-52 bombers on Hanoi and Haiphong in December 1972 that produced a final cease-fire agreement.

When the date for a cease-fire seemed certain, *Time* commemorated the 2,810,000 Americans who served in Vietnam from March 1965 until January 1973: "If the majority of them performed bravely and well—and they did—their sacrifices were somehow tragically diminished by the very ambiguity of the war, its often enraging purposelessness."[91] Certainly, the newsmagazines gave their readers a sense of the purposelessness of the war from autumn 1967 afterward. Combat coverage throughout much of the 1965–1967 buildup phase reinforced the idealized image of the American soldier: brave, noble, self-sacrificing, and stoic. Early in the war, heroic soldiers saved their comrades from a fanatic enemy, medics sacrificed themselves to rescue the wounded, and aviators braved withering groundfire to attack targets; late in the war, everyone just wanted to survive and go home, and heroes disappeared from newsmagazine pages. The voices quoted from Vietnam had altered their tone from determination and duty to despair and dissatisfaction.

Newsmagazine articles responsibly balanced the tales of battlefield bravery with graphic imagery to inform readers about the brutality of war. *Newsweek, Time,* and *U.S. News & World Report* also made sure their readers recognized the contributions of African Americans on the battlefield. They occasionally told their readers that Americans behaved dishonorably by killing prisoners and looting, and they did not shirk from reporting the disintegration of the military during the latter years of war. Generally, the newsmagazines placed the conduct of military personnel within the context of American society: antiwar attitudes, drug usage, racial militancy, and racism. However, they conveyed these images to their readers reluctantly, usually waiting until government officials had revealed the problems. Journalists knew what was going on before Congress and the Defense Department issued reports, though. While coverage in *Newsweek, Time,* and *U.S. News & World Report* adequately portrayed combat in Vietnam, it failed to provide sufficient information about the conditions affecting Americans at war and the ultimate effects of national policy on the people who fought.

---

91. "U.S. after Viet Nam," *Time,* November 6, 1972, p. 22.

4

American Ways of War
Firepower and Futility

American ways of war in Vietnam caused controversy from the start. America went to war with the latest in modern weaponry: cluster bombs and napalm, chemical defoliants, computer-controlled artillery, helicopters, motion and thermal sensors, night-vision scopes, and the world's largest bomber—the B-52, which dropped thirty tons of bombs from an altitude beyond sight and hearing of those below. Firepower, mobility, and technology formed an operational triad for American commanders. Military doctrine had prepared them to fight a conventional war in Europe, however, not an insurgency in Asia. Almost from the start, controversy arose concerning military strategy and tactics in Vietnam. The specter of the world's mightiest industrial nation bombarding an agrarian society in northern Vietnam and pummeling the countryside of southern Vietnam aroused opposition in the United States and Europe. Also, a divisive debate erupted among military commanders, strategists, and policymakers regarding the appropriateness and effectiveness of military methods.

Newsweek, Time, and *U.S. News & World Report* thoroughly reported, and engaged in, the debate about military methods. Antiwar demonstrations and congressional dissent on war policy gradually affected military strategy and tactics in Vietnam, but the internal debate among planners and policymakers had more immediate consequences. Factions formed and quarreled within the Defense Department, military headquarters in Saigon, and the National Security Council over the choice of warfare for Vietnam, whether to wage attritional war, adopt counterinsurgency techniques, or establish an enclave network.¹ Belief in the United States' ultimate superiority on the battlefield because of its war technology convinced many in the military hierarchy that the attritional strategy would triumph. *Newsweek, Time,* and *U.S. News & World Report* eventually chose sides, and the factional dispute over military strategy and tactics in Vietnam played out in the newsmagazines. The dispute concerned the best way to fight the war, dominate the battlefield, and force the communists to negotiate a settlement or, preferably, withdraw into the remote regions of southern Vietnam.

Attritional warfare dominated military operations from summer 1965 through autumn 1968. The attritional warfare faction included General Westmoreland, senior Army generals at the Pentagon, most senior presidential advisors in the Johnson administration, and, until summer 1967, the secretary of defense, Robert S. McNamara. Attritional warfare relied on artillery, aerial bombardment, special ordnance, and search-and-destroy/sweep operations to inflict heavy casualties on the guerrillas, stop their reinforcement and resupply from the north, eliminate storage depots, and obliterate fortified sites. Although attritional warfare prevailed until late 1968, counterinsurgency warfare had influential proponents. The counterinsurgency faction included Marine Corps generals and second-tier Army commanders in Vietnam and some strategists in the Defense Department. Counterinsurgency warfare relied on squads and platoons stationed in villages to deny the Vietcong access to residents; its strategic purpose was to protect villagers and to provide time for so-called pacification teams to build allegiance to the southern government by offering agricultural assistance, medical treatment, education, and improvements in living conditions. A third faction, the enclave faction, included State Department policymakers, some military strategists, and, by summer 1967, the secretary of defense; its strategic purpose was to create secure zones around cities and densely populated coastal areas to permit the southern government to establish its authority.²

The newsmagazines initially accepted the premise that American superiority in weaponry and technology would defeat the communists. The longer

---

1. For a discussion of the factions and strategic preferences within the Defense Department and military hierarchy and among policymakers, see the *Pentagon Papers,* Senator Gravel ed., vols. 3–4.

2. This summary was derived from a variety of sources, including Westmoreland, *A Soldier Reports; Pentagon Papers,* 3:408–17; Herring, *America's Longest War,* 175–79; Maclear, *Ten Thousand Day War,* 133.

the war went on, however, the more frequently newsmagazines evaluated military methods and eventually displayed factional favoritism. Each newsmagazine had aligned itself with a faction by the end of summer 1965. *Newsweek,* which reminded its readers that political action was equal in importance to military action, favored the counterinsurgency group initially, and later in the war argued for an enclave strategy to reduce American casualties while the Vietnamese assumed responsibility for combat. *Time,* which believed that superior weaponry and modern technology would defeat the communists, and *U.S. News & World Report,* which preferred immediately intensified and unrestricted warfare, both sided with the attritional group; but *U.S. News & World Report* later advocated the counterinsurgency approach in the south because conventional military methods apparently were not effective. By selectively presenting information favorable to a strategic preference and by incorporating commentary on military methods in articles about combat, each newsmagazine delivered to its readers an appreciably different perspective on the conduct of the war. These factional alignments further distinguished the newsmagazines from network television news programs, which did not offer viewers editorially distinct presentations on strategy and tactics.[3]

Factional bias displayed by *Newsweek, Time,* and *U.S. News & World Report* potentially influenced the perceptions of millions of readers on the conduct of the Vietnam War, an important consideration because military methods provoked public discourse. Congress, antiwar activists, and ordinary citizens expressed concern about the American casualty rate, Vietnamese civilian casualties, the purpose of aerial bombardment of northern Vietnam, and the lack of discernible progress on the battlefield. Strategy and tactics mattered, especially from summer 1965 until troop withdrawals began in summer 1969. Despite technological superiority and advanced weaponry, the United States faced incredible resistance from communist military units in the south and steadfast refusal to negotiate a settlement by the Democratic Republic of Vietnam in the north. Claims of progress by the Johnson administration and military commanders seemed dubious to many Americans, and antiwar demonstrations attracted more participants.[4] Failure was not

3. Bailey, "Vietnam War," determines that only ABC presented politically conservative commentary concerning the Vietnam War, but this pertained to support for intervention, not the conduct of the war. Scholars do not indicate that network news programs offered markedly different interpretations of strategy and tactics.
4. Melvin Small, *Johnson, Nixon, and the Doves,* 82–88.

apparent, however, until late 1967. Conventional warfare methods succeeded at first. By adhering to military doctrine, commanders secured the coastal and inland enclaves during summer 1965, battled the guerrillas in the adjacent countryside during autumn, then entered the enemy's highland and mountain bastions during winter 1965–1966. With the operational triad of firepower, mobility, and technology accomplishing major objectives, the military command in Saigon continuously expanded its operational role. ARVN was pushed aside, relegated to a security role at provincial capitals and its own camps. The American military relied on aircraft, equipment, and machinery that required a level of maintenance and training the Vietnamese did not have, which compelled the United States to fight the war its own way.[5]

Attitudes and preferences developed gradually in the newsmagazines. Judgments on military methods emerged in distinct patterns. *Newsweek* doubted the practicality and purpose of search-and-destroy/sweep operations in guerrilla warfare, and commented in spring 1966, "The U.S. has now given up any pretense of fighting a counterinsurgency war." A year later, *U.S. News & World Report* observed, "Despite the dozens of textbooks on guerrilla warfare prepared by Westerners, and despite training schools for U.S. troops, the U.S. Army still lacks the flexibility that is the main ingredient of counterguerrilla attacks." *Time* acknowledged the limits of modern weaponry during the first summer of war, saying, "[T]anks are all but useless in Mekong Delta swamps; jets lack the endurance for close-support actions; heavy artillery is rarely on hand when the V.C. strike." Soon, though, *Time* adopted the attitude it would hold for the next few years: "Day and night, screaming jets and prowling helicopters seek out the enemy from their swampy strongholds in southernmost Camau all the way north to the mountain gates of China."[6]

A debate resounded within the corridors of the Pentagon regarding application of firepower. Some military commanders opposed massive firepower because it needlessly inflicted casualties among farmers and villagers. Some also worried that kin and survivors of victims would be resentful and hostile toward American troops. According to a postwar survey of 111 commanders

5. Kinnard, *War Managers*, 42–44.
6. "Then and Now—The Difference," *Newsweek*, March 14, 1966, p. 42; "Bigger War Ahead in Vietnam?" *U.S. News & World Report*, March 27, 1967, p. 29; "Status & Strategy," *Time*, August 6, 1965, p. 28; "A New Kind of War," *Time*, October 22, 1965, pp. 28–29.

who had served in Vietnam, 71 believed the amount of aerial bombardment "about right" and 63 believed the same about artillery support; however, 31 and 33 commanders, respectively, thought the American military had used "too much" bombardment and artillery. The former Army general who conducted the survey expressed surprise that "a substantial minority of the generals themselves felt that there was too much firepower."[7] To reduce civilian casualties, military planners established numerous free-fire zones, a formal designation for areas considered Vietcong strongholds. To establish a free-fire zone required the forcible removal of farmers and villagers from areas equivalent to townships in the United States. Residents who refused to leave these zones were at considerable risk because the free-fire classification permitted warplanes, artillery, and infantrymen to fire upon any Vietnamese without warning. This policy, too, generated opposition among some officers who realized that many rural Vietnamese absolutely would not abandon the farms and villages where their families had lived for generations.[8]

Newsweek, beginning in summer 1965, intermittently informed readers about civilian casualties caused by American firepower, an issue *Time* considered a minor consequence of war and *U.S. News & World Report* deemed overblown. *Newsweek* and *Time* explored the effects of artillery, bombs, and chemicals on the ecology of Vietnam. *Time* told readers in early 1968 that defoliants had no lasting effects and caused no harm to animals and humans; *Newsweek* published its first lengthy article on the subject in early 1971, informing readers that long-term environmental damage had occurred.[9] *Time* believed the mobility provided by helicopters would win the war, and the magazine's articles from summer 1965 through autumn 1967 indulged in hyperbolic tribute to tactical operations by the First Air Cavalry Division. *Time* also presented firepower positively, informing readers that intensive artillery fire and aerial bombardment were necessary despite the risk to noncombatants. *U.S. News & World Report,* although similar to *Time* in its endorsement of firepower and other components of attritional warfare, questioned the deployment of American troops in remote areas where guerrillas had the advantage.

Newsweek, Time, and *U.S. News & World Report* reported the war in

---

7. Kinnard, *War Managers,* 47.
8. Kahin, *Intervention,* 407–8.
9. "Defoliating Vietnam," *Time,* February 23, 1968, p. 70; "The Blight that Failed," *Newsweek,* January 11, 1971, p. 79.

significantly different ways throughout American military intervention. *Newsweek* emphasized the evident contradiction between the American style of conventional warfare and the enemy's guerrilla warfare. Also, its dominant tone from summer 1965 onward expressed criticism of and skepticism about the effectiveness of military methods. Finally, it recognized that civilian casualties caused by American military action posed a serious moral and political issue. *Time*'s jingoistic rhetoric from spring 1965 through summer 1967 described American military methods as unquestionably superior. It offered readers repeated descriptions of special ordnance, technological devices, and weapons, suggesting that war technology would defeat the guerrillas. Finally, *Time* articles prior to summer 1967 rarely evaluated the overall conduct of the war, instead treating each search-and-destroy/sweep operation discretely. *U.S. News & World Report* insisted that unrestricted warfare was justified, without regard to civilians in the countryside, but it also blamed American commanders for not adapting to the situation in Vietnam. Whatever their differences, the newsmagazines had let readers know by autumn 1967 that American military methods had not defeated the Vietcong and People's Army. After withdrawal of American troops began in summer 1969, newsmagazine judgments on military methods concentrated on aerial bombardment of northern Vietnam and the performance of ARVN.

Operation Rolling Thunder

Newsmagazine readers understood from the tone of articles early in the war that the United States, an industrial giant and a technological leader, would prevail against communist guerrillas supported by northern Vietnam, an agrarian nation, and supplied long-distance by the Soviet Union and China. *Time* boasted: "[A]ll South Viet Nam thrums and bustles today with the American presence. It is not only the presence of 440,000 American fighting men but the astonishing buildup in a once-primitive land of all the means—and more—to fuel, feed and keep armed the fighting men. Dredging out ports and rivers, bulldozing roads and jet strips, the U.S. has created virtually from scratch a vast command, communications and supply network able to support and supply not only present U.S. needs but practically any that may arise in the future." *Newsweek* described this scene in Vietnam: "The whoosh of aircraft on the shiny new aluminum runways, the clatter of bulldozers and graders, the clouds of saffron dust rising over the new military roads, have become as much a part of the American buildup as the crack of rifles or the heavy whir of helicopters." *U.S. News & World Report* provided an example of the machinery of war: "Army engineers are taking jungles away from the Viet Cong with special plows. In the area around Saigon alone, these plows have cleared more than 80,000 acres of jungle that once gave the Viet Cong impregnable bases and headquarters."[10]

American ways of war inflicted death and injury on both combatants and civilians. More tons of bombs dropped on Vietnam than on Germany during World War II, and one scholar describes the aerial campaign as "the greatest flood of firepower against a nation known to history."[11] American warplanes, including B-52s and fighter-bombers, dropped millions of bombs, let loose countless canisters of napalm, and sprayed rockets on communities, farms, forests, and fortifications. Gunships and helicopters strafed real and suspected guerrillas. Artillery shells burst across the countryside. An estimated 80,000 to 140,000 civilians in southern Vietnam and another 55,000 to 180,000 civilians in northern Vietnam died from American firepower; tens of thousands more civilians died in Cambodia and Laos.[12] Anger and qualms about civilian casualties inflicted by American firepower contributed to antiwar attitudes in the United States.[13] The newsmagazines offered their readers contradictory interpretations on the role that firepower played. *Time* was transformed from an ardent advocate of firepower at the war's start to a caustic critic at war's end.

Newsweek, Time, and *U.S. News & World Report* all chronicled the use of firepower, particularly during 1965–1967 when military commanders and strategists placed so much faith in modern weaponry. Articles often referred to firepower's battlefield benefits, but only occasionally informed readers about consequent widespread devastation to nonmilitary targets and casualties among noncombatants. Typically, the newsmagazines did not mention

10. "Arrow of Thunder," *Time,* May 12, 1967, pp. 24–26; "The Military—'We Can Win It,'" *Newsweek,* April 18, 1966, pp. 28–31; "'The Coin Has Flipped Over to Our Side,'" *U.S. News & World Report,* November 27, 1967, p. 52.
11. Gabriel Kolko, *Anatomy of a War: Vietnam, the United States, and the Modern Historical Experience,* 200.
12. Spector, *After Tet,* 207; Maclear, *Ten Thousand Day War,* 241; James P. Harrison, "History's Heaviest Bombing"; Ben Kiernan, "The Impact on Cambodia of the U.S. Intervention in Vietnam," 225. According to Democratic Republic of Vietnam officials, no official statistics on casualties, either military or civilian, were recorded.
13. Kolko, *Anatomy of a War,* 174–75; Small, *Johnson, Nixon, and the Doves,* 25, 31–34.

civilian casualties in southern Vietnam in articles primarily devoted to descriptions of combat or special tactical operations. Seventeen newsmagazine articles, or 3 percent of the total on military operations, concerned civilian casualties caused by American firepower. *Newsweek* published ten such articles beginning in summer 1965, while *Time* published four articles and *U.S. News & World Report* three articles. Dozens of articles, however, reported the battlefield devastation wrought by bombs, shells, and rockets. Also, numerous articles pertained to Operation Rolling Thunder, the daily bombing of northern Vietnam. These articles clearly displayed editorial separation. Each newsmagazine delivered a different interpretation of the effectiveness and purpose of aerial bombardment that targeted sites in the Democratic Republic of Vietnam.

No aspect of the Vietnam War inspired more debate and dissension than Operation Rolling Thunder. Every day, weather permitting, dozens of American warplanes from Navy aircraft carriers and Air Force bases in Thailand and southern Vietnam attacked targets from the 17th parallel northward, including Laos, a neutral nation. That the world's most powerful nation was relentlessly pummeling a small, poor country aroused some Americans to protest the bombardment campaign and prompted some members of Congress to criticize the Johnson administration. Operation Rolling Thunder lasted from spring 1965 to autumn 1968. President Nixon resumed bombardment of the Democratic Republic of Vietnam in spring 1972, a decision that brought the resumption of congressional criticism.[14] *Newsweek* and *U.S. News & World Report* criticized Rolling Thunder for different reasons. *Newsweek* was skeptical that bombing could stop reinforcement and resupply of the guerrillas in southern Vietnam, and the magazine disliked the image of the United States attacking a weaker nation that had almost no industry or armament producers; *U.S. News & World Report* believed Rolling Thunder was ineffective because restrictions by the Johnson administration had given the northern government time to disperse its few factories and petroleum refineries. *Time* supported Rolling Thunder and told its readers the bombardment campaign had slowed reinforcement and resupply to the south. *Newsweek* and *Time* later criticized the Nixon administration for resuming the bombing of northern Vietnam.

14. Small, *Johnson, Nixon, and the Doves*, 31–34; Maclear, *Ten Thousand Day War*, 304–10; Herring, *America's Longest War*, 250–51.

Newsweek, which by 1966 skeptically viewed most methods applied by the American military in Vietnam, spoke with certainty regarding Rolling Thunder from summer 1965 onward. An article describing the increase in guerrillas in the south pointedly assigned blame. "For one thing, U.S. air strikes against North Vietnam have proved largely ineffective in stemming the infiltration of troops from the North; intelligence sources have recently concluded that there are now apparently no fewer than nine North Vietnamese battalions operating in South Vietnam," *Newsweek* reported. By summer 1966, *Newsweek* decided that Rolling Thunder had failed. "The Air War: Less Than A Success" declared a headline, and the accompanying article reviewed the objectives bombardment was supposed to have met. "Those purposes were to stem the rate of infiltration from the north and to convince Hanoi that it was in its own best interest to reach a negotiated settlement," the magazine noted. "Yet today, there are 50,000 more North Vietnamese troops in the south than there were six months ago, and Hanoi seems as far away from the peace table as ever." During a visit by Westmoreland to the United States in spring 1967, *Newsweek* chastised the general for his persistent advocacy of bombing the north. "The fact is that relatively few military targets remain untouched: some bridges and railroad yards inside Hanoi and Haiphong, the Haiphong docks, cement, plastics, lumber, fertilizer and other industrial plants with a limited contribution to the war effort," the magazine observed. A special summary on the war at the start of 1968 cited the bomb tonnage dropped on the northern nation and the destruction of bridges, roads, fishing boats, and trucks, but also noted the persistent stream of soldiers and supplies moving southward. "The material damage to North Vietnam . . . has been immense," *Newsweek* stated. "But what the bombing does not seem to have done is to weaken North Vietnam's over-all military position."[15]

U.S. News & World Report delivered a similar message about Rolling Thunder with a different rationale. "Thousands of tons of American bombs are dropping from the skies on Communist targets inside South Vietnam and north of the seventeenth parallel in Communist North Vietnam," the magazine wrote in 1966. "Those attacks are not widespread enough to be decisive.

---

15. *Newsweek:* "Vietnam: The New War," July 5, 1965, p. 31; "The Air War: Less Than a Success," August 29, 1966, pp. 21–22; "The Home Front," May 8, 1967, p. 35; "A Will of Steel?" January 1, 1968, pp. 25–26.

... Evidence is growing that the bombing thus far has not greatly hurt the North Vietnamese war effort." The magazine concluded in mid-1967, "Almost 2½ years of incessant—but strictly limited—air attacks over the North have had almost no noticeable effect on the war in the South."[16]

Time's readers received a much different picture of Rolling Thunder. "Streaking in like vengeful lightning bolts, the F-105 Thunderchiefs loosed their bombs, rockets and cannon fire on a North Viet Nam highway bridge, sent it crashing into a gorge," an article reported. "Speeding southeastward, they knocked out another bridge leading to Laos and long used by the Communists to send troops and supplies into South Viet Nam. With fuel and ordnance still to spare, the Thunderchiefs swung back north, destroyed a key railroad bridge in North Viet Nam." The prose indicated to readers that bombardment was both efficient and effective. Rolling Thunder made a real difference, according to *Time*: "Concentrating on lines of communication . . . , the U.S. raiders have increased their destruction of materiel headed south from an estimated 15% to 25%." *Time* made an inventory of destruction: 300 bridges destroyed; highways cut at 2,000 locations; railroad tracks blown up in 200 places. An attack on petroleum storage tanks near the northern port of Hanoi and on industrial sites near the capital of Hanoi warranted praise. "[The] American pilots who in one year have forged a brilliantly successful new tactical role for air power over Viet Nam, showed last week that the U.S. can indeed succeed," *Time* commented. "The operation was a triumph of tactical planning and destructive efficiency." More importantly to *Time*, Rolling Thunder had aided the war against the guerrillas. "Communist main force units, physically bruised, psychologically hurting and short of supplies because of the bombings, have avoided large-scale pitched battles for three months," *Time* stated in early 1967, months after *Newsweek* had concluded the opposite and months before *U.S. News & World Report* also judged Rolling Thunder a wasted effort.[17]

Disagreement among the newsmagazines over Rolling Thunder's effectiveness resembled the internal battle among policymakers, Defense Department planners, and CIA analysts that intensified during 1967. The effect of

---

16. "Ahead in Vietnam: A Bloody Stalemate?" *U.S. News & World Report,* April 11, 1966, pp. 36–37; "The Truth about War in Vietnam," *U.S. News & World Report,* July 31, 1967, pp. 40–43.

17. *Time:* "The Fighting American," April 23, 1965, pp. 22–25; "The Storm Breaks," April 15, 1966, p. 29; "The Red Napoleon," June 17, 1966, pp. 32–36; "Ripping the Sanctuary," July 8, 1966, pp. 11–16; "Wishing, Still Nothing," February 17, 1967, pp. 17–18.

the bombs falling in northern Vietnam and along the supply routes in Laos was difficult to determine because terrain, thick tree cover, and jungle foliage often obscured the details essential to damage assessments. The uncertainty about specific effects resulted in much speculation. The CIA, an autonomous entity, submitted a series of inconclusive judgments on the impact of Rolling Thunder on impeding the flow of reinforcements and supplies from the north, while the Defense Intelligence Agency, a military entity, submitted a series of definite judgments that the bombing had hindered the communists by destroying supplies and creating a logistical backup in the north.

An example of this interagency feud was a CIA report on aerial bombardment of "lines-of-communication" (LOCs) from northern Vietnam to the south. (Numerous reports written by the CIA, Defense Intelligence Agency, and policymakers referred to the network of highways, railroads, and trails as lines-of-communication, which became the focus of bombing attacks when infiltration by People's Army regiments increased from early 1966 onward.) The report was the first major statement by the CIA that Rolling Thunder was of doubtful value. However, a four-page summary submitted by an aide to national security advisor Walt W. Rostow listed almost two dozen items identified as inconsistencies in the CIA analysis. These inconsistencies, according to the aide, resulted from the CIA ignoring specific examples of success—such as the destruction of a "modern cement plant" and data showing that the "fertilizer and chemical industry ha[d] been curtailed"—and relying on a "selective use of evidence" to conclude that Rolling Thunder had not harmed the communists' war effort. To buttress the criticism of the CIA report, the aide cited Defense Intelligence Agency statements and supplemental charts that indicated severe damage to bridges, docks, and railroad tracks. The aide informed Rostow that the CIA's "presentation of the analysis may be deficient." Rostow reviewed the summary and wrote a memo to the president conceding that the effectiveness of Rolling Thunder "is a matter on which our judgments can honestly differ." The memo asserted that "the bombing of North Viet Nam has imposed these costs on North Viet Nam for its aggression," listed economic aid furnished by the Soviet Union to replace products destroyed by Rolling Thunder, and estimated the number of northern residents—600,000—required to repair the damage and rebuild the transportation system.[18]

18. "Some Comments on Rolling Thunder: The 1967 Campaign against LOCs," undated, and Rostow to President Johnson, memorandum, October 18, 1967, national security files, Rostow, box 6, LBJ Library.

Newsmagazine correspondents assigned to the Pentagon and White House knew about this internal battle among policymakers, military planners, and intelligence analysts. Their sources damned or praised the speculative conclusions being issued by the various agencies. Correspondents sent information to their respective newsrooms where editors decided what to leave out or downplay and what to publish. The historical record has determined that the sources favored by *Newsweek* and *U.S. News & World Report* judged Rolling Thunder correctly and *Time*'s sources did not. Defense Department strategists and CIA analysts had concluded by summer 1967 that aerial bombardment of northern Vietnam impeded but did not reduce reinforcement and resupply of the Vietcong and People's Army in the south. Secretary of Defense McNamara returned in July 1967 from his ninth trip to Vietnam to tell the president and a select group of senior advisors that Rolling Thunder had made no difference. "We have destroyed more, but what we destroyed has less effect on the war in the South," McNamara said. The secretary delivered the same message a month later to a Senate committee, and he recommended to President Johnson the curtailment of Rolling Thunder. Tet 1968 finally convinced nearly everyone in the Johnson administration and strategists in the Defense Department that three years of nearly continuous bombardment had failed. "It was now clear that bombing alone could not prevent the communists from amassing the materiel, and infiltrating the manpower necessary to conduct massive operations if they chose," stated a special Defense Department report popularly known as the Pentagon Papers.[19]

None of the newsmagazines or network news programs paid attention to the issue of civilian casualties in the Democratic Republic of Vietnam until *New York Times* reporter Harrison Salisbury visited the north in December 1966 and disclosed widespread destruction to neighborhoods near Hanoi. Newspapers in Britain and Europe had reported the occurrence of civilian casualties from aerial bombardment during summer and autumn 1966, but the major American news organizations had carried only brief references to the subject and had dismissed the foreign articles as propaganda or exaggerations. Salisbury was the first American journalist from a mainstream newspaper to visit northern Vietnam, and his articles created a furor because the

---

19. McManus and Magnuson interviews; McNamara to President Johnson, memorandum, and Tom Johnson's notes of meetings, July 12, 1967, box 1, LBJ Library; *Pentagon Papers*, 4:20–71, 235. See also Herring, *America's Longest War*, 175–79.

Johnson administration had assured journalists that almost no civilian casualties resulted from Rolling Thunder.[20] Nearly six months before the *New York Times* articles, *Time* had informed readers that Air Force and Navy bombardment had spared neighborhoods located within military targets, creating "islands surrounded by a sea of discriminate destruction."[21] *Newsweek*, *Time*, and *U.S. News & World Report* repeated what the *New York Times* reported, but each magazine emphasized that attacks on Hanoi and Haiphong had produced only a small number of casualties.[22] *Time* reminded its readers, "During the past year alone, Viet Cong terrorists have methodically murdered more than 3,000 civilians in the South." A photograph accompanying the article showed dead and injured victims of a terrorist bomb in Saigon, but the caption did not say whether it was a recent incident or a file photo.[23]

For the remainder of the Rolling Thunder campaign, all three newsmagazines insisted that casualties were minor in terms of the intensity of the bombing. "By all accounts, civilian casualties have been small considering the scope of the raids; this appears to be partly because of the effective protective measures taken by the North Vietnamese and partly because the U.S. bombing attacks are not indiscriminate terror raids of the World War II type," *Newsweek* stated. *Time* referred sarcastically to concerns for heavy casualties: "The increased pounding of the North evoked a flurry of stories that civilians had been wantonly killed and homes destroyed in Hanoi. There was talk that the raids signaled a new and sinister phase of escalation."[24]

Resumption of full-scale aerial bombardment of northern Vietnam in 1972 brought a dramatically different response from *Newsweek* and *Time* (but not *U.S. News & World Report*). *Time*, previously an ardent supporter of Rolling Thunder, now caustically criticized the decision to resume bombing. *Time* articles during the final year of the war contained commentary completely uncharacteristic of its articles from a few years earlier. The magazine

20. Wyatt, *Paper Soldiers*, 152–56.
21. "The Red Napoleon," *Time*, June 17, 1966, p. 36.
22. "Civilians Weren't the Target, but . . . ," *Newsweek*, January 9, 1967, p. 17; "Flak from Hanoi," *Time*, January 6, 1967, pp. 13–15; "Bigger War in the New Year—And No End in Sight," *U.S. News & World Report*, January 9, 1967, p. 13.
23. "Flak from Hanoi," *Time*, January 6, 1967, pp. 13–15.
24. "A Will of Steel?" *Newsweek*, January 1, 1968, pp. 25–26; "Racing the Monsoon," *Time*, September 1, 1967, pp. 18–19.

adopted a tone of disbelief regarding the Nixon administration's justification for the attacks: "In fact, there is no conclusive evidence that the 158,000 GIs still in Viet Nam are in any immediate peril." *Time,* which had previously dismissed international criticism of Rolling Thunder, now expressed awareness of the problem. "The step-up in the air war would inevitably renew the ugly worldwide image of the U.S. once again clobbering the North from the skies," an article warned. The magazine no longer maintained that warplanes bombed with pinpoint accuracy. "Since April 6, when Nixon officially reinstated mass bombing of the North, aerial attacks on civilian targets have become all too common," *Time* noted. "American jets in search of visible targets have destroyed countless hospitals, churches and even cathedrals, as well as residential suburbs." The Nixon administration, disturbed by the critical attitude of a formerly reliable Republican ally, assigned senior advisors—including Henry Kissinger, the national security advisor—to speak with *Time* correspondents. H. R. Haldeman, a senior presidential aide, wrote that the articles "are trying to create the impression . . . that the President did this in a moment of anger."[25]

The transformation of *Time* from a supporter of Operation Rolling Thunder to a critic of bombardment in the north happened for the same competitive reasons that caused the newsmagazines to create separate editorial attitudes early in the war, only the rationale had reversed. By the late 1960s, *Time* perceived *Newsweek* as a real competitor rather than a distant also-ran. *Time*'s doctrinaire anticommunism and its enthusiasm for the Vietnam War had possibly cost it readers among politically moderate Americans and younger adults. Beginning in 1967, *Time* purposely lessened its ideological tone. Top executives believed that blatant ideology was bad for business. Another factor affecting *Time*'s transformation was the realization that aerial bombardment of northern Vietnam sullied the image of the United States. Also, public opinion, which had increasingly turned against the bombing, mattered to the magazine. "A lot of people, particularly in Western Europe, who are not totally unsympathetic to some American effort and presence in Viet Nam, . . . are very much against the bombing," Hedley Donovan,

---

25. "Striking with a 'Dynamic Defense,' " *Time,* January 10, 1972, p. 27; "Vietnamization: A Policy Under the Gun," *Time,* April 17, 1972, pp. 34–39; "Living Inside a Bull's Eye," *Time,* October 23, 1972, p. 42; H. R. Haldeman to Herb Klein, Ron Ziegler, and Chuck Colson, memorandum, May 15, 1972, White House special files, Haldeman name file, box 2, Nixon Project.

Time-Life editor, said. "And I think this is increasingly true of an important layer of the opposition in this country."[26]

Newsweek, which had doubted the effectiveness of Operation Rolling Thunder but had not considered the issue of civilian casualties serious, berated the Nixon administration for renewing the bombing, mining the harbors of northern ports, and bringing B-52 bombers into the raids on cities. *Newsweek* faulted the rationale: "With the risk of civilian casualties so high, why then did the U.S. launch its close-in saturation raids?" Lengthy descriptions of damaged neighborhoods filled articles, which mentioned schools, hospitals, and churches in ruins. "It was the heaviest bombing campaign in the history of warfare, and the relentless American air attacks on North Vietnam took a toll beyond the massive human and material wreckage in Hanoi and Haiphong alone," *Newsweek* wrote.[27] The magazine's adversarial stance in 1972 arose from its previous pattern of skeptical commentary concerning Rolling Thunder. While *Newsweek* had accepted the military's word during the 1965–1968 bombardment campaign that every effort was made to keep civilian casualties to a minimum, the magazine evidently had no tolerance for the renewal of a strategy that had so obviously failed before.

One critic has accused *Newsweek* and *Time* of inaccurate coverage of the so-called Christmas bombing attacks on Hanoi and Haiphong in 1972. Martin F. Herz, a former State Department official, reviewed *Newsweek* and *Time* articles from the two-week period of the bombardment and determined that both newsmagazines distorted the extent of damage to nonmilitary areas and casualties to civilians caused by bombs from high-flying B-52s. Herz concluded that both newsmagazines let their political viewpoints skew their coverage.[28] *Newsweek* and *Time* did emphasize destruction to nonmilitary areas in Hanoi and Haiphong, and they accepted casualty figures issued by the government of northern Vietnam. Both magazines suggested that B-52s could not bomb precisely from their altitude of thirty thousand feet. The historical record confirms that approximately 1,600 civilians died in Hanoi from the bombing because military targets were encircled by residential

---

26. Baughman, *Henry R. Luce,* 193–94; Gans, *Deciding What's News,* 190–93; Donovan oral history, 99.

27. "Diplomacy by Terror," *Newsweek,* January 8, 1973, pp. 10–12; "What Went Wrong?" *Newsweek,* January 1, 1973, pp. 8–12.

28. Martin F. Herz, *The Prestige Press and the Christmas Bombing, 1972: Images and Reality in Vietnam,* 54, 64–65.

neighborhoods; in Haiphong the targets were set apart. Some scholars, including Herz, agree with the Nixon administration argument that these casualties were moderate considering the scope of the bombardment.

At the time, *Newsweek* and *Time* presented the Christmas bombing attacks as inexcusable. The editorial viewpoints of *Newsweek* and *Time* regarding the bombing of northern Vietnam had developed since spring 1972, so this stance during the final weeks of the war seemed logical. Editors and correspondents at each magazine had decided that past statements by American military commanders and government officials concerning precision bombing were misleading, if not outright deceptive. Also, having learned a lesson from the December 1966 articles in the *New York Times* on evidence of severe damage to nonmilitary areas, neither *Newsweek* nor *Time* could ignore statements from northern Vietnam on civilian deaths.

"Moral Problems"

American firepower in southern Vietnam received much attention from the newsmagazines, too. Firepower against the enemy on the battlefield received criticism only when its effectiveness was doubted, but firepower against enemy positions—real or suspected—received divided treatment. *Newsweek, Time,* and *U.S. News & World Report* articles routinely mentioned the incredible amount of artillery shells fired at the enemy when guerrillas attacked or when American troops assaulted fortified positions. "The gunners opened the breeches and took aim through the open barrels straight into the faces of the steadily advancing Viet Cong," *Time* reported, referring to the point-blank use of artillery. "The three batteries fired more than 2,200 shells." A major operation in the mountainous provinces near the Laotian border typically relied on firepower to assist infantry. "The Marines withdrew and let the air and artillery knock off the top of the hill, blasting away foliage and great chunks of earth and rock," *Time* wrote, citing the successful conquest of a hilltop bunker complex. "Both hills had been mercilessly shelled, bombed and burned off." *Time* intermittently advised readers that aerial bombardment was crucial. "Never before has tactical air power been used so intensively to help fight a ground war," an article stated. *Newsweek* also portrayed aerial bombardment on the battlefield positively. "The great majority of military experts agree that the use of air strikes in direct support of allied soldiers in South Vietnam deserves chief credit for making the war militarily unlosable," an article stated. "And it seems equally clear that close air support has played an important role in boosting the fighting spirit of American ground troops." *Newsweek* reported the absolute necessity for firepower under certain circumstances. "Hemmed into a circular wooded area, the battalion called for air support as it beat off wave after wave of suicidal attacks by the North Vietnamese," an article related. *U.S. News & World Report* emphasized the continued importance of artillery and aerial bombardment after troop withdrawals began and infantry operations were reduced. "Instead, the massive firepower of the U.S. military machine is being brought into play," the magazine observed, mentioning the substitution of bombs and shells for infantrymen.[29]

B-52 bomber missions in southern Vietnam generated disagreement within the military concerning their effectiveness. "Even the deepest tunnels are not safe from the 1,000-lb. bombs of the Guam-based B-52s, falling in sticks neatly bracketed to decapitate a small mountain," *Time* wrote in autumn 1965. "Critics snorted that it was overkill run riot, using elephants to swat mosquitoes. But the point was to hit the V.C. without warning (the B-52s fly so high that they are seldom seen or heard by their targets) in the heart of their eleven major strongholds, keep them edgy and off balance." On another occasion, *Time* reported, the B-52s "jackhammered a Viet Cong radio and communications center." *Newsweek* questioned whether the B-52s were a showpiece weapon or a valuable instrument of war in Vietnam. "The raid on the Iron Triangle and its aftermath made plain just how difficult it is to measure the immediate results of the B-52 attacks," *Newsweek* wrote. "No one knows for certain, but most U.S. military men are convinced that the mammoth bombers kill very few Viet Cong." Late in the war, *Time,* after its attitude adjustment, regarded the B-52s as a menace. "The U.S. has apparently decided on a policy of massive and calculatedly destructive airpower as a substitute for manpower," *Time* observed, describing a B-52 attack in the Mekong Delta on a suspected Vietcong camp that instead killed and injured dozens of farmers. "In the American effort to eliminate this elusive, wandering enemy—numbering

29. "Gathering Intensity," *Time,* March 31, 1967, p. 36; "Efficient Thunder," *Time,* May 12, 1967, pp. 24–26; "Quiet No More," *Time,* August 12, 1966, p. 20; "The B-52s," *Newsweek,* October 25, 1965, p. 41; "Fury at Ia Drang: Now the Regulars," *Newsweek,* November 29, 1965, p. 22; "Vietnam: As Shooting Dies Down," *U.S. News & World Report,* October 27, 1969, p. 35.

5,000 by the officer's estimate—the bombs are dropping night and day on the friendly Vietnamese of Dinh Tuong."[30]

Shells from howitzers and bombs from aircraft exploded on farmhouses, fields, hamlets, and trails. Most often, firepower destroyed fortified bunkers and positions from which guerrillas fought American infantrymen. Sometimes, it missed the intended targets, killing or injuring children, men, and women. Sometimes, firepower blasted rural homesteads simply because American troops suspected the structures sheltered guerrillas or because they did not want to take any chances. And, on occasion, firepower was an instrument of terror employed in areas where guerrillas operated; this harassment-and-interdiction tactic, called H&I by the troops, called for the firing of artillery shells randomly during the night.[31] The creation of free-fire zones supposedly had removed all residents friendly to the southern government, or at least not actively supporting the Vietcong. The newsmagazines reported the wholesale relocation of sizable sectors of the population in the provinces without delving into the social effects of American policy. "Part of [Operation] Hickory's mission is to remove the estimated 11,000 villagers living in the DMZ and resettle them farther south, thus creating a free bombing zone in the buffer strip," *Time* succinctly reported. *U.S. News & World Report* more cavalierly described a resettlement operation:

> The aim of Operation Cedar Falls is to remove more than 8,000 peasants from the area and resettle them in government-supervised refugee camps. And while the experience was an unpleasant one for some of the GI's, they did their best to make it as painless as possible for the uprooted.
> Even as the last of the evicted still poked around their wood and thatch huts assembling their belongings, U.S. troops began to burn and bulldoze their villages to the ground. And when all the peasants and their huts are gone, the Iron Triangle—once a sanctuary where the Viet Cong swam freely as fish in a sea—will be declared a 'free-fire zone.' Then, the whole area will be watched constantly by spotter planes and helicopters, and anyone caught in the triangle will be fair game.[32]

---

30. "A New Kind of War," *Time,* October 22, 1965, p. 39; "The Storm Breaks," *Time,* April 15, 1966, p. 28; "The Military—'We Can Win It,'" *Newsweek,* April 18, 1966, pp. 28–31; "Rolling Backward Again," *Time,* September 11, 1972, p. 24.

31. Spector, *After Tet,* 198–202; Stanton, *American Army,* 85–86.

32. "Demilitarizing the Zone," *Time,* May 26, 1967, pp. 24–25; "Assault on the Iron Triangle," *U.S. News & World Report,* January 23, 1967, p. 39.

The reference to an "unpleasant" experience for the soldiers contrasted dramatically with the narrative on Operation Cedar Falls written by Jonathan Schell for the *New Yorker* in July 1967. In "The Village of Ben Suc," Schell described the casual brutality of American soldiers as they attacked and occupied a community thirty miles northwest of Saigon. *New Yorker* readers learned that thousands of villagers, all designated "hostile" because the Vietcong had controlled Ben Suc for years, were taken by trucks to a relocation center where no shelters existed and little water was available.[33] Schell's version of events hardly seemed like the "painless as possible" operation described in *U.S. News & World Report*.

Newsweek exhibited the most interest in civilian casualties caused by American firepower. Beginning in summer 1965, months before the other newsmagazines alerted readers to the hazards posed to ordinary Vietnamese, and extending to winter 1967–1968, *Newsweek* published eight articles concerning the issue compared to three articles in *Time* and two in *U.S. News & World Report*. "In dozens of southern villages, bewildered peasants found themselves forced to cower in their improvised bomb shelters or risk being caught in a rain of death," *Newsweek* wrote. "And all too often, the men in the planes overhead had no way of knowing whether their bombs were hitting Viet Cong, noncombatants—or nobody at all." *Newsweek* cited a CBS report on Marines who set fire to thatched huts in a village because nearby snipers had shot at them, and the magazine compared that incident with destruction from bombs and shells. The article mentioned that such events rarely occurred, then commented, "Yet for the U.S. to allow such incidents to multiply would pose serious practical as well as moral problems." Another article featured an interview with Edward G. Lansdale, a noted counterinsurgency expert who had directed a program in the Philippines that suppressed an agrarian rebellion during the 1950s. Lansdale spent several weeks in Vietnam to evaluate American policy, and criticized the use of conventional warfare methods. *Newsweek* emphasized his opinion that "the recent trend toward hit-or-miss bombing and the burning of villages" would alienate the Vietnamese. The other newsmagazines had a different perspective on alienation. "Planes are known to attack only when guerrillas fire at them," *U.S. News & World Report* commented. "So peasants blame the air attacks on the Viet Cong." *Time* advised its readers, "The Reds are less and less welcome

33. Jonathan Schell, "The Village of Ben Suc," *New Yorker*, July 15, 1967.

in villages, since the villagers are learning that their presence may well bring the planes."[34]

Policymakers in Washington reacted swiftly to news coverage about civilian casualties. A special meeting of representatives from the presidential press office, Defense Department, United States Information Agency, and State Department convened in summer 1965 to discuss an official response and to coordinate future government statements. "Alleged maltreatment of Vietnamese civilians and civilian facilities is a moral and humanitarian concern for many Americans," a memo noted. "We must recognize this as a serious, long-run problem." A participant from the Defense Department recommended that government officials should remind journalists that American firepower killed civilians in Vietnam accidentally while the Vietcong deliberately assassinated and terrorized residents. This comparative theme subsequently appeared in *Time* and *U.S. News & World Report*. "[E]very use of napalm against armed enemy troops, far less a brutal act than Viet Cong beheading of helpless women, triggers criticism and protest around the world," *U.S. News & World Report* wrote. *Time* told readers, "Last year alone, some 11,000 innocent civilians were killed or kidnaped by the Viet Cong in their calculated campaign of terrorism."[35] *Time* repeatedly relied on this comparison when reporting civilian casualties from American military action.

By the final year of the war, the complete transformation of *Time* could be seen in an article on civilian casualties resulting from an increase in Air Force and Navy missions. The magazine, which had previously taken a hint from the Defense Department to refer to Vietcong terrorism whenever possible, now alerted readers to regard government statements warily. "To counter possible reaction at home and abroad, the White House ordered up a kind of pre-emptive public relations strike that emphasized Communist villainy," *Time* commented. Much earlier, *U.S. News & World Report* had also acknowledged the consequences of unrestrained application of firepower. In the wake of Tet 1968, the magazine noted that tactics should be reevaluated. "The U.S. may have to reduce reliance on one of its greatest assets, artillery and

---

34. "Strictly Military," *Newsweek*, August 16, 1965, pp. 30–32; "Old Lover," *Newsweek*, August 30, 1965, p. 29; "What It Would Take to Turn the Tide in Vietnam," *U.S. News & World Report*, July 12, 1965, pp. 46–48; "A New Kind of War," *Time*, October 22, 1965, p. 39.

35. Memorandum of discussion, August 10, 1965, national security files, Vietnam country file, box 197, LBJ Library; "Why U.S. Isn't Winning a War," *U.S. News & World Report*, April 1, 1968, pp. 44–48; "A Limit on War," *Time*, October 1, 1965, pp. 38–39.

bombing firepower," *U.S. News & World Report* wrote. "Much Vietnam fighting is done in and around populated areas. Indiscriminate bombing or shelling can create as many Viet Cong as it kills."[36]

With thousands of civilian victims every month, the paucity of articles in the newsmagazines regarding death and destruction in the countryside might seem hard to explain. Evidently, it was a matter of access and proximity. Correspondents were unaware of the extent of the casualties because the areas most affected were in enemy strongholds inaccessible to journalists. "The result was we couldn't go where the artillery was laying down fire," says Nicholas Horrock, who reported for *Newsweek*. "I don't think the American people understood what we were doing. The soldiers did." Several correspondents say their exposure to rural Vietnam was restricted because, by necessity, they accompanied American troops on patrols and tactical operations. Correspondents did not witness death and destruction in rural villages beyond the battlefield. They did see firepower targeted at known enemy locations. "I went where the action was, and the action was in the boonies [remote rural areas], looking for Charlie," says James Wallace, of *U.S. News & World Report*. "Most of the time they [American soldiers] called in air support and artillery to take out machine guns and mortars that were hammering them." In addition, correspondents assumed that the Vietnamese who stayed in free-fire zones had done so for a reason. "On the one hand, you knew that the people still in the villages basically were hostile," says Burton Pines of *Time*, explaining the assumptions that guided military operations in free-fire zones. "On the other, you also knew that in a war, any war, civilians get hurt. My experience was, the men in the field did their damnedest to not recklessly blast the hell out of a place." Horrock believes that correspondents focused too much on combat coverage. "We really could have done the civilian side better, much better," he says. "The destruction, the tragic effect on the people. The method we used to fight the war was devastating, so devastating to the country."[37]

Not until November 1971 did a newsmagazine correspondent investigate the discrepancy between the number of enemy dead claimed and the number of enemy weapons seized, a sure indicator of civilian deaths. A *Newsweek*

---

36. "Vietnamization: A Policy Under the Gun," *Time*, April 17, 1972, pp. 34–39; "Why U.S. Isn't Winning a War," *U.S. News & World Report*, April 1, 1968, pp. 44–48.

37. Horrock, Wallace, and Pines interviews.

correspondent checked statistics for Operation Speedy Express, a months-long mission in the Mekong Delta some three years earlier. The Army claimed the Ninth Infantry Division had killed 11,000 guerrillas and captured 700 weapons, an incredible gap. No journalists sought an explanation at the time. The *Newsweek* correspondent spent two months gathering information, then suffered through five months of delay by editors who doubted the news value of an old event. The article, "Pacification's Deadly Price," finally ran in summer 1972 and stated that "a staggering number of noncombatant civilians" had died, perhaps 5,000 Vietnamese.[38]

The belated realization by the newsmagazines that heavy casualties had occurred among Vietnamese in the countryside probably can be attributed to the gradual reduction in American involvement. With so few American casualties from 1971 onward, correspondents paid more attention to the suffering of Vietnam's residents.

"Elephants Chasing Rabbits"

During the first two years of formal military intervention in Vietnam, the Army and Marine Corps sent into the countryside modern infantry units with highly trained personnel using an abundance of equipment that provided firepower and mobility. American commanders and government policymakers fully recognized the unusual conditions in Vietnam, but they exuded confidence regarding the ability of the world's most modern military to defeat guerrillas. The newsmagazines conveyed this confidence, although each candidly alerted readers to potential flaws in the American approach to war in Vietnam. *Newsweek* wondered in midsummer 1965 whether conventional infantry units should venture beyond the secure coastal enclaves established at Da Nang, Qui Nhon, and Nha Trang. "On the face of it, this strategy [enclave security] seems unexceptionable," the magazine wrote. "Nevertheless, it does raise one vital problem that has never been adequately discussed by U.S. officials. This is the wisdom of shifting the emphasis that was placed, under the Kennedy Administration, on specially trained, elite anti-guerrilla fighters to the current reliance on regular U.S. troops."[39]

Each newsmagazine viewed the American approach to war differently.

---

38. Knightley, *First Casualty*, 399–400; "Pacification's Deadly Price," *Newsweek*, June 19, 1972, pp. 42–43.
39. "Vietnam: The New War," *Newsweek*, July 5, 1965, p. 32.

Infantry operations, particularly search-and-destroy/sweep missions, were portrayed as successful most often in *Time* and less often in *U.S. News & World Report*, while *Newsweek* found success ephemeral. *Time* offered colorful visions of coordinated operations in which American troops dominated the battlefield. *U.S. News & World Report* offered assurances that each major mission disrupted the guerrillas, cost them quantities of supplies, and caused enemy casualties. *Newsweek* offered examples of ineffectual attempts to fight an unconventional war by conventional methods. To *Time*, Americans were the hunters and guerrillas the prey: "In the foothills of the Chu Pong massif, practically in Cambodia's backyard, the brigade found its quarry." To *Newsweek*, Americans were fighting the wrong war: "U.S. commanders found that many of the tactical concepts religiously taught in America's top military schools simply did not work in the rugged jungles and mountains of Vietnam." To *U.S. News & World Report*, Americans were well-equipped but ill-prepared: "It is partly the way Americans go to war that restricts U.S. response to revolutionary struggles."[40] By providing consistent commentary on military operations in southern Vietnam, the newsmagazines affected their readers' perceptions of the chances for success.

Time focused on the impressive might of the American military. "The view at night was spectacular," an article reported. "From offshore, the 8-in. guns of the cruiser *St. Paul* flashed out barrages of shells up and down the enemy lines. U.S. warplanes, dropping parachute flares that hung in the sky like chandeliers, swooped in on their targets with bombs and bright orange seas of napalm." *Time* declared Operation Attleboro a success in autumn 1966, reporting nine hundred Vietcong killed in combat. "Some 16,000 U.S. troops traded blows with an elusive communist enemy that remained mostly hidden in this forest vastness, emerging occasionally to do vicious, bloody battle," an article stated. "So far, most of the blood was Red." *Newsweek*, however, found these large-unit tactics problematic. "[W]hen the Americans and their Vietnamese allies tried to spring the trap, it was the same old story: the Viet Cong main force was no longer there," the magazine wrote. "'These things take too long to crank up,' grumbled one senior U.S. soldier about the massive operation." Unlike *Time*, *Newsweek* indicated its suspicion

---

40. "The Guardians at the Gate," *Time*, January 7, 1966, pp. 13–21; "The Military: A Revolution in Thinking, Tactics, and Character," *Newsweek*, July 10, 1967, pp. 45–46; "Why U.S. Isn't Winning a War," *U.S. News & World Report*, April 1, 1968, p. 44.

about American claims of enemy casualties. "At the end of the week, with the operation still in progress, the Marines were claiming hundreds of enemy dead. But once again, the main body of Viet Cong appeared to have evaded the trap and to have sifted away into the neighboring hills," *Newsweek* wrote about Operation Harvest Moon in December 1965. The magazine reminded readers in early 1966 that too many tactical operations accomplished little: "[B]ig conventional sweeps are described even by those who command them as a game of elephants chasing rabbits. What our elephants succeed in doing is flushing the rabbits out of their holes and tunnels where they can be shelled and bombed. But the 'traps' sprung on the North Vietnamese regiments and VC battalions seldom trap anything much."[41]

Each newsmagazine covered Operation White Wing, a major tactical operation, in February 1966. The operation sent 12,000 troops into the forests of the coastal plain in I Corps, the military region adjacent to the demilitarized zone separating northern and southern Vietnam. "As White Wing rolled on," *Time* reported, "[the commander] from time to time fluttered up in his chopper for a bird's-eye view of the battle. It was quite a scene. Over the coastal checkerboard of the 5,000 advancing U.S. troops, silver spotter planes drifted, directing the fire of artillery batteries, whose guns wafted silver-blue smoke into the air." *U.S. News & World Report* stated, "Almost every day American troops discover huge stocks of rice, weapons, medicines and other material cached in jungle hideouts." *Newsweek* perceived Operation White Wing much differently: "Somewhat disheartened by the performance of his unit, one First Cav colonel conceded: 'We're like elephants chasing rabbits.' What he didn't say, however, was that the U.S.'s rabbits—the Special Forces teams—found the enemy rabbits, but that the elephants were unable to follow through."[42]

Newsmagazine articles described the futility and frustration associated with major tactical operations. "Weeks sometimes go by when as many as 16 major U.S. operations are under way—and no major contact is made any-

41. "Waiting for the Bugles," *Time* October 21, 1966, p. 46; "The Giant Spoiler," *Time*, November 18, 1966, pp. 34–39; "No Victory, No Defeat," *Newsweek*, October 25, 1965, p. 36; "One Kind of Routine," *Newsweek*, December 20, 1965, p. 34; "Then and Now—The Difference," *Newsweek*, March 14, 1966, p. 42.

42. "The Biggest Week," *Time*, February 11, 1966, pp. 28–29; "Ahead in Vietnam: A Bloody Stalemate?" *U.S. News & World Report*, April 11, 1966, p. 37; "Rabbits and Elephants," *Newsweek*, February 21, 1966, p. 36.

where because the enemy is ducking battle," *Time* noted. "The Reds, as usual, had faded into the bush," another article stated. *Newsweek* described an expedition into the countryside near Saigon in August 1965 by thousands of paratroopers with the 173rd Airborne Brigade. "When the operation ended four days later, the 173rd had killed one guerrilla and captured two," the magazine reported. "As for the main body of the Viet Cong, they had undoubtedly heard about the operation long in advance and chosen not to fight. That they do only on their own terms." *Newsweek* focused on the issue much more than the other newsmagazines, usually citing a lack of contact with guerrillas to affirm its viewpoint on the ineffectiveness of conventional warfare methods. "The more than 25,000 troops involved in Operation Junction City continued for the second week to search in vain for an estimated 10,000 North Vietnamese regulars thought to be in the area," the magazine wrote in March 1967. *U.S. News & World Report* intermittently observed that the countryside remained contested territory, a region where the Vietcong and People's Army waited for opportunities to attack. The magazine described a fierce battle for two hills near Khe Sanh, a mountain village, in May 1967. American troops took the hills, but a People's Army regiment retained control of adjacent ridges. "[N]ow that the battle has been won at high cost, the Marines still don't have enough men to occupy the hills permanently," the magazine commented, indicating that another battle would result—which it did eight months later when the communists laid siege to Khe Sanh.[43]

The newsmagazines also provided straightforward coverage of major tactical operations. These articles reported information provided by military sources, without alternative judgments. *Newsweek* reviewed a year's worth of major tactical operations in late 1966, reciting statistics and summaries provided by the military: Operation Masher/White Wing "smashed the Viet Cong's crack Yellow Star Division"; Operation Hawthorne "spoiled the plan of an enemy regiment to launch an offensive"; Operation Hastings/Prairie killed 800 guerrillas and captured 254 "modern Russian weapons"; Operation Attleboro killed 1,000 guerrillas. *Time* also published statistical evidence of success, citing captured material: "250 tons of enemy rice, medical

43. "Taking Stock," *Time*, July 14, 1967, pp. 20–21; "There Is No One Else," *Time*, August 6, 1965, pp. 17–19; "A Long, Hot Walk," *Newsweek*, August 16, 1965, p. 33; "Sweep and Countersweep," *Newsweek*, March 13, 1967, p. 50; "A Key Victory for Marines—But Was the Battle Necessary?" *U.S. News & World Report*, May 15, 1967, pp. 8–10.

supplies, and cigarettes"; "2,000,000 lbs. of rice, 80 rocket launchers, 25 machine guns, 481 Claymore-type mines, large quantities of rifles, pistols, oil, clothing, even 116 bicycles."[44]

Commentary on attritional warfare appeared more frequently by summer 1966. *Newsweek* reflected the concerns of some battalion and brigade commanders whose frustration with search-and-destroy/sweep operations cast doubt on a key element of American strategy, while *Time* and *U.S. News & World Report* reflected the viewpoints of senior officers at command headquarters in Saigon whose confidence in the concept of conventional warfare held firm. Although the newsmagazines offered somewhat different interpretations regarding the effectiveness of military strategy and tactics, each provided an accurate representation of American conduct of the war. Throughout the first three years of formal military intervention, search-and-destroy/sweep operations dominated operational action, although most American casualties resulted from ambushes and firefights involving small units, such as platoons and companies.[45] This reliance on conventional warfare had some benefit. The Vietcong main-force units that steadily attacked cities and ARVN camps from summer 1965 through spring 1966 withdrew into the forests and mountains, from which smaller groups launched harassment raids against American sites. The number of small-scale combat incidents more than doubled from winter 1965–1966 to winter 1966–1967, an indication that Vietcong main-force units preferred not to challenge American troops except under extremely favorable or emergency conditions. Also, the search-and-destroy/sweep operations created a high degree of security in territory immediately around cities and important military sites.[46]

But conventional warfare failed to extend security into the countryside. The dominance of search-and-destroy/sweep operations placed thousands of troops in the countryside temporarily, but only the positioning of these troops permanently in small units near villages would have offered security to the southern government's pacification teams. One military historian has concluded that the commitment of large numbers of troops to lengthy operations in remote areas actually permitted the Vietcong to move more freely

---

44. "The American Way of War," *Newsweek,* December 5, 1966, pp. 49–53; "Bigger & Uglier," *Time,* July 9, 1965, pp. 20–21; "The Giant Spoiler," *Time,* November 18, 1966, pp. 34–39.

45. Ronald H. Spector, "Perception and Reality in America's Military Performance in Vietnam, 1965–1970," 154–55, 162.

46. Andrew F. Krepinevich, Jr., *The Army and Vietnam,* 188–89.

into the villages closer to provincial capitals and other cities. In addition, the pressure exerted on the Vietcong brought regiments of the People's Army southward from the Democratic Republic of Vietnam, which resulted in costly encounters for the Americans.[47] Lastly, the massive sweeps by infantry battalions did not disperse the guerrillas or inhibit their freedom of movement. They returned when the Americans went back to camp. Search-and-destroy/sweep operations definitely damaged the enemy by capturing munitions and supplies, blowing up bunkers, and forcing the communists to flee or fight. But these accomplishments had limited benefits because the communists received new munitions and supplies, built new bunkers in different locations, and regrouped in the same forests and mountains. For the United States to have occupied the communist strongholds in southern Vietnam would have required an additional 400,000 troops than were ultimately deployed.[48] *U.S. News & World Report* succinctly stated the problem in late 1965. "Once a battle is considered over—unless it's fought in a productive, populated area—U.S. forces withdraw to established bases," the magazine wrote. "The results of victory are never clearly apparent." Many commanders of brigades and divisions believed Westmoreland relied too much and for too long on search-and-destroy/sweep operations and should have dispersed troops to strengthen security for pacification teams. *Newsweek* reflected that viewpoint in late 1966: "That, of course, raises the question of whether the U.S. way of war—with its reliance upon masses of materiel and technological improvisation—can be adapted to complex political ends."[49]

Newsweek was echoing the conclusion of a report to the Army chief of staff in spring 1966 by a special committee of officers. The chief of staff had instructed the committee to evaluate the attritional warfare strategy implemented by Westmoreland the previous year. The officers recommended less emphasis on search-and-destroy/sweep operations. More troops should protect villages while self-defense militia received training from American advisors. Plainly, the officers said, attritional warfare should yield to an enclave strategy

---

47. Ibid., 188.
48. Kinnard, *War Managers*, 41–42.
49. "Fighting Gets Tougher—So Does American GI," *U.S. News & World Report*, December 13, 1965, p. 41; "The American Way of War," *Newsweek*, December 5, 1966, p. 53. Douglas Kinnard surveyed about a hundred Vietnam unit commanders on a variety of topics. Nearly six out of ten thought search-and-destroy operations should never have been conducted or should have ceased after a year. Also, nearly three out of ten thought large-unit operations generally should have ended after a year, while four out of ten thought large-unit operations never should have been used (*War Managers*, 45).

that included a counterinsurgency component, officially called pacification. Westmoreland dueled with the Pentagon over whether his strategy already contained provisions for territorial security and a self-defense program. Nothing really changed. A follow-up study by the Army in May 1967 found that Westmoreland relied overwhelmingly on search-and-destroy/sweep operations, with pacification a minor element. *U.S. News & World Report* reported the reliance on multibattalion tactics: "These aggressive maneuvers are running at three times the rate of a year ago."[50]

Of the newsmagazines, only *Newsweek* had directly criticized Westmoreland. "There are those who would contend that Westmoreland is something less than a brilliant strategist," an article commented.[51] Westmoreland reacted to criticism of his strategic plan by complaining to McNamara and President Johnson. The general wondered whether people in the Defense Department and White House were questioning his leadership. A discussion of news stories occurred at a meeting attended by the president, secretary of defense, chairman of the Joint Chiefs of Staff, presidential press secretary, and Westmoreland in summer 1967. "The President said he has never heard anybody who has ever been critical of General Westmoreland in any way," the notes recorded.[52] Johnson's remark hardly seemed credible. Factionalism regarding strategy had divided the military hierarchy, Defense Department strategists, and Johnson administration policymakers since 1965.[53] Westmoreland's immediate superior, the Army chief of staff, was among those senior military commanders who "questioned the wastefulness and apparent fruitlessness of search and destroy operations."[54] Critics existed in Vietnam, too. Correspondents who developed sources with infantry units heard complaints from officers about the tactics mandated by headquarters in Saigon. "We were getting criticisms of strategy from people in the field, colonels and below," says Wallace of *U.S. News & World Report*. "It wasn't just gripes. We thought it was valid."[55]

A week after the Tet 1968 offensive demonstrated the capability of the guerrillas to penetrate the security zones surrounding cities and major mili-

50. Herring, *LBJ and Vietnam*, 73–74; Krepinevich, *Army and Vietnam*, 180–83; "Decisive Battles Near in Vietnam War?" *U.S. News & World Report*, May 1, 1967, p. 53.
51. "The American Way of War," *Newsweek*, December 5, 1966, pp. 49–50.
52. Tom Johnson's notes of meetings, July 13, 1967, box 1, LBJ Library.
53. *Pentagon Papers*, vols. 3 and 4; Herring, *America's Longest War*, 175–79.
54. Herring, *LBJ and Vietnam*, 44.
55. Wallace interview.

tary bases, the *Time* bureau chief in Washington interviewed President Johnson about speculation that Westmoreland would be replaced. "There has never been a period when I have had greater confidence in General Westmoreland than now," the president told *Time*'s John Steele.[56] Six weeks later the Defense Department announced that Westmoreland would become Army chief of staff—in effect, a promotion—and appointed a successor, Gen. Creighton W. Abrams, the deputy commander in Vietnam. *Time* blithely stated, "Until the Tet offensive, Westmoreland's judgment had never been seriously questioned." Newsmagazine correspondents in Saigon and Washington attempted to learn whether the change in command would bring a new strategy. *Time* mentioned in an introductory profile of Abrams, "He might also reduce the massive-area type of search-and-destroy operations and concentrate instead on an increased use of reconnaissance patrols—throwing in his battalions only if the patrols hit paydirt." *Newsweek* learned that Johnson knew very little about Abrams and did not even know his name, a detail it did not publish.[57]

Tet 1968 also prompted reappraisals by *Time* and *U.S. News & World Report* regarding military methods. *U.S. News & World Report* wrote, "The U.S. is paying dearly for years of illusion in Vietnam—the illusion that a revolutionary struggle could be handled with conventional warfare, that firepower could win back a countryside where an enemy political infrastructure was firmly entrenched." *Newsweek,* reviewing the record of failure that culminated in the Tet offensive, advised readers, "Inevitably, this raised an even more perplexing question about the effectiveness of General Westmoreland's aggressive search-and-destroy tactics." The magazine speculated about what Abrams would do: "It would not be at all surprising if the U.S. command in Saigon laid less emphasis in the coming months on costly search-and-destroy operations against the enemy." This and other *Newsweek* articles emphasized the difference between Westmoreland's decisions and those of Abrams. The theme was that Abrams recognized the peculiar characteristics of warfare in Vietnam while Westmoreland never did. A *Newsweek* article several months after Westmoreland relinquished command to Abrams credited his successor with focusing on defense of the cities, refusing to commit troops to "isolated outposts like Khe Sanh," reducing by two-thirds the number of infantrymen

---

56. Tom Johnson's notes of meetings, February 9, 1968, box 1, LBJ Library.

57. "End of the Tour," *Time,* March 29, 1968, p. 21; "A Changing of the Guard," *Time,* April 19, 1968, pp. 25–32; Charles Roberts oral history, LBJ Library, 1:39.

assigned to fortifications along the demilitarized zone, and implementing other "visible changes in American military tactics" that pushed the communists deep into the countryside. This article finally provoked a response from an exasperated chairman of the Joint Chiefs of Staff. "You should know that there is an insidious effort being undertaken in the press to derogate Westy as a commander," wrote Gen. Earle Wheeler to Abrams. Articles about the apparent improvement in the military situation, Wheeler stated, attributed "the change in the situation entirely to you . . . by denigrating Westy's efforts prior to your assumption of command."[58]

The accuracy of newsmagazine coverage of tactical operations during 1968–1969 was questionable, according to historians. Articles from summer 1968 onward focused on the small-unit warfare Abrams had implemented. *Newsweek* reported that Abrams deployed battalions rather than brigades, and that infantry platoons regularly operated alone in the countryside. "The bulk of the units are kept constantly on the move, scouring the countryside in search of weapons caches and carrying out night ambushes along enemy infiltration routes," *Newsweek* wrote. *Time* described the methods. "Under the direction of Abrams, the U.S. has evolved a potent mix of tactics for keeping Communist troops consistently off balance," an article stated, noting the presence of hundreds of infantry squads and platoons in the countryside. "The most vital ingredient in the mix is maneuverability." *U.S. News & World Report* observed, "[I]nstead of seeing battalion and multibattalion sweeps of long-time Communist hideouts in the Vietnamese jungles, you see U.S. patrols from three men up to perhaps a company nose into every nook and cranny of this country."[59] Historians have determined that Abrams indeed switched tactics, but not until troop withdrawals began in summer 1969. Abrams continued large-unit warfare through spring 1969.[60] Also, infantry units continued to attack fortified positions and hilltops, which caused heavy casualties; approximately 22,950 Americans died during the sixteen months after the start of the Tet 1968 offensive. Not until the battle for Ap

58. "Why U.S. Isn't Winning a War," *U.S. News & World Report*, April 1, 1968, pp. 44–48; "Hanoi Attacks," *Newsweek*, February 12, 1968, p. 30; "After Westy," *Newsweek*, April 1, 1968, p. 45; "A General without Illusions," *Newsweek*, October 21, 1968, pp. 48–49; General Wheeler to General Abrams and Admiral McCain, message, October 16, 1968, national security files, Vietnam country file, box 99, LBJ Library.

59. "Defending Saigon," *Newsweek*, July 22, 1968, p. 34; "The Strategy and Tactics of Peace in Viet Nam," *Time*, March 28, 1969, pp. 18–25; "Vietnam: As Shooting Dies Down," *U.S. News & World Report*, October 27, 1969, p. 35.

60. Krepinevich, *Army and Vietnam*, 253–55.

Bia, which became known as Hamburger Hill, did the military abandon its preference for traditional assaults on entrenched enemy outposts.[61] The newsmagazines appear to have accepted the premise that a new chief commander meant new methods. By the time small-unit warfare actually dominated military action in autumn 1969, the newsmagazines had relegated American infantry operations to a low priority.

Helicopters and War Technology

The image of a helicopter came to symbolize the Vietnam War. Almost every documentary and movie about the war had scenes with helicopters ferrying troops to battle, evacuating the wounded, and hovering over the ground while a gunner scanned the grassland or jungle for the enemy. An icon of the war was the picture of a helicopter on a rooftop landing pad with a long line of children, men, and women desperately waiting to board as Saigon fell to the communists in April 1975. The helicopter symbolized more than the war itself. It stood for the superiority of American technology in Vietnam.[62] Twenty-two articles appeared in *Newsweek, Time,* and *U.S. News & World Report* pertaining to the military role of helicopters, with sixteen articles published between summer 1965 and spring 1968, the period when helicopters were perceived as the wonder weapon in Vietnam. Despite the criticism and skepticism they showed toward military methods generally, the newsmagazines treated helicopters with respect. Not until late in the war were readers informed about the serious liabilities associated with helicopters.

Other war technology also received attention, especially from *Time,* which wrote about weaponry in an awestruck tone. Articles extolled the lethality of ordnance and the wondrous capability of various electronic devices. *Time's* rapturous prose introduced an article in summer 1966 beneath the headline "Charge of the Air Cav":

Half a league, half a league, Half a league onward—Alfred Lord Tennyson

Not a single cavalryman carried a saber, instead they cradled automatic rifles in their arms. No plumed, defiant foe fell to their swift assault, only scrawny, half-naked guerrillas.

---

61. Spector, *After Tet,* 182–83.
62. See Karnow, *Vietnam,* 436–38; Fitzgerald, *Fire in the Lake,* 492.

Air Cav troopers, using the strategy of General Custer's day, have struck swiftly and destructively at the enemy's food supplies: more than 1,000,000 lbs. of rice have been systematically destroyed in the Air Cav's first year of action.

Its 430 choppers, flying from a carefully cropped launch pad outside An Khe, have carried men and whole batteries of snub-nosed 105s and 155s [artillery] into places no one would have imagined.... As a result the Air Cav moves faster and hits harder than any army since Genghis Khan's.[63]

Newsweek and *U.S. News & World Report* never indulged in similar rhetoric, but each newsmagazine accepted the argument that helicopters would be instrumental in winning the war. "The First Cavalry, hopefully, is the U.S. Army's answer to guerrilla warfare in the jungle," *Newsweek* wrote. "The old concepts of capturing and holding terrain are gone. First Cavalry is interested only in finding and destroying enemy personnel." *Time* praised the mobility aspect: "Thanks to the helicopter, the U.S. had found a way to overpower the guerrilla fighter with his own methods: speed and surprise." *U.S. News & World Report* recognized the significant advantages the machine provided. "Vietnam has been called the first 'helicopter war,'" an article noted. "It is the choppers that give the U.S. Army a mobility never before equaled in warfare."[64]

Helicopters performed miracles, according to the newsmagazines. *Newsweek* offered a dramatic account of a reconnaissance patrol ambushed by the Vietcong several miles from Danang. Isolated and encircled, the patrol radioed for help. "Minutes later, U.S. helicopters carrying reinforcements were whirling overhead and the now outclassed Viet Cong quickly vanished into the bush," *Newsweek* wrote. On another occasion, a fierce battle at Plei Me seemed certain to end in defeat for a combined force of American and Vietnamese soldiers. A narrow highway bracketed by tall hills was the only route reinforcements could use—except for helicopter troopers. "It was the newly arrived 1st Air Cavalry that came charging—and by rotors not roads," *Time* reported, and their arrival dispersed the guerrillas. Helicopter pilots became the knights of the air, the glamorous aviators similar to the daring young

---

63. "Charge of the Air Cav," *Time,* September 23, 1966, p. 31.
64. "The War No One Wants—Or Can End," *Newsweek,* August 9, 1965, p. 19; "The Red Napoleon," *Time,* June 17, 1966, p. 34; "Why U.S. Isn't Winning a War," *U.S. News & World Report,* April 1, 1968, p. 44.

men of World War I. Pilots wore cowboy hats and customized their uniforms, a privilege accorded them because of the risks they encountered. "Among Army men in South Vietnam, however, few risk their lives more regularly than the pilots and crewmen of the 'Hueys,'" *Newsweek* stated. "For the Viet Cong, the choppers make fat targets as they hover just off the ground and, proportionately, casualties among helicopter crewmen have run higher than in any other branch."[65]

The aptly named First Airmobile Cavalry Division arrived in Vietnam in summer 1965 with 18,000 soldiers and several hundred helicopters. At a mobilization ceremony for the Army's first helicopter-borne infantry unit, "Defense Secretary McNamara sounded like a proud father," *Time* reported. Now infantry was "freed from the tyranny of terrain," *Newsweek* declared. During the next two years, the newsmagazines intermittently reviewed the incredible effect the helicopter had on warfare. "Riding in 430 helicopters, they came to South Viet Nam as the lethal, leapfrogging heralds and exemplars of a new concept of air mobility in waging ground war," *Time* wrote. *Newsweek* lauded the "revolution in jungle warfare that has been wrought by the American helicopter." Unlike the French troops a decade earlier who had depended on reinforcements and supplies transported by convoys, American troops relied on assistance from above. "No longer are the Communists able to employ their favorite tactic of launching a large-scale attack against an isolated outpost and then ambushing the overland convoy sent in to lift the siege," *Newsweek* stated. The potential for battlefield success seemed a certainty. "The First Cav has practically rewritten the book on counterinsurgency warfare," *Newsweek* concluded. *U.S. News & World Report* indicated the confidence commanders had in the new unit. "In mid-September, the First Cavalry Division—a helicopter-borne air-mobile division—landed in South Vietnam and moved directly to a well-protected base of operations near the high plateau region 260 miles north of Saigon to confront the Reds where they are reputed to be strongest," the magazine reported.[66] Significantly,

---

65. "A New Ball Game?" *Newsweek*, May 3, 1965, p. 53; "The Red Napoleon," *Time*, June 17, 1966, pp. 32–36; "Patrols, Pilots, and the PX," *Newsweek*, May 24, 1965, p. 48.

66. "The Commitment," *Time*, June 25, 1965, p. 31; "Whirling Dervishes," *Newsweek*, December 13, 1965, p. 28; "Digging Out the V.C.," *Time*, September 29, 1967, pp. 38–39; "Barring the Door," *Newsweek*, June 27, 1966, p. 42; "The American Way of War," *Newsweek*, December 5, 1966, pp. 49–53; "Tide Turning in Vietnam War?" *U.S. News & World Report*, September 27, 1965, p. 35.

the attitude of the newsmagazines toward helicopters in Vietnam was almost entirely positive during the same period that articles expressed doubts about key components of American military methods.

Helicopter warfare had a downside, however. Helicopters were extremely difficult to fly, and crashes due to a combination of poor weather and pilot error were not uncommon. Helicopters required extensive maintenance, and even a minor malfunction could cause loss of control. Lastly, helicopters had minimal armor to keep overall weight low, and a heavy-caliber bullet striking a rotor blade, hydraulic valve, or almost any mechanical linkage could down the aircraft. Correspondents knew full well the dangers of travel aboard the Hueys and Chinooks. "Helicopters weren't that safe," Rudolph Rauch, of *Time*, says. "If they didn't fall apart and crash, they were always being shot at."[67]

Newsmagazines rarely covered the limitations of helicopters. *Newsweek*, ever the skeptic, first mentioned the downside in an article concerning a major tactical operation that had failed to produce any contact with guerrillas, primarily because of a delayed airlift of soldiers to block an escape route. "Part of the problem was that the much-vaunted mobility of the First Cav wasn't all it was cracked up to be," *Newsweek* noted. "For one thing, the First Cav's helicopters can be reduced to semi-paralysis by a low cloud ceiling in a mountainous area. For another, the division's hundreds of choppers require a staggering amount of logistical support." *U.S. News & World Report*, which took every opportunity to chastise the military for inefficient use of personnel, mentioned the problem of mechanical upkeep. "[T]he choppers must have bases for repairs and fuel," an article reported. "A typical Army assault-helicopter company has 31 assigned aircraft and about 300 men. The main responsibility of 131 of those men—nearly half the company—is maintenance and repair. They often serve their year's tour in Vietnam without firing a shot." *Time* informed readers in early 1971, "Next to the Viet Cong, the helicopter has been the greatest threat G.I.s have had to face in Viet Nam." The article cited 2,450 deaths from accidental crashes and 2,800 deaths from shootdowns; both casualty tolls included helicopter crews and passengers. Despite all the dangers and the drain on resources, helicopters continued to earn tributes from the newsmagazines late in the war. "In the opinion of many military experts, the helicopter has been the difference between a humiliating U.S. defeat in Vietnam and whatever chance remains of attain-

---

67. Stanton, *American Army*, 92–93; Rauch interview.

ing some more satisfactory outcome," *Newsweek* commented. *U.S. News & World Report* stated, "Helicopters also have turned near-defeats into striking victories and have changed the face of non-nuclear warfare, not only in Vietnam, but for the future."[68]

Information about war technology appeared more often in *Time* than in the other newsmagazines. *Time* published encomiums to weaponry in July, October, November, and December 1965.[69] One article stated "the once-cocksure Viet Cong found themselves choking in a new kind of war." *Time* extolled the inventory of the American arsenal: an antipersonnel bomb that erupted with razor-sharp shards; a "beehive" artillery shell that spewed thousands of tiny steel darts; a lightweight flak vest for protection against shrapnel; an aircraft gunship with a six-barreled machine gun that shot six thousand bullets a minute ("can slash a swatch of jungle to salad in moments"); perimeter surveillance radar for detecting enemy soldiers in forest and jungle; computer-equipped airborne command aircraft to coordinate troop deployment, direct artillery fire, and identify targets; an electrically controlled land mine for detonation with maximum effect; and the latest lethal infantry weapons—grenade launcher, easily portable machine gun, and rapid-fire rifle. *Time* revealed to readers the wizardry of a night-vision rifle scope, a helicopter-borne infrared optical scanner to detect humans and equipment, and a high-flying supersonic reconnaissance aircraft with special cameras to locate hidden enemy positions.[70] And although *Time* criticized the Nixon administration for resuming aerial bombardment of northern Vietnam in spring 1972, it could not resist praising the "laser-guided and electro-optical 'smart' bombs" the American warplanes dropped on targets. "Dropped from high altitudes—rather than on the low-level runs that were necessary to ensure accuracy for unguided 'dumb' bombs—the new armaments have made the war far less perilous for American pilots," *Time* reported. "They have also given flyers

68. "Rabbits and Elephants," *Newsweek*, February 21, 1966, p. 36; "Why U.S. Isn't Winning a War," *U.S. News & World Report*, April 1, 1968, p. 44; "The War within the War," *Time*, January 25, 1971, p. 35; "'Just Say It Was the Comancheros,'" *Newsweek*, March 15, 1971, pp. 39–44; "Lessons U.S. Has Learned in the 'Helicopter War,' " *U.S. News & World Report*, November 23, 1970, pp. 49–50.

69. *Time*: "Bigger & Uglier," July 9, 1965, p. 47; "A New Kind of War," October 22, 1965, pp. 28, 38–39b; "Deeper & Wider," November 19, 1965, pp. 34, 39; "Technology of War," December 3, 1965, p. 31.

70. *Time*: "Judicious Dribs & Drabs," July 21, 1967, p. 31; "Taking the Night from Charlie," May 31, 1968, p. 39.

the assurance that they can eliminate military targets without the fear that their bombs may fall wide of the mark."[71]

Newsweek and *U.S. News & World Report* paid far less attention to war technology except as it influenced strategy and tactics. Only one lengthy article in *Newsweek,* a year after military intervention commenced, explained in detail the various types of modern weaponry the American military had employed in Vietnam. The magazine usually informed readers that war technology and modern weaponry did not help much. *U.S. News & World Report* blamed technology for shifting manpower from infantry units. "The U.S., according to veteran officers, has more rear-echelon support troops per rifleman on the fighting line than any other army in the world," an article noted. "Better or different use of these rear-echelon troops is sharply limited unless the U.S. decides to fight in a radically different manner." Throughout the war, the magazine reminded readers that only a small percentage of troops were infantrymen.[72]

Although certain types of technology fascinated *Time* and earned some mention in *Newsweek* and *U.S. News & World Report,* none of the newsmagazines devoted much space to the spraying of chemical defoliants on the Vietnam countryside. Five articles, or less than 1 percent of the total for military operations, pertained to defoliants, with *Newsweek* publishing three and *Time* and *U.S. News & World Report* one each. *U.S. News & World Report* first reported the use of defoliants in autumn 1966, and stated that the chemicals were "harmless." *Time* allocated a full page in early 1968 to the subject. The article reported the spraying of 50 million pounds of herbicides on a million acres during 1967. "The defoliant herbicides do not concentrate in animal tissue," *Time* stated, citing a study by an agricultural research institute. A risk existed for environmental damage, the article noted: "Complete defoliation could also cause laterization, the destructive process that occurs in some tropical soils when removal of vegetation exposes them to erosion and sunlight." *Newsweek* cited the same institute study, but also

---

71. "Nixon at the Brink over Viet Nam," *Time,* May 22, 1972, p. 27; "New Arms, More Bombs," *Time,* June 5, 1972, p. 29.

72. "The Military—"We Can Win It," *Newsweek,* April 18, 1966, pp. 28–31; "Why U.S. Isn't Winning a War," *U.S. News & World Report,* April 1, 1968, pp. 44–48. *U.S. News & World Report* introduced its readers to warfare technology early, just a month after deployment of combat units, with extensive details ("In Vietnam, a 'Blank Check' to Try Out New Weapons," April 12, 1965, p. 38).

quoted other scientific researchers to reach a contradictory conclusion that the defoliants caused "irreparable damage."[73] The reason *Time* and *Newsweek* found the topic newsworthy was a public controversy generated by two American biologists whose article in a political activist journal predicted long-term environmental damage and physical harm to rural residents of southern Vietnam. Both magazines used information from a White House source to rebut aspects of the article.[74]

A later *Newsweek* article relied on a report from scientists who volunteered to study the environmental effects of defoliants in Vietnam. "The team reported it could find no conclusive evidence that the defoliants affected the health of the civilian population, or that they had caused any striking increase in the number of birth defects," the magazine stated. This article appeared in summer 1972, with the headline "When the Landscape Is the Enemy," and it covered damage done by defoliants, bombs, shells, and specially designed bulldozers that scraped brush and trees for hundreds of yards away from the perimeters of artillery bases and infantry camps to eliminate hiding places for guerrillas. "In Vietnam, on a scale unprecedented in the history of warfare, the landscape itself has become an enemy subjected to systematic destruction," *Newsweek* wrote. "In order to get at the elusive Communists, the U.S. has ravaged jungles with millions of tons of bombs and shells, sprayed thousands of acres of farmlands and forests with deadly herbicides and sent teams of giant bulldozers to cut huge swatches through the jungles."[75] The article appeared two years after the Nixon administration ordered a ban on Agent Orange, the principal defoliant, so named because it was stored in orange barrels. Scientific concern about defoliants surfaced initially in the mid-1960s, then increased during 1969.[76] Correspondents had seen the defoliated roadsides, and some had visited the Air Force squadrons that sprayed the chemicals, but none were concerned that defoliants might have harmful aftereffects and that defoliation might cause long-term environmental damage. "One subject I really should have pursued was the spraying,

---

73. "End to Hanoi's Jungle Sanctuary?" *U.S. News & World Report*, October 3, 1966, p. 21; "Defoliating Viet Nam," *Time*, February 23, 1968, p. 70; "The Blight that Failed," *Newsweek*, January 11, 1971, p. 79.

74. Untitled document countering statements by biologists, December 4, 1967, office files, Fred Panzer, box 427, LBJ Library.

75. "When the Landscape Is the Enemy," *Newsweek*, August 7, 1972, pp. 24–26.

76. Lewy, "The Question of American War Guilt," 357–58.

the chemical spraying," says William J. Cook, of *Newsweek.* "I knew people who did it. It didn't get me interested. It should have."[77]

Newsweek, Time, and *U.S. News & World Report* devoted much space to military operations and methods, strategy, and war technology. The preponderance of commentary by each newsmagazine either accepted or rejected American military doctrine applied in Vietnam. Depending on the editorial viewpoint, American ways of war symbolized genius and determination or arrogance and ignorance. *Time* accepted the idea that modern weaponry would decimate and demoralize the enemy. It expressed certainty that war technology promised an effective, efficient way to wage war. *Time* praised the application of lethal ordnance, enthused over B-52s and avionics, marveled at the gadgetry and machinery, and romanticized the exploits of the helicopter. To *Time,* the operational triad of firepower, mobility, and technology would prevail under any conditions. *U.S. News & World Report* regarded American military doctrine differently. It blamed reliance on technology for inducing commanders to forsake fundamental principles of warfare and for diverting too many troops from combat duty to maintenance and logistical roles. *U.S. News & World Report* believed that intensive aerial bombardment and deployment of an immense force of infantrymen would overwhelm the enemy. *Newsweek,* however, never wholeheartedly accepted the premise that any quick-fix solution would win. Although its articles exhibited the same fascination with helicopters as *Time* (without the rapture), the magazine recognized both the limitations of modern weapons and their awful consequences to people in the countryside. *Newsweek* consistently referred to the moral question raised by the use of firepower. Unlike *Time,* which saw war technology as beneficial, and *U.S. News & World Report,* which saw it as detrimental, *Newsweek* saw war technology as a malevolent distraction which deceived Americans into thinking that machinery could triumph over ideals. *Time* changed its attitude late in the war, responding to public opinion and the realization that firepower had only prolonged the war, not affected its outcome. *Newsweek,* though, spoke early and consistently on behalf of Americans whose conscience could not accept the death and destruction inflicted on civilians in Vietnam. "Somehow, Americans brought up in a society that depends so heavily on technology seem to find it easier to take another man's life by mechanical means," *Newsweek* wrote.[78]

77. Cook interview.
78. "Song My: A U.S. Atrocity?" *Newsweek,* December 8, 1969, p. 37.

American Ways of War

Articles on war technology in the newsmagazines manifested an ambivalence in society toward technological development, which had accelerated tremendously after World War II. On one hand, Americans wanted to be the first to land a man on the moon to demonstrate national—and ideological—supremacy; on the other, they knew that money spent on the space program instead could help many citizens who lived in poverty. On one hand, they realized that the first generation of computers in the workplace and a wave of automation in basic industry, such as steel- and auto-making, increased productivity; on the other, they feared the loss of human judgment and the diminution of skilled labor. On one hand, they remained faithful to the idea that machinery brought progress; on the other, they suspected technocracy. On one hand, they knew that modern weaponry saved the lives of American troops, and felt that this justified its use; on the other, they saw the dead and maimed children and adults whose villages and farms had been bombed and shelled—scenes which bothered the national soul. Somehow, as public dissatisfaction with the war grew year by year, Vietnam became embroiled in a cultural conflict over the ultimate result of technological development.[79] The war heightened tension about automatic processes, impersonal devices, and remote-control systems. *Newsweek, Time,* and *U.S. News & World Report* reflected the schisms in society about the effects of technology.

Debate on American ways of war in Vietnam continued for years. Documents, memoranda, and reports circulated among military commanders, strategists, and policymakers arguing for different strategy and tactics to salvage the situation. Some contended that excessive firepower alienated many Vietnamese because of its carnage and disillusioned many Americans because of its cruelty; others believed that restrictions on the application of firepower forestalled victory. Some considered attritional warfare and conventional military methods to be wrongheaded; others assumed that alternative methods were deficient and could not defeat a disciplined adversary. Every one of these arguments appeared in the pages of *Newsweek, Time,* and

---

79. Michael Adas, *Machines as the Measure of Men: Science, Technology, and Ideologies of Western Dominance,* 404–5, discusses the historical connection in the American mind between machinery and progress. William Hardy McNeill, *The Pursuit of Power: Technology, Armed Force, and Society since A.D. 1000,* 376–77, notes the increasing distrust of technocracy during the 1960s. Lewis Mumford, *The Myth of the Machine,* comments on public disaffection toward automation, computers, and other forms of technological development during the 1960s.

U.S. News & World Report during the Vietnam War. Yet each newsmagazine favored certain factions and viewpoints to the exclusion of others, which prevented readers of any one periodical from obtaining the breadth of the debate occurring within the military hierarchy and the policymaking establishment.

5

Determination, Doubt, Despair

Americans, whether policymakers or private citizens, rarely agreed on Vietnam during the 1960s. At a White House conference in September 1963 to discuss the worrisome communist insurgency and latest crisis in southern Vietnam, President John F. Kennedy listened to reports from a State Department diplomat and a Marine Corps general. Kennedy had sent the diplomat and general on a fact-finding mission to assess the situation in Vietnam, where 16,000 American military personnel advised and trained the southern army. A summer of dramatic and violent protests in Saigon by Buddhist militants opposed to the national government had further weakened an already unpopular regime. The general spoke first, describing the situation as hopeful because the army had continued to fight the guerrillas and performed capably despite the turmoil. The diplomat spoke next, describing the situation as hopeless because the disturbances had paralyzed the government and diverted the army from the war in the countryside. Then the president asked, "The two of you did visit the same country, didn't you?"[1]

The same question certainly applied in April 1966 when *U.S. News & World Report* and *Newsweek* published decidedly different perspectives on the military situation in Vietnam, where 220,000 American troops waged war. One week, *U.S. News & World Report* posed the provocative headline question, "Ahead in Vietnam: A Bloody Stalemate?" The next week, a *Newsweek* headline proclaimed, "The Military—'We Can Win It.'" Although the magazines had obtained information from similar sources, primarily commanders

---

1. Lloyd C. Gardner, *Pay Any Price: Lyndon Johnson and the Wars for Vietnam*, 82; Karnow, *Vietnam*, 293; David Kaiser, *American Tragedy: Kennedy, Johnson, and the Origins of the Vietnam War*, 250–51. Kaiser has the most detailed account of the White House conference.

in Vietnam and senior officers at the Pentagon, *U.S. News & World Report* chose to emphasize anonymous criticisms that restrictions on military operations had cost the United States an opportunity for victory, while *Newsweek* focused on predictions that superior firepower and technology would prevail. These contrary conclusions seemed to prove a point *Time* had made several weeks earlier about the Vietnam War: "It is simply confusing."[2]

Contradictory assessments of the military situation in Vietnam often appeared in *Newsweek, Time,* and *U.S. News & World Report,* a clash of perspectives that conveyed the ambiguity of the war itself and the editorial prerogatives of the newsmagazines. Unlike previous wars fought by the United States, warfare in Vietnam rarely resulted in the permanent conquest or occupation of territory and almost never produced tangible evidence of lasting success. Without such proof, disagreement existed among policymakers and within the military hierarchy about progress on the battlefield and the prospect for triumph. The lack of an official consensus on the military situation let each newsmagazine determine the status of the war based on its own viewpoint.

The eight-year war in Vietnam lasted through two presidential administrations, during which constant internal bureaucratic and political maneuvers shaped Vietnam policy. The newsmagazines, too, occasionally shifted their editorial viewpoints to reflect changes in the attitudes of their sources, editors, and readers.[3] *Time* provided optimistic assessments of the war and typically downplayed or ignored altogether serious concerns about the military situation from summer 1965 until midsummer 1967; then, from autumn 1968 through spring 1972, it positively portrayed the effort to improve the Vietnamese army and insisted the southerners could stand alone after the Americans had gone, despite indications the army could not withstand a major enemy attack. *Newsweek* issued occasional skeptical judgments on military efforts from autumn 1965 onward and more consistently doubted the military could win the war, although it did not become defeatist in tone until early 1968; later, *Newsweek* was negative about the Vietnamese army ever becoming capable of fighting on its own. *U.S. News & World Report* initially expressed optimism that a strategy of all-out warfare would defeat the

---

2. "Ahead in Vietnam: A Bloody Stalemate?" *U.S. News & World Report,* April 11, 1966, p. 36; "The Military—'We Can Win It,'" *Newsweek,* April 18, 1966, p. 30; "The New Realism," *Time,* February 18, 1966, p. 19.

3. See Montague Kern, Patricia W. Levering, and Ralph B. Levering, *The Kennedy Crises: The Press, the Presidency, and Foreign Policy,* 195–98.

communists, but by spring 1966 it persistently criticized the policy of gradual military escalation and was the first to state the war would not be won, a theme it repeated until autumn 1967; later, the magazine supported the plan to improve the Vietnamese army, and offered scant critical coverage.

However, a rare period of editorial convergence among the newsmagazines during summer 1967 alarmed President Lyndon B. Johnson and his national security assistant, Walt W. Rostow. *Newsweek, Time,* and *U.S. News & World Report* had concluded by midsummer that a military stalemate existed in southern Vietnam. References to a lack of progress on the battlefield and the prospect of indefinite, inconclusive warfare brought rebuttals from the president. When the *New York Times* also wrote that evidence of a stalemate was obvious, Johnson agreed to a plan by Rostow to foster positive news coverage in the newsmagazines and on the nightly newscasts broadcast by ABC, CBS, and NBC. The propaganda campaign, orchestrated by Rostow, made available to newsmagazine correspondents and other journalists some specially commissioned reports from the Defense Department and CIA that demonstrated progress in Vietnam. Documents included material designated "secret" and "confidential," which ordinarily prohibited public disclosure.[4] The campaign had mixed results, influencing *U.S. News & World Report* but not *Newsweek* and *Time.* An unintended consequence was a bitter backlash by journalists when the Tet 1968 military offensive by communists apparently contradicted the message of victory that Johnson and Rostow had concocted.

Aside from the special effort in 1967, presidential advisors and policymakers in the Johnson and Nixon administrations regularly monitored newsmagazine coverage of the Vietnam War. The Johnson administration also created the Public Affairs Policy Committee for Vietnam and an ad hoc council, the Tuesday Luncheon Group, both of which occasionally focused on newsmagazine articles. Articles in *Newsweek, Time,* and *U.S. News & World Report* sometimes prompted discussions or rebuttals. "They were useful to follow," Rostow said.[5] Memoranda and reports from both the Johnson and

---

4. Rostow remembered concentrating the campaign on "the national media," which to him meant the newsmagazines, television networks, *Life* magazine, the *New York Times,* and the *Washington Post* (Rostow interview). For more on the propaganda campaign, see Small, *Johnson, Nixon, and the Doves,* 122–23, and Herring, *LBJ and Vietnam,* 142–46.

5. White House central files, name files for George Christian, Robert Kintner, Robert Komer, Frederick Panzer, and Walt Rostow, LBJ Library; Tom Johnson's notes of meetings, n.d., LBJ Library; Public Affairs Policy Committee for Vietnam, national security files, Vietnam country file, box 197, LBJ Library; Christian, Reedy, and Rostow interviews.

Nixon administrations reveal that articles on the military situation generated specific responses from officials, who either refuted or praised the judgments of the newsmagazines.[6]

The different perspectives of the newsmagazines from autumn 1965 to summer 1967 and the brief period of agreement on the military situation from midsummer into autumn of that year made critical and skeptical commentary on the military situation available to readers of *Newsweek, Time,* and *U.S. News & World Report* several months to a year before ABC, CBS, and NBC provided similar commentary. The newsmagazines had decided by the end of summer 1967 that a different policy for Vietnam was necessary and that military victory seemed unlikely—judgments that appreciably preceded the Tet 1968 communist offensive, an event generally identified as the point when media coverage of the war turned negative. Some scholars have argued that the news media became critical of Vietnam policy during Tet 1968 when journalists sensed the war could not be won or because opposition to the war was the "political fashion." Indeed, most major newspapers and all three network television news programs waited until Tet 1968 to recommend new policy and to declare that victory was not possible. A survey by the *Boston Globe* in February 1968, during the Tet offensive, showed that sixteen of thirty-nine major American daily newspapers supported the Johnson administration's policy in Vietnam while nineteen opposed it. Scholars have also suggested that the news media lost faith in the war after the American people did, which public-opinion polls indicated was prior to Tet 1968. These conclusions about the timing of negative news coverage and editorial criticism of Vietnam policy perhaps apply to the television networks and some metropolitan newspapers, but not to *Newsweek, Time,* and *U.S. News & World Report*.[7]

---

6. Hundreds of documents at the LBJ Library deal with responses to newsmagazine articles and contacts with newsmagazine correspondents and editors. A considerably smaller number of documents from the Nixon Presidential Materials Project deal with similar topics.

7. Peter Braestrup discusses the negative, or defeatist, tone that dominated television news programs during February and March 1968 (*Big Story,* 510, 517–19). Daniel C. Hallin writes that television news commentary became more critical during Tet 1968 (*"Uncensored War,"* 161–66), and Herring (*America's Longest War,* 200–203) and Fitzgerald (*Fire in the Lake,* 525–26) both state that most media coverage turned critical during Tet. Stanley Karnow refers to television network news programs during Tet 1968 that advocated a prompt negotiated settlement because military triumph seemed improbable (*Vietnam,* 547–48). The *Boston Globe* survey ("The U.S. Press and Its Agony of Appraisal," February 18, 1968, pp. 5F–7F) is reported in "Shifting on the War," *Newsweek,* March 25, 1968, p. 84.

Confidence and Caution

It took several months for the newsmagazines to offer assessments of the military situation in Vietnam after the American military buildup began. Initially, correspondents focused almost exclusively on the drama of combat involving Americans against southern communist guerrillas, known as the Vietcong, and northern communist soldiers, who infiltrated in ever-increasing numbers. "When I first went to Vietnam, they [editors] were looking for hot shit, bang-bang copy," says William J. Cook, a *Newsweek* correspondent in Vietnam for eleven months. Cook realized that though the Vietcong suffered setbacks on the battlefield, they retained their political control. His editors preferred to focus on combat at the time. "Policy was not in the scheme of things," Cook says. *Time* also placed priority on combat coverage. "We had a political guy to keep an eye on the Saigon government, an embassy guy for policy matters, and two of us handled the military action," says Burton Pines, a *Time* correspondent who spent nineteen months in Vietnam. "When there was a lot of action, a third man would come in." James Wallace, who sometimes functioned as a one-person bureau for *U.S. News & World Report,* affirms that combat had priority. "I went where the action was, and the action was in the boonies looking for Charlie [the enemy]," he says.[8]

Gradually, the combat coverage became somewhat repetitive. Beginning in autumn 1965, each newsmagazine offered assessments of the military situation in articles constructed around dramatic narratives of combat. *Time* noticed an immediate turnaround of the military situation. "Today South Viet Nam throbs with a pride and power, above all an esprit, scarcely credible against the summer's somber vista," an article declared. "The Viet Cong's once-cocky hunters have become the cowering hunted as the cutting edge of U.S. firepower slashes into the thickets of Communist strength." *U.S. News & World Report* offered a less exuberant judgment, written in its staccato style. "Almost overnight, there's been a big change in Asia's jungle war," the magazine stated. "Struggle isn't over by a long shot, but, after years of gloom, there are reasons for optimism." *Newsweek* provided a sober assessment: "In fact, if the military situation was improving, that improvement was being achieved primarily by increased expenditure of U.S. lives and materiel." The

---

8. Cook, Pines, and Wallace interviews. By late 1968, interest in combat coverage declined, although interviews with other correspondents for *Newsweek* and *Time* who reported the war's later years reveal that combat coverage remained a priority until most American troops had departed by mid-1971.

magazine also wrote, "The Vietnamese war has often been called a 'dirty little war,' but a war that bids fair to tie up more than a quarter of a million U.S. troops can hardly be termed 'little' any longer."[9]

The difference in perspectives sharpened from autumn 1965 onward, after American troops established secure zones around the major cities and ports in southern Vietnam. *Time* described steady progress late in 1965: "The new feel and direction of the war are sufficiently tangible to lead some officials in Washington to ask whether [peace] negotiations may after all prove unnecessary, even undesirable." *U.S. News & World Report*, however, reminded readers about the temporary nature of a battlefield victory. "Once a battle is considered over—unless it's fought in a productive, populated area—U.S. forces withdraw to established bases," an article stated. "The results of victory are never clearly apparent." *Newsweek* exhibited outright pessimism: "U.S. and Vietnamese ground troops slogged through the bloody routines of a war that now seems likely to extend itself almost indefinitely, both in time and intensity."[10]

The arrival of more American troops raised expectations for success, especially during 1966 when deployment to Vietnam increased in-country personnel from 184,000 to 385,000. Army and Marine Corps infantry seemed to be everywhere in southern Vietnam. Numerous reconnaissance patrols scoured the countryside to detect guerrillas and their camps, while large-scale tactical operations sent thousands of troops on two types of missions: search-and-sweep, which flushed the enemy from rural strongholds; and search-and-destroy, which eradicated bunkers, storage sites, and occasionally hamlets where guerrillas or their supporters lived. These large-unit operations usually produced no significant combat, but the presence of Army and Marine Corps battalions challenged the guerrillas in their strongholds for the first time since the insurgency began in 1959.[11] American troops killed thousands of guerrillas, destroyed huge caches of supplies, established bases

---

9. "A New Kind of War," *Time*, October 22, 1965, pp. 28–29; "Tide Turning in Vietnam War?" *U.S. News & World Report*, September 27, 1965, p. 35; "GI's Pour In—And the War Looks Up," *Newsweek*, October 4, 1965, p. 38; "One Kind of Routine," *Newsweek*, December 20, 1965, p. 34.

10. "Winning Instead of Wishing," *Time*, November 5, 1965, p. 31; "Fighting Gets Tougher, So Does American GI," *U.S. News & World Report*, December 13, 1965, p. 41; "One Kind of Routine," *Newsweek*, December 20, 1965, p. 34.

11. Stanton, *American Army*, 80–89.

in enemy bastions, and seized strategic hilltops. Americans built modern airfields, bigger ports, and gigantic depots. Most journalists assigned to Vietnam, and those who visited on one- or two-week tours at government expense, saw the operational record and logistical buildup as evidence of a successful strategy. *U.S. News & World Report* certainly did: "It is clear now that the Communists are losing the war." Another of those swayed by the influx of men, machinery, and weaponry was the editor of *Newsweek,* Osborn Elliott, who had visited Vietnam early in 1965 and returned a year later. "What had impressed me the year before was the professionalism and dedication of the Green Berets," Elliott wrote in his autobiography. "Now it was the sheer massiveness of the American presence."[12]

When the Johnson administration announced a comprehensive strategy for the Vietnam War early in 1966 at a planning conference in Honolulu, reaction by the newsmagazines reflected their different perspectives on the war. The new strategy resulted from several assumptions: that real military progress had occurred during the previous year; that security for certain crucial rural areas would be established within a year; that destruction of half the guerrilla strongholds in the countryside would occur; and that the southern army would protect all secure rural areas.[13] *Time* accepted these premises: "The U.S., having gone to extraordinary lengths to seek peace in Viet Nam, has now prepared to win the war in that unhappy country." *U.S. News & World Report* dismissed the idea that American troops had gained the upper hand. The military situation was quite the contrary, the magazine said: "The hope is that 300,000 American troops will be enough to insure that a military disaster can be avoided in South Vietnam." *Newsweek* devoted several paragraphs to a straightforward explanation of specific components of the strategy. Then the magazine asked, "Is it, indeed, a grand design—or merely another pipe dream, the latest in a long series of unsuccessful Washington blueprints for victory in Vietnam?"[14]

Military displeasure with presidential restrictions surfaced at the Honolulu conference. *U.S. News & World Report* wrote, "The President was told

---

12. "Reds Don't Talk Peace—What's Holding Them Up?" *U.S. News & World Report,* November 8, 1965, p. 44; Elliott, *World of Oz,* 93.

13. Maclear, *Ten Thousand Day War,* 145–46; Stanton, *American Army,* 84–85.

14. "The New Realism," *Time,* February 18, 1966, p. 21; "New Roadblocks on the Way to Peace," *U.S. News & World Report,* February 14, 1966, pp. 31–32; "After the Pause: Motion or Progress?" *Newsweek,* February 14, 1966, p. 21.

that a decisive military victory in South Vietnam could not be achieved with fewer than 600,000 troops, all-out air attacks on Hanoi and Haiphong, blockade of the North and expansion of the war into Laos and possibly Cambodia and Thailand." Then the magazine suggested that this strategy had received insufficient consideration: "That course is dead, vetoed by the President." *Newsweek* defended presidential restrictions by describing the recommendations as unreasonable. "Even as he ordered the air strikes against the north resumed, LBJ rejected—for the time being—every one of the more extreme options opened to him by his Pentagon planners," an article commented. "Allied troops would not be deployed across the 17th parallel into Laos to interdict the Ho Chi Minh Trail. There would be no amphibious invasion of the North Vietnamese coast to open a second front, no nuclear ultimatums to Hanoi or Peking." *Time* concentrated on the issue of targets in northern Vietnam, hinting that some restrictions interfered with strategic goals. "Beyond the need for additional aircraft, Air Force planners insist that the North can only be bombed effectively if they have permission to hit 'source' targets—oil dumps to keep trucks from rolling rather than the trucks themselves or the roads they negotiate, thermal and hydroelectric plants to starve small workshops of power rather than the shops themselves, ammunition factories to cut production rather than smaller, harder-to-hit ammo dumps," the magazine explained.[15]

The Honolulu conference became a watershed for newsmagazine commentary on the military situation in Vietnam. Speculative forecasts on the duration of the war and the ultimate number of troops sent to Vietnam appeared within weeks and continued into the summer. The military command hierarchy wanted it known that the timetable set by the president and the secretary of defense, Robert S. McNamara, seemed unrealistic.[16] *U.S. News & World Report* ventured first into the fray. "Officials agree that, if the new strategy is to proceed successfully, it will require not only an effort of five to seven more years, but a sustained level of fighting in the countryside, more billions in nonmilitary aid and enormous patience at home," an article

15. "Vietnam War's New Strategy—Will It Work?" *U.S. News & World Report,* February 21, 1966, p. 32; "After the Pause: Motion or Progress?" *Newsweek,* February 14, 1966, p. 20; "The String Runs Out," *Time,* February 4, 1966, pp. 25–26.
16. For more on the insistence by the Joint Chiefs of Staff and Westmoreland on more troops, more intensive aerial bombardment, and more authority to attack border regions in Cambodia and Laos, see Herring, *LBJ and Vietnam,* 30–42.

explained. The possibility that intervention could last into the 1970s presumably surprised most readers. *Newsweek* informed its readership a few weeks afterward about the variance between the Johnson administration's rosy prediction and military reality. "The three-year period mentioned in Washington as that needed to win in Vietnam seems wildly optimistic," the magazine commented. "Five to seven years would appear more realistic—assuming, of course, that China does not enter the conflict."[17]

The factional alignments of the newsmagazines became more apparent after the Honolulu conference. *Time* supported the war policy of Johnson, McNamara, and Dean Rusk, secretary of state. This policy stipulated the gradual escalation of aerial bombardment of northern Vietnam, meaning that the list of targets was periodically broadened to persuade the communist leadership in Hanoi to enter into negotiations for a peace settlement or face the destruction of its industry, ports, transportation network, and utilities; an incremental buildup of the American military in southern Vietnam; and no expansion of infantry operations into Cambodia or Laos, mainly because Johnson worried about provoking China to intervene. *Time* also endorsed the attritional-warfare strategy of General Westmoreland. Attritional warfare in southern Vietnam relied on battalions and brigades for search-and-destroy/sweep operations, intense firepower from artillery and warplanes, and relentless bombardment of a trail network in Laos to interrupt infiltration of reinforcements and supplies. Attritional warfare governed American military operations from autumn 1965 through winter 1968–1969. *Newsweek* aligned itself with dissenters among policymakers who thought bombardment of northern Vietnam served no worthwhile military purpose and harmed the international image of the United States. By summer 1967, McNamara also had adopted this outlook. *Newsweek* also endorsed the faction that favored counterinsurgency warfare rather than attritional warfare. This faction included General Abrams, then the deputy commander in Vietnam; most Marine Corps commanders in Vietnam; and civilian analysts at the Department of Defense. Counterinsurgency warfare emphasized platoons for hamlet security to permit so-called pacification teams from the southern government in Saigon to bring agricultural improvements, education, and health care to rural residents. *U.S. News & World Report* presented

---

17. "Vietnam War's New Strategy—Will It Work?" *U.S. News & World Report,* February 21, 1966, p. 32; "Then and Now—The Difference," *Newsweek,* March 14, 1966, p. 42.

the viewpoint of military hard-liners, primarily the Joint Chiefs of Staff, who wanted more intensive bombardment of northern Vietnam, deployment of up to 700,000 troops, activation of military reserve units to meet manpower requirements, and presidential permission to invade border regions of Cambodia and Laos to eliminate enemy sanctuaries. Westmoreland also wanted to attack the sanctuaries.[18] By selectively presenting information favorable to a factional preference and by incorporating commentary on military methods in articles about combat, each newsmagazine delivered to its readers an appreciably different perspective on the war.

American casualties steadily climbed during the second summer of intervention, and newsmagazine articles reflected the terrific infighting between the hard-liners and the Johnson-McNamara-Rusk group.[19] *Time* told readers the war might continue until 1974 and require a commitment of 750,000 troops. *Newsweek* mentioned 750,000 troops, too, and predicted the war might go on until 1976, resulting in 100,000 American dead. *U.S. News & World Report* published two articles forecasting up to a million troops in Vietnam until 1971.[20] No newsmagazine attributed the estimated troop requirements to an identified source. The Defense Department documented that the 750,000 figure came from a formal military analysis provided by a general to some journalists.[21] The background briefing by the general signified an effort by the military hierarchy to make its case to the public for an end to the gradual escalation policy.

Different Perspectives

Time, until summer 1967, painted a picture of triumph on the battlefield and an enemy on the defensive, except for an occasional brief acknowledgment that not all was going well. The approach of the first anniversary of for-

18. See the *Pentagon Papers,* vols. 3 and 4, for discussions of the factions and strategic preferences within the Defense Department and military hierarchy and among policymakers, and of conflicts within the Defense Department regarding restrictions on military operations in Cambodia and Laos from 1965 to 1969. Kinnard, *War Managers,* 116–19, discusses resentment among military strategists for Johnson's refusal to activate reservists.

19. Gardner, *Pay Any Price,* 43; *Pentagon Papers,* 3:290.

20. "The Prospect Ahead," *Time,* August 19, 1966, pp. 17–18; "Numbers Game," *Newsweek,* August 22, 1966, pp. 64–67; "Has U.S. 'Missed the Boat' in Vietnam?" *U.S. News & World Report,* June 27, 1966, pp. 38–39; "Is End of Vietnam War in Sight?" *U.S. News & World Report,* July 25, 1966, p. 28.

21. Herring, *LBJ and Vietnam,* 35, 50.

mal military intervention brought recognition of the need for visible signs of progress. "For one thing, as the size and cost of the U.S. commitment grows, Americans will understandably expect their forces to go beyond containment and start reclaiming territory," *Time* noted. "So far, the results have been less than spectacular." After a series of large-unit military operations in the central highlands and the provinces around Saigon apparently caused heavy casualties to Vietcong units, *Time* told its readers to discount congressional criticisms of policy. "The war, therefore, is not going badly—although one would hardly realize it, judging by what comes out of Washington," an article declared. "The beginnings of success can be seen." Part of the problem, according to the magazine, was impatience. "Six months ago, many had expected that so large a surge in manpower would produce dazzling results," it commented. *Time* believed the sweeps of battalions and brigades into rural areas paid long-term dividends. "On the ground, American fighting men are not only taking on wily veterans of guerrilla warfare but are also inflicting losses that no foe can afford to take indefinitely," an article concluded.[22]

According to a succession of *Time* articles, the guerrillas withdrew from their remote strongholds, leaving the Americans in control. "The relative quiescence of the Communists on the battlefield is less satisfying than it is annoying to U.S. commanders, who are spoiling for a fight they are confident they can win," *Time* wrote. Marine Corps infantrymen had created several fortified camps near the demilitarized zone and in the northwestern provinces by this time, while U.S. Army paratroopers and the First Air Cavalry Division had moved into strategically located positions farther inland from the coastal enclaves. "The Americans from their hilltop positions control all the major corridors to the south," *Time* asserted. Actually, American troops never controlled the access routes and infiltration corridors that snaked through Laos into southern Vietnam. Enemy reinforcements and supplies increased continually whenever operations by the Vietcong and People's Army required it.[23]

Despite its upbeat assessments of military operations, *Time* bluntly informed its readers to expect a long war. "The war is undeniably going well

---

22. *Time:* "The Guardians at the Gate," January 7, 1966, p. 20; "No Cure in Consensus," June 10, 1966, p. 32; "An Alltime High for Action," May 27, 1966, p. 27; "Ripping the Sanctuary," July 8, 1966, p. 17.

23. "The Red Napoleon," *Time,* June 17, 1966, p. 32; "Waiting for the Bugles," *Time,* October 21, 1966, p. 46; Maclear, *Ten Thousand Day War,* 118–20, 185.

for the Allies," *Time* wrote. "Yet there is little prospect that it can be won easily or soon." The Vietcong relentlessly attacked American outposts, ambushed American patrols, and returned to former sites whenever American troops shifted to another area. Ominously, too, the communist cadres in the countryside remained intact. "Most important of all, the Viet Cong's control of the villages, where four out of five Vietnamese live, has hardly been touched," *Time* stated in autumn 1966. Still, the magazine wished the communists would face reality: "They should realize by now that they cannot win the war, cannot drive out the U.S., and are bogged down in considerable trouble besides."[24]

Wishful thinking affected *Time* editors for several more months, a period when the American death toll escalated dramatically and the presence of northern communist soldiers in the south increased substantially. "Communist main force units, physically bruised, psychologically hurting and short of supplies because of the bombings, have avoided large-scale pitched battles for three months," *Time* stated. Another article insisted, "The military situation in Viet Nam gave ample cause for confidence." The magazine refused to modify its positive outlook, partly because its senior corps of editors had risen through the ranks while the zealous anticommunist Henry Luce ran the Time-Life empire and partly because *Time*'s managing editor, Otto Fuerbringer, firmly believed the United States would win. Luce had let the managing editor exercise complete authority to shape news coverage.[25] "Top editors at *Time* had power," says former associate editor Ed Magnuson. "*Time* was launched as a magazine with a point of view and unlike general newspapers it always expressed opinions in those stories involving such basic issues as politics [and] national security." *Time* kept the faith as summer 1967 neared. "Forced to rationalize defeat after defeat in South Viet Nam, the Viet Cong and the North Vietnamese army have been desperately searching for a major military victory or psychological victory," the magazine argued in an article about a fierce and costly battle involving Marines near Khe Sanh, the site of a lengthy siege months later.[26]

Newsweek, from early 1966 to summer 1967, was mostly positive about

24. "Which Way?" *Time,* October 14, 1966, p. 31; "Why Ho Keeps Saying No," *Time,* November 11, 1966, pp. 30–31.

25. "Still Wishing, Still Nothing," *Time,* February 17, 1967, p. 18; "Pulling Together," *Time,* March 31, 1967, p. 17; Baughman, *Henry R. Luce,* 149–50, 186–88.

26. Magnuson interview; "Arrow of Death," *Time,* May 12, 1967, pp. 24–26.

the results of combat involving Americans against Vietcong and the People's Army, but regularly mentioned serious problems concerning the inability of American troops to establish security beyond the coastal enclaves and referred to the apparent ineffectiveness of efforts to reduce infiltration from northern Vietnam. Elliott, *Newsweek*'s editor at the time, later explained that although senior editors at the magazine wanted military intervention to succeed, they believed the methods were ineffective. Gradually, reports filed from Vietnam influenced *Newsweek* editors in New York. "As the war ground on, most of *Newsweek*'s correspondents came to agree that things were not going well," Elliott recalled.[27]

Newsweek mixed confidence with caution during the first year of intervention, warning that the United States risked repeating the futility a dozen years earlier of the war in Korea (June 1950 to July 1953). "The U.S. role in the Vietnamese war has already lasted longer than that [Korea], and by last week it was abundantly clear that the U.S. must go on a partial war footing to provide the men, money and materiel for a struggle that could go on with no end in sight," *Newsweek* wrote. The war in Korea had produced a stalemate on the battlefield for the final two years, mainly due to the participation of hundreds of thousands of soldiers from communist China. A massive attack by Chinese soldiers in November 1950 across the Yalu River, which separated China from Korea, imperiled the entire American and United Nations force for many weeks. Some senior assistants and advisors in the Johnson administration, and the president himself, feared direct military involvement in Vietnam by the Chinese, which did send thousands of laborers to northern Vietnam to rebuild bridges and roads targeted by American warplanes. A serious reaction by the Soviet Union also was possible. Johnson always emphasized the risk of provoking the Chinese and Russians. "The north was a minor power, but LBJ never stopped thinking about its two superpower sponsors," Rostow said. Some strategists believed that intervention by China would produce a stalemate in Vietnam. Others believed the topography of Vietnam and the vast areas of remote, inaccessible forests and mountains made it impossible to defeat the guerrillas.[28]

Newsweek referred to the Korean War during the first year of intervention

27. Elliott, *World of Oz*, 90–91, 111.
28. "New and Serious Decisions," *Newsweek*, July 26, 1965, p. 19; Rostow interview; Robert Buzzanco, *Masters of War: Military Dissent and Politics in the Vietnam Era*, 159–60; Levine, *Struggle for Southeast Asia*, 82.

in Vietnam more than did the other newsmagazines. Seven editions of *Newsweek* contained commentary that likened Vietnam to Korea, compared to three editions of *Time* and two of *U.S. News & World Report*.[29] A *Newsweek* article two weeks after the first deployment of American combat troops to Vietnam reported that planners had prepared a response should northern Vietnam send its soldiers south across the demilitarized zone, just as northern Korea had done. "Then, the word is, the U.S. is prepared to send in 250,000 men to hold the line at the 17th parallel," the magazine stated. "Which, of course would mean another Korea—at least." In July, *Newsweek* reported the existence of a contingency plan to place "between 250,000 and 320,000 men, to hold a line of defense at the 17th parallel" if China intervened.[30] Realistically, the 17th parallel that separated northern and southern Vietnam had no resemblance to the 38th parallel dividing northern and southern Korea. The demilitarized zone partitioning Vietnam ended on the west at the border with Laos, a neutral country with mountainous and heavily forested terrain conducive to infiltration; the zone in Korea passed through a peninsula and ended on the west at the Yellow Sea, an expanse of water easy to monitor.

The cautionary tone in *Newsweek* reflected profound concern among some of the Army's emeritus generals regarding combat on the mainland of Asia. James Gavin, Matthew Ridgway, and Maxwell Taylor, each a distinguished commander and esteemed tactician with experience in World War II and Korea, at various times advised against deploying infantry troops to Vietnam.[31] *Newsweek* referred to a warning by Gavin in a *Harper's* article that "a land war in Asia" must be avoided. *U.S. News & World Report* also cited the general's warning. *Newsweek* had mentioned the phobia about a "land war in Asia" when American troops first ventured beyond the enclaves during sum-

29. *Newsweek:* "Marines and a Message," March 22, 1965, pp. 37–38; "Anxious Days," June 21, 1965, p. 44; "New and Serious Decisions," July 26, 1965, p. 19; "Strictly Military," August 16, 1965, pp. 30–32; "Fury at Ia Drang: Now the Regulars," November 29, 1965, p. 21; "Whirling Dervishes," December 13, 1965, p. 28; "Voices of Dissent," January 31, 1966, p. 34. *Time:* "Status & Strategy," August 6, 1965, pp. 28–30; "The Face of Victory," August 27, 1965, pp. 18–19; "Winning Instead of Wishing," November 5, 1965, p. 31. *U.S. News & World Report:* "What It Would Take to Turn the Tide in Vietnam," July 12, 1965, pp. 46–48; "Vietnam War's New Strategy—Will It Work?" February 21, 1966, pp. 31–38.

30. "Marines and a Message," *Newsweek*, March 22, 1965, p. 38; "New and Serious Decisions," *Newsweek*, July 26, 1965, p. 19.

31. *Pentagon Papers*, 3:16–17; Karnow, *Vietnam*, 19, 561.

mer 1965. "For inch by inch, the war in Vietnam is becoming what many Americans have dreaded ever since Korea: an American war on the mainland of Asia," the magazine stated. *Time,* however, used an analogy to the Korean War to dispel the notion that Vietnam would be another exercise in futility. *Time* praised the battlefield performance of American troops, a demonstration not only of their courage but evidence that "smashed also was the myth that the U.S. can't fight on land in Asia."[32]

Although it regarded intervention in Vietnam warily, *Newsweek* accurately summarized the situation early in 1966. "[T]here have been some notable successes and the military picture in Vietnam today is hardly as ominous as some home-front warriors insist," it remarked. "Although Saigon still fully controls only a quarter of the country, the Viet Cong and the North Vietnamese regulars have not launched a major main-force attack since the first of the year." *Newsweek* assured its readers that artillery, helicopters, and infantry tactics had made a difference. "It was no longer simply a guerrilla struggle fought on enemy terms," the magazine declared. "It was a brand-new war. Long-time skeptics . . . have come to be cautiously optimistic about the purely military prospects." Several months later, an article described a scene in a secure area: "The province's fields are once again green with growing rice, houses have been built and new schools, bridges and roads have replaced those blown up by the Viet Cong." An upbeat year-end review informed readers about the progress some 360,000 troops had attained. It had been "exactly one year since Communist forces last felt willing—or able—to mount a major offensive action," *Newsweek* reported. "It is now possible to discern a strategic pattern to the war. And in a strictly military sense, that pattern is remarkably favorable to the U.S."[33]

Newsweek, however, exhibited pessimism when it looked beyond the battlefield: "American combat troops have not yet fully adjusted to the problems of fighting a paramilitary war with heavy political overtones." *Time* mentioned this same flaw nine months later. *Newsweek* again referred to the

32. "Voices of Dissent," *Newsweek,* January 31, 1966, p. 34; "Should U.S. Fight Land War in Asia?" *U.S. News & World Report,* April 25, 1966, p. 21; "Anxious Days," *Newsweek,* June 21, 1965, p. 44; "Strictly Military," *Newsweek,* August 16, 1965, p. 30; "The Face of Victory," *Time,* August 27, 1965, pp. 18–19.

33. *Newsweek:* "After the Pause: Motion or Progress?" February 14, 1966, p. 21; "The Military—'We Can Win It,'" April 18, 1966, pp. 28–31; "How Goes Pacification?" September 19, 1966, p. 63; "The American Way of War," December 5, 1966, p. 49.

ideological aspect of the war when it focused on the deployment of the Twenty-fifth Infantry Division and an infantry brigade to the Mekong Delta, a populous region where the bulk of the southern rice crop was grown. The magazine viewed the assignment of American troops to the delta as "a make-or-break test of whether U.S. troops and methods of warfare can be adapted to the essentially political task of winning the allegiance of village peasants." *Newsweek* edged into sarcastic disdain for the military's penchant for rosy analyses: "Down the sterile, echoing Pentagon corridors rumbled The Latest Word: Communist military strength in South Vietnam was continuing to diminish." The article then listed four news items about recent fierce combat and massive military operations against the Vietcong and People's Army, all of which indicated the strong presence of communists. "If enemy strength was indeed decreasing, that fact had not yet made much difference to the men on the sharp end of the war," *Newsweek* remarked.[34]

Near the start of summer 1967, at almost the same point that *Time* described the communists as desperate, *Newsweek* offered an opposite outlook: "The only hope of a peaceful solution now lies in endless months of battlefield attrition." But the attritional warfare strategy adopted by Westmoreland apparently had failed. *Newsweek* stated, "The U.S., however, will never attain its objectives in South Vietnam so long as infiltration from the north continues—and infiltration cannot be halted by bombing raids against the north." The magazine also issued an ambivalent evaluation of the person responsible for military operations in the south: "There are those who would contend that Westmoreland is something less than a brilliant strategist."[35]

U.S. News & World Report reported battlefield successes with the effusiveness of *Time* and judged war policy with the wariness of *Newsweek,* but differentiated itself from the other newsmagazines by harping on the rift between government policymakers and military leaders. Most articles presented the position of American headquarters staff in Saigon and senior officers at the Pentagon, specifically the Joint Chiefs of Staff. As the most militaristic and ultraconservative newsmagazine, *U.S. News & World Report* considered the military situation problematic because of indecision by civilians.

34. "After the Pause: Motion or Progress?" *Newsweek,* February 14, 1966, p. 20; "Wanted: More Men in Viet Nam," *Time,* November 18, 1966, p. 39; "World of Water," *Newsweek,* December 19, 1966, p. 56; "The Sharp End," *Newsweek,* November 28, 1966, p. 36.

35. *Newsweek:* "Escalation Again—By Both Sides," May 1, 1967, pp. 19–20; "How to End the Bombing and De-Escalate," May 15, 1967, p. 43; "The American Way of War," December 5, 1966, pp. 49–50.

U.S. News & World Report began its campaign of criticism a year after the military buildup began. "JCS [Joint Chiefs of Staff] wants military commanders in Vietnam to have more say-so, not tied by bonds of 'management directives' from inexperienced civilians in Washington," an article revealed, without naming its sources. The Johnson administration had indeed forced military planners to list potential targets for aerial bombardment in northern Vietnam, some of which the president and key policymakers would authorize, and to keep infantry operations within the borders of southern Vietnam. The military hierarchy sought unrestricted aerial attacks against the north and permission to pursue the enemy into Cambodia and Laos. "Military men in Vietnam, trained to win wars, want a more ambitious 'winning strategy,'" *U.S. News & World Report* told readers. "Increasingly, they find themselves out of harmony with the President and his advisers, calling the shots from 9,000 miles away."[36]

Johnson and McNamara gradually expanded the list of northern targets from bridges, highways, railroads, and warehouses. American warplanes bombed petroleum-storage sites, electric-power plants, and factories. *U.S. News & World Report* relayed reaction from anonymous military commanders who "insist[ed] the bombings came too late to do much good." An analysis by the CIA agreed with the military. Meanwhile, Westmoreland and military planners continued to lobby for faster deployment of combat troops and to increase the number beyond the 400,000 personnel privately promised by the Johnson administration. *U.S. News & World Report* stated that "demand is growing in Saigon for U.S. to get in with more of everything."[37]

Senior officers at the Pentagon made known their displeasure with the restrictions. A spate of articles appeared in July and August 1966 in *Newsweek*, *Time*, and *U.S. News & World Report* informing readers that 600,000 to 750,000 troops were necessary to win the war, which could last until the early 1970s—unless the policy of gradual escalation ended.[38] *U.S. News & World Report* warned later that failure to immediately deploy the additional

---

36. "Ahead in Vietnam: A Bloody Stalemate?" *U.S. News & World Report*, April 11, 1966, pp. 36–37; *Pentagon Papers*, 3:20, 71, 90, 408–17; "Ahead in Vietnam: A Bloody Stalemate?"

37. "Bigger Bombing: Where Will It Lead?" *U.S. News & World Report*, July 11, 1966, p. 31; *Pentagon Papers*, 3:20, 71, 90, 408–17; "What It Will Take to Win the War," *U.S. News & World Report*, August 22, 1966, p. 23.

38. "Is End of Vietnam War in Sight?" *U.S. News & World Report*, July 25, 1966, p. 28; "The Prospect Ahead," *Time*, August 19, 1966, p. 17; "Numbers Game," *Newsweek*, August 22, 1966, pp. 64–67.

troops would "allow the war to drag along at whatever pace Hanoi chooses." Several weeks passed without any action from the Johnson administration. *U.S. News & World Report* predicted that Westmoreland would have no choice but to "start leveling off" military operations and reduce "plans for seeking out organized Communist forces and annihilating them." Finally, according to the magazine, "A new antiguerrilla campaign, long-planned and about to be launched, will be slowed down by the shortage of U.S. troops for that drive." In summer 1967, *U.S. News & World Report* made the same argument. "The U.S. has not been able to mount a major offensive operation since Junction City last February," an article asserted. "At least one big operation planned for the spring was postponed because there were not enough troops available."[39]

Military headquarters in Saigon supplied statistical data to prove that the situation favored the United States. Without any territorial objectives in southern Vietnam to mark actual progress, such as the advance of a battlefront or the permanent seizure of a guerrilla stronghold, the military command in Saigon relied on statistics to substantiate its claims of success. Attritional warfare depended on reducing the infiltration rate, depleting the Vietcong and People's Army units, and capturing sizable caches of supplies and weaponry. The military command had no trouble verifying the number of ammunition boxes, rifles, and rice sacks hauled away by American troops, but tallying corpses proved problematic. The death toll for guerrillas supposedly was from an actual count of corpses, a procedure called a body count. Aerial bombardment of the trail network through Laos into southern Vietnam certainly killed many guerrillas, but a body count could not be obtained in enemy-controlled areas. Bombs dropped by B-52s and other warplanes undoubtedly killed many guerrillas, too, but an accurate body count could not be made from dismembered and shredded corpses. Infantry combat offered more opportunity for obtaining body counts, but American troops usually lacked the time or the incentive to thoroughly search the forests, hills, ravines, and swamps where bodies lay. Almost every encounter with the enemy produced many more dead guerrillas than Americans, according to official reports, and in the relatively few major battles guerrillas

---

39. *U.S. News & World Report:* "What McNamara Learned in Vietnam," October 24, 1966, 41; "New Plan for Vietnam War," November 7, 1966, 31–33; "Stalled War: Now What?" July 17, 1967, p. 25.

were killed at a rate several times higher than the American killed-in-action figure. For many months, journalists merely relayed the enemy casualty figures given to them.[40]

Until summer 1966, the newsmagazines routinely reported enemy casualty figures without qualification. Soon enough, though, correspondents and other journalists learned from personal observation or from military sources that the "body counts" were estimates based on extrapolation from known dead or simply guesswork. *Newsweek* signaled its suspicions by occasionally using "claimed" to qualify an enemy death toll or a phrase like "officers reported they had counted" so many enemy dead. *Time* used qualifying terms less often, but employed phrases like "counted 371 Communist dead" and "actual body count" when it wanted to highlight the death toll.[41] Distrust of body-count statistics extended to the Pentagon. An internal study by Defense Department analysts of enemy casualty figures for 1966 revealed a startling discrepancy with the total reported by Military Assistance Command in Saigon. Staff officers there had submitted a total death count of almost 55,000 guerrillas for the year, but analysts from the Pentagon interviewed numerous infantry officers about the individual body-count reports they had filed and discovered that the actual total was 19,500 dead. Obviously, body-count reports had inflated as the numbers went up the chain of command from platoon to company to battalion to brigade and higher.[42]

Statistical data fueled strategic planning for Vietnam. To succeed, attritional warfare required the steady depletion of enemy personnel. Official assessments of the overall military situation relied on sets of numbers for various categories. Sources fed information to newsmagazine correspondents in Saigon and Washington based on the data, which influenced commentary on the military situation in Vietnam. The conflict over Vietnam policy among analysts, planners, policymakers, and the military hierarchy worsened during winter 1966–1967. The military situation edged toward instability, with

---

40. Kinnard, *War Managers,* 70–75, and Maclear, *Ten Thousand Day War,* 164, explain the reliance on statistical data, including body counts. The general literature of the Vietnam War, including memoirs and military history, is replete with examples of factors affecting the body count.

41. "U.S. Dilemma: 'If Bomb It Must,' " *Newsweek,* May 29, 1967, p. 27; "Barring the Door," *Newsweek,* June 27, 1966, p. 42; "The Light that Failed," *Time,* June 10, 1966, p. 31; "The Battle for Hamburger Hill," *Time,* May 30, 1969, p. 27.

42. Hammond, *The Military and the Media, 1962–1968,* 317–18.

American units seemingly dominant for weeks on end, only to have enemy units resume the offensive. Infiltration from northern Vietnam accelerated rather than abated. Attempts to arrange peace negotiations failed.[43] Defense Department analysts and planners wondered if military intervention could subdue the insurgency.

McNamara and Johnson had not expected Westmoreland to keep raising the number of troops needed in Vietnam. By winter 1966–1967, Westmoreland was recommending 500,000-plus troops and later would ask for 600,000. Neither number promised a shorter war, however, with intervention forecast to last until the early 1970s. McNamara, who employed statistics for all major decisions, also felt aerial bombardment had failed. Most civilians and military personnel responsible for evaluating the overall situation in Vietnam distrusted the statistical data, which added to their uncertainty. *Newsweek* identified one concern: "One disheartening fact is that, after nine months of major American operations in Vietnam, there are now an estimated 240,000 Viet Cong and North Vietnamese in the field—more than when the U.S. assumed its combat role."[44]

Specter of Stalemate

A dozen years separated the Korean War from the Vietnam War, but Americans' memory of prolonged, inconclusive warfare in Korea affected government policy, military strategy, and public opinion from the instant a Marine Corps brigade deployed to southern Vietnam in March 1965.[45] By midsummer 1967, with thousands of troops dead and military progress uncertain, articles appearing first in *U.S. News & World Report,* then *Newsweek,* and finally *Time* had described the Vietnam War as a stalemate. *U.S. News & World Report,* a persistent critic of Johnson's policy of gradual military escalation and restrictions on targets in northern Vietnam, had stated in several articles that all evidence pointed to a battlefield stalemate. *Newsweek,* a critic of American military methods, alluded to the repetitive cycle of attack and counterattack. *Time,* an ardent supporter of war policy, reluctantly conceded that the

43. Berman, *Lyndon Johnson's War,* 22–23; Herring, *America's Longest War,* 175–79.
44. Kinnard, *War Managers,* 70–72; Krepinevich, *Army and Vietnam,* 184–86; "The Draft: The Unjust vs. the Unwilling," *Newsweek,* April 11, 1966, p. 31.
45. Kathleen J. Turner, *Lyndon Johnson's Dual War: Vietnam and the Press,* 147; Hunt, *Lyndon Johnson's War,* 69, 101; Robert Buzzanco, "The American Military's Rationale against the Vietnam War," 563–69.

communists controlled most of the countryside. All told, the newsmagazines referred to a stalemate in seventeen articles from April 1966 through August 1967.[46] To policymakers and presidential advisors already worried about an erosion of political support for military intervention, these articles potentially associated Vietnam with the Korean War, which had ended in a two-year battlefield stalemate. Politicians, policymakers, and military leaders regarded the Korean War as a disastrous experience for the United States, and they believed the public wished to avoid another war like it.

In mid-July, President Johnson, referring to "the stalemate creature," arranged a special news conference at the White House where General Westmoreland, who was in Washington for consultation with policymakers, emphatically announced that "stalemate is a complete fiction" and "completely unrealistic."[47] The news conference was the first held by Johnson in the private residential area of the White House, thus indicating the priority he gave to the issue. Three weeks later Johnson told a newspaper columnist, "There is no truth in the stalemate theory."[48] That same week, however, the *New York Times* published a front-page analysis, which continued inside on a full page, describing the situation in Vietnam as a stalemate.[49] Because the *New York Times* often set the agenda for network television news programs and many newspapers, its focus on the stalemate theme already presented by *Newsweek, Time,* and *U.S. News & World Report* made it more likely that news programs on ABC, CBS, and NBC would join the chorus.[50] This prospect

---

46. *U.S. News & World Report* first called the war a "stalemate" on April 11, 1966, and it repeated that description on June 27, 1966, and on January 9, May 1, May 15, July 17, and July 31 of 1967. *Newsweek* first described a stalemate situation on December 19, 1966, and then used similar descriptions for the military situation in 1967 editions of May 8, July 10, July 17, August 14, and September 4. *Time* cited a stalemate scenario on June 30, 1967, and similarly described the military situation on July 14, August 18, and August 25 of the same year.

47. Max Frankel, "Generals Agree with President on Build-up Issue," *New York Times,* July 14, 1967, sec. 1, p. 1; Associated Press, "LBJ Displays 'Unity' over Viet Buildup," *Denver Post,* July 14, 1967, sec. 1, p. 1.

48. President Johnson interview with Peter Lisagor, Tom Johnson's notes of meetings, August 4, 1967, box 1, LBJ Library.

49. R. W. Apple, "Vietnam: Signs of Stalemate," *New York Times,* August 7, 1967, sec. 1, p. 1.

50. Gans, *Deciding What's News,* 180, considers the *New York Times* the "standard setter" for the national news media, including the newsmagazines and television networks. Editors and producers often considered news coverage and placement in the *New York Times* verification of the importance of an event or issue.

distressed Johnson, to whom "stalemate [was] a fighting word."[51] The stalemate analogy also angered Rostow. "Vietnam was not Korea," Rostow said. "Our forces dominated the battlefield. 'Stalemate' applies to military forces in fixed positions, unable to advance either way. The Vietnam situation was an erroneous perception concerning a stalemate."[52]

Vietnam policy depended on further faith and patience of the American people while 470,000 troops in southern Vietnam sought the elusive goal of military superiority at the end of summer 1967. To refute the stalemate theme, the president authorized Rostow to reveal to certain journalists information from secret and confidential documents at the Department of Defense and CIA that listed statistics on tonnage of food, supplies, and weapons captured or destroyed, estimated the number of enemy killed, and predicted the gradual weakening of communist control in the countryside.[53] "LBJ just didn't believe our side of the story was getting out," Rostow said, explaining the disclosure of intelligence data intended to quantify progress. Also, the president met personally with journalists to argue his case, including fourteen meetings with newsmagazine correspondents and editors. Johnson invited personnel from *Newsweek, Time,* and *U.S. News & World Report* to the Oval Office and Rose Garden of the White House and to his ranch in Texas to persuade them the war was being won.[54] The entire effort coordinated by Rostow from midsummer through autumn 1967 amounted to a propaganda campaign directed at the newsmagazines and television network news programs, which had begun to adopt a more pessimistic tone about the Vietnam War.

Public proclamations of optimism contrasted with private discussions where candor permitted use of the word *stalemate*.[55] Newsmagazine judgments on

---

51. Apple, "Vietnam: Signs of Stalemate," sec. 1, p. 14.
52. Rostow interview.
53. National security files, Vietnam country file, box 98, and Rostow, box 6, LBJ Library. Both sources contain many documents from the CIA and Defense Department for background briefings to correspondents.
54. Rostow interview; president's appointments file, July–November 1967, LBJ Library; Rostow to White House staff, memo, August 9, 1967, national security files, Vietnam country file, box 7, LBJ Library. Johnson met with Mel Elfin, Kenneth Crawford, and Charles Roberts from *Newsweek;* Otto Fuerbringer, Hugh Sidey, and John Steele from *Time;* and John Sutherland from *U.S. News & World Report* (president's diary and diary backup log, boxes 71–75 and 83, LBJ Library).
55. Berman, *Lyndon Johnson's War,* 13–14.

the military situation accurately reflected the ongoing dispute within the bureaucracy. In late 1966, a memo to McNamara from an aide described "an escalating military stalemate" in Vietnam.[56] A report by the Joint Chiefs of Staff in May 1967 blamed the incremental troop buildup and restrictions on Operation Rolling Thunder, the designation for bombardment of northern Vietnam, for prolonging the war. A memo to Johnson from McNamara argued that the war could not be won, and asked the president to consider scaling back military operations.[57]

The word *stalemate,* or its equivalent, appeared occasionally in the newsmagazines by spring 1967. *U.S. News & World Report,* clearly the voice of the hard-liners, published seven articles focused on the stalemate theme from spring 1966 to midsummer 1967, several with provocative headlines: "Ahead in Vietnam: A Bloody Stalemate?" "Has U.S. Missed the Boat in Vietnam?" "Bigger War in the New Year—And No End in Sight"; "Stalled War: Now What?" "The Truth about War in Vietnam."[58] *Newsweek* raised the specter in late 1966 with a reference to persistent resistance by the Vietcong in the Mekong Delta: "As a result, the military situation was, at best, a stalemate." Later *Newsweek* articles referred to "the treadmill melancholy of the Vietnamese war," asserted that intervention had "produced only a standoff," and stated that "U.S. ground forces were stalled." A critique of the military situation led to a negative conclusion. "The Johnsonian strategy remained simply more of the same in the conviction that Hanoi's threshold of pain would inevitably be crossed," *Newsweek* wrote. "As a thesis, it seemed logical enough, but it had yet to prove its worth as a strategy."[59] *Time,* the staunchest supporter of Vietnam policy, abruptly discarded its optimistic tone during summer 1967, publishing four articles on the apparent stalemate. The magazine published the pessimistic assessments after the editor-in-chief at Time-Life,

---

56. *Pentagon Papers,* 4:47.
57. Berman, *Lyndon Johnson's War,* 11, 50–51.
58. *U.S. News & World Report* "stalemate" articles: "Ahead in Vietnam: A Bloody Stalemate?" April 11, 1966, pp. 36–37; "Has U.S. Missed the Boat in Vietnam?" June 27, 1966, p. 38; "Bigger War in the New Year—And No End in Sight," January 9, 1967, pp. 26–27; "Decisive Battles Near in Vietnam War?" May 1, 1967, p. 52; "Reds' Plan: Fight while Talking," May 15, 1967, p. 8; "Stalled War: Now What?" July 17, 1967, pp. 25–28; "The Truth about War in Vietnam," July 31, 1967, pp. 40–43.
59. *Newsweek:* "World of Water," December 19, 1966, p. 56; "A Nation at Odds," July 10, 1967, p. 19; "Now the Ninth Coming," July 17, 1967, p. 21; "The President in Trouble," September 4, 1967, p. 17; "The Home Front," May 8, 1967, p. 36.

Hedley Donovan, reprimanded *Time* managing editor Fuerbringer for excessive optimism. "Occasionally a kind of cheerleader tone turns up in our treatment of the war and Washington decisions about the war," Donovan wrote. "The effect is to make us sound like uncritical champions of an official line rather than thoughtful, independent supporters of a policy which, God knows, has its agonizing aspects."[60] Donovan, however, waited until Fuerbringer was on vacation in midsummer 1967 to mandate a different tone for *Time*.

Jason McManus, then an associate editor at *Time*, remembers the transformation: "The change was from optimism that the war could be won and enthusiasm for the war to increasing skepticism." McManus, whose job was to write articles for the World section, received an assignment in late July from Donovan, who substituted for Fuerbringer during vacations. Donovan wanted an article that would explain the problems with ARVN. This was *Time*'s first full recognition of serious flaws affecting the southern army: low morale, poor leadership, uneven quality, and reluctance to fight. "I was the one asked by Donovan to do the story, to start turning the battleship," McManus says. "I think in a way I was chosen for that because of my purity. I was not tainted by any of the posturing so many at the magazine had put forth on the war."[61]

Other articles mentioned the lack of real progress. *Time* remarked on the stalemate in the countryside where although "the V.C. may not be winning control of more villages, they are not losing many either." Another article stated, "More than anything else, the current talk of stalemate in Viet Nam stems from the disparity in the progress of the two wars," and explained that the war on the battlefield seemed successful while the war to eliminate Vietcong control of the countryside did not. "In recent months, it has become apparent that the war in Viet Nam is not going entirely according to the U.S. scenario for 1967," another article commented. "Part of the new unease about the state of the war stems from the fact that, for all the hard fighting over the past year, Communist forces in South Viet Nam are as strong as they were a year ago, if not stronger." *Time* doubted whether several important policy goals, including political stability, could be attained. "All of these

---

60. Donovan, *Right Places, Right Times*, 360.
61. McManus interview. The article McManus wrote was "Building Up the ARVN," *Time*, August 4, 1967, pp. 24–25.

aims require a continuing U.S. momentum of success on the battlefields, and of late that momentum unfortunately has flagged," it declared. Another article reported, "[N]o one envisions any dramatic breakthrough in the military balance very soon."[62]

Publication of the stalemate theme in *Newsweek, Time,* and *U.S. News & World Report* annoyed Rostow and Johnson. Their information from the embassy in Saigon, Westmoreland, and intelligence analyses convinced them the war could be won because the guerrillas had suffered enormous casualties and aerial bombardment had hampered infiltration. In July, Johnson and Rostow attended a special meeting on the military situation in Vietnam with McNamara, Rusk, and Richard Helms, the CIA director. In a candid discussion, they reviewed political tension within the Saigon leadership, widespread corruption in the southern government, a request by Westmoreland for more troops, a request by the Joint Chiefs of Staff to lift restrictions on Operation Rolling Thunder, the slow pace of the pacification program, and increasingly negative news coverage. "There is not a military stalemate," McNamara told the participants.[63]

After the meeting, Rostow suggested to Johnson the creation of a coordinated campaign to generate positive news coverage. The president and Rostow believed that the news media, particularly the newsmagazines, distorted the facts. They considered the newsmagazine coverage detrimental to their policy, and they worried that it might affect congressional and public support. Also, the *New York Times* began to develop the stalemate theme in early August. The television network news programs more often portrayed the military situation negatively, too. "If you tell people something often enough, they will begin to accept it as fact even though it isn't the situation," Rostow remembered years later. "They were creating doubt."[64]

The stalemate theme provoked a reaction from the Johnson administration

62. *Time:* "Reminiscence on a River," June 30, 1967, p. 28; "The Organization Man," August 25, 1967, p. 20; "Taking Stock," July 14, 1967, p. 20; "The Pressures Mount," August 18, 1967, pp. 12–13.
63. McNamara report on trip to Vietnam, July 12, 1967, Tom Johnson's notes of meetings, box 1, LBJ Library. This 16-page summary contains numerous quotations from McNamara but none from the other participants.
64. Rostow interview; Apple, "Vietnam: Signs of Stalemate," *New York Times,* August 7, 1967. Rostow thought the television network news programs set the media agenda. Rostow also considered *Newsweek* "a liberal journal" while *U.S. News & World Report* "spoke for the very conservative elements," and *Time* had "abandoned the war" (Rostow interview).

because it coincided with a momentous shift in public perception about the Vietnam War during summer 1967. The Gallup Poll asked participants in nationwide surveys for May, July, and October, "Do you think the United States made a mistake sending troops to fight in Vietnam?" In May, 37 percent of respondents answered yes and 50 percent no; in July, 41 percent answered yes and 48 percent no; in October, 46 percent answered yes and 44 percent no—the first plurality of "yes" responses since Gallup initially asked the question two years earlier. Americans were losing confidence. (Immediately after the Tet 1968 communist offensive, the Gallup Poll reported that 48 percent of respondents answered yes and 41 percent no to the same question.)[65] The pessimism was understandable that summer. The death toll of Americans in Vietnam often exceeded 200 a week, the Selective Service System conscripted 20,000 young men for military service each month, and Congress debated an income tax surcharge of 6 percent to finance the war.

To restore public confidence in Vietnam policy, Rostow directed other presidential aides to obtain analyses and reports from authoritative sources, including the CIA and Defense Intelligence Agency. Information from these sources then would be given to certain journalists. This violated official procedures, but Rostow hoped journalists would find the information credible. "Yes, we realized that to make our case we had to provide persuasive data," Rostow explained. "The press tended to focus only on the most visible aspects of the war and on discrete incidents. So much of what was being done was not visible, and the totality of the situation had to be shown." The effort involved several staff assistants, speechwriters, researchers, and secretaries, all assigned to the Vietnam Information Group, created in August 1967. Among the duties envisioned for the propagandists was to "[p]rovide background material to leak to correspondents regularly, with the President's approval."[66] Rostow, assisted by Robert Kintner, the presidential communications policy advisor, instructed other presidential assistants to meet with correspondents from *Newsweek, Time,* and *U.S. News & World Report* to furnish them with information that proved the United States was winning the war.[67] The campaign lasted until the end of 1967.

65. George H. Gallup, *The Gallup Poll: Public Opinion, 1935–1971.*
66. Rostow interview; George Christian to President Johnson, memorandum, August 22, 1967, and Tom Johnson to George Christian, memorandum, August 15, 1967, White House confidential file, FG 105, box 24, LBJ Library.
67. Rostow and Christian interviews. Christian, although not directly involved with the

Documents made available to newsmagazine correspondents included a specially commissioned analysis from the CIA. The analysis cited prisoner-interrogation reports, reconnaissance photographs, captured files from Vietcong and People's Army units, an evaluation of the pacification program, and a summary of political factionalism in southern Vietnam. A separate section detailed the damage done by Operation Rolling Thunder to northern Vietnam's economy, transportation system, and military facilities. "Allied forces have reversed the military situation since 1965 and smashed Communist hopes of a military victory," the analysis stated.[68] The upbeat analysis omitted any reference to the agency's conclusion that aerial bombardment had not substantially affected the capability of northern Vietnam to support warfare in the south, a judgment disclosed several years later in the Pentagon Papers, a secret study of policy decisions. Another document summarized aerial bombardment statistics relating to tonnage, targets, and damage assessments.[69] Several documents concerned rural hamlet security data for the pacification program. Data ranked thousands of hamlets according to their security status, from secure to contested to Vietcong-controlled. The documents showed progress, reporting that 67 percent of the southern population resided in secure areas and 42 percent of the hamlets were under government control; both percentages represented increases by half or better since 1965.[70]

Rostow wrote long memos from classified information provided to him as national security advisor and from personal contacts with military commanders. He distributed these memos to the president and presidential assistants for background briefings to journalists. Rostow emphasized some basic points: the accuracy of aerial bombardment; the extreme difficulty faced by guerrillas on infiltration routes; the large number of northern Vietnamese assigned to repair railroad tracks, roads, and bridges damaged or destroyed by bombardment; the amount of aid to northern Vietnam from the Soviet Union; the

---

campaign, remembered that several political assistants and policymakers who had regular contacts with journalists passed the information along.

68. Memorandum for the President, "A Record of Achievements in Vietnam," Central Intelligence Agency, September 9, 1967, national security files, Rostow file, box 6, LBJ Library.

69. Declassified secret report, undated, national security files, Vietnam country file, box 99, LBJ Library.

70. Hamlet Evaluation Security, November 30, 1967, White House central files, office files, Fred Panzer, box 427, LBJ Library.

presence of sanctuary areas in Cambodia and alternative infiltration routes there; improvements in the performance of the southern army; and statistical data on supplies and vehicles destroyed by bombardment.[71]

Rostow, however, selectively withheld information which confirmed suspicions that attritional warfare had failed. Journalists were not told about an estimate from the Military Assistance Command that placed the number of Vietcong and People's Army personnel in the south at 485,000, a dramatic rise from the estimated 300,000 personnel in 1966. The increase resulted from a bureaucratic triumph by the CIA, which insisted the order of battle must include Vietcong self-defense militia and political cadres because these guerrillas constituted a paramilitary force.[72] Rostow and Westmoreland realized the new order of battle would cause an uproar in Congress and the news media. They also doubted whether the rationale for previously excluding militia and cadres, which related to their defensive roles, should be acknowledged. "Danger is press will latch on to previous underestimate and revive credibility gap talk," Rostow informed the president, recommending that Westmoreland insert the order-of-battle statistics in the annual year-end review to lessen its impact.[73]

Some newsmagazine articles relayed the information supplied by Rostow and other presidential assistants. *Time* used the hamlet security data for an article on the apparently demonstrable success of the pacification program. It also presented the case that casualties would inevitably weaken the Vietcong and People's Army, making it possible for the southern army to handle primary responsibility for security in populated areas. *U.S. News & World Report* forthrightly informed readers about the source of its information, and added an advisory. "After months of stalemate and gloom, American officials are pouring out a flood of good news about Vietnam," an article noted. "Many Americans, misled by overly optimistic reports in the past, tend to be wary of accepting the latest information at face value." The magazine then credited search-and-destroy/sweep operations with forcing guerrillas to reduce their attacks in the central highlands and I Corps. Another article offered the conclusion that attritional warfare probably would succeed. "The

---

71. Memoranda from Rostow dated October 18, 1967, November 11, 1967, and November 27, 1967, national security files, Rostow file, box 6, LBJ Library.

72. Berman, *Lyndon Johnson's War*, 32–33.

73. Rostow to president, memo, November 21, 1967, national security files, Rostow file, box 1, LBJ Library.

way things are going, it will take 18 months to two years to subdue effectively the Communist war machine," *U.S. News & World Report* commented. *Newsweek,* like *Time,* accepted the argument regarding better security in the hamlets; a year-end review of the five military regions in southern Vietnam described military progress in four, with only the Mekong Delta region remaining impervious to American power.[74]

One consequence of the informational campaign during autumn 1967 was that attention was paid to Cambodia. Five newsmagazine articles featured pertinent details. "One development that increasingly troubles U.S. strategists is the supply line that the Communists have established through Cambodia to circumvent the dangerous U.S. bombings of the Ho Chi Minh Trail," *Time* reported in one of three articles it published about the neutral nation's role. "North Vietnamese and Red Chinese cargo ships are docking at the Cambodian port of Sihanoukville." *Newsweek* and *U.S. News & World Report* each carried one article with substantial details on Cambodia.[75] American troops would invade Cambodia in April 1970, igniting a wave of antiwar protests in the United States, which included the deaths of four students shot by National Guard soldiers at Kent State University in Ohio.

Despite the generous skepticism with which correspondents regarded information from the Johnson administration and military command, the release of classified information had an effect by the beginning of 1968. The newsmagazines began to accept the viewpoint that the Vietcong and People's Army had suffered horrendous casualties, a circumstance which would gradually deplete their ranks. When artillery shells blasted into the Marine base at Khe Sanh in January while thousands of People's Army soldiers besieged the garrison, thus inspiring immediate comparisons in the news media to the French defeat at Dien Bien Phu in 1954, the newsmagazines portrayed the intensifying combat as a prelude to a new phase of the war. "The ultimate aim of the new North Vietnamese aggressiveness may well be to put Hanoi

74. "Progress," *Time,* November 24, 1967, pp. 22–23; "Frontier Offensive," *Time,* December 22, 1967, pp. 15–16; " 'The Coin Has Flipped to Our Side,' " *U.S. News & World Report,* November 27, 1967, pp. 50–53; "As War Heats Up in Vietnam," *U.S. News & World Report,* January 8, 1968, p. 21; "How Goes the War?" *Newsweek,* January 1, 1968, pp. 17–26.

75. "Progress," *Time,* November 24, 1967, p. 23; "Frontier Offensive," *Time,* December 22, 1967, p. 16; "Rumblings on the Periphery," *Time,* January 5, 1968, p. 26; "Just a Baby Step," *Newsweek,* December 25, 1967, p. 38; "Cambodia—A Growing Base for Reds," *U.S. News & World Report,* December 11, 1967, p. 62.

in a more favorable position when it decides to negotiate," *Newsweek* stated. *U.S. News & World Report* decided that a series of battalion-size attacks on American outposts in mountainous terrain signaled desperation: "There is good reason to believe, as 1968 starts, that this year really is going to see the beginning of the end of the war here in Vietnam."[76]

Tet 1968

A few hours before dawn on January 31, 1968, the communists launched a series of attacks across southern Vietnam. Tens of thousands of communist soldiers assaulted cities and towns, military installations, government buildings, petroleum-storage depots, railway stations, airports, and communications facilities. Most attacks lasted two or three days, while others went on for a week and some longer. Urban warfare raged in several major cities, of which Hué and Saigon endured the most destructive combat. Hué, the former royal capital, was the cultural center of the south, and enemy occupation of the city, including an ancient fortress called the Citadel, was a traumatic ordeal; a counterattack by Marines and southern army soldiers took four weeks to reclaim the city. Saigon, the largest southern city and the national capital, became the focus of news coverage for its symbolic value. Not only was the center of government embattled, but a Vietcong squad invaded the U.S. Embassy compound and attacked Military Assistance Command headquarters. For dozens of American journalists who had spent most of their time in Saigon without ever taking fire or had wandered around the countryside unsuccessfully seeking combat, Tet 1968 brought the war to the streets outside their hotels. Newspapers with reporters in Saigon printed eyewitness stories of brutal fighting, and television network news programs broadcast dramatic scenes. Americans had rarely seen such images. Approximately 1,600 Americans died during the four weeks of intense combat that encompassed the Tet 1968 offensive. "In a war that had produced too many surprises, none stunned harder than Tet," historian Michael Maclear states.[77]

---

76. "Drawing the Noose?" *Newsweek*, February 5, 1968, pp. 39–40; "How and When the War May End," *U.S. News & World Report*, January 8, 1968, p. 21.

77. Maclear, *Ten Thousand Day War*, 202–3. Details on the offensive come from ibid., 200–204; Spector, *After Tet*, 25; and Stanton, *American Army*, 223–38. The effect of Tet 1968 on public opinion is arguable, and abundant scholarship on it has produced an array of conclusions.

Because the nightly news programs on ABC, CBS, and NBC had already delivered the trauma of Tet 1968 to the American public, the weekly newsmagazines constructed articles combining combat drama with military and political perspective. Each magazine reported statements by Westmoreland concerning heavy enemy casualties and the lack of any permanent tactical advantage for the guerrillas—a "military failure," according to the general. Each magazine also noted the courageous performance by American troops, which repulsed the guerrillas and immediately counterattacked to recapture territory seized by the enemy. And each magazine delivered to readers a sense of the chaos and savagery experienced by combatants and civilians.

Newsmagazine coverage received scathing criticism for inaccuracy, bias, and incompleteness in a book, *Big Story*, by Peter Braestrup, the former journalist in Vietnam who reviewed media performance during Tet 1968. Braestrup argues that the newsmagazines devoted too much space to the fighting in Hué and Saigon, which accounted for only a small percentage of casualties and combat. He concludes that the newsmagazines refused to accept Westmoreland's viewpoint, that articles downplayed or ignored the significant losses suffered by the Vietcong, and that the newsmagazines failed to recognize the rapid disappearance of main-force units from the battlefield and the constant tactical operations by American and southern army units as proof that Tet 1968 was a defeat for the guerrillas.

Braestrup, however, exaggerates the alleged misdeeds of the newsmagazines. Newsmagazine coverage, when compared with the historical record of the Tet 1968 offensive, presented an accurate account of the event. The magazines offered positive and negative information on the enemy operation, its strategic consequences, and social impact. Articles noted counteroffensive operations when they happened. Commentary clearly indicated that the guerrillas had sustained tremendous casualties which would prevent them from maintaining military operations. Commentary also emphasized the political and psychological effects of Tet 1968 on Congress and the American people. Braestrup sees this commentary as evidence of bias, but the newsmagazines expressly interpreted events and issues from a particular editorial viewpoint—an established practice by the 1960s.[78]

Initial commentary by the newsmagazines considered Tet 1968 to be only a temporary setback. "Shocking as the week's developments were, they were

---

78. Braestrup, *Big Story*, 121, 136–42, 510–15.

not likely to alter the fundamental American commitment to see the war through to an honorable conclusion or change the Administration's policy," *Newsweek* decided, although it recognized the probable public response. "For not unreasonably, Americans were asking how such an unprecedented display of Communist strength was possible after more than two years of massive U.S. military involvement in Vietnam." *Time* assessed the destruction and casualties inflicted by the enemy, specifying substantial losses at military bases, airfields, and government sites. "In that sense, and because they continued after five days of fighting to hang on to some of their targets, the Communists undeniably won a victory of sorts," the magazine wrote. Yet the number of guerrillas killed illustrated the high price paid for a temporary triumph. "In the end, however, the Communist victory may be classed as Pyrrhic," *Time* stated, and then alluded to the reaction in Washington: "To a capital lulled by repeated boasts that the military war was being won, the strength and duration of the Red offensive came as an unpleasant, even humiliating surprise." *U.S. News & World Report* respected the military aspects of the attacks. "This Red drive—in its initial days, at least—stunned U.S. officials with its precision and intensity," an article declared. "Despite defeats of the past year, the Communists showed they do not lack manpower—dedicated and skilled."[79]

Commentary on the significance of Tet 1968 obviously incorporated resentment toward the Johnson administration for its apparent deceit during the recent propaganda campaign. Newsmagazine editors and correspondents, and other journalists, reminded readers about the claims of progress. *Newsweek* reported Westmoreland's estimate of 31,000 enemy dead, the accuracy of which was "a matter deeply doubted both in Saigon and Washington." The article reviewed the vulnerability to attack of every southern city and all military installations. "But even that fact, painful as it was, did not disturb the U.S. psyche as much as the puncturing of countless official claims, made over a period of years, that the U.S. was winning," *Newsweek* wrote. "Just how misguided those claims had been was demonstrated with each passing day last week." A subsequent edition prominently mentioned that "Pentagon analysts reportedly slashed the Saigon command's claim" of

---

79. "Hanoi Attacks," *Newsweek*, February 12, 1968, pp. 24, 30; "Double Trouble," *Time*, February 9, 1968, pp. 15–16; "The General's Gamble," *Time*, February 9, 1968, p. 22; "As Climax Mounts in Vietnam," *U.S. News & World Report*, February 12, 1968, p. 23.

31,000 enemy dead to just 7,000. "This was not a negligible figure, but when compared with the heavy losses in U.S. and South Vietnamese ranks, it hardly could be said to reflect a stunning Allied victory," *Newsweek* noted, referring to the insistence by Westmoreland and the Johnson administration that Tet 1968 signified a defeat for the guerrillas. *Time*, alluding to the order-of-battle report that Rostow and Westmoreland had delayed releasing, remarked, "Nearly all military experts agree Westmoreland has underestimated Communist strength—or overestimated the effectiveness of Viet Nam's regular army and paramilitary units." Another article directly criticized the generals and policymakers who had manipulated statistics. "At the uppermost levels of the Administration and the Pentagon, where optimism has been endemic from the war's earliest days, officials were still trying to find something comforting in the recent Communist Tet offensive despite all of the evidence to the contrary," *Time* wrote. "Such statements sounded absurd." More to the point, the stalemate had ended. "Undeniably, [the enemy] now has the initiative throughout South Viet Nam," *Time* declared. *U.S. News & World Report* took the opportunity to assess the capability of the guerrillas and to challenge the assertion that most southern Vietnamese lived in areas controlled by the government. "The nationwide co-ordination of Red forces was demonstrated," the magazine reported. "So was the willingness of people in the countryside and cities to help the guerrillas in case after case."[80]

Newsmagazine coverage of Tet 1968 disturbed the Johnson administration, particularly *Time*'s statements and a lengthy *U.S. News & World Report* article that blamed the president and his advisors for restraining the military. "LBJ paid too much heed to media reports," says George Reedy, the former presidential press secretary who became a political advisor to Johnson in 1968. "With all that was going on, on Capitol Hill, in Vietnam, he was distracted by media reports. But he would not let it go." The president arranged a special meeting with *Time*'s Donovan, Fuerbringer, and John Steele, the Washington bureau chief. Johnson lectured the three journalists on the positive aspects of Tet 1968. He told them the southern populace did not join the attacks, the Vietcong had withdrawn to the

---

80. "Man on the Spot," *Newsweek*, February 19, 1968, pp. 33–34; "The Second Wave?" *Newsweek*, February 26, 1968, p. 33; "Picking Up the Pieces," *Time*, February 16, 1968, p. 20; "Critical Difference," *Time*, March 1, 1968, pp. 11–13; "On the Defensive," *Time*, March 1, 1968, p. 19; "As Climax Mounts in Vietnam," *U.S. News & World Report*, February 12, 1968, p. 25.

countryside again, southern army soldiers had fought bravely, and the pacification program had survived.[81]

Rostow ordered a thorough refutation of a *U.S. News & World Report* article that squarely blamed the Johnson administration for the Tet offensive. The magazine had devoted several columns in a mid-February edition to an interview with an unidentified "military authority" who repeated all the complaints from the generals in the Pentagon that previous articles had reported, which included a too-gradual escalation of bombardment and restrictions on military operations. *U.S. News & World Report* blamed "civilian advisers," primarily McNamara, and Johnson for ignoring advice from the Joint Chiefs of Staff. "Today, there still is no apparent plan, strategy or grand design for winning the war," the magazine stated. The article encapsulated the dispute between the military hierarchy and the Johnson-McNamara policy faction that had simmered since summer 1965.[82] Rostow knew that the magazine spoke for and to ardent anticommunists and political ultraconservatives. A response was necessary.

The fifteen-page rebuttal commissioned by Rostow was accompanied by a three-page summary, and it went to the president for review. Each criticism made by *U.S. News & World Report* received a two-part response: the first from the Joint Chiefs of Staff, the second from civilian analysts at the Defense Department. In most cases, the Joint Chiefs of Staff responses stated that the military had accepted presidential restrictions on military operations without concern that these would compromise the accomplishment of strategic goals. However, a major problem confronted Johnson and Rostow because the comments from analysts confirmed some statements by *U.S. News & World Report,* namely that several presidential restrictions had hindered timely prosecution of the war. Specifically, analysts focused on the issues of immediate deployment of massive numbers of combat troops versus incremental deployment and immediately intensive aerial bombardment of northern Vietnam versus gradual escalation of bombardment. The analysts concluded that the incremental buildup and gradual escalation of bombardment had reduced the effectiveness of military operations. Rostow decided not to confront *U.S. News & World Report.* "In my judgment," Rostow wrote

81. Reedy interview; William J. Jorden to President Johnson, memorandum, March 25, 1968, president's appointment file, diary backup, box 93, LBJ Library.
82. "A Showdown in Vietnam?" *U.S. News & World Report,* February 19, 1968, pp. 35–38; Levine, *Struggle for Southeast Asia,* 105, 110–11.

at the bottom of the summary, "under no circumstances should we use the systems analysis (SA) comments. They would split rather than unite the government."[83]

Time and *U.S. News & World Report* soon returned to the theme that Tet 1968 had exposed the lack of security in the countryside while also proving to be a costly defeat for the guerrillas, in effect affirming Westmoreland's viewpoint. Both magazines suggested that neither side had won. "But the present circumstances—the mood of the people, the fear in the cities, the setbacks in the countryside—all show how far the war is from being won anyplace in Vietnam," *U.S. News & World Report* wrote. "They also show the tremendous aftermath of a Communist offensive that was, technically, a military failure." *Time* reported a counteroffensive near Saigon by American and southern army battalions, telling readers it meant the resumption of tactical operations only five weeks after the massive enemy assault. Another article described the dramatically altered character of combat. "In attempting to go back on the offensive, the allies have found that the war has become even more frustrating," *Time* commented. "There are fewer big battles, but many more small firefights; the enemy seems to have scattered across the length and breadth of the country." *Newsweek* retained its skepticism, saying the offensive "forced thousands of allied troops to withdraw to the defense of the cities and laid bare the South Vietnamese countryside to Communist encroachments." A sixteen-page analysis of the war by *Newsweek* in mid-March produced this conclusion: "It now appears that the U.S. must accept the fact that it will never be able to achieve decisive military superiority in Vietnam."[84]

In fact, all three newsmagazines had accurately summarized the situation. The Vietcong had withdrawn to remote sanctuaries to recover from heavy casualties suffered during Tet 1968, and communist strategists in the northern Democratic Republic of Vietnam had decided to revert to small-unit warfare. The Tet 1968 offensive was supposed to trigger an uprising in the south against the government in Saigon, but it did not. Also, every target seized by

---

83. Paul H. Nitze to Rostow, memorandum, February 13, 1968, national security files, Vietnam country file, box 78, LBJ Library.

84. "Big Setback for U.S. in Vietnam," *U.S. News & World Report*, March 4, 1968, p. 25; "On the Offensive," *Time*, March 22, 1968, p. 25; "Hard Months on the Ground," *Time*, April 5, 1968, p. 21; "The Tet Offensive: How They Did It," *Newsweek*, March 11, 1968, pp. 64–65; "The Military Dilemma," *Newsweek*, March 18, 1968, p. 27.

the communists eventually was retaken by American troops and the southern army. Policymakers at the Defense Department, State Department, and White House had realized, too, that military superiority was not possible. Johnson learned in March from a senior advisory group that further troop buildups and more intensive bombardment of the north would not drive the communists from the battlefield nor compel them to negotiate.[85]

Braestrup offers evidence in *Big Story* that the national news media uniformly portrayed Tet 1968 as a turning point in the war, and specifically accuses *Newsweek* of "keeping up with political fashion" by adopting an antiwar tone because of the Tet offensive. He cites a CBS special report on February 27 by Walter Cronkite, television's preeminent journalist, and an NBC documentary on March 10 as reasons for *Newsweek*'s subsequent essay advocating a pullback to coastal enclaves, cessation of bombardment of the north, and peace negotiations. Cronkite told millions of viewers, "To say that we are mired in stalemate seems the only realistic, yet unsatisfactory, conclusion," and he recommended negotiations with the communists. The NBC documentary informed an audience that continuing the war was futile. At this point, *Newsweek* suddenly gave up on the war, according to Braestrup.[86] But in fact, the essay in mid-March, "More of the Same Won't Do," reiterated themes already published by *Newsweek* beginning in 1966. The essay said attritional warfare and bombardment of northern Vietnam had not succeeded, and that the enemy's nationwide offensive had demonstrated the ineffectiveness of American military strategy. "Indeed, simply to do more of the same might lead to more of the same kind of failure," *Newsweek* argued. The phrase "more of the same" had appeared during 1967 in articles criticizing military methods and war policy. *Newsweek* endorsed a negotiated settlement, which reinforced its previous statements that the war essentially was a political struggle.[87] Braestrup and other scholars who conclude that Tet 1968 was a turning point for news media commentary on the Vietnam War have erroneously included the newsmagazines. *Newsweek, Time,* and *U.S. News & World Report* provided readers with critical commentary and negative judgments about Vietnam policy and the military situation in that country months before Tet 1968.

---

85. Herring, *America's Longest War,* 198–203; Jeffrey Kimball, *Nixon's Vietnam War,* 52–53.
86. Braestrup, *Big Story,* 493, 523–25. Cronkite is quoted in William M. Hammond, *Reporting Vietnam: Media and Military at War,* 121.
87. "More of the Same Won't Do," *Newsweek,* March 18, 1968, pp. 23, 31–34.

Recovery and Withdrawal

The Vietcong and People's Army withdrew to their sanctuary areas in the mountains and valleys of southern Vietnam, the jungle terrain of Laos, and the forests of Cambodia by autumn 1968. Sporadic combat involving mainforce guerrillas caused serious casualties for Army and Marine Corps units until summer 1969. For the next two years, the guerrillas engaged in harassment attacks rather than tactical operations. Tet 1968 had depleted their ranks, and it had led to peace negotiations. A military-political strategy directed by the Hanoi government dictated that Vietcong and People's Army units should pressure American troops and ARVN to compel negotiators for the United States to accept certain conditions favorable to the communists. Meanwhile, vast areas of the countryside came under the control of the Saigon government for the first time. Numerous villages in the Mekong Delta had no Vietcong cadres, and populated areas along the coast were occupied by the southern army. The railroad line from Saigon to Danang reopened. Convoys traveled roads at night near major cities. Still, enough guerrillas remained active to threaten pacification teams and government officials in the countryside.[88]

The newsmagazines maintained different perspectives on the military situation. *Newsweek* believed the reduction in combat served a political goal for the north rather than taking it as evidence of success for the small-unit warfare initiated by General Abrams, who had succeeded Westmoreland in July 1968. Abrams focused on protecting the major cities in southern Vietnam while dispatching small infantry units into the countryside to set ambushes and attack Vietcong cadres. "On the surface, this Communist retreat to the countryside may seem a triumph for Abrams's urban strategy," *Newsweek* commented. "But it may also pose grave dangers now that a cease-fire may be only months away—at which point the men who sit on a piece of land will effectively control it." *U.S. News & World Report* believed the tide had turned. "The absence of the Communist main forces makes it possible for U.S. and South Vietnamese troops, working in small units, to turn their full attention to combating the guerrillas and their political organizations," the magazine reported. *Time* described the progress, too, but remained dubious. "Except for the communists, America's worst enemy in Viet Nam has been American official optimism," an article observed before summarizing a statistical analysis

---

88. David W. P. Elliott, "Hanoi's Strategy in the Second Indochina War," 89–91; Spector, *After Tet,* 279–91.

that placed 92 percent of the southern populace in secure communities. "Some students of the war have long questioned the accuracy and significance of pacification statistics," *Time* wrote, an obvious allusion to the 1967 pacification statistics.[89]

The newsmagazines noticed the obvious improvement in the military situation in southern Vietnam from late 1968 through early 1971. The Vietcong and People's Army attacked American outposts less frequently, except for a brief offensive during early 1969. American casualties remained high until autumn 1969, but visible progress occurred. *Time* regained some of its optimism: "More roads are opened monthly: highway drives that would have been considered suicidal two years ago can now be made as a matter of course." *Newsweek*, which also cited safe travel and a governmental presence in rural villages, refused to concede that the long-term outlook had brightened because it found "no convincing evidence that the Viet Cong have suffered any real loss of military strength in the last few months."[90]

The military tried to persuade important editors that the tide had turned. Osborn Elliott, *Newsweek*'s top editor, toured Vietnam and received special treatment from the military, although he probably did not realize it. *Newsweek* correspondent Nicholas Horrock heard about it afterward. "I was doing a story about a helicopter outfit, just a short story about something they were doing that was different, and they had been in Cambodia and that sort of stuff," Horrock says. "So I get there and I'm interviewing, asking them questions, and one of these kids says, 'You know, you're the second guy from *Newsweek* who's been here. There was some guy and we had to go up and down Route One and just machine-gun everything for some guy from *Newsweek*.' It was Osborn Elliott, the editor. The Army wanted to take Oz out to show him someplace in the Delta and they didn't want anything to happen to him, so they sent this Cobra outfit [helicopter gunships] to shoot the hell out of everything, just to clear the way. That's what they did. They were very knowledgeable about rank, influence."[91]

With the military situation in southern Vietnam apparently stable, the

---

89. "A General without Illusions," *Newsweek*, October 21, 1968, pp. 48–49; "War's New Turn," *U.S. News & World Report*, November 25, 1968, pp. 33–34; "Viet Nam: The New, Underground Optimism," *Time*, December 12, 1969, pp. 14–15.

90. "Viet Nam: The New Underground Optimism," *Time*, December 12, 1969, pp. 14–15; "Easy Come . . ." *Newsweek*, March 3, 1969, p. 32.

91. Horrock interview.

Nixon administration decided in April 1970 to invade Cambodia to destroy the sanctuary areas. Unknown to the public and overlooked by the news media, the U.S. Air Force had extensively bombed eastern Cambodia for a year. The presence of many Vietcong and People's Army soldiers in sanctuary areas had resulted in pressure from the United States on the Cambodian government to send its army into the eastern region. A military coup ousted the royal leader of Cambodia in early 1970 and the army attempted to remove the communists, but a counterattack almost reached the capital city of Phnom Penh. At that point, American troops and ARVN invaded Cambodia. The invasion triggered antiwar protests in the United States, an outburst of congressional criticism, and editorial opposition in the news media.[92]

Only *U.S. News & World Report* endorsed the idea that the invasion of Cambodia would accomplish anything. An article thoroughly described the military operation, the destruction of supplies, and the swift movement by American troops through the eastern region. "Many Red units now are wandering leaderless throughout eastern Cambodia," the magazine declared. *Time* adopted a wait-and-see tone. "Despite talk of 'cleaning out' the sanctuaries, the tanks and heliborne troops had little chance of catching many of the 40,000 enemy troops (three-fourths of them North Vietnamese) who use the border areas for rest, refitting and training," the magazine reported. "They may well elude the current sweeps as they have avoided clearing operations in South Viet Nam for years." *Newsweek* regretted the expansion of the war. "The fallout on the Cambodian side has been nearly disastrous," it wrote. "The operation has actually intensified the North Vietnamese drive into western Cambodia."[93]

The withdrawal from Cambodia in July 1970 afforded an opportunity for analysis of the military situation. *Time,* although generally positive about the results, signaled its overall skepticism in the headline "Winding Up the Cambodian Hard Sell." The article acknowledged the seizure of numerous weapons and munitions, the destruction of depots, and the dispersion of the communists from their sanctuaries. "All this was done with fewer U.S. casualties than expected and with the most impressive show of competence yet

---

92. William Shawcross, "The Secret Bombing of Cambodia"; Henry Kissinger, "In Defense of the Nixon Policy."

93. "Smashing Red Bases," *U.S. News & World Report,* May 25, 1970, p. 32; "Raising the Stakes in Indochina," *Time,* May 11, 1970, pp. 15–16; "And So We Leave Cambodia," *Newsweek,* July 13, 1970, p. 29.

demonstrated by the South Vietnamese forces," *Time* noted. The magazine commented, though, that the Nixon administration had indulged in overblown rhetoric "to certify and canonize the success of the Cambodian venture." *Newsweek* recognized the damage done to the enemy and the surprise performance by ARVN, and judged the invasion a minor triumph. "Yet at best, [the results] would not necessarily mean that the incursions have altered the course of the war," it wrote.[94]

Cambodia was the last major military operation for American troops. Attention turned to the Vietnamization program, which was intended to improve the performance of the southern army. ARVN had functioned efficiently and bravely in Cambodia, but its record in southern Vietnam remained spotty. It could defend secure areas, but it could not sustain offensive operations. The steady withdrawal of American combat troops meant ARVN would soon stand alone on the battlefield. When it did operate on its own during the invasion of Laos in February 1971, its inability to capture important territorial objectives and its subsequent disastrous retreat illustrated the problem the Republic of Vietnam would have when American withdrawal was complete—which, observers thought, would probably be in summer 1973, if peace negotiations did not end the conflict sooner.[95]

All three newsmagazines dramatically reported the dismal performance by the southern army during the Laos invasion. They also questioned the purpose of the invasion, wondering why ARVN should risk its best troops in an operation that appeared doomed from the start.[96] *Newsweek* perceived even greater risks: "The U.S. seems to be slipping into a wide-ranging air war that could last almost indefinitely, adding steadily to the billions of dollars that have already trickled away, to the American death toll and to the roster of pilots held by the enemy." *Time*, too, questioned the wisdom of the Laos invasion: "Whatever the case, the operation suggested that in the process of re-

---

94. "Winding Up the Cambodian Hard Sell," *Time,* July 13, 1970, p. 7; "And So We Leave Cambodia," *Newsweek,* July 13, 1970, p. 22.

95. Kinnard, *War Managers,* 139–41; Maclear, *Ten Thousand Day War,* 182–83, 302–6.

96. "Laos: What Is the Objective?" *Newsweek,* March 8, 1971, pp. 14–15; "Slugging It Out," *Newsweek,* March 29, 1971, pp. 34–35; "Shadowboxing," *Time,* March 22, 1971, pp. 23–25; "Laos: The Bloody Battle to Get Out," *Time,* March 29, 1971, pp. 21–22; "Struggle in Laos—Biggest Test Yet for South Vietnam," *U.S. News & World Report,* March 15, 1971, pp. 20–21; "War Report: Upsurge of Optimism," *U.S. News & World Report,* March 22, 1971, p. 22.

treating from South Viet Nam, the U.S. was churning up all of Indochina even more thoroughly than it did when the big American buildup began half a decade ago."[97] The Nixon administration admonished the newsmagazines for their coverage. Presidential assistants communicated their displeasure. "The idea that the President is seeking a military victory in Indochina has again come to the fore with *Newsweek* being the most prominent source so far," a memo stated.[98] The White House contacted "friendly" newsmagazine correspondents, especially those with *U.S. News & World Report*, to urge positive commentary.[99]

The final assessments by the newsmagazines of the military situation in Vietnam appeared in 1972 after the Easter Offensive by the People's Army had routed ARVN in several provinces. The aftermath of the offensive was a steady deterioration of government control in areas deemed secure since 1969. *Time* voiced despair. "No one really expects Saigon to be able even to attempt to reverse the battlefield situation very soon," an article stated. "The immediate hope is that with U.S. air and naval power, the South Vietnamese will be able to maintain a stalemate." The magazine saw other signs of decline across the south. Vietcong and People's Army units moved toward provincial capitals and major cities, and the Saigon government transferred soldiers from the countryside to protect the more populated sectors. "As a result, there has been a sharp surge of small-scale fighting in the Delta, a region that the U.S. military once boasted had been virtually pacified; no fewer than 300 government outposts have been destroyed there since the offensive began," *Time* reported. *Newsweek* sensed a general collapse. "North Vietnamese forces now hold the initiative throughout the south," it reported. A headline in mid-May, "Vietnam: The Specter of Defeat," led to a summary of disastrous events throughout the south. Defeat was averted, but the military situation deteriorated steadily throughout the summer. *Newsweek* told readers that some provinces in the Mekong Delta again had fallen under the complete control of guerrillas, although the southern army retained nominal authority in several populous provinces. "But in most of the other delta

---

97. "The Last Big Push—Or a Wider War?" *Newsweek*, February 15, 1971, p. 24; "Indochina: A Cavalryman's Way Out," *Time*, February 15, 1971, p. 24.
98. Mort Allin to H. R. Haldeman, memorandum, February 23, 1971, White House special files, White House action memoranda, box 5, Nixon Project.
99. Charles Colson to H. R. Haldeman, memorandum, February 11, 1971, White House special files, staff member and office files, Colson, box 4, Nixon Project.

provinces, the Viet Cong are once again collecting taxes and gathering recruits either by persuasion or force," an article stated.[100]

To sum up, throughout the Vietnam War, the newsmagazines reflected information provided by sources who advocated certain viewpoints related to military and political policies. Each newsmagazine provided a distinctive perspective on the factors affecting conduct of the war. Readers received much information about the temporary results of battlefield success, tenacity of the enemy, and difficulty of military operations in jungles, mountains, and swamps. By the second summer of intervention, the newsmagazines had alerted their readers to the prospect of a long war that might require more than a half-million troops. *Newsweek* presented a far different picture of the military situation in Vietnam from autumn 1965 through midsummer 1967 than did *Time*, which offered generally optimistic assessments. *U.S. News & World Report* painted a pessimistic portrait of the situation from spring 1966 onward, blaming policymakers for hindering military operations. All three newsmagazines responded positively to an informational campaign by the Johnson administration in autumn 1967. While none uncritically accepted the data provided, *U.S. News & World Report* offered a more positive outlook during the weeks immediately preceding the Tet 1968 communist offensive. Newsmagazine performance during Tet 1968 denoted a belief that war policy had failed and the war somehow should end. Of the newsmagazines, *Time* presented the most inaccurate assessments of the military situation from summer 1966 until autumn 1967 and was late to react to indications that the communists had resumed their control of the countryside during 1971. *Newsweek* appraised the military situation most accurately for much of the war.

---

100. "Hanoi's High-Risk Drive for Victory," *Time,* May 15, 1972, p. 30; "New Arms, More Bombs," *Time,* June 5, 1972, pp. 28–29; "Nixon's Vietnam Gamble," *Newsweek,* May 22, 1972, p. 22; "Vietnam: The Specter of Defeat," *Newsweek,* May 15, 1972, pp. 20–22; "Back to the Big Muddy," *Newsweek,* August 21, 1972, pp. 21–23.

6

The War at Home
Debate and Dissent

> A whole generation of young Americans (and many of their elders) have had to re-examine their basic conceptions of America's world role and the nature of the Communist enemy—the legacy of the 1950s. If the ideological battle looked black and white in the monolithic days of John Foster Dulles and Joseph Stalin, it looks perplexingly gray today—especially in Vietnam, where the twin drives of Communism and nationalism fuse.
>
> —"A Nation at Odds," *Newsweek,* July 10, 1967

Newsweek, unlike *Time* and *U.S. News & World Report,* recognized that an era of doctrinaire anticommunism had ended during summer 1967 because of the Vietnam War. Until then, a twenty-year political consensus had assured presidents and policymakers that a majority of Congress, the news media, and the public would endorse economic and military support for noncommunist governments, even if they were authoritarian or autocratic. However, by summer 1967 the moral ambiguity of warfare in Vietnam and genuine concern about the purpose of intervention had generated dissent on war policy by many members of Congress, created editorial opposition to the war by several metropolitan newspapers, sparked protests on the campuses of elite and upper-tier universities, and brought antiwar demonstrations to the streets of some cities.[1] Editors at *Newsweek* sensed the national mood, and the magazine

---

1. Small, *Johnson, Nixon, and the Doves,* 25, 140–41; Gans, *Deciding What's News,* 202–3, 271–73; Hallin, *"Uncensored War,"* 50.

devoted almost the entire July 10 edition to the impact of the Vietnam War on American society after two years. The special report, "A Nation at Odds," covered forty-eight of sixty news pages. Separate articles focused on generational conflict, the inequity of military conscription, political divisiveness, social turmoil, and the tarnish to the international image of the United States.

Newsweek published its commentary on the breakup of the Cold War consensus amid a transition in public opinion on the Vietnam War. A series of public opinion polls by Gallup, Harris, and Roper indicated steep declines in confidence about the conduct of the war, the president's decisions, and war policy. The Johnson administration fully realized that support for the war had eroded sharply from spring through summer 1967. The president and his national security advisor, Walt W. Rostow, directed the military commander in Vietnam, General Westmoreland, and the ambassador there, Ellsworth Bunker, to visit the United States for a series of speeches to national associations and for meetings with congressional leaders, corporate leadership councils, and journalists. Westmoreland and Bunker returned stateside in November 1967. Rostow had a presidential press office assistant prepare for Bunker a two-page list of questions that journalists might ask.[2] Westmoreland met with journalists on five separate occasions during a ten-day visit. The general hoped to persuade news executives that U.S. troops had turned the tide of war. Westmoreland's comments included an ill-fated prediction that American troops could begin to leave Vietnam in 1969 because the Vietcong would not be a serious threat by then, a remark that haunted him when the Tet 1968 offensive erupted.[3]

As noted, Rostow also advised the president to meet with correspondents and editors for the newsmagazines. Johnson, known for his personal lobbying style, met on six occasions with *Newsweek* journalists, five with *Time*, and three with *U.S. News & World Report* from July through November 1967. Some sessions lasted an hour, some longer. George E. Christian, who was the presidential press secretary, remembers the effort to persuade newsmagazine correspondents to write positively about military progress and social changes in Vietnam and to remind editors that other presidents had dealt

---

2. W. Marvin Watson to Rostow, list, November 18, 1967, national security files, Vietnam country file, box 98, LBJ Library.

3. Herring, *LBJ and Vietnam*, 142–46; Turner, *Lyndon Johnson's Dual War*, 182–83.

with serious domestic political problems during wartime, notably Abraham Lincoln and Woodrow Wilson. "The plan was to counteract some of what the press was writing about the war—that no president had ever dealt with such divisiveness," Christian says. Johnson and his top assistants believed that the newsmagazines influenced the political attitudes of their respective readerships: *Newsweek*'s mainstream liberal constituency, *Time*'s mainstream conservative bloc, and *U.S. News & World Report*'s ultraconservative segment. "President Johnson used to say the opinion leaders in the country were the *New York Times, Washington Post,* the three networks, and the three newsmagazines," Christian explains. "His attitude was that all of those media outlets pretty well determined the media agenda all over the country." The plan by the White House was to persuade editors and correspondents from each newsmagazine that congressional dissent and antiwar demonstrations must not undermine war policy. Presidential advisors and staff did not expect the newsmagazines to ignore dissenters and demonstrators, but the idea was to emphasize to editors and correspondents that the majority of Congress and the public wished to stop the communists from taking control of southern Vietnam.[4]

Antiwar activities and the attendant news coverage interested presidents and policymakers. Negative coverage especially bothered Johnson. "He hated the criticism," says George Reedy, one of Christian's predecessors as press secretary. "Here he had set up all these restrictions on bombing, he personally picked the targets, he agonized over our dead boys—and he was vilified, hanged in effigy." In summer 1965, the Johnson administration created the Public Affairs Policy Committee for Vietnam, which included representatives from the Defense Department, State Department, U.S. Information Agency, and presidential press office. The committee met weekly until spring 1966 to discuss ways to respond to criticism and to rebut arguments made by antiwar activists. The committee also occasionally recommended that certain officials and policymakers schedule interviews with journalists to provide background information. Interview recommendations often listed correspondents for *Newsweek, Time,* and *U.S. News & World Report.*[5] Later in the war, President Nixon and his assistants also reacted to antiwar activities

---

4. Christian and Rostow interviews.
5. Reedy interview; meeting notes and memoranda, Public Affairs Policy Committee for Vietnam, national security files, Vietnam country file, box 197, LBJ Library.

and news coverage. They used different stratagems in an attempt to manipulate public opinion and the news media, specifically the newsmagazines. A clandestine effort organized letter-writing campaigns for publication in *Newsweek* and *Time,* while various presidential assistants met with the publisher of *U.S. News & World Report* for favorable articles.[6] Nixon authorized a series of private public opinion polls to determine attitudes on the troop withdrawal timetable, resumption of bombing in northern Vietnam, dropping mines in northern harbors, and the Vietnamization plan. Polls were conducted in advance of policy announcements, and data was given to friendly journalists for publication or broadcast.[7]

Whether antiwar demonstrations meaningfully influenced American public opinion remains a matter of conjecture. Some scholars argue that because many officials and policymakers in the Defense Department and State Department had attended elite universities, the antiwar activism among faculty at their alma maters caused them to question their decisions on Vietnam. Those with college-age children enrolled at upper-tier colleges and universities felt the tension in their own households.[8] Journalists working for national news media, many of whom had graduated from upper-tier universities, perhaps attached greater legitimacy to antiwar arguments because of their association with those prestigious campuses.[9] Over time, the antiwar movement broadened to include faculty and students at other universities, although only an estimated 2 percent of collegians were classified as activists by a CIA-FBI analysis in 1968. News coverage of the smaller demonstrations during 1965 and 1966 sustained antiwar activism and increased public awareness of the movement.[10]

---

6. H. R. Haldeman to Herbert G. Klein, memo, May 13, 1970, White House special files, Klein file, box 6, and Klein to Nixon, memo, January 27, 1972, White House special files, Klein file, box 4, Nixon Project.

7. Andrew Z. Katz, "Public Opinion and Foreign Policy: The Nixon Administration and the Pursuit of Peace."

8. Paul Joseph, "Direct and Indirect Effects of the Movement against the Vietnam War," 170–71.

9. Stephen Hess discusses attendance at elite and highly selective colleges and universities by journalists with national news media. Forty percent of Vietnam-era newsmagazine correspondents graduated from these institutions, and one-third had graduate degrees (*Washington Reporters,* 45).

10. Small, *Johnson, Nixon, and the Doves,* 62–68, 82–88, 126; Herring, *America's Longest War,* 173.

News coverage of antiwar activities in the United States created controversy at the time and inspired scholarly appraisals afterward. During the war, government officials and military commanders believed that coverage of antiwar demonstrations and criticisms by Congress convinced the Vietnamese communists to delay negotiations for a cease-fire because public support in the United States seemed tenuous only a year after American combat troops deployed. Also, a general belief developed that news coverage, especially on network television programs, encouraged further demonstrations by antiwar activists. Antiwar organizations scheduled events for maximum media exposure, and the leadership realized that news coverage disseminated their message to the general public, presumably aiding their cause. However, media attention caused friction among leaders of antiwar organizations, some of whom enjoyed their celebrity status. Of consequence, too, was the emphasis given by journalists to violence at antiwar demonstrations, often involving few activists but guaranteed prominent play because conflict constituted a basic news value. Leaders of some antiwar organizations recognized that this emphasis on the provocative behavior of extremists distorted public perception of the membership, and they worried that mainstream Americans would find these actions unacceptable, thereby harming their cause. Leaders of other antiwar organizations, though, fed the media appetite for outrageous conduct, hoping it would enhance their political power.[11]

Postwar scholarship of news coverage of antiwar activities has concentrated on the "framing" of articles and film segments on network television news programs. Framing analyses have determined that news coverage narrowly focused on the confrontational aspects associated with antiwar activities, whether it was speakers shouting epithets at opponents, demonstrators inciting others to commit vandalism, or marchers fighting with police. Framing thus directed readers and viewers to consider events in terms of situational confrontations rather than their broader challenges to national ideology. Framing also restricted the portrait of antiwar activists to those with scraggly hair, unkempt appearance, or "costumed" apparel, meaning flag-draped clothing and facial paint, which conveyed to readers and viewers the idea that only people on society's fringe were protesting the war. Finally,

11. Todd Gitlin, examining the effect of news coverage on an antiwar organization, concluded that journalists and extremists manipulated each other and that the celebrity status accorded some antiwar activists harmed the movement (*The Whole World Is Watching: Mass Media in the Making and Unmaking of the New Left*, 11–23, 29, 119, 154, 183, 273).

narrative frames set the activities of antiwar organizations against standards for patriotism and social order.[12]

Of the three newsmagazines, *Newsweek* exhibited the most sensitivity about the moral anguish created by the war. Except during the first year of the war, *Newsweek* refrained from portraying antiwar activists as extremists without a legitimate cause; by mid-1966, the magazine was showing the inclusiveness of the antiwar movement by mentioning the involvement of a variety of citizens, while recognizing that extremists tended to provoke confrontations. *Time* and *U.S. News & World Report*, and most mainstream news organizations, persisted in presenting antiwar activists and dissenters in Congress as unpatriotic or leftist political extremists. Most of the mainstream news media fixated on disruptive behavior and extremist rhetoric, but *Newsweek* also reported that a majority of demonstrators behaved lawfully and responsibly. Clearly, *Newsweek*'s prior criticism of military operations and methods in Vietnam, especially Operation Rolling Thunder, and its attention to civilian casualties from American firepower had contributed to tolerance for opposition to the war by summer 1967. *Time* and *U.S. News & World Report*, meanwhile, persistently chided congressional critics of war policy. *Time* ridiculed Senators J. William Fulbright, the chairman of the Foreign Relations Committee, and Robert F. Kennedy, the late president's younger brother, for their early dissent. *Time* and *U.S. News & World Report* also questioned the patriotism of antiwar activists, and both magazines emphasized the probable harm to the war effort that protests caused.

"Vietniks" and Appeasers

Fissures appeared in the Cold War consensus soon after Operation Rolling Thunder started and combat units arrived in Vietnam in March 1965. During the final weeks of spring semester, a series of small antiwar demonstrations, called "teach-ins," at elite private and public universities in New England and New York City attracted news coverage. Sponsors of some events

---

12. Gitlin concludes that news coverage suggested "the New Left was dangerous to the public good" (*Whole World Is Watching*, 29). Hallin, studying network news programs, writes that from 1965 to 1967 antiwar activists sometimes were portrayed as cowards and traitors (*"Uncensored War,"* 193–96). Douglas M. McLeod and J. K. Hertog discuss the framing of demonstrators "as an isolated minority" who deviated from acceptable behavior ("The Manufacture of Public Opinion by Reporters: Informal Cues for Public Perceptions"). Small states that media emphasis on violence at antiwar demonstrations caused most Americans to reject the movement (*Covering Dissent*, 162).

had invited advisors and policymakers from the Johnson administration to explain the rationale for military intervention, but these speakers were booed or harangued by antiwar activists. These incidents prompted the administration to avoid future sessions. "As a general rule, US officials will not participate in teach-ins, but will attempt to meet the requirement for speakers for responsible unofficial university forums and for university-sponsored symposiums," a White House memo recommended.[13] Concerned citizens sent 82,300 letters and telegrams regarding Vietnam policy to the White House and State Department from March through July.[14] By autumn 1965, tens of thousands of people had attended antiwar demonstrations in several major cities and university communities across the country. The primary motivation for most participants in antiwar demonstrations from spring 1965 through summer 1966 was to protest the aerial bombardment of northern Vietnam. Demonstrators later protested the American death toll, the physical harm and psychological trauma caused to southern Vietnamese from American military action, and the principle of military intervention.[15]

The debate over the war divided opponents and proponents into "doves" and "hawks," labels that appeared during the first year and became media shorthand for the duration. Doves, named for the bird of peace, wanted an immediate, unconditional end to aerial bombardment of northern Vietnam, a reduction of American combat operations in southern Vietnam, and disengagement when the southern ally seemed capable of self-defense. Hawks, named for the bird of prey, advocated an aggressive military strategy to defeat the Vietcong and to force the communist regime in northern Vietnam to withdraw its army from the south. Schisms on war policy initially formed within influential or highly visible segments of American society: faculty at elite and upper-tier colleges and universities; members of Congress; editorial writers and columnists for newspapers; prominent clergy and social activists; and celebrity actors, artists, authors, and performers. Doves and hawks used their position and social status to proselytize peers, policymakers, presidential advisors and assistants, and the public.[16] Gradually, schisms developed

---

13. Memorandum for the record, August 23, 1965, Public Affairs Policy Committee for Vietnam, national security files, Vietnam country file, box 197, LBJ Library.

14. Summary report of public affairs activities, August 13, 1965, Department of State, national security files, Vietnam country file, box 197, LBJ Library.

15. Small, *Johnson, Nixon and the Doves*, 68, 25, 31–32, 62–63.

16. Joseph examines the connections between elite universities and policymakers, concluding that antiwar protests at the elite campuses had a disproportionate effect on those

among corporate executives and labor union leaders, other journalists and academics, and ordinary citizens, whose discussions with family and friends about the war often turned argumentative. Not everyone was a dove or a hawk. Many people believed it their patriotic duty to accept government policy on Vietnam despite their doubts about the wisdom of military intervention in a country with apparently insurmountable political and social problems. *Newsweek, Time,* and *U.S. News & World Report* reported the duel between doves and hawks, inserting commentary on this homefront war. This commentary helped to establish an identity for each newsmagazine. "The hawks had *U.S. News* and the doves had *Newsweek,*" Christian remembers. "*Time* wanted to save Vietnam from communism. We all did."[17]

Newsweek sensed the public mood about the Vietnam War early. An article in summer 1965, "The War No One Wants—Or Can End," summarized the qualms many Americans felt about the prospect of warfare in Asia. Appearing three months after *Time*'s declaration on "the right war in the right place at the right time," the *Newsweek* headline illustrated the difference in attitude between the two newsmagazines. This attitude affected news coverage of antiwar activists and critics of Vietnam policy. *Newsweek* recognized the extremist element within the antiwar movement, but offered perspective. "High-strung and polemic, these anti-America Americans have seized on the U.S. role in Vietnam to justify their own deep-seated antipathy to a society they consider cruel, materialist and insensitive," an article observed. "The anti-Americans are a minority of a minority, of course, but they have been influential beyond their numbers in introducing an unwelcome edge of hysteria to domestic politics." The magazine then described other participants in antiwar demonstrations: "[T]he dissenters include some of the most respected and articulate people in the land: clergymen, professors, doctors, artists, lawyers and congressmen. Though many are young and some are hippies, they are not simply an angry band of alienated kids or an exuberant tribe of drop-outs." Violence by a small number of antiwar activists distressed the majority of demonstrators "who now found their cause somehow

---

who set policy in Washington, partly because faculty from elite universities tended to publish opinion pieces in the prestige press ("Direct and Indirect Effects of the Movement," 170–71). Small discusses public antiwar activities by persons in the artistic community (*Johnson, Nixon, and the Doves,* 89, 127) and dissension among the nation's political and social elite (52–53, 140–41, 225–28).

17. Christian interview.

sullied by the more extreme and more foul-mouthed of their colleagues," *Newsweek* explained. The article commented that the more militant antiwar activists "seemed exhilarated" by violent confrontations with police, and *Newsweek* predicted that they wanted "the opportunity to act out their convictions" in future demonstrations.[18]

Time sought to isolate antiwar activists from the political mainstream. "While catcalling Vietnik demonstrators in recent weeks have suggested that a sizable segment of U.S. opinion disagrees, every opinion poll to date has shown resoundingly that vastly greater numbers of Americans recognize and support the nation's Asian policy," an article stated, using a variation of *beatnik*, a name applied to members of a counterculture movement from the 1950s, to refer to antiwar activists. A description in *Time* of a major antiwar rally in autumn 1967 stated that the demonstrators "swarmed" into the streets, and described "ranting, chanting protesters" consisting of "hard-eyed revolutionaries and skylarking hippies; ersatz motorcycle gangs and all-too-real college professors; housewives, ministers, and authors; Black Nationalists in African garb—but no real African nationalists; nonviolent pacifists and nonpacific advocates of violence." *Time* referred to participants from "fragmentary fringe groups," took note of a leader's "wild-haired" appearance, and mentioned "red and blue Viet Cong flags" fluttering beneath the "marbled gaze of Lincoln's statue."[19]

Time showed special hostility toward Benjamin Spock, the famous pediatrician and author who was a prominent antiwar activist. A photo caption listed Spock and his wife as "notables," but placed quotation marks around the word to question the credibility of that status. A remark by Spock to demonstrators—"The enemy is Lyndon Johnson; the war is disastrous in every way"—was said to have been "cried," rather than "declared" or some more suitable verb. *Time* often used verbs and adjectives to attribute irrational attitudes to antiwar activists. "Speakers caterwauled in competition with blues and rock bands as the demonstrators jostled across the lawns," the newsmagazine stated, and "Aroused by acrimony and acid-rock, the crowd

---

18. "The War No One Wants—Or Can End," *Newsweek*, August 9, 1965, p. 17; "Viet Nam: The Right War at the Right Time," *Time*, May 14, 1965, p. 30; "A Nation at Odds," *Newsweek*, July 10, 1967, pp. 19–20, 29; "Dissenting from the Dissenters," *Newsweek*, November 6, 1967, p. 26.

19. "Seven Days of Zap," *Time*, November 5, 1965, pp. 31–35; "The Banners of Dissent," *Time*, October 27, 1967, pp. 23–27.

moved exuberantly out" toward its destination. A boxed sidebar article on the march on the Pentagon noted that activists convened in a theater that was "normally a pad for psychedelic frolics."[20]

Time also pointedly crafted an article that contrasted Air Force pilots flying a dangerous mission over northern Vietnam with demonstrators criticizing aerial bombardment on the same day: "In the U.S., professors at Harvard, Syracuse and Western Reserve universities held all-night 'teach-ins,' protesting U.S. policies in Viet Nam." Another article mentioned a backlash from patriotic citizens. "If anything, the 'get-out-of-Viet Nam' protesters have had the unexpected catalytic effect of arousing a degree of support for the war that had not previously been apparent," *Time* wrote. "At dozens of U.S. universities, students and faculty have scheduled 'bleed-ins' to provide blood for the fighting men in Viet Nam. . . . In New York, where 10,000 demonstrators marched three weeks ago in protest against the U.S. role in Viet Nam, 25,000 counter-demonstrators jammed Fifth Avenue last week in its support." *Time* analyzed the potential benefit for peace negotiations from a five-week suspension of Operation Rolling Thunder, then commented, "The President and his advisers were aware that no matter when the bombing was resumed, there would be howls of protest from an assortment of students and statesmen, professors and preachers."[21]

U.S. News & World Report concentrated on the theme that antiwar demonstrations encouraged the Vietnamese communists to continue the war. "They are persuaded by the recent demonstrations in the U.S. that this is an unpopular war at home, and that most Americans are against it," an article stated. "There is agreement among most thoughtful observers here [Saigon] that the Communists are very impressed by the antidraft and antiwar demonstrations in the U.S., and that they are counting on those demonstrations to affect the U.S. will to fight." The magazine gave big play to a commentary headlined "Civil Disobedience: Prelude to Revolution?" Other articles cited the adverse effects of demonstrations on military morale. The magazine indicated that demonstrators had subverted the military effort. "Americans in Vietnam, in growing numbers, feel that the U.S. public and the Johnson Administration have exhausted their patience with the war and

---

20. "The Banners of Dissent," *Time,* October 27, 1967, pp. 23–27.
21. *Time:* "The Fighting American," April 23, 1965, pp. 22–25; "Seven Days of Zap," November 5, 1965, pp. 31–35; "The String Runs Out," February 4, 1966, p. 23.

are now working for a face-saving way out at truce talks in Paris," asserted one article. *Time* also cited the detrimental impact of antiwar sentiment. "Hanoi [is] misled by the noisy dissent of antiwar groups in the U.S.," an article stated. Dissension and criticism should be considered a facet of democracy, not an indication of weakness, *Time* argued. "They [the communists] are convinced that the U.S. does not have the will and patience to wage a protracted, highly expensive war and seize upon every scrap of U.S. domestic protest to prove it," another article commented. "While Hanoi probably no longer believes that it can drive out the Americans, it still believes that it can wear them down to the point of quitting."[22]

The emphasis by *Time* and *U.S. News & World Report* on violence, radical behavior, extremist oratory, and the unusual clothes worn by some antiwar demonstrators aimed to stigmatize the antiwar movement. Both magazines wanted their readers to consider such activities as unpatriotic and unacceptable during wartime, and both imagined that their readers already regarded antiwar demonstrations as such. Because the two magazines appealed to a mainstream conservative and an ultraconservative readership, respectively, *Time* and *U.S. News & World Report* reinforced those viewpoints.[23] Also, the editors themselves typically held the beliefs their magazines expressed. "The magazine had succeeded because we had established a large audience which accepted our way of looking at things," says Jason McManus, who was a senior editor at *Time*. "If we found conduct outrageous or unacceptable, our readers would, too. As the war went on, our attitudes toward protestors and dissenters changed, as did those who read *Time*."[24]

Extremists, radicals, and scruffy activists were easy targets for *Time*, but a certain level of hypocrisy governed its treatment of male college students who preferred not to make war. *Time* took care not to offend its solidly middle-class readership, the parents of the baby boomers then entering college. While a tiny percentage of male antiwar activists set fire to their Selective Service conscription cards to symbolize refusal to serve and a quarter-million others

22. "Reds Don't Talk Peace—What's Holding Them Up?" *U.S. News & World Report*, November 8, 1965, pp. 44–45; "It's More than a Shooting War for American GIs," *U.S. News & World Report*, October 30, 1967, p. 66; "The War without a Goal: Mood of Americans in Vietnam," *U.S. News & World Report*, June 24, 1968, 31; "Which Way?" *Time*, October 14, 1966, pp. 31–32; "Why Ho Keeps Saying No," *Time*, November 11, 1966, p. 31.
23. Graber, "Content and Meaning."
24. McManus interview.

broke the law by not registering with Selective Service at age eighteen, far more young men legally avoided conscription through deferments for college students.[25] During the wartime years, only 23 percent of male college graduates enlisted or were drafted into the military, compared to 45 percent of high school graduates who did not attend college or who lost their deferments by dropping out of college. (In addition, a minority of military-age men actually served in Vietnam. Of all conscripted and enlisted military personnel from 1965 through 1972, only 24.9 percent served in Vietnam or in direct support roles, such as aboard Navy ships in the South China Sea or Gulf of Tonkin and at Air Force bases in Thailand; the remaining 75.1 percent served in noncombat areas in Asia, Europe, and the United States.)[26] *Time* explained in an article on "draft ducking" by male collegians that many were "bothered and puzzled by the meaning of the Viet Nam struggle." Unlike their fathers and uncles who served in World War II, these collegians applied for permanent exemptions from Selective Service by falsifying personal details, including claims of homosexuality, bedwetting, or psychological problems that required treatment. *Time,* while not condoning such methods, offered a sympathetic account of bright young men who merely wanted to begin their careers or attend graduate school without interruption. "They are not Vietniks, or frenzied protesters," the magazine declared. "Indeed, they pay little or no attention to the thin demonstration fringe."[27] *Time* did not apply derogatory descriptions to them.

Newsweek dealt with the same topic, but compared activists who risked prison by refusing military induction and who demonstrated against the war to the collegians who sought unwarranted exemptions rather than acting on moral principles. "All the dodgers and all the demonstrators were protesting the hard way—and getting their lumps for it," *Newsweek* wrote. "But a far greater proportion of draft-age young men were playing it the cool 1960s way—not avoiding the draft by illegal means, but calculatingly and quite legally outwitting it. They were lining up to join home-based National Guard units, flocking to the graduate schools, making sudden decisions for the Peace Corps, getting all possible mileage out of every possible ailment, even trying to flunk the mentals at Army examinations." *Newsweek* also raised the

25. Maclear, *Ten Thousand Day War,* 232.
26. Baskir and Strauss, "The Draft and Who Escaped It."
27. "Greeting," *Time,* June 3, 1966, pp. 21–24.

touchy issue of middle- and upper-class privilege. Describing confrontations at several colleges between campus officials and the Students for a Democratic Society, the magazine devoted space to Selective Service policy that set requirements for college credit hours and grade-point average. "Out of the turmoil came loud—and sometimes contradictory—complaints that the draft is unjust (because it might take some students) and undemocratic (because, by exempting most students, it throws the burden of the war on the blue-collar poor)," *Newsweek* explained, using parenthetical comments to make the point.[28]

Congressional critics of Vietnam policy received nasty treatment in *Time*, neutral treatment in *Newsweek*, and virtually no attention from *U.S. News & World Report*, which instead quoted senators and representatives who advocated heavier bombing and expansion of military operations beyond southern Vietnam. *Time* reported that a bloc of sixteen senators who had consistently opposed aerial bombardment of northern Vietnam and urged a limit on troop deployment sent a formal message to the Hanoi government clarifying their position. The senators wanted the communists to know that although they preferred a negotiated settlement to continuation of the war, their criticisms of policy in no way meant they favored troop withdrawal. *Time* commented wryly, "The Senators who signed wanted to let their constituents know that they were not giving aid and comfort to the enemy"—a phrase traditionally associated with traitors. Another *Time* article noted the opposition of a few senators to a supplemental budget request for the war. One senator "seemed almost hysterical" during his speech, according to *Time*. The hawks in Congress relied on *U.S. News & World Report* to deliver their message. Typical of the newsmagazine's approach was an article based only on interviews with hawks who urged a "fight to win" policy, an article on a senator's speech for "stepped-up" aerial attacks on northern Vietnam, and an article on another senator's conclusion that antiwar demonstrations and congressional dissent caused leaders in most noncommunist nations of Asia to doubt the commitment of the United States to Vietnam. *Newsweek* avoided sympathetic coverage of hawks and critical coverage of doves. Articles mentioned unhappiness among Republicans whenever Johnson emphasized his desire for a negotiated peace settlement rather than complete victory and

28. "The Draft: The Unjust vs. the Unwilling," *Newsweek*, April 11, 1966, p. 30; "The War Comes to the Campus," *Newsweek*, May 23, 1966, p. 29.

unhappiness among liberal Democrats whenever Johnson escalated the war. "While Senate Democratic liberals made plans to keep the peace pressure on the President with a series of floor speeches, conservative Republicans were hatching their own strategy," *Newsweek* reported. "Floor speeches by de-escalators are likely to be the major immediate focal point of Congressional unhappiness over the course of the war."[29]

Prior to the breakup of the Cold War consensus during 1967, most mainstream newspapers resembled *Time* in their harsh words for early dissenters in Congress on war policy. Congressional criticism prior to summer 1967 was difficult for many journalists to accept because it seemed inappropriate. Cold War ideology had conditioned journalists and the public to question the motives of anyone who doubted the wisdom of fighting communism at certain times and in certain places.[30] Not that criticism of presidential decisions hadn't occurred. President Truman fired General MacArthur after a dispute about strategy during the Korean War, and some members of Congress, notably Republicans, had denounced Truman. However, Truman's congressional critics never questioned the purpose of the war. Dissent in Congress over the Vietnam War had focused on strategy initially, primarily from Republicans who wanted more aggressive action. Then, liberal Democrats asked whether the United States was on the wrong course by preserving the authority of a corrupt military hierarchy in southern Vietnam to combat communism. This concern had surfaced previously regarding policy toward autocratic regimes in Latin America and Asia, but all the pent-up dissatisfaction burst forth because of Vietnam.[31]

Two senators in the vanguard of dissent, J. William Fulbright and Robert F. Kennedy, were portrayed as icons of questionable conduct in *Time* and *U.S. News & World Report*. *Time* persistently derided Fulbright, a Democrat from Arkansas. As chairman of the Foreign Relations Committee and a sponsor of the original resolution that authorized military intervention, Fulbright assumed a leading role in criticizing the conduct of the war just

29. "To Hanoi with Candor," *Time,* May 26, 1967, pp. 13–14; "The Wartime Leader," *Time,* May 14, 1965, p. 24; "Way Congress Sizes Up War," *U.S. News & World Report,* January 31, 1966, pp. 28–31; "The Battle over U.S. Policy in Vietnam," *U.S. News & World Report,* February 28, 1966, pp. 40–48; "Brooke Shifts His Outlook," *U.S. News & World Report,* April 3, 1967, p. 15; "The Road Past North C Pier," *Newsweek,* June 28, 1965, p. 20; "After the Pause: Motion or Progress?" *Newsweek,* February 14, 1966, p. 19.

30. Hallin, *"Uncensored War,"* 116–22.

31. Karnow, *Vietnam,* 487–91, 503; Small, *Johnson, Nixon, and the Doves,* 82–98.

weeks after combat troops deployed. Fulbright sought an end to Operation Rolling Thunder and a limit on the number of troops sent to Vietnam.[32] A *Time* article reported a speech by the senator, then commented, "Without saying a single unkind word about the Communist aggressors, Fulbright urged a negotiated settlement." *Time* also supplied this information about Fulbright: "Bland persistence is the hallmark of the Arkansas Democrat, who was once denounced by Harry Truman as 'that overeducated Oxford s.o.b.'" Fulbright could not understand the reason for taking a stand in Vietnam, *Time* decided. "Put simply, it is an emotional and intellectual reluctance to believe that Communism is a monolithic doctrine of belligerence based on a fanatical dream of world domination," the magazine stated.[33]

Fulbright scheduled a hearing on the war in early 1966 at which various scholars, former policymakers and advisors, and retired military generals testified. *Time* wrote contemptuously of one notable witness, George F. Kennan, a former State Department planner who was the prime strategist for the containment policy. Kennan said the United States should not worry too much about Vietnam because it had little economic or strategic value, and the commitment of a such a large military force there seemed inordinate. Kennan's statement represented "an attitude that evokes distant echoes of Neville Chamberlain's dismissal of Hitler's plans to rape Czechoslovakia as 'a quarrel in a far-away country between people of whom we know nothing,'" *Time* wrote. "Indeed, the testimony before Fulbright's committee pointed up a curious fact. Many liberal interventionists who were so ready to fight for Europe before World War II have become virtual isolationists today." *Time*'s comment comparing Kennan to the British prime minister whose appeasement policy allowed Hitler to proceed with actions that would result in World War II was incredibly damning. *U.S. News & World Report* also decried the dovish attitude in Congress. "One group of critics in Congress—the 'liberals'—have been yearning for any kind of settlement, complaining that the U.S. is bringing nothing but destruction to Vietnam, and is heading for war with Red China," the magazine observed. *Newsweek* did not chastise Fulbright for his challenges to presidential decisions on Vietnam. The magazine reminded its readers that Fulbright "has always fancied the role of the

---

32. Small, *Johnson, Nixon, and the Doves*, 53–54; Turner, *Lyndon Johnson's Dual War*, 156.
33. "The Wartime Leader," *Time*, May 14, 1965, p. 24; "The Commitment," *Time*, June 25, 1965, pp. 25–31.

iconoclast, the lonely dissenter" because "it fits his coolly critical temperament." The senator considered the risk to his political future slight when "the nation may well have everything to lose" if war policy was not challenged, *Newsweek* remarked.[34]

Kennedy, a Democrat from New York, joined the ranks of congressional critics in early 1966.[35] Kennedy warned that China and the Soviet Union might unite to oppose the United States in Vietnam. *Time* selected an analogy in his speech for special attention. "Reaching for a description of the U.S. role in Viet Nam, Bobby misquoted Roman Historian Tacitus—and ludicrously mislabeled him 'one of their generals'—as saying, 'We made a desert and we called it peace,' " an article commented. *Time* consistently referred to Kennedy as "Bobby" until he was assassinated in June 1968; it did not use first names for other senators. *Newsweek* occasionally referred to Kennedy as Bobby, but this was more to distinguish him from his younger brother Teddy, also a member of Congress, than to denigrate him as *Time* did. *U.S. News & World Report* described Kennedy and his congressional allies as "leftists," and cited Kennedy's "political partisans" in the news media and academe who promoted the senator's presidential aspirations.[36] Kennedy also had opponents among journalists. Many journalists thought him an opportunist.[37] *Newsweek* mildly rebuked Kennedy for his self-appointed role as peacemaker in early 1967. Kennedy had gone to Paris to meet privately with officials from northern Vietnam, an act that infuriated Johnson. "Whatever he might have contributed to the quest for peace, his adventures in Europe succeeded mainly in sparking up that other war—the one between the Administration and Robert F. Kennedy," *Newsweek* noted. A subsequent showdown in the White House between the president and Kennedy was showcased in *Newsweek*.[38]

34. "The New Realism," *Time,* February 18, 1966, pp. 19–20; "Vietnam War's New Strategy—Will It Work?" *U.S. News & World Report,* February 21, 1966, p. 32; "Advice and Dissent" *Newsweek,* February 21, 1966, p. 30.

35. Karnow cites Kennedy's criticism of the resumption of Operation Rolling Thunder in January 1966 as the definite break with the Johnson administration (*Vietnam,* 485).

36. "To Hanoi with Candor," *Time,* May 26, 1967, pp. 13–14; "Cards on the Table," *Time,* May 5, 1967, p. 18; "Will Bobby's Friends Trip Up LBJ in '68?" *U.S. News & World Report,* April 10, 1967, pp. 53–54.

37. Gerard J. DeGroot, *A Noble Cause? America and the Vietnam War,* 174–75.

38. "Bobby Abroad," *Newsweek,* February 13, 1967, pp. 34–35; "Facedown," *Newsweek,* February 20, 1967, p. 32.

Time and *Newsweek* offered different perspectives on an unusual appearance before Congress by General Westmoreland. In spring 1967, a time when the war was not going well but was not yet going disastrously, Johnson invited Westmoreland to address Congress, a blatantly political tactic by the president to elicit a public gesture of support by senators and representatives. The general appeared in full-dress uniform with rows of service ribbons on his chest. "The tall, tanned soldier held Congress in thrall," *Time* declared. "He was the paradigm of the professional military man—dark hair fringed with grey, jaw square and trim." The magazine noted the historic circumstances, too. "His very presence in the House was unprecedented—no other military commander had ever addressed a joint meeting of Congress in the midst of a conflict that he was still directing," *Time* reported. Westmoreland engaged in domestic politics when he spoke about antiwar demonstrations and other dissent, an unmistakable reference to those in Congress who questioned war policy, and when he asserted that such actions harmed troop morale in Vietnam and encouraged the communists to prolong the war. *Time* did not find his comments inappropriate. "Yet, judging from the reaction he [Westmoreland] might just as well have called for a suspension of the Bill of Rights," *Time* wrote. Some senators did find the general's comments inappropriate, and they told journalists he should have talked solely about military matters. At first, only Democrats chastised Westmoreland for venturing into the political realm, but two Republicans later issued statements that the general had erred. "Within hours, a fresh platoon of protesters—this time Republicans—had managed to screw up ample courage," *Time* remarked of the delay. *Newsweek* also observed the historic event, but with another viewpoint: "More damagingly, others contended that the President was compromising America's traditional relationship between the civilian and the military by using the battlefront commander to lobby Capitol Hill and the public for the Administration's Vietnam policy."[39]

Transformation

Time dropped its derisive tone by the end of summer 1967. The summertime shift in public opinion had occurred, the secretary of defense had told Fulbright and other senators that Operation Rolling Thunder had failed, the

39. "Cards on the Table," *Time*, May 5, 1967, pp. 17–19; "The Home Front," *Newsweek*, May 8, 1967, p. 32.

war had mired in a stalemate—and *Life,* the corporate partner of *Time,* advocated a bombing halt and a negotiated settlement in autumn 1967. Word that *Life* intended to publish an editorial rejecting established Vietnam policy shocked the Johnson administration. Although a separate publication from *Time,* the two magazines shared bureaus around the world and some correspondents wrote for both. *Time* and *Life* had enthusiastically endorsed military intervention in Vietnam. Eventually, though, *Life* indicated that the war would be too costly to endure in terms of national prestige and casualties.[40] *Time* remained steadfast until summer 1967 when Hedley Donovan, editor-in-chief for the Time-Life Corporation, instructed its managing editor to moderate the tone.[41] But moderation in *Time* did not mean abandonment of its support for the war, so *Life*'s editorial in October 1967 effectively separated the two magazines editorially. "The proposal was to do a *Life* editorial, but that, to some extent, committed *Time* and *Fortune* also, so editors from both *Time* and *Fortune* were in these discussions," Donovan recalled.[42] The imminent *Life* editorial warranted discussion at a meeting the president had with the secretary of defense, secretary of state, CIA director, national security advisor, and presidential press secretary.[43] Donovan immediately heard from the White House. "Johnson got wind of it and wanted to send Dean Rusk to New York to argue with us," Donovan wrote, adding that he declined to meet with the secretary of state. An aide informed the president, "Hedley Donovan has asked John Steele to talk to the President about the *Life* editorial."[44] Johnson met with Steele, *Time*'s bureau chief in Washington, to request his help in dissuading Donovan from publishing the piece.[45] The editorial, which Donovan wrote, represented a symbolic moment for the Cold War consensus. Donovan acted after the disclosure of testimony by McNamara to a Senate committee in August 1967 that Operation Rolling Thunder had not achieved meaningful results.[46]

40. Baughman, *Henry R. Luce,* 193–94; Braestrup, *Big Story,* 41–42; Karnow, *Vietnam,* 489.
41. Donovan, *Right Places, Right Times,* 320.
42. Hedley Donovan, *Roosevelt to Reagan: A Reporter's Encounters with Nine Presidents,* 103; "The Case for Bombing Pause Number 7," *Life,* October 20, 1967, p. 4; Donovan oral history, 94–96.
43. Tuesday luncheon group, Tom Johnson's notes of meetings, October 11, 1967, box 1, LBJ Library.
44. George Christian to President Johnson, memorandum, October 10, 1967, White House central files, Ex PR 18, box 360, LBJ Library; Donovan, *Roosevelt to Reagan,* 103.
45. President's appointment file, John Steele name card, LBJ Library.
46. Donovan oral history, 99.

With public evidence of disillusionment within the Johnson administration over military methods and with the growing sense that the war could not be won, the Cold War consensus steadily collapsed. "The war went on too long without any definite accomplishments," Rostow said.[47] Certainly, Tet 1968 confirmed the suspicion of many Americans that the war could not be won, and the cumulative effects of the combat toll for Americans, unease about civilian casualties from aerial bombardment in northern and southern Vietnam, and the domestic turmoil associated with the war contributed to a reassessment of the ideology that had led to military intervention. Yet the United States remained at war for almost five more years. While military operations and peace negotiations continued, public opinion still mattered to presidents and policymakers. Antiwar demonstrations grew larger from autumn 1967 through spring 1970. Mainstream news media advocated stopping aerial bombardment of northern Vietnam altogether and setting a limit on the number of American troops in southern Vietnam.[48]

The total loss of consensus by spring 1968 failed to produce dramatic transformations in the newsmagazines, although *Newsweek* daringly advocated a radical shift in Vietnam policy just six weeks after Tet 1968 started. *Newsweek* outlined a plan to end the war, yet avoided mentioning troop withdrawal. Set beneath the headline "More of the Same Won't Do," the plan stipulated an end to Operation Rolling Thunder and adoption of an enclave strategy. "Under this plan, the U.S. would stop its large-scale search-and-destroy operations and withdraw its major forces from the sparsely populated borders of South Vietnam—particularly from the area just below the Demilitarized Zone," *Newsweek* recommended. "Such a step would mark explicit recognition by the U.S. that it is fighting a primarily political war, and that its first duty is to protect the great majority of South Vietnamese who live in the coastal cities and in the Mekong Delta." *Newsweek* published its plan six months before Operating Rolling Thunder ceased and sixteen months before troop withdrawal began, which essentially ended large-unit warfare for the Americans. *Time* waited until summer 1971, when 239,000 troops remained in Vietnam, to advocate complete withdrawal by spring 1972. "If it is now safe for us to trade with China and safe to negotiate an ABM [antiballistic missile] agreement with Russia, it should be safe, at last,

47. Rostow interview.
48. Herring examines dissension within the higher echelons of the Johnson administration (*America's Longest War,* 175–79). Small discusses the editorial transformation of the prestige press (*Johnson, Nixon, and the Doves,* 9).

to bring our soldiers home from Viet Nam," *Time* commented.[49] The loss of consensus had no effect on *U.S. News & World Report*, which never advocated withdrawal and restricted its critique of American failure in Vietnam to postmortem analyses of military methods.

One scholar of wartime journalism, Peter Braestrup, cites the *Newsweek* plan as evidence that the magazine had dramatically changed its editorial viewpoint on the war because of the Tet offensive. Braestrup concludes that *Newsweek* and other national news organizations overreacted to the offensive, which in turn pressured Johnson and policymakers to decide to seek a negotiated settlement. Braestrup argues in *Big Story* that media hysteria made it impossible for the Cold War consensus to hold. But in fact the American public refused to abandon the war effort for at least two years after Tet. A series of public-opinion polls by various nationwide survey organizations from autumn 1969 through autumn 1970 indicated that only 19 to 22 percent of respondents favored immediate troop withdrawal while 31 to 39 percent favored a phased withdrawal until a cease-fire agreement was reached.[50] *Big Story* suffers from a limited study period, which causes Braestrup to miss *Newsweek*'s persistent criticism of military methods beginning in spring 1966 and growing more assertive from summer 1967 onward.

Critical commentary on the war by *Newsweek* during 1966 and 1967 caught the attention of Donovan and others at Time-Life. With previous evidence that editorial policy at *Time* dissuaded some readers from renewing their subscriptions and an awareness that many Americans only halfheartedly supported the war, Donovan pushed for moderation. His memorandum to Fuerbringer, *Time*'s managing editor, in summer 1967 recommended that the magazine adopt a more rational voice that recognized the shift in public mood. *Time* risked distancing itself from its mainstream readership. Although *Time*'s subscriptions and newsstand sales substantially increased during these years, *Newsweek* grew at a proportionally greater rate, not necessarily because it treated Vietnam policy more critically but because it had become a favorite of the media crowd. Donovan urged editors "to take *Newsweek* more seriously."[51] Time-Life executives realized that national advertisers re-

---

49. "More of the Same Won't Do," *Newsweek*, March 18, 1968, p. 23; "Coming to Terms with Viet Nam," *Time*, June 14, 1971, pp. 28–30.

50. Braestrup, *Big Story*, 41–43; John E. Mueller, *War, Presidents and Public Opinion*, Table 4.5 series.

51. Donovan, *Right Places, Right Times*, 360, 321.

garded *Newsweek* as the "hot" newsmagazine because it attracted a younger readership with its coverage of popular culture and its less blatantly opinionative style. *Time* seemed "too stodgy" and "too narrow politically."[52]

The election and inauguration of Richard M. Nixon coincided with a new phase in antiwar activism. Organizers reacted to the public perception fostered by the news media that extremists dominated the movement. In 1969 a dramatically different strategy evolved to encourage ordinary citizens to protest the war. Organizers designated October 15 as Moratorium Day. Simply by not going to work or attending classes, any person could protest the war. Organizers asked moratorium participants to attend prayer vigils in their communities, to march in Washington, or to otherwise gather together in a public place so they would be a visible presence. The sincerity of the organizers, who recruited thousands of volunteers—with ordinary haircuts and clothing—to spread the word throughout the nation, and the idea that every American community could be involved, appealed to many people. Millions of citizens skipped work and school, and they conducted vigils or marched in their communities; hundreds of thousands of people gathered in Washington, D.C.[53]

Network television news programs broadcast minimal coverage of Moratorium Day, while the newsmagazines devoted three- to five-page layouts to the event. One reason for television's inattention to a symbolic demonstration by a cross-section of the population was the intimidation of the networks by Vice President Spiro T. Agnew, who had lambasted the national news media for liberal bias, including an antiwar attitude. As an industry regulated by the Federal Communications Commission, the networks decided not to aggravate the Nixon administration by giving priority coverage to Moratorium Day.[54] The newsmagazines had no such considerations. Most noteworthy was *Time*'s portrayal of the "thousands of Americans who have never thought to grow a beard, don a hippie headband or burn a draft card" demonstrating "their dismay and frustration over Viet Nam." The catcalling Vietniks had vanished from the magazine's pages. Instead of re-airing its suspicions that antiwar demonstrations impeded the war effort or interfered

---

52. Grunwald, *One Man's America*, 354–59. Gans describes the attitude among Madison Avenue advertising agencies in 1968 that *Newsweek* had an edge over *Time* (*Deciding What's News*, 73–74).
53. Small, *Johnson, Nixon, and the Doves*, 183–85.
54. Ibid.; Karnow, *Vietnam*, 598.

with peace negotiations, *Time* portrayed the event as a reminder to Nixon to deliver on his campaign promise the previous year to end the war. "Nixon now seems to have raised false hopes, and this week's Moratorium may be only the beginning of the price he must pay for doing so," the magazine commented. "Unless he can assert new leadership and rally much of the nation in some unforeseen way, Nixon's timetable for a withdrawal from Viet Nam will surely have to be speeded up." *Newsweek* appreciated the participation of a wide spectrum of citizens, but hinted that too many had waited too long to show their opposition. "[I]ronically, the peace movement has sprung to life just at the time when the allied military situation in Vietnam seemed more promising than it has in months," an article observed. "What's more, American battle deaths are at a three-year low as a result of informal orders to U.S. commanders to bring down American casualties." *U.S. News & World Report* reported Moratorium Day without embellishment, affirming that the parade in Washington was orderly and that marchers acted peaceably. But a month later, the magazine asserted that the Moratorium Day coalition included many communists, several of whom helped organize the event.[55]

The participation of some *Newsweek* staffers in Moratorium Day events in New York City had an unanticipated effect on the magazine's correspondents in Saigon. "A *Newsweek* editor and some of the writers went to a peace protest on their lunch break, lit candles, and carried signs," says Nicholas Horrock, who was one of those correspondents. "All of the *Newsweek*ies up on Madison Avenue were very liberal and against the war, of course. They went out to lunch, protested, and came back and edited the Vietnam copy. They were photographed and quoted in the news. So I'm dealing with all these guys [military sources in Saigon] who are killers, and they wouldn't talk to us." Horrock soon reestablished rapport with his sources. Antiwar attitudes were indeed held by much of the magazine's staff, according to Osborn Elliott, editor-in-chief during the Vietnam era. "Most of *Newsweek*'s writers, researchers, and editors were by then strongly opposed to the war, but a few editorial people, and many more on the business side of the magazine, felt quite differently," Elliott wrote.[56]

55. "Strike against the War," *Time*, October 17, 1969, pp. 17–22; "Nixon and the Moratorium," *Newsweek*, October 20, 1969, pp. 26–31; "Vietnam: As Shooting Dies Down," *U.S. News & World Report*, October 27, 1969, pp. 29–31; "As War Protests Hit a Crest," *U.S. News & World Report*, November 24, 1969, p. 28.

56. Horrock interview; Elliott, *World of Oz*, 101–2.

Newsmagazine commentary that assigned responsibility to Nixon for public dissatisfaction with Vietnam policy angered the president and his assistants, affirming their longtime distrust of most journalists.[57] H. R. Haldeman, presidential chief of staff, reminded administration officials that *Newsweek, Time,* the *New York Times,* and the *Washington Post* epitomized "the hostile press." Haldeman ordered the officials responsible for media policy to find friendly journalists who would inform the public about this situation.[58] Haldeman also instructed White House assistants to find ways to indirectly influence public perception of policy achievements by the Nixon administration. One idea involved organizing Republican loyalists to write Donovan regarding their displeasure with *Time*'s negative tone. Upon review, however, that suggestion was rejected. "It was felt that a large mail campaign directed to Hedley Donovan would not be credible in light of the subject matter and the elapsed time," a memo stated. "We did initiate one letter (copy enclosed) which is a detailed critique of the subject and may have a chance of reaching Mr. Donovan."[59] Several weeks later, a modified approach began. "Activated the letters-to-the-editor apparatus against *Time* (at least ten letters)," an aide informed Haldeman.[60] The letter-writing effort involved the College Republican National Committee. This group had success placing letters in *Newsweek* from autumn 1969 through spring 1970. The writers submitted the letters under their own names but did not identify themselves as members of the College Republican group. One edition of *Newsweek* unknowingly published three letters from the group, and another edition had four such letters.[61]

Presidential culpability for a resurgence in violent antiwar demonstrations was the theme of *Time*'s and *Newsweek*'s coverage of protest in May 1970. The invasion of Cambodia by American troops and ARVN to destroy enemy depots and camps intensified antiwar activities, especially at college campuses. Vandalism and arson inflicted serious damage to offices and classrooms. Then, a unit of the Ohio National Guard shot several students at Kent State University during a confrontation with antiwar demonstrators. Four students

57. Small, *Johnson, Nixon, and the Doves,* 17–18.
58. Haldeman to Herbert G. Klein, memo, February 4, 1970, White House special files, Klein file, box 1, Nixon Project.
59. Klein, follow-up report on action memorandum 468, June 20, 1970, White House special files, Klein file, box 5, Nixon Project.
60. Jeb S. Magruder to Haldeman, memo, July 22, 1970, White House special files, Klein file, box 5, Nixon Project.
61. Klein to Nixon, memos, October 30, 1969, and June 19, 1970, White House special files, Klein file, box 3, Nixon Project.

died and nine were wounded; many of the victims were innocent bystanders who were hit by bullets that passed over the demonstrators. A chain reaction of campus riots swept the country, closing 450 colleges and universities two weeks before their semesters ended.[62] *Time* focused on the cause of the violence. "[E]ven if the Cambodian expedition should accomplish more than now appears likely, it has already destroyed far more American resources of morale and cohesion than any North Vietnamese supplies could be worth," the magazine declared. Another article explicitly faulted Nixon for provoking unrest. A few paragraphs reviewed the president's justification for the invasion, which linked military necessity, national honor, and national resolve. "But the manner in which he did it seemed deliberately designed to divide the country further," *Time* concluded. "[Nixon] made a glib, not to say demagogic, connection between foreign aggression and domestic dissent. Said he: 'We live in an age of anarchy both abroad and at home.'" *Newsweek* blamed Nixon, too. "[T]he Cambodian invasion bespoke a President perilously insensitive to the expectations of millions of his countrymen that the war would be steadfastly wound down rather than suddenly cranked up," an article commented. "This was not the standard of leadership that the country seemed badly to need, nor was it the standard of leadership that Mr. Nixon had promised to supply."[63]

Criticizing a president for Vietnam policy decisions marked an about-face for *Time*, which from 1965 to 1967 had ridiculed those who refused to support Johnson's decisions. Congress, formerly a special target, now received some respect. "Viet Nam dangerously concentrated the nation's power in the presidency, with Congress relegated to a kind of restive passivity," *Time* stated. Previously, the only occasions on which the magazine had found fault with a president were those that pertained to inaction rather than action. "Lyndon Johnson had waited dangerously long before acting on the problem," *Time* had stated in a 1966 review of the decision to intervene in Vietnam. But the Nixon presidency represented an undesirable shift in authority. The resumption of bombing in northern Vietnam and the mining of harbors in the wake of the Easter Offensive in 1972 worried *Time*: "The way that decision was reached illustrates with disturbing clarity the President's

---

62. Small, *Johnson, Nixon, and the Doves*, 202.
63. "At War with War," *Time*, May 18, 1970, pp. 6–8; "The New Burdens of War," *Time*, May 11, 1970, p. 10; "Mr. Nixon's Home Front," *Newsweek*, May 18, 1970, pp. 26–28.

total domination of the vital arena of war and peace—and the total lack of effective checks and balances under a Constitution that is in other respects so careful to prevent arbitrary action." The so-called Christmas bombing of Hanoi and Haiphong also distressed the magazine. "More than ever before, it is the President's war; the public, the Congress, much of the bureaucracy are mere spectators, not asked or expected to participate," *Time* said.[64]

Newsmagazine articles on antiwar activities and criticism of Vietnam policy made up a fraction of total news media coverage. Americans received impressions on antiwar activists and policy critics from a variety of sources, notably television, so it cannot be determined what effect the commentary in *Newsweek, Time,* and *U.S. News & World Report* had on public perception. The Johnson administration cared what the newsmagazines published, though. "You shouldn't consider any single source as more important than another in its effect on the public," Rostow said. "We [the presidential staff] thought too much of the *New York Times* and the magazines, and we reacted to television. We saw a general movement in the press against the war."[65]

In sum, newsmagazine coverage of antiwar activities and criticism of Vietnam policy differed from that of other news media. News coverage in other media typically exaggerated the level of violence associated with antiwar activities and overstated the role extremists played in antiwar organizations. In addition, news coverage of antiwar activists and policy critics framed dissent in terms of political deviancy, which degraded its legitimacy. These news coverage patterns existed for most of the Vietnam War, with some moderation beginning in autumn 1969 after the Cold War consensus collapsed. But an emphasis on violence continued throughout the war in the news organizations examined by several scholars. Among the newsmagazines, only *U.S. News & World Report* consistently conformed to the journalistic performance observed in other news organizations. Its coverage persistently portrayed antiwar activists and policy critics as outside the political and social mainstream, and the magazine clearly considered their activities detrimental to the war effort. *Time* conformed to general news media performance from 1965 to 1968, when its commentary pointedly derided and ridiculed antiwar

64. *Time:* "U.S. after Viet Nam," November 6, 1972, pp. 21–22; "The Guardians at the Gate," January 7, 1966, p. 13; "Nixon at the Brink over Viet Nam," May 22, 1972, p. 11; "More Bombs than Ever," January 1, 1973, p. 12.
65. Rostow interview.

activists and congressional critics of Vietnam policy. But *Time* altered its tone dramatically from late 1969 onward, especially by affixing responsibility for domestic turmoil on the president rather than on activists, which it had done previously. *Newsweek,* after briefly conforming to the pattern seen in other news media, provided more balance and perspective on the antiwar movement than did the other newsmagazines. *Newsweek* offered an inclusive portrait of demonstrators, recognized the adverse effect the war had on society, and maintained the viewpoint that dissent had a legitimate purpose.

7

"Our" Vietnamese and the "Other"

[W]hy don't *our* Vietnamese fight as well as *their* Vietnamese?
—"A Nation at Odds," *Newsweek,* July 10, 1967

The United States intervened in southern Vietnam convinced that capitalism, democracy, and modernization would prevail in a war against communism. Articles in *Newsweek, Time,* and *U.S. News & World Report* reflected faith in this ideology during the Vietnam War. "For the first time, millions of Vietnamese have been exposed to modern methods and machinery," *Newsweek* reported. "Also, now that the farmer has seen what modernization can do, he—like his city cousin—wants bigger and better things from the government." *Time* explained the scope of the effort: "American aid is apt to rise higher still as the U.S. underwrites the construction of the schools, power stations, hospitals, roads, ports, and communications systems that are essential for the creation of a viable nation and a healthy unified economy."[1] Policymakers and planners devised a military strategy to suppress the communist insurgency while special programs transformed Vietnam's economy and society. The result would be a new Vietnam, an anticommunist bulwark for Southeast Asia. This grand plan derived from modernity theory, which guided the American foreign policy establishment from the mid-1950s throughout the Vietnam War. The theory held that sustainable economic progress resulted in social reform, transforming a "backward" nation into a

---

1. "Revolution without Plan," *Newsweek,* February 9, 1970, p. 37; "Pilot with a Mission," *Time,* February 18, 1966, p. 31.

participant in the world economy and eventually resulting in a democratic political system. Scholars and theorists in academe worked with the Commerce Department, Defense Department, State Department, and a variety of agencies responsible for international programs. The influence of modernity theory on American policy in Vietnam was profound.[2]

Success, however, depended on the cooperation of the Vietnamese ally and defeat of the Vietnamese enemy. When intervention failed disastrously, American policymakers and planners believed "our" Vietnamese had proven inferior to the "other" Vietnamese. Americans, from officers in the field to military commanders and embassy officials in Saigon, typically considered the southern Vietnamese incapable and reluctant to fight. American military advisors and troops admired the fighting ability and spirit of the southern guerrillas, called the Vietcong, and the People's Army from northern Vietnam.[3] Wartime portrayals of the Vietnamese ally and enemy published by the newsmagazines during the war echoed this judgment.

Newsweek, Time, and *U.S. News & World Report* clearly considered the Vietnamese ally a poor partner and the Vietnamese enemy a formidable foe. Most articles portrayed the ally—the southern government in Saigon, southern army, and southern society—as corrupt, fractious, inept, indifferent toward the war, and resistant to adopt new ways. Most articles portrayed the enemy—the southern guerrillas, northern communist government in Hanoi, and northern army—as brutal, devious, fanatical, subhuman, and warlike. The newsmagazines constructed portrayals of the Vietnamese from American sources throughout the war, sources directly involved with policy and programs for Vietnam. They relied on embassy officials, military advisors and commanders, policymakers, senior presidential assistants, and planners

---

2. For more on modernity theory, see Berman, *Influence of the Carnegie, Ford, and Rockefeller Foundations,* 112–20; Hunt, *Ideology and U.S. Foreign Policy,* 159–161; Apter, *Rethinking Development,* 16–23; So, *Social Change and Development,* 17–19, 29–31; Berger, Berger, and Kellner, *Homeless Mind,* 7–9; Luke, *Social Theory and Modernity,* 212–22. For the theory's influence on policy, see Fifield, *Americans in Southeast Asia,* 323–326; Levine, *Struggle for Southeast Asia,* 94–99; Kahin, *Intervention,* 68 and 143–144; Said, *Culture and Imperialism,* 289–292; Berman, *Influence of the Carnegie, Ford, and Rockefeller Foundations,* 123.

3. Kinnard, *War Managers,* 67, 138–41; Maclear, *Ten Thousand Day War,* 132–33, 144–49; Robert D. Schulzinger, *A Time for War: The United States and Vietnam, 1941–1975,* 120–23, 133–37, 189–92; Spector, *After Tet,* 73–77, 108; Stanton, *American Army,* 83–84. General attitudes of Americans toward the Vietnamese are also discussed in Fitzgerald, *Fire in the Lake,* and Karnow, *Vietnam.*

in the Defense Department and State Department for explanations of why success in Vietnam eluded the United States despite billions of dollars in economic and military assistance and the ultimate presence of 540,000 American troops.[4] These explanations rarely expressed doubt in American ideology, and the newsmagazines failed to sufficiently explore the cultural chasm separating Americans and Vietnamese.

Articles published by *Newsweek, Time,* and *U.S. News & World Report* provided much information on difficulties caused by the Vietnamese, but scant information on American misconceptions. Of the more than two hundred newsmagazine articles that contained information about the southern government, military, and society, 72 percent had predominantly negative connotations. Of the several dozen articles containing information about the Vietcong and northern People's Army, 83 percent described a fierce, indomitable opponent. Newsmagazine articles also ascribed subordinate political status to both the Vietnamese ally and enemy. The ally required American guidance and protection; the enemy served communist masters in the Soviet Union and China. In the pages of *Newsweek, Time,* and *U.S. News & World Report,* the Vietnamese were surrogates in a struggle between capitalism and communism.[5]

Americans rarely doubted their ideology or strategy, but they often doubted the capability of the Vietnamese to learn new ways.[6] Condescension, contempt, and disdain characterized the American attitude toward the Vietnamese, an attitude the newsmagazines displayed. *Newsweek, Time,* and *U.S. News & World Report* had almost no reason to challenge American ideology during most of the Vietnam era. Until the early 1950s, the Marshall Plan had helped western Europe recover economically from World War II and had limited the influence of communism there, while the formerly authoritarian

---

4. Cloud, Pines, Rauch, McManus, Cook, and Horrock interviews confirmed the reliance on American sources for information about the Vietnamese or to substantiate the personal observations of correspondents in Vietnam.

5. Said, *Culture and Imperialism,* 189–90, discusses American insensitivity to other cultures and inability to recognize the worth of certain values inherent to other cultures. The subordinate status assigned by American officials to the Vietnamese is discussed in Kimball, *Nixon's Vietnam War,* 120–22; Fifield, *Americans in Southeast Asia,* 173–74; and Levine, *Struggle for Southeast Asia,* 11–12, 103–4.

6. Mark Bradley, "An Improbable Opportunity: America and the Democratic Republic of Vietnam's 1947 Initiative," 15–18; Fitzgerald, *Fire in the Lake,* 492–98; Maclear, *Ten Thousand Day War,* 142–49.

nation of Japan had emerged by the mid-1960s as the dominant economic power in Asia after adopting economic, political, and social reforms stipulated by the United States. American ideology, with its origin in the self-defined concept of mission and the self-declared sense of exceptionalism that had shaped international policy for decades, touted the benefits of capitalism, democracy, and modernization during the Cold War. The United States especially targeted the former colonial nations of Africa and Asia. The core ideological concept postulated that economic power eventually equated to political power, and that therefore prosperity led to participatory democracy. Modernization enabled capitalism to flourish, creating a bureaucratic state dedicated to the development of commercial agriculture or industrialization for purposes of international trade and committed to institutional control of the economy and society. The foreign policy of the United States induced recipients of aid to adopt the American model for their private and public sectors. Every lesson learned during the American transformation from a nation of farmers to a nation of corporate empires would accelerate the process for Third World nations.[7]

The newsmagazines reported the Vietnam War through an ideological prism, which influenced the construction and presentation of news. Newsmagazine articles on the Vietnamese government, military, and society exhibited the Cold War myopia, ethnocentrism, cultural bias, and racism embedded in American ideology. Journalists and their sources—military personnel, policymakers, and strategists—had grown up in a society that prized European culture and ideals. The role of the United States as leader of the anticommunist bloc had contributed to an ethnocentric perspective. The racist viewpoints that had dictated foreign policy in Asia and Latin America since the 1890s had conditioned Americans in Vietnam to see themselves as guardians and mentors, not as partners.[8] The newsmagazines reflected the

7. Edward McNall Burns, *The American Idea of Mission: Concepts of National Purpose and Destiny,* 47–48; Hunt, *Ideology and U.S. Foreign Policy,* 160–62.

8. For Cold War myopia, see Hunt, *Lyndon Johnson's War,* 105; Fifield, *Americans in Southeast Asia,* 182–86, 257–258; Levine, *Struggle for Southeast Asia,* 35–36, 113–14. For ethnocentrism, see Gans, *Deciding What's News,* 202; Luke, *Social Theory and Modernity,* 222; Said, *Culture and Imperialism,* 46–47. For cultural bias and racism, see Alexander DeConde, *Ethnicity, Race, and American Foreign Policy: A History,* 63–68, 103–4; Arthur Power Dudden, *The American Pacific: From the Old China Trade to the Present,* 147–50; Emily S. Rosenberg, *Spreading the American Dream: American Economic and Cultural Expansion, 1890–1945,* 21–28, 44–45, 86; Burns, *American Idea of Mission,* 187–189; Selig S. Harrison, *The*

cultural and social milieu within which they functioned and conveyed the attitudes and beliefs of their news sources. Other national news media generally exhibited the same influences, although scholars have yet to specifically examine portrayals of Vietnamese on network television news programs or in articles by the Associated Press, United Press International, and other news services.[9] Portrayals of the Vietnamese during the war potentially influenced millions of readers whose perceptions derived to some extent from the newsmagazines.[10] The dominant theme in *Newsweek, Time,* and *U.S. News & World Report* during the Vietnam War was the inferiority of the Vietnamese ally to the Vietnamese enemy. Newsmagazine articles encoded information according to culturally determined standards, using evocative terms and symbolic descriptions familiar to readers, thus communicating in a code understood by sender and receiver. By using references their readers would understand, the newsmagazines often distorted and stereotyped the Vietnamese.[11]

The Southern Government and Society

For many readers during the mid-1960s, their first exposure to Vietnamese culture and society came from *Newsweek, Time,* and *U.S. News & World Report.* From the mid-1950s onward, the majority of American newspapers virtually ignored international news except for dramatic coverage of crises, disasters, revolutions, and wars. In addition, newspaper editors allocated far more space to news from Europe than to news from Asia when publishing

---

Widening Gulf: Asian Nationalism and American Policy, 33–35; Thomas J. McCormick, *China Market: America's Quest for Informal Empire, 1893–1901,* 109–11.

9. The tendency of journalists to reflect the dominant political paradigm is examined in Donohue, Tichenor, and Olien, "Guard Dog Perspective"; Gans, *Deciding What's News,* 203; Kern, Levering, and Levering, *Kennedy Crises;* Stocking and Gross, *How Do Journalists Think?* 13–17. See also Hallin, *"Uncensored War,"* 9, 50; Hammond, *The Military and the Media, 1968–1973,* 3–5; Wyatt, *Paper Soldiers,* 49; Gans, *Deciding What's News,* 202.

10. William Watts has determined that most adult Americans based their opinions on events, issues, and people in Asia on information from newsmagazines, newspapers, and television news programs, not on books or specialized journals (*The United States and Asia: Changing Attitudes and Policies,* 13–15).

11. Zhongdang Pan and Gerald M. Kosicki, "Framing Analysis: An Approach to News Discourse"; Bird and Dardenne, "Myth, Chronicle, and Story"; Entman, "Framing"; Pamela J. Shoemaker and Stephen D. Reese, *Mediating the Message: Theories of Influence on Mass Media Content,* 49.

copy from the Associated Press, United Press International, and other news services.[12] People who wanted some sense of international events and issues subscribed to newsmagazines. In-house marketing studies for *Time* during the early 1970s indicated that its readers and *Newsweek*'s wanted to be "knowledgeable" about current events and issues. Ninety percent of subscribers read the world/international section, and nearly four-fifths subscribed for "analysis" of the news.[13] The weeklies probably provided most of the information that readers encountered about the Vietnamese. Throughout the war, however, the newsmagazines published contradictory messages. On the one hand, the government in Saigon must act autonomously; on the other, the Vietnamese must accede to American policy and operate programs by American standards.

The newsmagazines conveyed images of the Vietnamese without providing context. After American troops deployed to southern Vietnam, *Time* described an upcoming lunar new year holiday. "The Vietnamese festival of Tet combines the qualities of Christmas and the end of Ramadan, the Hindu feast of lights and the pagan rites of spring," an article explained. "Before Tet begins, the good spirits of forest and stream, garden and hearth, head for the stars to report to the Emperor of Jade, thus leaving the world to the evil offices of fork-tongued devils and scaly trolls." Taken literally, the description suggested reverence for a primitive, superstitious fable rather than simply a popular holiday celebration. *Newsweek*, failing to explore the consequences of nearly a century of French colonization on Vietnamese governance, informed readers about the ally's governmental system: "Hardly a nation in the modern sense of the word, South Vietnam is not only the home of conflicting creeds and religions, but also a collection of semi-autonomous regions ruled over by military commanders who exercise the power of medieval warlords."[14] In other words, Vietnam had yet to become a twentieth-century civilization.

The United States embarked on a nation-building effort in Vietnam dur-

---

12. Cohen cites a 1960 study of international news published in the *New York Times, Chicago Tribune, Milwaukee Journal,* and two daily newspapers in Madison, Wisconsin (*The Press and Foreign Policy,* 117). Hohenberg examines international news coverage in six metropolitan daily newspapers during summer 1964 (*Between Two Worlds,* 420–21).

13. Lieberman Research, "How *Time* Subscribers Feel about *Time* Magazine," February 1971, and "A Study of Consumer Attitudes toward *Time* Magazine and Other News Media," July 1973.

14. "The Devils of Tet," *Time,* February 17, 1967, pp. 27–28; "A Civil War within a War?" *Newsweek,* May 30, 1966, pp. 43–44.

ing the Eisenhower administration of the 1950s. American policymakers assumed the role of patron-mentor to the Vietnamese based on their experience in China a decade earlier. Because the China experience had ended in defeat for the American-sponsored regime, the plan for Vietnam included a provision for sustained pressure to enact social reforms, primarily the distribution of land to farmers in order to lessen the appeal of communism, which promised common ownership of farmland. The program for Vietnam also embraced modernization, calling for the creation of a centralized bureaucracy to supervise government programs and an organized economy to engage in international commerce.[15] Essential social reforms never were enacted by the Diem government before his overthrow and assassination in autumn 1963, but the modernization process had begun. A bureaucratic hierarchy functioned in the republic's government and military, expansion of commercial agriculture occurred, and enrollment in urban schools increased tremendously.[16]

American policymakers and planners modeled modernization programs in Vietnam on other efforts elsewhere. Economic-development programs emphasized agricultural export products and manufacturing. Other programs trained government officials, or prospective bureaucrats, to become better administrators to enhance their supervision of the economy and society.[17] Much of the official and academic rhetoric early in the Vietnam War endorsed this approach. A political science scholar told colleagues at a national conference, "It is a major effort of the AID [Agency for International Development] program to try to transfer American technology abroad, to try to help other countries to imitate us."[18] Few critics in the United States suggested prior to the early 1970s that American ideology represented a form of

15. Dudden examines the paternalistic attitude U.S. policymakers had toward China (*American Pacific*, 192–93); Harrison explains the nation-building concept (*Widening Gulf*, 25); James Peck argues that the American experience in China and the modernization principle both shaped U.S. policy in Asia ("The Roots of Rhetoric: The Professional Ideology of America's China Watchers," 50).

16. Jeffrey Clarke, "Civil-Military Relations in South Vietnam and the American Advisory Effect," 188.

17. Apter, *Rethinking Development*, 22–24; Berman, *Lyndon Johnson's War*, 112–115; Hunt, *Lyndon Johnson's War*, 57; W. Scott Thompson, "Anti-Americanism and the U.S. Government" (paper presented at a symposium of the American Academy of Political Science, *Anti-Americanism: Origins and Content*, Lancaster, PA, 1988).

18. Bartlett Harvey, "The World Impact of American Technology" (paper presented at a symposium of the American Academy of Political Science, *American Civilization—Influence on Foreign Policy*, Lancaster, PA, 1965).

neocolonialism or neoimperialism. Some evidence already indicated that modernization caused serious economic problems for many nations, including incredible debt and social turmoil, but criticism from within the establishment was muted.[19]

Administrators of economic-development and rural-assistance programs introduced the Vietnamese to technology from the United States, taught them how to use it and maintain it, and then created vocational and managerial training systems for efficient adaptation to American methods. *Time* recognized the challenge. "By any standard, the U.S. has taken on an enormous task. Actually, it is an art in which the U.S. should excel, considering its success in revitalizing the war-scarred Western European nations and Japan," an article noted. "The difference is that those countries were already mature national states with well-developed economies." *Time* emphasized the scope of the effort: "U.S. aid will be needed for everything from installing social justice in the hamlets and combatting inflation to improving farm practices and—most important—inspiring in South Viet Nam's 16 million war-weary people a sense of nationhood."[20] The entire effort presumed, of course, the inefficiency of existing methods and the desire of the Vietnamese to emulate a foreign culture.

Another influence on American policymakers was the several successful efforts against communists and radicals in other countries during the 1950s: an agrarian rebellion in the Philippines immediately after World War II had gradually diminished from a threat to a nuisance; anti-American radical governments in Guatemala and Iran had fallen to organized opposition coordinated by the CIA; Greek communists had lost a civil war; communist-supported rebels in Congo had retreated; and the British had prevented communist guerrillas from taking control in Malaya.[21] Soon after military intervention began in Vietnam, *Time* assured readers that a similar strategy of economic, military, and social programs would cause "the gradual petering out of guer-

19. Walden Bello, David Kinley, and Elaine Elinson, *Development Debacle: The World Bank in the Philippines;* Berman, *Influence of the Carnegie, Ford, and Rockefeller Foundations,* 13–14; Lawrence B. Krause, *U.S. Economic Policy toward the Association of Southeast Asian Nations: Meeting the Japanese Challenge,* 31–68.

20. "Pilot with a Mission," *Time,* February 18, 1966, p. 29. For the importation of Western methods to societies in Africa and Asia, see Adas, *Machines as the Measure of Men,* 303, and Hunt, *Ideology and U.S. Foreign Policy,* 160–61.

21. Levine, *Struggle for Southeast Asia,* 53–58; Maclear, *Ten Thousand Day War,* 50–53; Kahin, *Intervention,* 68–70.

rilla attacks—as they petered out without ceremony in Greece, the Philippines, Malaya and the Congo." Some of these successes had relevance to Vietnam, but not all. Nationalism, ethnic animosity, religion, and rural-urban antipathy affected anticommunist campaigns to varying degrees in the other countries. Policymakers and strategists, however, generalized the experiences to formulate a comprehensive anticommunist plan rather than one tailored specifically for Vietnam. Further complicating the situation in Vietnam was the presence of large ethnic groups, specifically the Chinese, Khmers, and Montagnards, each with its own political agenda.[22]

Because the Diem government had started the modernization process, American policy from 1965 onward promoted capitalism and democracy. Capitalism received impetus from a variety of economic-aid programs that encouraged the importation of consumer merchandise and industrial machinery. The key component of economic aid, known as the commercial import program, worked very well. American subsidies kept the prices of imports affordable, enabling ordinary Vietnamese to buy a variety of apparel, houseware, and electronic products. The import program expanded the retail and service sectors, thereby enlarging the middle class, which presumably would be keen to fight communism. Vietnamese in the south became dependent on affordable imported consumer products, and the subsidy program became more expensive every year for the United States to maintain. Newsmagazine readers received almost no information about this program. Instead, the newsmagazines focused on traditional forms of assistance linked to modernization. *Newsweek,* for example, wrote about an AID effort in a rural area that concentrated on "digging wells [and] building roads" to enable villagers to irrigate crops and more easily transport the harvest to marketplaces.[23]

High hopes and good intentions for Vietnam soon mired in cultural quicksand. When programs failed to produce results, when machinery fell into disrepair from improper maintenance, when equipment and supplies vanished, and when the Vietnamese did things their own way, Americans concluded that the Vietnamese could not adapt to modern ways. "U.S. officials are

22. "In Quest of Peace," *Time,* January 14, 1966, pp. 32–33; Fifield, *Americans in Southeast Asia,* 63–64, 244–47; Levine, *Struggle for Southeast Asia,* 58–63; Harrison, *Widening Gulf,* 10–13.
23. Kahin, *Intervention,* 85–88; Herring, *America's Longest War,* 62–63; "The 'People Rush,'" *Newsweek,* January 6, 1969, pp. 26–27.

questioning whether, except in a strictly military sense, Americans can be expected to operate effectively in such a totally alien society as Vietnam," *Newsweek* wrote. Newsmagazine articles focused on problems with economic aid programs. "Corruption, by universal testimony, is still the rule rather than the exception with South Vietnamese officials," *Newsweek* commented in an article on the thriving market in stolen imported products. Food shipments to impoverished farm families sometimes disappeared. *Newsweek* described the theft of ninety thousand pounds of wheat after administrative responsibilities had been transferred to the Vietnamese: "Vietnamization has meant that, where an American adviser might have held the key to the local warehouse, it is now the South Vietnamese province chief who can open its doors." Evidence indicated, however, that American officials tolerated corruption and thievery because influential Vietnamese benefited.[24]

Rudolph Rauch wanted to write about economic development, but his editors at *Time* preferred to focus on combat. "I was very interested in the economy of Vietnam, and would try to do economic stories," Rauch says. His methods for gathering information typically involved personal observation of Americans working with the Vietnamese, interviews with both, and background briefings with American program administrators. "They [Americans] definitely were frustrated by so many things," Rauch says. "The war itself made progress almost impossible. Then the day-to-day details required so much attention, just to keep an eye on everything, to keep things functioning." Rauch filed information about all aspects of the economic programs he had the opportunity to report on, including work by Vietnamese to learn new techniques. Still, the American viewpoint dominated. "We [the Americans] just seemed so better organized and efficient," Rauch says. Eventually, late in the war Rauch stopped writing economic articles. "It made no sense to worry about raising ducks in Vietnam when the communists were going to be in control," he says.[25]

The question of whether the Vietnamese could govern themselves figured prominently in American policy. Based on the belief in a racial hierarchy of capability for governance and responsible behavior, American policymakers in the 1960s continued the tradition of doubting the ability of Asians to

24. "The Key Task," *Newsweek,* January 1, 1968, pp. 23–24; "Quartermaster to the VC," *Newsweek,* January 10, 1972, p. 23; Levine, *Struggle for Southeast Asia,* 119; Maclear, *Ten Thousand Day War,* 145–46.

25. Rauch interview.

handle their own affairs. State Department officials and policymakers had filed reports in the late 1940s that referred to the Vietnamese as "children" and "unfit for self-government." Dean Acheson, secretary of state in the Truman administration, and John Foster Dulles, secretary of state in the Eisenhower administration, also considered the Vietnamese unable to form a government resistant to communist subterfuge. American attitudes remained constant into the 1960s, relying on stereotypes associated with Asians: childlike and culturally backward.[26] *Time* described a visit by Premier Nguyen Cao Ky to a rural community. "Ky and his wife Mai intended to show their interest in the peasants," the magazine reported. "It would have worked well, except that Ky and Mai arrived in matching jet-black flight suits, purple scarves, flight boots and blue flying caps. The villagers were struck dumb. 'Good God,' said a watching American, 'they look like Captain and Mrs. Midnight.'" *Time* reported that the American ambassador lectured Ky on democracy. "During a luncheon two weeks ago, [Ellsworth] Bunker gave the Premier a stern talking-to, warning him that he was undermining the fairness and legality of the coming elections," an article stated. *Newsweek* informed readers without irony about the perceived relationship between Bunker and the president of Vietnam: "Thieu has increasingly spurned the ambassador's advice, and the caution and restraint that Bunker instilled in his prize pupil have begun to wear off. Considering the volatile political situation that he has created out of what looked like a winning position to begin with, Nguyen Van Thieu may yet wish that he had hung onto the apron strings a little longer."[27] *Newsweek* presented the premise that Thieu, a fortyish former army general who had risen to the top leadership position by dint of personal ambition, intelligence, and shrewdness, somehow needed tutelage in domestic politics from an American diplomat.

Several factors contributed to the construction of these portrayals in the newsmagazines, including, as noted, the United States' ethnocentric perspective and racist viewpoints. But not all portrayals of the Vietnamese ally

---

26. Bradley, "Improbable Opportunity," 16; Kahin, *Intervention*, 68; Adas, *Machines as the Measure of Men*, 305–6; Hunt, *Ideology and U.S. Foreign Policy*, 162. In an examination of the postwar occupation of Japan by the American military, John W. Dower says the Americans considered the Japanese eager pupils who wished to adopt new ways (*War without Mercy: Race and Power in the Pacific War*, 303–4).

27. "Pilot with a Mission," *Time*, February 18, 1966, p. 28; "Thieu on Top," *Time*, July 7, 1967, pp. 23–24; "No Ky and a Big Win," *Newsweek*, August 16, 1971, p. 30.

constructed by the newsmagazines resulted from American arrogance—sometimes, it was simply ignorance. When formal military intervention began in March 1965 in southern Vietnam, only a handful of academic specialists at American universities knew much about its culture or society and only a few dozen Americans could speak fluent Vietnamese.[28]

Journalists, too, arrived in Vietnam with almost no knowledge of its culture and society, nor did they attempt to learn. Although the Defense Department offered a brief introductory course to journalists on the history of Vietnam, few bothered to attend. James Wallace, describing his preparation to go to Vietnam as a correspondent for *U.S. News & World Report*, says: "I volunteered to go there because it was the top story, a war. When they told me I got the assignment, I went to the library to see where the hell it was." Journalists had little professional incentive to study the culture and society of Vietnam because they and their editors preferred to focus on Americans. Newsmagazine correspondents fit this profile. "The Vietnamese angle was under-written," Stanley Cloud says. "We were concerned about our soldiers and our role in the war." Cloud, however, attempted to get a sense of Vietnamese society when he became *Time*'s Saigon bureau chief in 1971. "The first thing I did on arrival in Saigon was spend six weeks on a trip around Vietnam," he says, explaining that he traveled with an interpreter. "We stayed in [army] hotels: that is, cheap hotels where they sometimes bivouacked South Vietnamese troops, almost totally out of contact with Americans. It was an incredibly enlightening experience. It shaped all that I did in Vietnam afterward." Cloud relied on this immersion in another culture to provide context when he assumed his duties as bureau chief, which made him responsible for covering the American embassy and senior officials in the Vietnamese government.[29]

Interviews with six newsmagazine correspondents who reported from Vietnam during the war revealed that all had scant knowledge of the country's culture and society and all had minimal fluency in the language. "We couldn't speak the language, so we couldn't talk to the people when the situation allowed," says Nicholas Horrock, who reported for *Newsweek*. Of the six correspondents, two were fluent in French, one in French and German,

---

28. Hess, *United States' Emergence*, 62–63; Levine, *Struggle for Southeast Asia*, 152.
29. Elegant, "How to Lose a War," 74; Wallace interview; Wyatt, *Paper Soldiers*, 143–44; Cloud interview.

one in German, and two spoke only English; the four who spoke foreign languages had acquired them in courses taken in college. French fluency certainly had relevance in Vietnam, given its colonial past, but most Vietnamese did not speak French; the few who did usually came from affluent families, either landowners or merchants, or from the military officer corps and former colonial bureaucracy. This meant that French-speaking journalists could converse with only a narrow spectrum of the populace. "I could not speak a word of Vietnamese, but I could speak French," says Rauch. "I could go out and speak to the province chiefs and the senior army officers." Wallace was typical of most correspondents and other journalists in that he became self-taught in the Vietnamese language. "I never spoke really good Vietnamese, but I spoke better Vietnamese than anybody else around," says Wallace, who spent nearly five years in-country. "I spoke well enough to get around."[30]

The development of democracy in Vietnam proved much more frustrating for Americans than the introduction of capitalism or modernization. An entrenched plutocracy of landowners and merchants dominated society while the military exercised nominal political power.[31] At the time of formal military intervention in March 1965, 1 percent of landowners held 44 percent of the farmland and 60 percent of all farmers were tenants.[32] Economic dominance meant political control. For purposes of public image and national prestige, the United States pressured the southern military's generals to create a constituent assembly to draft a democratic constitution, preferably including a provision for redistribution of land. Popular elections then would start the democracy phase. First, however, a stable government was needed. By spring 1965, several military coups had ousted the different generals and civilians who had occupied the presidential palace in Saigon during the eighteen months after the overthrow of Diem. "The only visible change has been that, with each new government, a new and larger group of military politicians gets a crack at the graft and corruption," *Newsweek* commented. Another coup in June 1965, two months after military intervention began, brought a stern rebuke from the American ambassador to senior army officers

30. Horrock, Rauch, and Wallace interviews.
31. Fitzgerald, *Fire in the Lake*, 72–77, 332–35; Karnow, *Vietnam*, 150–51, 230–36.
32. Harrison, *Widening Gulf*, 104; Levine, *Struggle for Southeast Asia*, 87–88; Mark Selden, "People's War and the Transformation of Peasant Society: China and Vietnam," 372–73.

in Saigon.[33] No more coups occurred, and the latest general to occupy the presidential palace, Nguyen Cao Ky, promised an election, which was held in September 1966, to select a constitutional convention.

Even the first steps toward the American goal of a representative government were an occasion for scorn. "Full of self-importance, the delegates drafted and debated for days," *Time* wrote, describing the historic national convention in Saigon that produced the republic's first democratic constitution. "Indeed, for the first few months, the antics seemed particularly appropriate to the hot, humid Opera House." *Newsweek* offered less than reassuring evidence that the Vietnamese understood the democratic concept: "'I've forgotten what the election is for,' commented a candid citizen in the province of Vinh Long. 'But I will vote. It is the responsibility of a citizen to vote.' Then, as he nodded into his midday siesta, he suddenly remembered the point of voting. 'I will elect a representative to write a constitution,' he declared triumphantly."[34] Vietnamese society included merchants, laborers, clerks, farmers, students, teachers, and others, but *Newsweek* chose to represent the ally with the voice of an uninformed, sleepy villager whose immediate concern was a nap.

The Johnson administration worried that journalists were not paying attention to democratic development. A memo to press secretary George Christian concerned the telling of this side of the story: "It is just as important to show what brave, resourceful men are doing in the villages of Vietnam; what democratic politicians and American diplomats in Saigon are trying to do in making the government less corrupt and more responsive to the people."[35] American policymakers wanted the national legislative and presidential election of late summer 1967 to show the world that democracy existed in Vietnam, but the State Department and Johnson's advisors had rigged the election. Under pressure from American officials, Ky agreed to withdraw from the presidential campaign and run as vice president for Thieu; the Thieu-Ky ticket won the election with only 35 percent of the popular vote, hardly a mandate. A neutralist candidate finished second with 17 percent of the vote.

33. "Vietnam: Correcting the Crucial Error," *Newsweek,* September 12, 1966, pp. 48–49; Karnow, *Vietnam,* 380–86.
34. "Vote of Confidence in a Civilian Future," *Time,* March 24, 1967, p. 22; "Pregnant Choice," *Newsweek,* September 19, 1966, p. 58.
35. Harry C. McPherson, Jr., to George Christian, memo, October 4, 1967, White House central files, Ex PR 18, box 360, LBJ Library.

Despite disappointment with the winning ticket's low plurality, the Johnson administration scored a public relations triumph. A team of international observers monitored polling places and the counting rooms where ballots were delivered, and worldwide news coverage touted the honesty of the election. *Time*'s managing editor, Otto Fuerbringer, was summoned to the president's ranch in Texas and agreed to a personal request from Johnson to be an observer. Fuerbringer returned from Vietnam to discuss the election with Johnson at a White House luncheon.[36] *Time* judged the prospect of a Thieu-Ky government: "To be sure, some South Vietnamese were disturbed by the prospect of continued rule by the military men who have run the country for the past two years. But most U.S. officials are convinced that at the present stage of South Viet Nam's political development, and with a war under way, a freely elected Thieu-Ky team is the surest guarantee of continued stability." Strangely, seventeen months later *Newsweek* remarked that the freely elected government impeded prospects for peace. "Already one senses the first inchoate stirrings of a Southern-based, peace-oriented opposition to Thieu," an article observed. "The U.S. may thus find itself in the paradoxical and unenviable position of having to help subvert a government of its own creation."[37]

Time likened democratic principles in Vietnam to American ideals. "Without the universal human urge for freedom, the South Vietnamese would not still be fighting—regardless of all U.S. military help," an article stated. "The concept of freedom is vastly different in Asia, of course." *Time* then explained that freedom in Asia meant self-governance—that is, not a communist government that took orders from Moscow or Beijing—rather than individual liberty. "For the short term, the Administration will do everything in its power to help a beleaguered nation build the sort of society it wants free from external interference," *Time* wrote, referring to the threat from the northern communists, not the United States. *Newsweek* recommended empowerment of rural residents who lived under the supervision of administrators appointed by the Saigon government. The magazine suggested elections for village administrators: "They offer the opportunity to begin the process of convincing the Vietnamese people that their revolution

---

36. President's appointments file and daily diary, July 11, 1967, LBJ Library; memo to Johnson, September 6, 1967, White House central files, Ex PR 18, box 360, LBJ Library; president's appointments file, September 6, 1967, LBJ Library.

37. "Thieu on Top," *Time*, July 7, 1967, p. 24; "What If Saigon Won't Make a Deal?" *Newsweek*, December 16, 1968, p. 41.

may finally be realized—and, incidentally, that they can be trusted with responsibility."³⁸

When the first popularly elected national assembly convened in November 1967, *Time* commented, "The result will likely be a pure, if noisy, laboratory in democracy for some time to come, and plenty of advice will be needed all around." Americans stood ready to advise. Yet years later, the laboratory had not yielded the anticipated results. "Deputies have taken unconscionably long to act on some key bills and have cut the heart out of others: the lower house, for example, eviscerated the crucial land-reform proposal by preserving the right of landlords to keep large portions of land worked by their tenants," *Time* reported in 1970. Despite an awareness that the primary attraction of communism to most farmers was the envisioned redistribution of land in areas controlled by the southern guerrillas, no significant redistribution happened until late 1969—and then only in selected villages chosen for a special rural security, or pacification, program.³⁹

Democratic principles never took hold, at least from an American perspective. Rauch spent several weeks during autumn 1971 reporting the national elections for *Time*. "The whole thing was a fraud," he says. "The effort to create an honest political infrastructure was doomed to failure. I don't think it was stated so boldly in the magazine, just that there was a healthy degree of skepticism presented." *Time* indeed made known it doubted that Thieu and others had protected electoral integrity. "The President's swollen 94.3% vote ran absurdly far ahead of the 35% that he won in 1967 and the 50% that he had said he would regard as an adequate expression of popular support in this year's balloting," the magazine wrote.⁴⁰

Although the United States purportedly supported democracy in Vietnam, American officials dreaded the disunity that political dissension caused. Students rioted in Saigon to protest a military conscription law that ended exemptions for males enrolled in college. To prevent other riots, the government ordered students to the countryside where they labored in rural con-

---

38. "Czechoslovakia and Viet Nam," *Time* August 9, 1968, p. 24; "The New Realism," *Time*, February 18, 1966, pp. 19–22; "Vietnam: Correcting the Crucial Error," *Newsweek*, September 12, 1966, p. 49.

39. "A Stake Worth Fighting For," *Time*, November 3, 1967, p. 25; "Thieu Faces the Kindergarten," *Time*, January 12, 1970, p. 20; Harrison, *Widening Gulf*, 92–93; Herring, *America's Longest War*, 231; Kimball, *Nixon's Vietnam War*, 95–97; Spector, *After Tet*, 185–86.

40. Rauch interview; "Too Good to Be True," *Time*, October 18, 1971, p. 43.

struction projects. "Since June, 9,000 students from Saigon's high schools and university have been hard at work for the first time in their lives," *Time* commented in 1965, stating that the government program was modeled after the Peace Corps operation. "With sleeves rolled up and sweat rolling down, the students are building privies, schools and roads in 18 Vietnamese provinces." *Newsweek* reminded readers that affluent Vietnamese students had avoided military service while American troops were dying. "In Saigon and other major towns, draft dodging is near endemic," an article stated. "Bribes are offered to officials for deferments (the going rate: $275)."[41]

The new constitution gave Americans some hope that the prospect of political participation would satisfy the Buddhist activists whose agitation almost provoked a civil war in spring 1966. Buddhists had led the effort to force Diem from office, and the unrest had resulted in the dismissal of the highest-ranked Buddhist general, a corps commander at Hué named Nguyen Chanh Thi. *Time* presented the ouster favorably. "The ambitious little general," the magazine commented, was the "chief rival for power" to Ky. *Time* called Thi "the canny and insubordinate warlord of the five northernmost provinces." For two months, the Vietnamese army practically stopped fighting the guerrillas and northern army while various regiments and brigades fought among themselves or in occupied cities to quell riots. With almost 300,000 American troops in-country and a death toll of 500 a month, the Johnson administration feared the effect on public opinion of the turmoil the Buddhists had caused. Newsmagazine coverage of the rebellion excoriated the Buddhists. *Newsweek,* referring to "the tangled skein of Vietnamese political life," defined the conflict. "Among other things, it concerned an elemental clash between the military professionals, politicians and religious groups over who would ultimately control the country," an article stated. "But it was also about two proud and stubborn men—Nguyen Cao Ky, an erstwhile playboy pilot turned politician, and Thich Tri Quang, a shrewd and secretive monk who has played a leading role in the overthrow of no fewer than four South Vietnamese governments." *Newsweek* portrayed Quang as a mysterious professional troublemaker, and accompanied an article on the rebellion with a photograph of a dead American being lifted into a helicopter—in case anyone had missed the point that Americans were dying

---

41. "A Problem to Rival the War," *Time,* September 3, 1965, pp. 28–29; "One Kind of Routine," *Newsweek,* December 20, 1965, p. 35.

while the southern Vietnamese quarreled. *Time* went a step further, characterizing the leader of Buddhist dissidents in a manner certain to evoke a negative response from readers. An article reported that Quang spoke animatedly, "thrusting his jaw forward like an emaciated Mussolini." Another article showed just as little restraint. "[Quang] has long been South Viet Nam's mysterious High Priest of Disorder," *Time* commented. "Wily and ruthless, Delphic and adept, he is the best of breed of a new kind of backroom bonze. In the murky world of Oriental mysticism and Saigon's immemorial intrigue, these robed and shaven men have emerged as the new Machiavellis of the Vietnamese political scene. Tri Quang is unquestionably their prince."[42]

American anger, frustration, and resentment toward the Vietnamese rose as the death toll mounted during summer 1967. Americans in Vietnam represented a wealthy, technologically superior, and modern nation, yet the people of Vietnam ignored them. Military advisors and civilian administrators viewed themselves as teachers thwarted by stubborn students who refused to learn the correct ways. Advisors, embassy personnel, and AID workers vented their displeasure to journalists.[43] *Newsweek* published a two-page litany of complaints about Vietnam's government and military in September 1967. The article, entitled "Vietnam: Last Chance?" and written by Everett G. Martin, the magazine's Saigon bureau chief, blamed the Vietnamese for hindering the war effort with their corruption, incompetence, and indifference. Martin advocated placing ARVN under direct American command and ending all aid unless Americans were given authority to remove Vietnamese officials and generals from their positions for poor performance. "In this way, the Congress would guard U.S. self-interest and give proper recognition to the fact that, despite all the U.S. effort, the South Vietnamese can still deprive us of victory," he wrote.[44]

The article caused an uproar. The U.S. embassy in Saigon informed the State Department that "Vietnamese political figures have become increasingly sensitive about Vietnamese sovereignty." The telegram continued, "Most

---

42. "The Storm Breaks," *Time,* April 15, 1966, pp. 21, 28; "The Military—'We Can Win It,'" *Newsweek,* April 18, 1966, p. 28; "A Civil War within a War?" *Newsweek,* May 30, 1966, pp. 38–44; "The Light that Failed," *Time,* June 10, 1966, p. 39; "Politician from the Pagoda," *Time,* April 22, 1966, pp. 25–30.

43. Fitzgerald, *Fire in the Lake,* 493; Hammond, *The Military and the Media, 1962–1968,* 297–98.

44. "Vietnam: Last Chance?" *Newsweek,* September 25, 1967, pp. 64–65.

Saigon newspapers commented briefly and negatively on the Martin article. *Tien* [a major daily newspaper] commented that if Martins recommendations were accepted, 'All Vietnamese soldiers, including Gen. Thieu and Gen. Ky, would desert immediately and would move out together to set up a zone of resistance against the American army.' . . . *Tien* then went through Martins conclusions, one by one, and rejected them all." Martin had succeeded in directing attention to the frustration of American military officers whose impatience and anger toward the southern army was no secret. The embassy report acknowledged that American headquarters had discussed placing ARVN under direct command: "The utility of a joint command arrangement has been considered many times and discarded as impractical."[45]

The newly elected Thieu-Ky government informed the American embassy that it would not renew Martin's visa upon expiration. *Newsweek*'s editor, Osborn Elliott, asked the State Department to prevent the Vietnamese from forcing Martin to leave. Dean Rusk, the secretary of state, relayed the message to the embassy. "*Newsweek* requests that the State Department take every appropriate step to assure that these visas are renewed since the action raises most serious questions concerning press coverage of the war," his telegram said. "We expect repercussions in US press circles if GVN [the government of Vietnam] persists in refusal renew Martins visa." Telegrams ensued from the embassy, the State Department, and the president's national security advisor, Walt Rostow. The criticisms and recommendations in the article "collectively constituted [a] mouthful Vietnamese would not swallow," an embassy telegram stated. Embassy officials learned just how angry the Vietnamese were when a Vietnamese official visited with an embassy political counselor. The official "expressed concern at increasing number of American statements from official and private sources criticizing GVN and Vietnamese performance and capabilities and asserted there was a growing tendency of American advisers in various fields simply to take over functions rather than prepare and assist Vietnamese in performing them more efficiently," the embassy reported.[46] Nevertheless, the Vietnamese renewed Martin's visa a few months later.

45. U.S. embassy in Saigon to State Department, telegram, October 13, 1967, national security file, Vietnam country file, box 98, LBJ Library.

46. State Department to U.S. embassy in Saigon, telegram, January 3, 1968, and U.S. embassy in Saigon to State Department, telegram, October 13, 1967, national security file, Vietnam country file, box 98, LBJ Library.

Newsmagazine articles cited the apparent ineptitude of the Vietnamese to cope with basic matters. "Even Saigon itself, once a graceful and gracious French city, is sadly strangling," *Time* noted. "Garbage is rarely collected and mountains of sidewalk filth have accumulated. Potholed streets go unrepaired, bus service is unpredictable, goods scarce, housing either unavailable or astronomical in price." This was the kind of coverage that angered Vietnamese officials. "They read the magazine as soon as copies arrived," Rauch says. "They let you know immediately if they felt you had insulted them. They hinted they would revoke your visa and you would have to leave, but they didn't." A unit of Vietnam's national police surreptitiously tracked the information filed by journalists from Saigon. Horrock remembers an incident in autumn 1970. "I wrote a story about urban decay . . . the shanties, the garbage, the awful conditions," he says. "I sent the story off. Thieu had a press guy, very good English speaker. I got a call from this guy to remonstrate with me about my story. He mentioned that Thieu was considering stopping distribution of *Newsweek*. And the story hadn't run—it had been cut at the last moment, and Thieu's guy didn't realize it because he'd read my file they'd copied."[47]

American interests remained uppermost until the very end of military intervention. Peace negotiations appeared stalled during 1972 because Thieu would not agree to several provisions of a proposed cease-fire, including the presence of opposition representatives in a coalition government. *Time*, in an article headlined "Is Thieu Necessary?" stated, "Thieu, with the long war in Indochina winding slowly toward some sort of resolution, has become the sticking point in any serious peace discussions." *Newsweek* reported that Henry Kissinger, President Nixon's national security advisor, had waited days to visit Vietnam's president to discuss proposals, while Vietnamese government officials ordered newspapers in Saigon to protest American acquiescence on some issues. *Newsweek* commented, "Thieu was demonstrating his intransigence in a variety of Oriental ways."[48] From beginning to end, the newsmagazines gave readers contradictory messages concerning the necessity for establishing an autonomous government in Vietnam and the desire for American policy interests to prevail.

47. "Pilot with a Mission," *Time,* February 18, 1966, p. 26; Rauch and Horrock interviews.
48. Herring, *America's Longest War,* 244–45, 251–52; Kimball, *Nixon's Vietnam War,* 342; "Is Thieu Necessary?" *Time,* June 5, 1972, pp. 28–30; "A Deal with Hanoi, a Duel with Thieu," *Newsweek,* October 30, 1972, pp. 24–25.

The Southern Military

Newsmagazine coverage of the Army of the Republic of Vietnam alternately conveyed admiration or contempt, hope or despair. *Time* especially praised the ARVN during the first year of intervention. "Saigon's forces were doing some hunting of their own in the Mekong Delta," one article noted, and another said, "Government soldiers also fought hard and bravely." But *Newsweek* bluntly stated, "All too often, the Arvins (a nickname for Vietnamese troops, drawn from the title Army of the Republic of Vietnam) have displayed stupendous ineptitude, as well as a distressing reluctance to fight."[49] A pattern emerged in newsmagazine coverage of Vietnam's army: from spring 1965 through spring 1966, articles offered a balance of negative and positive portrayals; from summer 1966 through autumn 1968, coverage was mostly negative; from winter 1968–1969 through summer 1970, coverage turned positive; from autumn 1970 onward, negative coverage dominated.

This pattern reflected the shift in attitudes among American military personnel and policymakers. During the early stage of intervention, the Americans were confident that ARVN could be strengthened while American troops destroyed, or at least crippled, the main-force guerrilla units that had so decisively beaten the southern army during 1964 and 1965. Later, when it became obvious that ARVN commanders resisted changing their operational methods, the Americans expressed their frustration. Optimism followed the Nixon administration announcement that ARVN would receive modern weaponry and assume primary responsibility for combat to allow withdrawal of American troops, a policy called Vietnamization. Ultimately, the southern army would have to fight the southern guerrillas and northern military alone. When most American combat troops had gone by mid-1971, ARVN suffered a series of military setbacks against the Vietcong and People's Army, which brought a negative reappraisal. *Newsweek* and *Time* relayed these alternating impressions to their readers.

Notably absent from newsmagazine articles were perspectives from the Vietnamese military. Cultural ignorance and lack of language fluency limited correspondents, who could neither empathize with the Vietnamese point of view nor develop an effective network of sources outside the American establishment. Most correspondents had only a cursory knowledge of the history

---

49. "The Jungle Marxist," *Time*, July 16, 1965, pp. 24–28; "Technology of War," *Time*, December 3, 1965, p. 31; "Buddying Up," *Newsweek*, August 14, 1967, p. 28.

of Vietnam, and that was limited to the 1945–1954 war for independence from France. Like other American journalists who typically served a twelve- to eighteen-month assignment in Vietnam,[50] most newsmagazine correspondents had neither the time nor inclination to learn much about the Vietnamese.

Coverage of the Vietnamese had lower priority than coverage of Americans, and the work schedule of newsmagazine correspondents dictated that they concentrate on producing copy rather than learning about the customs and values of Vietnam. Even late in the war when American combat troops had departed, correspondents often reported on the activities of American advisors and relied on advisors for information about ARVN. "Most of the Americans had left," says Rauch of his arrival in Saigon in July 1971. "I worked through the advisors to get an idea how Vietnamization was proceeding, whether it would work." However, some correspondents also made an effort to evaluate ARVN through personal observation. During the six weeks that Cloud spent traveling to various ARVN camps, outposts, and training centers, he learned much about the capability of the southern army. Accompanied by an interpreter, Cloud saw the living conditions of the soldiers, watched their officers on duty, and observed infantry and logistical operations. He realized the severity of the problems affecting ARVN, and understood that the program of Vietnamization had not materially improved the army.[51]

Corruption, cowardice, desertion, and incompetence affected Vietnam's army throughout American military intervention. Occasionally, ARVN combat units fought bravely, and its death toll amounted to 107,000 by the time the Republic of Vietnam collapsed in April 1975. Overall, however, the performance of the army disappointed American military commanders and policymakers, although their public statements did not reflect what they told journalists. The ARVN performed poorly for several reasons: senior officers usually were chosen for command positions based on political allegiance, not military competence; officers supplemented their pay with bribes and kickbacks from businesses in their command regions in return for extra protection against the guerrillas or favoritism in receiving mandatory commercial licenses; officer candidates were required to have some college education,

---

50. Wyatt, *Paper Soldiers*, 143–44.
51. Rauch and Cloud interviews.

which restricted the officer corps to affluent and influential families; soldiers received such low pay that many of them stole pigs, poultry, and rice from farmers to sell for money or give to their families; and in a typical year approximately 20 percent of soldiers deserted, which meant units constantly were undermanned.[52]

Cultural tension also played a part in the American-Vietnamese military relationship. American advisors and military commanders had trained for offensive warfare, emphasizing aggressive tactics, individual initiative, and rapid deployment; Vietnamese commanders preferred defensive warfare, depending on cautious maneuvers and minimum exposure to the guerrillas. In July 1965 *Newsweek* explored the dual mandate for General Westmoreland to establish secure military zones and to improve ARVN. The magazine quoted an anonymous associate of the general: "[T]here's a limit to how much you can push Asiatics and Westy could lose them as he drives forward." Also, American embassy officials, program administrators, and military commanders operated under clearly delineated organizational authority, a system that usually resolved conflict by compromise, while Vietnamese commanders usually acted in a variety of roles that incorporated civil, military, and political responsibilities, which seriously impeded conflict resolution. "Far too many battalion, regimental and divisional commanders are more interested in becoming 'mandarins' and setting up private empires than in fighting," *U.S. News & World Report* remarked in July 1967.[53]

The balanced phase of coverage of the ARVN by the newsmagazines from spring 1965 through spring 1966 reflected an effort by the Johnson administration to persuade the American public that Vietnam was an able ally that needed help temporarily until it could resume responsibility for combat. An eight-page report prepared by the Defense Department for policymakers in 1966 summarized the status of ARVN and offered specific points to mention to journalists. The theme of the report was that improvement would occur, but it would take several years. "The central problem has been—is

---

52. Herring discusses the incompetence and poor combat performance of ARVN (*America's Longest War*, 57–59) and provides casualty statistics (256); Levine discusses favoritism and political factors (*Struggle for Southeast Asia*, 94); Maclear discusses corruption, conscription inequity, and poor leadership (*Ten Thousand Day War*, 132–49).

53. "Vietnam: The New War," *Newsweek*, July 5, 1965, p. 34; Maclear, *Ten Thousand Day War*, 147–48; Spector, *After Tet*, 108; "The Truth about War in Vietnam," *U.S. News & World Report*, July 31, 1967, p. 42.

today—and will be for a long time to come—a shortage of well-trained, well-motivated, aggressive and dedicated leaders," the report stated. "This problem is not susceptible to a rapid solution." *Time* had stated the essence of this theme in autumn 1965. "The U.S. buildup has indeed been decisive in halting the Viet Cong drive toward victory—but in large part because it has given the South Vietnamese, whose 600,000-man army continues to bear the brunt of battle, the help they need to go on fighting," an article noted. "It remains very much their war." *Newsweek* observed several weeks later, "Despite the massive buildup of U.S. forces in Vietnam, it is still the Army of the Republic of Vietnam (ARVN) which is doing a preponderance of the fighting—and dying." *Newsweek* also cited the need to create a better officer corps. "What is less certain is whether this sorely beset and war-weary force still has the capacity to defeat the Viet Cong," the article continued. "In the main, however, most officers blame the failures of the government troops not on the individual [soldier] but on the lack of leadership, a problem plaguing every segment of Vietnamese society."[54]

The newsmagazines offered a simplistic vision of American-Vietnamese relationships throughout 1965. *Time* reported the attitude of a Marine Corps advisor to an ARVN battalion: "'These Vietnamese are brave people,' he says. 'You go out on operation and—well—maybe things aren't done quite the way you want them to be. But then, in the middle of a battle, one of these little characters comes grinning up to you and hands you a hot cup of coffee." *U.S. News & World Report* offered a synopsis of the experience of an American soldier on duty in Vietnam. "Within weeks he builds up an intense loyalty to his buddies, then an attachment for the South Vietnamese," an article stated. "Soon, he takes up their cause with near-missionary zeal." A photograph accompanying the article showed American and Vietnamese soldiers together on patrol, and the caption stated, "Americans work well with South Vietnamese allies in field, respect them as fighters." *Newsweek*, too, informed readers that American troops respected their ally. "U.S. troops in the field almost universally reject the view expounded in some quarters that the government soldiers are little more than a pack of cowardly and ineffective puppets," said a December 1965 article. However, *Newsweek* had presented

---

54. Department of Defense, fact sheet, 1966, national security files, Vietnam country file, box 98, LBJ Library; "A New Kind of War," *Time,* October 22, 1965, p. 39; "One Kind of Routine," *Newsweek,* December 20, 1965, pp. 34–35.

a different picture in autumn 1965 in an article about a combined military operation involving 13,000 troops that resulted in no contact with guerrillas. "And even more heatedly, lower ranking Americans blamed it all on security leaks in the South Vietnamese Army," *Newsweek* declared. "The Viet Cong, many GI's charged, had been forewarned in plenty of time to fade away into the forested hills."[55]

By summer 1966, the newsmagazines were consistently reflecting disenchantment with the ARVN. *Time* analyzed the redeployment of American troops to the Mekong Delta when it became clear that the Vietnamese could not remove the Vietcong. "Since the rice-rich Delta must be cleaned out if the war is to be won, what is clearly required is American manpower and gunpower," *Time* wrote. *Newsweek* revealed that statements by American military commanders and policymakers belied their actual opinions. "Despite all the upbeat talk from Saigon and an ambitious retraining program, some South Vietnamese troops are still, by the testimony of American observers, feared by the peasants as rapists and thieves—almost as destructive as the Viet Cong," *Newsweek* reported.[56]

Disappointment with the southern army extended to its role in the pacification program, an American-directed effort to establish secure zones around clusters of villages. The program forcibly moved hundreds of thousands of farm families from their ancestral homesteads to fortified villages; then teams of specially trained government personnel arrived in the villages to build wells and irrigation systems, teach children to read and write, provide medical care, and supply a variety of agricultural and technical advice. Most importantly, local militia units manned perimeter bunkers at night to defend against guerrillas, and army units patrolled the area to keep guerrillas away. "The South Vietnamese Army, whose responsibility it is, cannot or will not provide the security needed to allow the pacification teams to go to work," *U.S. News & World Report* noted. This simplistic explanation for failure omitted several factors contributing to problems with the pacification program. Modeled after a similar program the British had used in a successful

---

55. "The Fighting American," *Time,* April 23, 1965, p. 23; "Fighting Gets Tougher—So Does American GI," *U.S. News & World Report,* December 13, 1965, pp. 39–41; "One Kind of Routine," *Newsweek,* December 20, 1965, pp. 34–35; "No Victory, No Defeat," *Newsweek,* October 25, 1965, p. 36.

56. "And Now the Delta," *Time,* August 19, 1966, p. 27; "The Home Front," *Newsweek,* May 8, 1967, p. 35.

anticommunist campaign in Malaya a few years earlier, the pacification plan seemed crucial to victory in Vietnam.[57] But despite public statements by the president, secretary of defense, and Vietnamese ambassador in early 1966 that pacification would receive priority treatment, the program never interested American military commanders and remained without a central coordinator until summer 1967.[58]

The newsmagazines expressed skepticism from the start. "In the 12 years the U.S. has been directly involved in Vietnam—since the Geneva accords of 1954—at least six pacification programs have been started and all have failed," *U.S. News & World Report* observed. "Some senior American advisers are confident the idea will work this time. Optimism among others is muted." *Newsweek* listed basic faults at a village its correspondent visited in September 1966. "A development team had been in the village for two months, and yet its census was not complete, and none of the prescribed grievance sessions—supposedly a key to the mind of the villagers—had been held," an article noted. "An ARVN officer explained that if U.S. troops assigned to the area departed, 'the Viet Cong would overrun us.'" Several years later, *Time,* too, displayed skepticism, reporting a serious discrepancy between the official total of 92 percent of the population living in secure villages and the unofficial total of 60 percent that most American officials mentioned. With the departure of American combat troops in the last summer of the war, the pacification effort collapsed. *Time,* citing the inability of ARVN to protect provincial capitals, wrote the plan's epitaph: "Meanwhile, pacification programs and other nonmilitary matters are being quietly set aside."[59]

Newsweek provoked a major controversy in October 1967 with a lengthy and derogatory piece about the ARVN, just two weeks after a similar furor erupted over its "Last Chance" article recommending that Americans take complete control of the war. Entitled "Their Lions—Our Rabbits," the article, replete with quotes from anonymous sources, informed readers:

---

57. "The Truth about War in Vietnam," *U.S. News & World Report,* July 31, 1967, p. 41; Herring, *America's Longest War,* 85–86, 89–90; Kolko, *Anatomy of a War,* 133–37.
58. Herring, *LBJ and Vietnam,* 73–74.
59. "Vietnam War's New Strategy—Will It Work?" *U.S. News & World Report,* February 21, 1966, pp. 31–32; "How Goes Pacification?" *Newsweek,* September 19, 1966, pp. 58, 63; "Vietnamization: Policy Under Fire," *Time,* February 9, 1970, pp. 25–26; "Hanoi's High-Risk Drive for Victory," *Time,* May 15, 1972, p. 30.

> At Dak To in the central highlands of Vietnam, an entire South Vietnamese regiment has taken itself out of action in order to concentrate upon supplying the 173rd U.S. Airborne Brigade with beer, prostitutes and laundry service. A Vietnamese Ranger unit performs a similar function for the Fourth U.S. Division near Pleiku.
>
> ... [A]n uncomfortably large number of South Vietnamese fighting men have virtually opted out of the war, leaving the field to their big American brothers.
>
> In each of the past three months, U.S. combat deaths have exceeded those of the South Vietnamese. Total American casualties now regularly outrun the South Vietnamese draft call, and in August alone the U.S. drafted more men than South Vietnam had in the previous six months.[60]

Defense Department cable messages, White House memorandums, and numerous telephone conversations immediately ensued upon publication of the article. An Army general issued a five-page classified report with data to rebut the contention that ARVN units had "opted out" of combat. The report listed specific tactical operations, casualty statistics, and summary analyses.[61] Walt Rostow wrote to Katherine Graham, publisher of *Newsweek,* to protest the article and to refute its theme. Rostow also wrote a memo to Johnson. "I should like your permission to make available to Mrs. Graham the attached sober evaluation of the improvement in the Vietnamese military over the past several years," Rostow wrote, referring to another Defense Department document. "It is quite a contrast to the shallow journalism of *Newsweek.*" Graham's response to Rostow supported her magazine's article and referred to the variety of sources the correspondents used to write the story. "It suggests why men who have worked with the South Vietnamese—and who know the slow and complex process through which an army derived from a developing society improves—take a quite different view than your men," Graham wrote.[62]

The bad reputation of the southern army generated initial skepticism about the Nixon administration's policy of Vietnamization. "Knowhow and firepower ... cannot replace spirit," *Time* commented in March 1969. "The

60. "Their Lions—Our Rabbits," *Newsweek,* October 9, 1967, pp. 44–50.
61. Military Assistance Command Office of Information document, October 11, 1967, national security files, Vietnam country file, box 99, LBJ Library.
62. Rostow to Johnson, memo, October 24, 1967, and Graham to Rostow, letter, October 27, 1967, national security files, Vietnam country file, box 98, LBJ Library.

best ARVN units certainly do not lack spirit—but the best are relatively few." *Newsweek* noted a year later, "To a great many observers, Vietnamization looks like an illusion or worse." The newsmagazines rarely questioned whether ARVN should be modeled on American military methods and organization. "Militarily, the thrust of Vietnamization appears to be an effort to remake the South Vietnamese forces in the image of their American patrons," *Newsweek* commented. "But so far, in terms of leadership, fighting habits, equipment and logistics, it is not a very good copy." The newsmagazines reported that newer models of helicopters and aircraft would not be sent to the Vietnamese because of their inability to learn how to operate and maintain the sophisticated equipment. *Newsweek,* describing an ARVN helicopter base in March 1971, observed, "The only machines that the Vietnamese maintenance crews were hosing down were their own Honda motorcycles."[63]

Two important military events occurred after most American combat troops had gone: in February–March 1971, ARVN invaded Laos, a neutral nation which the Democratic Republic of Vietnam had used as a major infiltration route for years; and in April–May 1972, the People's Army launched an intensive attack on the northern provinces of the Republic of Vietnam, an operation nicknamed the Easter Offensive by Americans. Both events were disastrous for ARVN. Having modeled their tactics on American doctrine, the Vietnamese relied on intensive firepower to succeed; in Laos, however, the terrain and weather negated firepower. In addition, the poor maintenance methods of the Vietnamese steadily reduced the availability of artillery and aircraft. *Newsweek* had previously identified the problem with Vietnamization: "[T]he South Vietnamese Army has been created by the U.S. Army in its own image, and the best ARVN units know no way of fighting save the American way." American helicopters evacuated ARVN from Laos when the People's Army counterattacked, and American aircraft delayed the enemy's advance. "That the ARVN withdrawal was not yet a rout was due very largely to U.S. airpower," *Time* reported. *Newsweek* commented, "When the fighting died down, the ARVN troops seemed to be scurrying back toward their own border." These articles upset the Vietnamese. Rauch recalls that

---

63. "The Strategy and Tactics of Peace in Viet Nam," *Time,* March 28, 1969, pp. 18–25; "The War in Vietnam," *Newsweek,* February 9, 1970, p. 34; "Saigon's Choppers: A Crash Waiting to Happen," *Newsweek,* March 29, 1971, pp. 34–35.

his visits to army units were tense. "The Vietnamese weren't really that glad to have us unless the Americans made them have us," he says. "They felt we made them look bad, that somehow we were responsible for their losing their hold on the country."[64]

The Easter Offensive humiliated ARVN, with a few exceptional units steadfastly resisting. Rauch flew by helicopter into An Loc, a besieged city bravely defended by an infantry brigade. "That was three days of more or less being constantly in danger," he remembers. "Eighteen hundred artillery shells the first day. The LZ [landing zone] was hot coming in, and they were shooting at us going out." Rauch's commitment to getting the story was not rewarded. "I remember I had to get out on a Friday to file," he says. "I got back to Saigon and filed, but they trimmed quite a bit because it was so late." An Loc was an isolated case. The southern army fell apart during the onslaught. People's Army infantry, supported by numerous Russian-made tanks, rolled from the highlands and mountains in the northern provinces. "None of the terror-stricken ARVN units put up much of a struggle," *Time* stated, singling out an infantry division near Quang Tri. "Immobilized by fear, the South Vietnamese hunkered down in their bunkers, refusing even to man their 24 artillery pieces." *Time* presented disturbing images of a routed army: "The headlong retreat turned into a rampage, [and] soldiers who had not eaten in two days looted stores in broad daylight. By night, gangs of deserters started fires and fought drunken skirmishes in the streets." *Newsweek*'s correspondents described scenes at Hué of "drunken soldiers milling around the streets" and at Quang Tri of soldiers "desert[ing] in droves, abandon[ing] their wounded." The magazine forecast a bleak future: "Despite a belief that the South Vietnamese Army has improved considerably, the fact remains that its ability to handle an all-out assault is now more questionable than ever."[65] American warplanes killed thousands of People's Army infantry and destroyed many tanks and artillery, thus preventing a complete collapse in May 1972.

64. "Fostering Another Illusion?" *Newsweek,* December 2, 1968, p. 41; "Laos: The Bloody Battle to Get Out," *Time,* March 29, 1971, p. 21; "Slugging It Out," *Newsweek,* March 29, 1971, pp. 34–35; Rauch interview.

65. Rauch interview; "Settling in for the Third Indochina War," *Time,* May 8, 1972, pp. 28–30; "Hanoi's High-Risk Drive for Victory," *Time,* May 15, 1972, pp. 12–13; "Another Ordeal for Hué," *Newsweek,* May 15, 1972, pp. 23–25; "Hanoi Attacks—And Blasts a Dream," *Newsweek,* April 10, 1972, p. 42.

The Northern Government

Cold War myopia shaped newsmagazine coverage of the Vietcong and Democratic Republic of Vietnam during the early years of American military intervention. *Newsweek, Time,* and *U.S. News & World Report* represented the viewpoint of American policymakers and strategists who believed the southern guerrillas and northern Vietnamese acted in tandem with China, with a lesser degree of involvement by the Soviet Union. Readers hardly ever encountered an argument that the communists in Vietnam were waging a war of reunification rather than a campaign to further the interests of a communist conspiracy masterminded by China and the Soviet Union. The domino theory, which predicted that a triumph by communists in one nation imperiled other nations in Southeast Asia, was used to justify intervention in southern Vietnam to prevent regional dominance by the Chinese. But this theory overlooked the centuries of hostility between the Vietnamese and Chinese, and the awareness by the communist government in Hanoi that China placed its own interests above those of Vietnam.[66]

The newsmagazines relied exclusively on American military officers and government officials for information concerning northern Vietnam, the northern army, and the southern guerrillas. Until the Cold War consensus began to dissolve in 1967, these sources presented a portrait of an international communist conspiracy seeking victory in southern Vietnam to advance a strategic goal, namely the conquest of Southeast Asia. Actually, although communist doctrine formed the foundation of northern Vietnamese actions, the war in Vietnam was intended primarily to unify a country arbitrarily partitioned by Britain, China, France, the Soviet Union, and the United States in 1954 to end a war of independence from colonial governance. Later, especially after the death of Ho Chi Minh, the newsmagazines downplayed the idea that the Vietnamese enemy was acting as a surrogate for the Soviet Union and China. But in general, the newsmagazines presented the Vietnam War within the framework of the ideological contest between communism and capitalism, similar to the performance of ABC, CBS, NBC, the *New York Times,* and other mainstream national news organizations.[67]

---

66. Hunt, *Lyndon Johnson's War,* 105. Maclear quotes historian Arthur Schlesinger, Jr., on the belief of the Kennedy and Johnson administrations that the Vietcong and Democratic Republic of Vietnam were pawns of China (*Ten Thousand Day War,* 135).

67. Bernhard, "Clearer than Truth"; Bindas, "Strains of Commitment"; Gans, *Deciding What's News,* 202; Hallin, *"Uncensored War,"* 49–50; Levine, *Struggle for Southeast Asia,* 81; Schiller, *Mind Managers,* 119–20.

References to the influence of China on the northern Vietnamese and to the domino theory appeared repeatedly in the pages of the newsmagazines during the war. To the newsmagazines, and to the policymakers and strategists who provided them with information, China determined the course taken by the Democratic Republic of Vietnam, and together the two communist nations would threaten all of Southeast Asia unless the United States protected southern Vietnam. *Time* explained that the strategic purpose of military intervention was "to blunt the growing threat of Communist China." *Newsweek* perceived a partnership between the People's Republic of China and northern Vietnam: "Not without some logic, the leaders in Hanoi and Peking remain firmly convinced that they can win an eventual triumph in Vietnam." *U.S. News & World Report* detailed a "Hanoi-Peiping alliance" to challenge the United States in Asia.[68]

Some senior American officials genuinely believed that the Democratic Republic of Vietnam functioned as a surrogate for an expansionist China, while others exploited a residual public fear and suspicion of the communist Chinese government stemming from the Korean War experience. Influential members of the Johnson administration sincerely worried about military intervention by China.[69] Johnson had another worry. "LBJ wasn't just fighting a Third World nation," Rostow said. "He was fighting a Third World nation supported by two nuclear powers. China and the USSR had nuclear weapons. LBJ had that in his mind. He was afraid of a wider conflict." Newsmagazine articles regarding the creation of secure coastal enclaves at Da Nang and Nha Trang in summer 1965 alluded to lessons learned during the Korean War when Chinese soldiers encircled thousands of American troops near the Yalu River in autumn 1950 and forced a hurried evacuation of thousands more. "If the U.S. strongholds should be overwhelmed by Red troops—Viet Cong, North Vietnamese or even Chinese—American troops and equipment could still be evacuated to seaward, rather than surrender to the enemy," *Time* wrote.[70]

Domino-theory scenarios presented in the newsmagazines suggested

---

68. "The New Realism," *Time*, February 18, 1966, p. 20; "Vietnam: The New War," *Newsweek*, July 5, 1965, pp. 30–32; "Reds Don't Talk Peace—What's Holding Them Up?" *U.S. News & World Report*, November 8, 1965, p. 45.

69. Herring, *America's Longest War*, 279. Maclear states that Dean Rusk and Henry Cabot Lodge, Jr., American ambassador to southern Vietnam, expected China to intervene if the United States threatened northern Vietnam (*Ten Thousand Day War*, 95–96).

70. Rostow interview; "Status & Strategy," *Time*, August 6, 1965, p. 29.

vulnerability elsewhere in the region. "Were Hanoi to conquer the South and unify it under a Communist regime, Cambodia and Laos would tumble immediately," *Time* declared. "After that, the U.S. would be forced to fight from a less advantageous position in Thailand to hold the rest of Southeast Asia." *Newsweek,* describing the halt of a People's Army offensive in Cambodia, attributed the action to confidence in an inevitable victory. "As far as anyone could tell, Hanoi's view seemed to be that as long as the South Vietnamese phase of the war in Indochina was still on, the other dominoes could wait," the magazine stated. *U.S. News & World Report* warned about the effect of American disengagement: "North Vietnam's potential for conquest is such that a wholesale American withdrawal from Vietnam might result in Hanoi turning to the rest of the Indo-China Peninsula."[71]

The newsmagazines offered more than conformist commentary. Their descriptions of the northern Vietnamese and Vietcong resembled propagandistic rhetoric. Guerrillas and communist officials were portrayed as brutal, cruel, fanatic, sinister, untrustworthy, and warlike. Most depictions of the enemy employed hateful imagery or reinforced racist stereotypes of the era associated with Asians. Pejorative labels were attached to guerrillas and communist officials, encouraging readers to infer that the enemy lacked human qualities, a common propaganda technique.[72] Such descriptions were routinely included in articles from spring 1965 through summer 1969, after which the tone became progressively muted in *Newsweek* and *Time.* In spring and summer 1971, respectively, these magazines stopped using the term "enemy" to identify the communists; *U.S. News & World Report* used "enemy" through the entire war. Of particular interest is the dramatic difference in the way *Time* first profiled the leader of the communist north, Ho Chi Minh, in summer 1965 and its treatment of him upon his death in September 1969—a transformation from the personification of communist evil to nationalist hero.[73] Also, each newsmagazine commonly referred to Minh by his first name,

---

71. "The Guardians at the Gate," *Time,* January 7, 1966, pp. 13–14; "Cambodia: Caught in a Cross-Fire," *Newsweek,* May 4, 1970, p. 25; "Pullout from Vietnam," *U.S. News & World Report,* January 27, 1969, pp. 36–37.

72. Journalistic framing, labeling, and inference are discussed by Entman, "Framing," 52; Herman and Chomsky, *Manufacturing Consent,* 29, 302–3; and Stocking and Gross, *How Do Journalists Think?* 13–17.

73. "The Jungle Marxist," *Time,* July 16, 1965, pp. 24–28; "The Legacy of Ho Chi Minh," *Time,* September 12, 1969, p. 22.

Ho; similar familiarity never was applied to leaders of the southern government, Nguyen Cao Ky and Nguyen Van Thieu, or to other northern leaders, such as Vo Nguyen Giap, the military leader.

As mentioned, newsmagazine correspondents had no contact with the Vietcong, People's Army, or northern Vietnamese officials during the war. Unlike the *New York Times,* no newsmagazine sent a correspondent to the Democratic Republic of Vietnam while American troops fought in the south. Therefore, all information pertaining to the enemy came from Americans in Vietnam and from Vietnamese with the southern government and army. The correspondents' lack of fluency in Vietnamese greatly restricted their contact with neutralist or oppositional figures who might have contradicted other sources. Even when speaking with southern Vietnamese, correspondents relied on interpreters to translate questions and answers, which made the information they obtained somewhat suspect because interpreters sometimes had political agendas of their own, either as government agents or communist sympathizers.

Indeed, *Time* experienced acute embarrassment several years after the communists won when the magazine learned that the interpreter for its Saigon bureau had simultaneously held the rank of a Vietcong colonel.[74] The interpreter, Pham Xuan An, was gathering intelligence on the southern government and military while working for *Time.* "He had massive influence on us," Burton Pines says. "So many stories were based on information he supplied. He fed us lies. We lied to our readers." Cloud and Rauch disagree with Pines concerning the impact An had on articles published in *Time.* "His information was good," Cloud says. "He gave us information not available from ordinary sources we had. I have no reason to doubt, even now, that everything he told us was true." All three men say An functioned for *Time* both as an interpreter and a stringer, or part-time journalist, obtaining information from various sources for the bureau. He traveled with *Time* correspondents when they visited ARVN units, toured the provinces to speak with villagers, and contacted officials with the southern government. He also occasionally provided information from Vietnamese who did not wish to be seen talking with Americans. "He was very good at giving us insights we would have missed," says Rauch, who covered the national elections with An in 1971.[75]

74. Morley Safer, *Flashbacks: On Returning to Vietnam,* 175–81.
75. Pines, Cloud, and Rauch interviews.

The most valuable work An performed for *Time* occurred during the latter months of 1972. "An had a source, someone he said was with the South Vietnamese government, who had incredibly accurate details on the cease-fire agreement," Cloud says. *Time* published the only newsmagazine article containing all nine provisions of the cease-fire agreement to which the United States, Democratic Republic of Vietnam, and Provisional Revolutionary Government, or Vietcong, concurred in October 1972. Because the Republic of Vietnam refused to accept the provision allowing the People's Army to remain within southern boundaries, however, the agreement did not take effect. Two months later, after intensive American aerial bombardment of Hanoi and coercive pressure on the Saigon government, essentially the same cease-fire agreement ended American military intervention. "We [*Time*] were the only one with the details," Cloud says. "We reported the whole situation accurately, from beginning to end." Although the historical record supports Cloud, the revelation that a Vietcong colonel was on *Time*'s payroll caused much anguish for a magazine that had espoused a militaristic anti-communist philosophy.[76]

The newsmagazines maintained an adversarial tone toward the enemy throughout the war. During the latter phase of military intervention, however, in *Newsweek* and *Time* the enemy became more of a worthy foe. Also, later articles clearly indicated that the Democratic Republic of Vietnam was acting autonomously, not as a pawn in an international communist conspiracy. Compared with coverage of the southern Vietnamese ally, which emphasized negative traits and conduct, articles regarding the Vietcong, People's Army, and northern communists generally focused on their bravery and tenacity. Readers understood that the United States faced a formidable enemy.

Time, which favored personalization of political issues, delivered its analysis of the enemy leader in a lengthy article, "The Jungle Marxist," in summer 1965:

> Hanoi last week was ready for total war. So was Ho Chi Minh, the goat-bearded god of Vietnamese Communism and, at 75, Asia's oldest, canniest Red leader.
> Once South Viet Nam fell, Ho could turn his attention to extending Vietnamese control over Cambodia, Thailand and Laos. As one historian

76. Cloud, Magnuson, Pines, and Rauch interviews; "A Summary of the Nine Points," *Time*, November 6, 1972, p. 16.

observes: "The Vietnamese have contributed very little to Asian culture, and quite a bit to its violence."

The West cannot countenance his Communist expansionism for fear that it will eventually inundate the rest of Southeast Asia. It will take a lot more than his guile and staying power to emerge a victor in Southeast Asia.[77]

Without bothering to clarify whether it was all Vietnamese or merely the northern Vietnamese who had not done much for Asian culture other than inflict misery, *Time* went on to explain why the communist government in Hanoi dared to confront the United States. According to the magazine, the northern Vietnamese needed the rice paddies of the Mekong Delta for food, desired to expand communist domination across the peninsula, and hoped to accomplish reunification of Vietnam without the assistance of the Chinese, who historically had considered Vietnamese territory a fiefdom. Certainly, much of the article accurately summarized centuries of Vietnamese history and decades of anticolonial warfare, but *Time* minimized both the personal leadership of Ho and the accomplishments of the northern communists by exaggerating the role played by the Soviet Union in the liberation struggle and by implying that the Hanoi regime would not have begun the southern insurgency unless China had authorized it. On the contrary, the Chinese communist leadership had pressured Hanoi to instruct the southern communists to negotiate membership in a coalition government in Saigon rather than fight a long insurgency.[78]

The newsmagazines failed to credit Ho and his colleagues in northern Vietnam for directing their own revolution, developing a unique political doctrine, and maintaining national autonomy. Obviously, sources within the Defense Department, State Department, and presidential administrations shaped newsmagazine portrayals of the Vietnamese communists, but some policymakers and strategists within the government and scholars in academe possessed knowledge that would have offered an alternative version had correspondents contacted them.[79] Ho and the communist leadership in northern

---

77. "The Jungle Marxist," *Time*, July 16, 1965, pp. 24–28. For a discussion of *Time*'s personalization method, see Baughman, *Henry R. Luce*, 45–46, 60.

78. "The Jungle Marxist," *Time*, July 16, 1965, pp. 24–28; Kolko, *Anatomy of a War*, 156–57. See also Fitzgerald, *Fire in the Lake*, 47–49, and Karnow, *Vietnam*, 99–103.

79. Bradley, "Improbable Opportunity," 3–4, 7–9, 16–17; William Duiker, "Waging Revolutionary War: The Evolution of Hanoi's Strategy in the South, 1959–1965," 32–35.

Vietnam had taken control of the anticolonial campaign during the 1940s and had organized an independent government in summer 1945. During the immediate postwar period, France restored its colonial authority with help from the United States. The war for independence from 1946 to 1954 in areas controlled by the communist organization, called the Vietminh, generated tremendous popular support for two reasons: the communists' policy of land redistribution, which transferred ownership of small tracts to hundreds of thousands of farmers by forcibly taking acreage from larger landowners; and an appeal to national self-determination that focused on evicting the French rather than on communism. The Vietminh was, first and foremost, a communist organization based on Marxist-Leninist principles, but its popularity among rural residents and its absolute control of the revolt against France placed Ho and his colleagues in a position that allowed them to create a special ideology distinct from communism in China and the Soviet Union.[80]

Another factor separating the northern Vietnamese from China and the Soviet Union was their awareness that the communist superpowers had betrayed them at the Geneva Conference in 1954, compelling the Vietminh to accept partitioning at the 17th parallel rather than unification.[81] American policymakers and strategists knew all this, but the newsmagazines never explained these rifts in the communist bloc. *Time,* however, published an assessment of Ho upon his death in September 1969 that explained the relationship of northern Vietnam with the communist superpowers. "[Ho] had come to represent a form of 'national Communism' that left him out of both the Chinese and Soviet orbits, but prompted both powers to court him," *Time* wrote. "Ho Chi Minh's life was dedicated to the creation of a unified Viet Nam, free from foreign control, and the 19 million people of his tortured land suffered mightily from his devotion to that vision."[82] The overall tone of admiration contrasted dramatically with *Time*'s previous description of a "goat-bearded god" whose "guile" had made him the would-be conqueror of Southeast Asia.

---

80. For discussions of the rural-urban division affecting the anticolonial campaign and the difficulty noncommunist nationalists had in opposing the French without aligning with the Vietminh, see Fitzgerald, *Fire in the Lake,* 86–89, and Levine, *Struggle for Southeast Asia,* 84–85.
81. Kahin, *Intervention,* 55–61.
82. "The Legacy of Ho Chi Minh," *Time,* September 12, 1969, p. 22.

Time persisted in ascribing to China a keen interest in fighting the Americans. "Red China . . . offered for the umpteenth time to send volunteers at the request of the guerrillas," an article reported, referring to a request by the Vietcong for volunteers from the north a few months after American combat troops arrived. Another article noted the aid China provided. "Quietly but unmistakably, the quality, quantity and firepower of the Viet Cong weapons have risen in recent months until in many cases they constitute a fresh and bothersome threat to U.S. units," *Time* wrote. "Thanks mainly to Red China, which supplies 80% of their weapons, the Viet Cong are now equipped with flamethrowers, rifle grenades, 12.7-mm. antiaircraft machine guns and 120-mm. mortars, in addition to the Russian rockets." The article went on to list other weaponry, including AK-47 rifles, that the Vietcong possessed.[83] Technically accurate because most weaponry for the Vietnamese communists arrived via China, the article did not specify where the weaponry originated—the Soviet Union. China had given the Vietnamese communists its surplus weapons for years, but had depleted its inventory by 1966. The Soviet Union then became the primary supplier to the Vietcong and People's Army of antiaircraft artillery and missiles, howitzers, machine guns, and rifles. *Time* and *Newsweek* failed to report this significant transition because their sources in the U.S. government preferred to view the Russians as ideologically moderate and the Chinese as ideologically militant.[84]

Newsmagazine articles speculated on Chinese and Soviet influence among the leadership in Hanoi. "Students of Vietnamese affairs have detected signs that Ho, in feeble health at 75, is now no more than a ceremonial figure," *Newsweek* wrote. "The power, they say, resides in an uneasy alliance of three factions: a pro-Soviet group . . . the pro-Peking ultras [militants] . . . and the party apparatus." Articles hinted that infighting among the Hanoi leadership prompted by the Chinese and Soviet governments would produce a replacement upon Ho's death who either would carry on the war, which China supposedly wanted, or negotiate a settlement, which the Soviet Union supposedly wanted. With the war dragging on, though, those hopes faded. "[T]here is no evidence whatever that factional differences have yet led any member of the North Vietnamese hierarchy to urge a settlement on anything

---

83. "The Senate on Viet Nam: Anxiety & Assent," *Time*, August 13, 1965, pp. 15–16; "Vote of Confidence in a Civilian Future," *Time*, March 24, 1967, pp. 22–24.

84. Levine, *Struggle for Southeast Asia*, 99–100; Maclear, *Ten Thousand Day War*, 124–25.

less than Hanoi's terms: a U.S. withdrawal leading ultimately to a unified, Communist Vietnam," *Newsweek* later concluded. *Time,* too, doubted whether factionalism affected the enemy leadership. "It was once fashionable among Hanoiologists to divide the North Vietnamese leadership into hawks and doves, hard-lining pro-Chinese and more flexible pro-Moscow factions," an article noted. "The pressures of all-out war have long since buried such fine distinctions, if they ever existed at all." *U.S. News & World Report,* agreeing that China seemed unable to persuade its junior partner to negotiate a settlement with the United States, found other reasons for such puzzling independence. "Among the experts in Saigon on how Asian Communists think, there seem to be strong indications that the answer lies in either (1) a misjudgment of America's determination to stay, or (2) an inability to find a face-saving way to agree on talks, or (3) Oriental deviousness," the magazine stated. This racist characterization, founded on a stereotypical western notion of the inherent cunning of Asians, hardly was an isolated case in the newsmagazines.[85]

Newsmagazine commentary on factions in Hanoi, militancy in Beijing, and moderates in Moscow had significance. The newsmagazines carried the messages of American policymakers and strategists who had constructed a war policy predicated on a demonstration of resolve, similar to that seen in Korea, and third-party diplomatic pressure, similar to that seen at the Geneva Conference of 1954. China and the Soviet Union surely could coerce their client state, the Democratic Republic of Vietnam, to settle. When it finally dawned on policymakers and strategists that the northern Vietnamese fully intended to fight their own war, they had to explain what went wrong.[86] The newsmagazines adjusted to these revisions in Cold War thinking as the war progressed.

The northern Vietnamese, on their own, had decided in early 1959 to prepare for an insurgency in the south. Several thousand southerners who had moved north after the partitioning in 1954 were ordered to return to

---

85. "Refreshed by the Pause," *Newsweek,* January 31, 1966, p. 34; "A Will of Steel?" *Newsweek,* January 1, 1968, pp. 25–26; "Victory in the Valley," *Time,* November 24, 1967, p. 34; "Why Ho Keeps Saying No," *Time,* November 11, 1966, pp. 30–31; "Reds Don't Talk Peace—What's Holding Them Up?" *U.S. News & World Report,* November 8, 1965, p. 45. Dower examines racist stereotyping during World War II when the Japanese were pictured as "mirror opposites" of Anglo-Americans because of their supposed cunning, irrationality, and inhuman behavior (*War without Mercy,* 29).

86. Fifield, *Americans in Southeast Asia,* 287; Levine, *Struggle for Southeast Asia,* 81, 102–7.

their home villages. They had trained in indoctrination techniques, guerrilla warfare methods, and cadre organization. They took up residence in the places where their aunts, uncles, and cousins had remained behind. The returnees lectured their neighbors on revolutionary ideology, promised them ownership of land, and recruited those who wanted to fight the Diem regime. Over the years, they built a strong network of cadres. Corruption in the southern government, excessive farm rental fees, and the generally arrogant attitude of government officials in the provinces persuaded many rural residents to join the cause. *U.S. News & World Report* described the infiltration process. "The majority of these infiltrators are civilian, rather than military," the magazine noted. "Many are South Vietnamese who went North for special training—as teachers, doctors, nurses, mechanics, political organizers. Their assignment is to return to their home villages and use their new skills to make themselves important to the villages, then organize Viet Cong cells."[87]

Insurgents followed a policy of terrorism, too, assassinating anticommunist village leaders and threatening harm to rural Catholics who would not accept communism. *Newsweek* described one cadre leader as "ruthless enough to enforce his movement's authority with torture and terror."[88] The insurgents formed a coalition organization, the National Liberation Front, which included noncommunists. The communists controlled the coalition, however, and the southern government applied the name Vietcong to the insurgents, a derogatory reference which implied that they were common laborers. By winter 1964–1965, the Vietcong controlled most of the inland provinces, the Mekong Delta, and large sections of the coastline in the Republic of Vietnam. Farmers in areas controlled by the Vietcong received land from evicted landlords, and the promise of ownership appealed to many farmers elsewhere.[89]

To support the insurgency, the government in Hanoi assigned thousands of workers to clear a network of trails through the mountainous and jungle terrain of Laos so soldiers and supplies could move north-south. The northern

---

87. "It's More than a Shooting War for American GIs," *U.S. News & World Report*, October 23, 1967, p. 37.

88. "Profile of the Viet Cong," *Newsweek*, April 12, 1965, p. 40.

89. For the formation of the Vietcong, see Herring, *America's Longest War*, 68; Levine, *Struggle for Southeast Asia*, 86; and Maclear, *Ten Thousand Day War*, 55–56, 172–83. For land distribution policy, see Fitzgerald, *Fire in the Lake*, 208–11; Harrison, *Widening Gulf*, 90–93; Kolko, *Anatomy of a War*, 130.

communist leadership dispatched People's Army units to the south beginning in autumn 1964. American military intervention in spring 1965 resulted in the eventual deployment of infantry regiments and then several entire divisions, and most infiltrators were northerners from summer 1965 onward. Officials in Hanoi informed China and the Soviet Union about their activities because northern Vietnam depended on each for fuel, industrial machinery, weaponry, and supplemental food, but neither the Chinese nor the Russians endorsed the insurgency.

Johnson advisors and aides, and sources in the State Department and Defense Department, told journalists about infiltration from the north, communist dominance of the insurgency, and other details that revealed northern control of operations in the Republic of Vietnam. "The Viet Cong function as part of a massive, well-oiled machine with controls that stretch northward from the smallest hamlet all the way to Hanoi," *Time* reported. Such language, of course, echoed the position of the U.S. government, which was that an external power directed the insurgency. "The National Liberation Front . . . makes every effort to avoid the appearance of Communist domination," *Newsweek* stated. But, it continued, "[f]ew Vietnamese on either side doubt that the ultimate direction of the rebellion lies with Hanoi or that its real guiding spirit is 'Uncle Ho.'" *Time* disparaged a public statement from the southern communists regarding a request for help from the north. "Squawking to North Viet Nam, the Viet Cong requested enough volunteers to 'step up the resistance of the war ten times,'" an article reported. "The request, of course, was a mere formality, since Hanoi is estimated to have 10,000 regulars in the South already."[90]

In sum, the newsmagazines reinforced the official viewpoint that the Democratic Republic of Vietnam served the interests of international communism rather than its own limited goal of national reunification. Articles inadequately explained the ideological and political factors that separated northern Vietnam from China and the Soviet Union. The supply of weaponry and general assistance from the communist superpowers was presumed to signify control over the actions of the Hanoi government, despite abundant evidence that a similar relationship between the United States and the Saigon government had not given Americans much leverage to dictate policy.

90. "The Organization Man," *Time*, August 25, 1967, pp. 22–23; "Profile of the Viet Cong," *Newsweek*, April 12, 1965, p. 41; "The Senate on Viet Nam: Anxiety & Assent," *Time*, August 13, 1965, pp. 15–16.

Southern Guerrillas, Northern Military

In the pages of the newsmagazines, American troops in Vietnam battled creatures, not humans. A sinister, subhuman enemy violated the rules of war by executing the wounded on the battlefield, mutilating the dead, and slaughtering innocent civilians. The newsmagazines described the Vietcong and People's Army with terms calculated to evoke loathing and revulsion in readers. Unlike the portrayals of American troops, which emphasized the individuality of combatants, portrayals of guerrillas attributed certain traits to all: discipline, fanaticism, ruthlessness. The newsmagazines relied on familiar images to enable readers to form pictures in their minds of the enemy. *Time* called the Viet Cong "[t]hose faceless little men in black pajamas." Rhetorical structure, framing, and inductive judgment constructed a reality for millions of Americans whose perceptions of the war were influenced by the newsmagazines.[91]

The three newsmagazines gave similar descriptions of the guerrillas. *Newsweek*, for example, published these phrases: "the Viet Cong slowly extended their tentacles into larger and larger areas of South Vietnam"; "U.S. Marines moved cautiously into a guerrilla-infested valley"; "surrounding swarms of guerrillas"; "guerrilla-infested hills"; "the subterranean network of political officers, tax collectors and intelligence gatherers which constitutes the guerrillas' shadow government."[92] *Time* typically applied terms like "Red-infested villages," "this elusively diabolical Red enemy," "Red butchery," "guerrilla-infested area," and "Red-rife Central Highlands," and wrote "in this dark, watery world, the enemy lurks like a predatory pike"; "the Reds have burrowed out a honeycomb of underground tunnels and fortifications"; "North Vietnam's 22nd Regiment slithered up the hill"; "a Communist-infested border area the size of New Jersey."[93] *U.S. News & World Report*, like *Time*,

---

91. "The Organization Man," *Time*, August 25, 1967, p. 21. Gamson, "News as Framing," examines the relationship between framing and intent. Graber, "Content and Meaning," discusses the construction of reality by journalists. Walter Lippmann explores the use of stereotypes by journalists to simplify events and issues (*Public Opinion*, 29). Pan and Kosicki, "Framing Analysis," analyze the persuasive effects of rhetorical structure. Carlin Romano explains the relationship between inductive judgments and journalistic assumptions ("The Grisly Truth about Bare Facts," 65–66).

92. *Newsweek*: "Profile of the Viet Cong," April 12, 1965, p. 41; "A New Ball Game?" May 3, 1965, p. 53; "A Marine Victory—and 'Optimism,'" August 30, 1965, p. 32; "No Victory, No Defeat," October 25, 1965, p. 36; "The Key Task" January 1, 1968, pp. 23–24.

93. *Time*: "There Is No One Else," August 6, 1965, p. 16; "Status & Strategy," August 6, 1965, pp. 28–29; "Waiting for the Bugles," October 21, 1966, p. 54; "The Bloody Hills,"

attached the Cold War designation for all communists to the Vietcong and People's Army, thus removing their national identity: "Red guerrillas," "Red-infested region," "Red troops and agents."[94]

By using provocative terminology to describe the enemy, the newsmagazines served a propaganda function rather than an informative one.[95] Their descriptions likening the guerrillas to an infestation of vermin and insects or to other creatures repeated the propaganda techniques promoted by the American government against the Japanese during World War II. Newspaper and magazine illustrations, government posters, and movie cartoons routinely depicted the Japanese as apes and rodents.[96] Based on the stereotyping of Asians long associated with American thought, caricatures of the Vietnamese enemy also contained imagery with potent symbolism. In addition, the newsmagazines and other mainstream news organizations followed the recommendation of the American military in not referring to northern Vietnamese combatants as the "People's Army." Defense Department officials believed that name lent too much stature, and that the American public would more easily understand references to the "North Vietnamese Army," or NVA.[97]

All combatants in the Vietnam War practiced cruelty and savagery. The execution of wounded on the battlefield, brutality and mistreatment of prisoners, mutilation of corpses, and infliction of civilian casualties occurred often.[98] *Newsweek, Time,* and *U.S. News & World Report* all reported such incidents committed by American troops or caused by military methods, publishing twenty-six articles on the subject from summer 1965 through winter 1972– 1973, or 4.5 percent of all articles pertaining to American military operations. The newsmagazines published fourteen articles containing information about incidents committed by the guerrillas or caused by their ter-

---

June 11, 1965, p. 34; "Bigger & Uglier," July 9, 1965, pp. 20–21; "The Guardians at the Gate," January 7, 1966, p. 20; "The Strategy & Tactics of Peace in Viet Nam," March 28, 1969, pp. 19–20.

94. *U.S. News & World Report:* "What It Would Take to Turn the Tide in Vietnam," July 12, 1965, p. 48; "Bigger War in the New Year—And No End in Sight," January 9, 1967, p. 27; "North Vietnam's Plight," December 22, 1969, p. 38.

95. Herman and Chomsky, *Manufacturing Consent,* 302–3; Van Dijk, *News as Discourse,* 11–13, 141.

96. Dower, *War without Mercy,* 9.

97. Faulkner, "Bao Chi," 149–50.

98. Spector, *After Tet,* 207–21; Stanton, *American Army,* 82–86.

rorism against civilians, representing 17.9 percent of all articles pertaining to Vietcong and People's Army military operations; another twelve articles mentioned combat incidents and terrorism by the guerrillas in an attempt to place criticism of American actions in context.

The newsmagazines and other news organizations reported atrocities committed by the guerrillas based on official reports released by the Military Assistance Command, usually accompanied by photographs. Of a terrorist bombing of a restaurant in Saigon, *Newsweek* wrote, "For the Viet Cong, this wanton murder was the triumph of the week." Combat reporting in *Newsweek* conveyed the savagery of war. "Some of the American wounded, caught by the enemy, had apparently been given the coup de grace with a bullet in the head," an article stated. Another article graphically described a grisly scene. "Both marines played dead, but when the North Vietnamese plunged a bayonet into the second marine and he groaned, the soldiers shot him through the head," *Newsweek* informed readers. The first Marine, "jabbed three times by bayonets, refused to cry out, and the North Vietnamese—now convinced that he was dead—took his watch and cigarettes and moved off."[99]

Time paid close attention to enemy conduct. "Last month three U.S. marines and eight South Vietnamese captured by the Viet Cong on a patrol 80 miles southwest of Danang were savagely executed," an article reported. "One American was shot six times in the face at close range. Another's face was hacked beyond recognition with a machete." A firefight between the First Cavalry and People's Army in a mountain valley produced this description: "After overrunning the out-gunned Americans, the North Vietnamese moved methodically across the platoon's battleground, shooting in the head any American still left alive." *Time* cited the assassination of "no fewer than 15,000 local village chiefs" and stated the Vietcong "regularly heave grenades into sidewalk cafés, detonate plastic bombs in hotels." Another article, based on a statement from the Saigon government, repeated the theme. "South of Saigon, in the Mekong Delta, the nature of the enemy was laid bare in a gruesome incident," *Time* commented. "A Vietnamese force discovered 25 prisoners of the Viet Cong, mostly civilians and three of them women, shot in their chains at Phu Lam." *U.S. News & World Report* cited the effect on

---

99. *Newsweek:* "Vietnam: The New War," July 5, 1965, p. 34; "Slaughter at Loc Ninh," November 13, 1967, p. 44; "The Roughest Yet," August 8, 1966, p. 30.

combatants of battlefield atrocities. "American troops fighting North Vietnamese regulars in the central highlands have seen their wounded comrades dragged into the brush by their captors and executed," an article stated. "Cleaning up the battlefield, they are sickened by the sight of American bodies—tied head and foot and shot through the head."[100]

Yet, despite attention to individual atrocities, *Newsweek* and *U.S. News & World Report* virtually ignored the major atrocity of the war at Hué during the Tet 1968 offensive. Vietcong cadres executed at least 2,800 residents of the former imperial city and possibly 4,700 residents, almost all of them municipal and national government officials, teachers, and anticommunist nationalists from the professional and technical occupations.[101] *Newsweek* did not publish any separate articles on the massacre, although it became known in April 1968. Instead, the magazine devoted several paragraphs to explaining the presence of execution squads in an article primarily focused on urban warfare in Hué, which raged for weeks. *Newsweek* neither specified the extent of the massacre nor clarified whether civilians had died from combat-related causes or executions.[102] *U.S. News & World Report* also paid little attention to the atrocity. Like many other journalists, James Wallace, the magazine's correspondent, generally dismissed reports about a massacre in Hué because of confusion and distrust. "It sounded like a real piece of propaganda at first," Wallace says, "one of those stories to make the communists look worse than they were. Fighting up there had been so bad it was hard to tell who'd done the killing. I didn't go to Hué for a lot of reasons, being so busy with everything else going on." *Time* published two articles on the massacre. "Since Tet, more than 1,000 bodies have been uncovered in 19 separate mass graves," the magazine reported. "Many were beheaded, some were mutilated, nearly all died with their hands tied behind their backs. Worst of all, many were buried alive in groups of 10 to 15, eyes open."[103] Peter Braestrup, in his examination of news coverage of Tet 1968, criticizes *Newsweek* and *Time*, among other major news organizations, for failing to

---

100. "The Guardians at the Gate," *Time*, January 7, 1966, p. 19; "Mass Kidnaping," *Time*, December 2, 1966, p. 37; "Rolling Thunder—And Murder in Chains," *Time*, April 15, 1966, p. 29; "Fighting Gets Tougher—So Does American GI," *U.S. News & World Report*, December 13, 1965, p. 40.

101. Braestrup, *Big Story*, 209–17; Karnow, *Vietnam*, 525.

102. "Sad, Sad Hué," *Newsweek*, April 8, 1968, pp. 48–49.

103. "Picking Up the Pieces," *Time*, February 16, 1968, pp. 32–34.

develop information about the massacre. His period of study ends on March 30, 1968, however, and does not include *Time*'s lengthy article in May examining the scope of the atrocity.[104]

Numerous newsmagazine articles indirectly paid tribute to the guerrillas, but the newsmagazines also insisted that the Vietcong and People's Army could not withstand American military power. Combat coverage routinely portrayed an enemy willing to suffer horrendous casualties while confronting American troops, and the repetitive cycles of intense combat proved difficult for the Americans. Vietcong and People's Army units broke contact on the battlefield when they accomplished their mission, then disappeared to replenish. "Resident V.C. have outsmarted Chu Lai's marines so far, and the local population of perhaps 20,000 Vietnamese is sullen and treacherous," *Time* stated. Combat coverage relating to American troops often alluded to their desperation when attacked. The newsmagazines, though, also intermittently mentioned the desperation experienced by guerrillas. "Deserters already are reporting a declining faith in ultimate Red victory, which needs bolstering by massive intervention from North Viet Nam or Red China," *Time* wrote in summer 1966. Several months later, an article pictured tension between guerrillas and the populace they depended on. "Hungry, wet and hurting, the Viet Cong have turned from wooing to coercing the local peasantry to get food, money and fresh recruits," *Time* observed. "Increasingly, interrogated defectors and prisoners assess the war as a stalemate." Another article mentioned the tension between northern and southern guerrillas. "Viet Cong fighters resent the intrusion of the Northerners, who often assume command positions despite their youth and inexperience," *Time* wrote. "Captured Communist documents tell of locals who refuse to give shelter, medical treatment and even directions to Hanoi's soldiers."[105]

Newsmagazine articles on the combat status of Vietcong units and tension with replacements from the People's Army originated from American military officers in Saigon and CIA personnel.[106] These articles accurately summarized many of the conditions affecting the guerrillas, but comments on poor morale or despair were inaccurate. Military intelligence officers had

104. "Mass Murder at Hué," *Time*, May 10, 1968, p. 37.
105. *Time:* "Status & Strategy," August 6, 1965, p. 29; "The Red Napoleon," June 17, 1966, pp. 32–36; "Why Ho Keeps Saying No," November 11, 1966, pp. 30–31; "North Viet Nam: Year of the Dog," January 26, 1970, pp. 24–25.
106. Cloud and Rauch interviews.

learned to their surprise that most Vietcong and People's Army soldiers retained their faith in ultimate victory throughout the war, except for several months after the Tet 1968 offensive when an anticipated general uprising among the southern Vietnamese failed to occur.[107]

At last, during the final phase of the war, the newsmagazines recognized the fallacy of American ideology. "The disastrous American experience in Vietnam is the product of blundering and blindness, miscalculation and insensitivity—and perhaps, too, of an entire cast of cold-war thinking," *Newsweek* wrote. *Time* listed other reasons. "The fault lay not only with the three Presidents who prosecuted the war but with the executive elites with whom they surrounded themselves," an article declared. "This 'can-do' mentality, it may be, suffused the executive thinking, the very traditional American sense that an impelling will in harness to superior technology can solve any problem. That impulse reckoned without the devastating complexities of Viet Nam, and a culture based on values few in the U.S. understood."[108]

The belated acknowledgment that American policymakers and planners had erred revealed the narrow range of news sources for the newsmagazines during most of the Vietnam War. By not expanding their network of sources to include those who criticized the misconceptions inherent in American ideology but instead relying on sources who blamed the Vietnamese ally for failure, *Newsweek, Time,* and *U.S. News & World Report* distorted the consequences of efforts to transform the culture and society of Vietnam. Their portrayals of the Vietnamese ally and enemy derived from historical stereotypes of Asians embedded in American ideology and Cold War rhetoric.

---

107. Kolko discusses Vietcong cohesion and morale (*Anatomy of a War,* 258–59); Maclear (*Ten Thousand Day War,* 185) and Spector (*After Tet,* 77–79) examine desertion rates among the communists; Tran Van Tra explains the temporary effect on morale after the offensive ("Tet: The 1968 General Offensive and General Uprising," 47–51).

108. "Judgment at Fort Benning," *Newsweek,* April 12, 1971, pp. 27–28; "U.S. after Viet Nam," *Time,* November 6, 1972, p. 22.

8

Perspectives

In the early weeks of 1967, Jason McManus and three other *Time* editors received an invitation to lunch from Hedley Donovan, the successor to Henry Luce as editor-in-chief of all publications in the Time Inc. domain. McManus, an associate editor for the Nation section, was the junior person of the group; the others were Otto Fuerbringer, managing editor; Henry Grunwald, senior editor of the Nation section; and Richard Clurman, chief of Time-Life correspondents. The invitation came soon after President Johnson announced a pause for the lunar new year's holiday in Operation Rolling Thunder, the aerial bombardment campaign against northern Vietnam. The previous year Johnson had stopped the bombing for thirty-seven days in an effort to persuade the communist government in Hanoi to agree to peace negotiations. *Time* had not approved of the lengthy halt, and signaled its displeasure with an eight-page article that led off the first edition of 1966. The article concentrated on the harm done to the war effort by the halt, which allowed the enemy to repair bridges, railroad tracks, roads, petroleum-storage depots, and warehouses. In addition, reinforcements and supplies surged from northern Vietnam. "With no U.S. planes to harass them," the article stated, "200 trucks daily—10 times the pre-pause average—moved war materiel southward."[1]

McManus remembers the lunch. "Donovan schedules a special lunch Friday, closing day. The others were invited to talk about what position we should take on the latest pause, and because I was the writer I was asked along to hear the discussion," he says. "Fuerbringer was exceedingly hawkish.

---

1. "The Guardians at the Gate," *Time,* January 7, 1966, pp. 13–21.

He hated every bombing pause that came along. I am tickled pink about this lunch because I know that this will save me a lot of trouble. I, the writer, am going to hear the senior editor, the managing editor, the editor-in-chief discuss this thoroughly, then find out what Donovan wants to do. Then I'm home free. I'm not going to have to get the word from Grunwald, who probably got a translation from Fuerbringer, about what Donovan said.

"We had two cocktails, these guys ordered steak. They gossip about whether Marilyn Monroe and Bobby Kennedy had had an affair, and all sorts of stuff. Vietnam is not mentioned. And I need to be back at my desk at my typewriter writing this friggin' story. Finally, the coffee comes. I raise my hand, but at that point Donovan pushes his chair back from the table and says, 'I don't think I really will need any coffee today. I guess we're agreed we're for this bombing pause.' And turned on his heel, and left the room.

"I guess he didn't want to give Fuerbringer a chance to argue. Also, Donovan delivered the message in front of Grunwald so Fuerbringer, who could be quite sneaky, could not mistranslate the instructions. I'm ecstatic. I went back and wrote very confidently." The *Time* article stated, "Hanoi has been given plenty of chances to talk—and has repeatedly scorned them."[2]

The lunch in January was the first step toward the transformation of *Time* from hawk at the start of the Vietnam War to dove at the end, from ardent advocate of war to vitriolic critic of renewed escalation during the final months. By summer 1967, Donovan had instructed Fuerbringer to mute the magazine's stridently supportive tone, and the editor-in-chief himself supervised the writing of articles to achieve that purpose. *Time* changed slowly, but it changed of necessity, for ideological and economic reasons. The magazine was the creation of Luce, whose anticommunism was sincere and intense. Senior editors, most associate editors, and many correspondents accepted *Time*'s political viewpoint when they went to work for it. To expect dozens of people to change their attitude quickly was unrealistic, and Donovan was a realistic person. The process of transformation progressed at dozens of lunches and editorial conferences over the next couple of years.[3]

The change in tone at *Time* carried potential economic harm. The magazine was much larger and richer than *Newsweek* and *U.S. News & World Report*. If it moved too far too fast, *Time* risked losing readers, which would

---

2. McManus interview; "Toughened Mood," *Time*, March 10, 1967, p. 21.
3. Donovan oral history, 160–66, 94–96.

endanger its advertising revenue. Indeed, although *Time* proceeded slowly to adopt a more neutral tone in war coverage, some readers noticed the difference. A pair of specially commissioned market-research studies in the early 1970s found that 39 percent of *Time*'s subscribers judged the magazine "more liberal now" than previously and 15 percent disagreed with *Time*'s viewpoint.[4]

Media Messages

Americans received most of their news about the Vietnam War from newsmagazines, newspapers, and television network programs. Each source of information contributed to public discourse on the war and influenced, to some degree, individual perceptions of the war. Somehow, though, news coverage from Vietnam blurred together in the collective consciousness, forming a memory of an amorphous media that had brought home nothing but bad news. Years after an American helicopter lifted one last person from a desperate throng awaiting evacuation on a rooftop in Saigon and a People's Army tank smashed the gate of the presidential palace there, many Americans believe that newsmagazines, newspapers, and television—especially television—played a major role in losing the war. Public memory perpetuated this myth, a circumstance partly attributable to media retrospectives that emphasized atypical examples of wartime coverage.[5] However, scholarly examinations of news programs on ABC, CBS, and NBC and of articles in certain newspapers have determined that the actual journalistic performance of the time contradicts the myth. The journalistic performance of the newsmagazines also differed markedly from the popular recollection and from television coverage. Importantly, too, each newsmagazine presented the war in a substantially different manner than its competitors, which demonstrated the effect of marketplace competition on editorial policy. "We always

---

4. Lieberman Research, "How *Time* Subscribers Feel about *Time* Magazine," February 1971, and "A Study of Consumer Attitudes toward *Time* Magazine and Other News Media," July 1973.

5. Hallin states that according to the "nation's historical memory" journalists played an instrumental role in the loss of public support for military intervention in Vietnam, and he discusses the public preoccupation with figuring out why the United States lost the war (*"Uncensored War,"* 3–4, 9). Michael Schudson discusses collective memory and the media's role in its formation (*Watergate in American Memory: How We Remember, Forget, and Reconstruct the Past,* 3–4, 64–65).

took the view that we were editing for ourselves," McManus says. "That's very arrogant. If we were good editors, the readers would feel informed and be appreciative of what we were doing. If not, we'd get fired."[6]

Newspapers, network news programs, and newsmagazines delivered information on the Vietnam War according to their particular journalistic styles. Each style had advantages and disadvantages. Newspapers provided a daily summary of military and political events, with a weekly wrap-up of important developments; while timely, these stories often lacked context. Network news programs also supplied a daily summary, usually accompanied by generic film footage of the sights and sounds of military activity; however, these segments typically valued emotional over informational content. The newsmagazines blended commentary with descriptive details, attempting to add perspective to otherwise discrete events and complex issues, and usually attached a discernible viewpoint to the information.

Previous chapters have assessed the journalistic performance of newsmagazines for accuracy, impact, and tone. Accuracy was measured by comparing newsmagazine articles with the historical record. The effort by presidents and policymakers to influence newsmagazine coverage and their response to newsmagazine articles provided evidence of impact. Tone was exhibited in the commentary that appeared in newsmagazine articles and was identified using discourse analysis, which involves classifying thematic focus and recording textual symbols.

Accuracy varied among the newsmagazines, depending on the subject. *Newsweek* provided the most accurate portrayals of the war. It recognized the ineffectiveness of Operation Rolling Thunder within a year of military intervention, devoted attention to civilian casualties caused by American firepower, and identified fundamental flaws in American military methods from early 1966 onward. *Newsweek* also correctly noted the inappropriateness of organizing ARVN on the American military model. Coverage consistently identified problems affecting the leadership of the southern army and government, which contributed to the ultimate collapse in spring 1975. Finally, *Newsweek* realized the political and social ramifications of the war on American society, presenting a picture of a broad spectrum of citizens who wondered whether their country should be fighting in Vietnam. *Time* accurately reported the complexity of military operations, explained the role of warfare

---

6. McManus interview.

technology, and described the characteristics of American combatants. The magazine offered a more balanced portrayal of the southern army, taking care to report its exemplary actions as well as its dismal ones. *Time* also presented information concerning the political and social factors in the south that adversely affected effective governance. *U.S. News & World Report* accurately depicted the factionalism within the Johnson administration and Defense Department from summer 1965 until Tet 1968. Its commentary revealed the depths of the dispute over policy and strategy. It also identified the post-Tet effect on American military morale. All three newsmagazines accurately described combat, its savagery and the tactical advantage the guerrillas usually had in the countryside. The newsmagazines also correctly represented the cohesive quality of American combatants from 1965 to 1968, and chronicled the steady deterioration of combat units from 1969 onward.

Conversely, the newsmagazines inaccurately presented several aspects of the war. From summer 1965 until spring 1971, they focused obsessively on Americans at war, relegating the southern army to a minor participant when in fact ARVN suffered serious casualties throughout the period. *Time* misled its readers for the first two years of the war by distorting the impact of American warfare technology and military methods. *Time* presented a war of steady military progress rather than a war of temporary gains, regular setbacks, and continuous uncertainty. *U.S. News & World Report* myopically perceived a war without political or social factors, instead representing military action as the sole determinant of victory. The newsmagazines did not sufficiently explore the cultural and ethnic diversity of Vietnamese society, which diminished the capability of the southern government to wage war. Neither did they fully explain the consequences to Vietnamese society of American military intervention. They also neglected to report candidly the animosity and disrespect between many American military personnel and the Vietnamese, which affected the attitude and behavior of combatants. Scholars have concluded that American commanders, planners, and policymakers were well aware of the relationship of these issues to military operations and programs in Vietnam.

The impact of the newsmagazines mostly pertained to their judgments on the overall military situation in Vietnam. Presidential advisors and assistants routinely contacted correspondents, and editors on occasion, to discuss events and trends. Commentary on military operations and methods often prompted reactions in the form of memos and rebuttals. During the latter months of

1967 a full-fledged informational campaign coordinated by the Johnson White House sought to change the viewpoints of all three newsmagazines regarding the existence of a military stalemate. The Nixon administration also attempted to manipulate newsmagazine coverage, especially during 1971 and 1972 when American strategy depended on warplanes rather than infantry. Clearly, Nixon personnel regarded the newsmagazines as somewhat influential, given their effort to publish favorable letters to the editor from college Republicans. Among the newsmagazines, *Time* received the most attention during the Johnson administration. *Time* editors and correspondents regularly visited the White House and Johnson's ranch in Texas, and copious memos, letters, and personal notes between *Time* journalists and administration aides and assistants attested to the importance the magazine had because of its presumably mainstream conservative readership and largest circulation among the three newsmagazines. *Newsweek* received special attention from presidential personnel at certain points in the war, such as when it focused on civilian casualties from American firepower and questioned the purpose of aerial bombardment in the north. The Nixon administration reacted strongly to critical commentary in *Newsweek* and *Time* during the invasion of Laos in 1971 and the resumption of full-scale aerial bombardment of the north in spring 1972. *U.S. News & World Report* never received special attention from the Johnson administration, since it obviously endorsed a hardline military approach, nor from the Nixon administration, because it endorsed Nixon's policies wholeheartedly.

The tone of newsmagazine articles emanated from descriptive details, quotations, and stance adjectives, adverbs, and verbs. The tone associated with each newsmagazine reflected its editorial emphasis, an intentional effort to foster a distinctive identity. The newsmagazines changed their perspectives on the war depending on a perceived need to meet the expectations of a readership that presumably shared a similar viewpoint. *Newsweek* adopted a mainstream liberal viewpoint, initially supporting intervention but incrementally distancing itself from national policy. The magazine was the first, in winter 1966–1967, to indicate the improbability of a military triumph; the first, in spring 1968, to recommend an end to military operations in the countryside; and the first to criticize expansion of the war into Cambodia and Laos—but it also caricatured the Vietnamese as incapable of effective governance and reluctant to assume responsibility for the war. *Time* maintained a mainstream conservative viewpoint, obligating it to endorse and support military intervention because containment of communism was a tenet of the Cold War consensus. *Time* adamantly insisted, despite evidence to the contrary, that military methods had achieved progress, a position it did not abandon until summer 1967; derisively portrayed efforts by the Vietnamese to develop an effective government; and consistently excused the death and destruction caused by American military methods by constantly comparing the devastating effects of U.S. firepower to the terrorism inflicted by guerrillas. *U.S. News & World Report* cultivated an ultraconservative readership, making it an ardent advocate for a confrontational policy. The magazine narrowly defined the war in terms of a military problem, one that only Americans could solve; steadfastly denied that American firepower caused harmful consequences; and promoted doctrinaire anticommunist ideology throughout the war.

Commentary reflected information received from the source networks selected by the newsmagazines, choices based on compatible viewpoints. *Newsweek* relied on sources in the military and Defense Department who considered large-unit warfare a mistake, believed American firepower created hostility among the Vietnamese, and argued for a program of social reform and rural security to counter the guerrillas. *Time* depended on sources in the military, Defense Department, and presidential staff who expressed faith in American warfare technology and modern weaponry, regarded southern Vietnam as an embryonic democratic-capitalist society which would develop with proper guidance, and accepted the premise that military intervention entailed a long-term commitment. *U.S. News & World Report* developed sources in the military hierarchy and among senior policymakers who recommended a regional war to shield the south from northern aggression and proposed total military control over all aspects of the war.

However, notable changes in tone occurred in *Newsweek* and *Time* during the Vietnam War. *Newsweek* asserted itself early in the war, becoming the most consistent critic and skeptic among the newsmagazines about American military methods. At least a year before television network news programs indicated that a military victory probably could not be attained in Vietnam and fifteen months before *Time* reached the same conclusion, *Newsweek* informed its readers that U.S. strategy and tactics were ineffective. Moral questions were asked early and often by *Newsweek*. Although not rejecting the Cold War consensus, which considered containment of communism essential, *Newsweek* questioned American ways of war that possibly alienated the southern Vietnamese and definitely sullied the American image in the world community. Alone among the newsmagazines during Tet 1968, *Newsweek* called for a switch in policy. *Time* transformed its tone more dramatically, though, shifting from deferential supporter of presidential decisions during most of the Johnson administration to defiant critic of presidential actions during the Nixon administration. *Time* went from refusing to acknowledge moral questions about military methods to accusing American policymakers of reprehensible conduct.

Newsmagazine coverage of the Vietnam War cannot be isolated from coverage in newspapers and on television. Therefore, the precise contribution made by newsmagazines to public discourse during the war and the exact place that newsmagazine coverage occupies in public memory remain unknown. In some important ways, newsmagazine coverage from Vietnam closely resembled newspaper and television coverage: positive portrayals of American combatants predominated; American military operations, rather than ARVN operations, received primary attention; interest waned as American troops withdrew; and military activities mattered more than political and social factors. In other important ways, newsmagazine coverage went beyond that of newspapers and television. Newsmagazine articles regularly presented millions of Americans with descriptive depictions of combat, provided judgments on military methods applied against the guerrillas, and offered evaluations of the military situation. Combat coverage by the newsmagazines permitted readers to sense the awful nature of the war, candidly conveying the ferocity of battlefield encounters and providing graphic details about death and injury to combatants. Judgments on military methods informed readers about the application of doctrine, reviewing the success or failure of tactical operations and assigning blame or credit. Evaluations of the overall military situation allowed readers to consider the prospects for progress or for a conclusion at various points in the war, broadening the appraisals from strictly military factors to include political and social considerations. With a weekly publication schedule and correspondents at bureaus in Vietnam and Washington, the newsmagazines arguably delivered a more comprehensive representation of the war than either newspapers or television. Of particular importance, commentary by the newsmagazines on the conditions, conduct, and effects of warfare in Vietnam directly communicated pertinent perspectives to readers, whose opinions about the war undoubtedly owed much to the viewpoints expressed by *Newsweek, Time,* and *U.S. News & World Report.*

Sources

Newsmagazine Editions Cited

Newsweek: **1965**—March 22, April 12, May 3, May 10, May 17, May 24, June 14, June 21, June 28, July 5, July 26, August 9, August 16, August 23, August 30, October 4, October 25, November 8, November 29, December 13, December 20; **1966**—January 31, February 14, February 21, March 14, April 11, April 18, May 23, May 30, June 27, August 1, August 8, August 22, August 29, September 12, September 19, November 28, December 5, December 19; **1967**—January 9, February 13, February 20, March 13, May 1, May 8, May 15, May 29, July 10, July 17, August 7, August 14, September 4, September 18, September 25, October 9, November 6, November 13, November 27, December 4, December 25; **1968**—January 1, February 5, February 12, February 19, February 26, March 11, March 18, March 25, April 1, April 8, May 20, May 27, July 22, October 14, October 21, December 2, December 16; **1969**—January 6, March 3, March 10, June 2, June 9, July 7, August 18, September 8, October 20, December 1, December 8; **1970**—February 2, February 9, May 4, May 11, May 18, June 29, July 13, August 17; **1971**—January 11, January 25, February 15, March 8, March 15, March 29, April 12, August 16, October 25; **1972**—January 10, April 10, May 15, May 22, June 19, August 7, August 21, October 30; **1973**—January 1, January 8.

Time: **1965**—April 23, May 14, June 11, June 25, July 9, July 16, August 6, August 13, August 20, August 27, September 3, October 1, October 22, November 5, November 19, November 26, December 3; **1966**—January 7, January 14, February 4, February 11, February 18, April 15,

April 22, May 27, June 3, June 10, June 17, July 8, August 12, August 19, September 23, October 14, October 21, November 11, November 18, December 2; **1967**—January 6, February 17, March 10, March 24, March 31, May 5, May 12, May 26, June 30, July 7, July 14, July 21, August 4, August 18, August 25, September 1, September 29, October 6, October 27, November 3, November 24, December 1, December 22; **1968**—January 5, February 9, February 16, February 23, March 1, March 22, March 29, April 5, April 19, May 10, May 31, June 7, August 9; **1969**—March 28, May 30, June 6, September 5, September 12, October 17, October 24, December 5, December 12; **1970**—January 12, January 26, February 9, March 16, May 11, May 18, July 13, December 14; **1971**—January 25, March 1, March 22, March 29, April 12, April 19, June 14, October 18, October 25; **1972**—January 10, February 7, April 17, May 8, May 15, May 22, June 5, September 11, October 23, November 6; **1973**—January 1.

U.S. News & World Report: **1965**—April 12, July 12, September 6, September 27, November 8, December 13; **1966**—February 14, February 21, February 28, April 11, June 27, July 25, August 15, August 22, October 3, October 24, November 7; **1967**—January 9, January 23, March 27, April 3, May 1, May 15, July 17, July 31, October 23, October 30, November 27, December 11; **1968**—January 1, January 8, February 12, February 19, March 4, April 1, June 24, November 25; **1969**—January 27, October 27, November 24, December 15, December 22; **1970**—January 26, April 6, May 25, November 23; **1971**—January 25, March 15, March 22, June 7, November 15.

Interviews

George E. Christian, press secretary for President Lyndon B. Johnson from December 1966 to January 1969; telephone interview, tape recording, June 23, 1999.

Stanley W. Cloud, *Time* bureau chief in Saigon from September 1971 to December 1972; telephone interview, tape recording, September 29, 1999.

William J. Cook, *Newsweek* correspondent in Vietnam from October 1965 to September 1966; e-mail responses to questions and telephone interview, tape recording, November 19, 1999.

Nicholas Horrock, *Newsweek* correspondent in Vietnam from December 1968

Sources

to August 1969 and June to December 1970; telephone interview, tape recording, November 24, 1999.

Ed Magnuson, *Time* associate editor and senior writer for the Nation section from 1961 to 1965 and 1968 to 1973; e-mail responses to questions, October 18, 22, and 25, 1999.

Jason McManus, *Time* associate editor, World editor, and Nation editor, variously, from 1965 to 1973; telephone interview, tape recording, November 27, 2000.

Burton Y. Pines, *Time* correspondent in Vietnam from December 1968 to June 1970; telephone interview, tape recording, September 27, 1999.

Rudolph Rauch III, *Time* correspondent in Vietnam from July 1971 to October 1972; telephone interview, tape recording, September 23, 1999.

George Reedy, press secretary for President Johnson from March 1964 to July 1965 and presidential assistant February 1968 to January 1969; personal interview, August 13, 1997, Milwaukee, Wisconsin.

Walt W. Rostow, national security assistant to President Lyndon B. Johnson from April 1966 to January 1969; personal interview, June 9, 1999, Austin, Texas.

James N. Wallace, *U.S. News & World Report* correspondent in Vietnam from July 1967 to May 1973; telephone interview, tape recording, November 23, 1999.

Books and Articles

Adas, Michael. *Machines as the Measure of Men: Science, Technology, and Ideologies of Western Dominance.* Ithaca, NY: Cornell University Press, 1989.

Altheide, David L. *Qualitative Media Analysis.* Thousand Oaks, CA: Sage Publications, 1996.

Anson, Robert Sam. *War News: A Young Reporter in Indochina.* New York: Simon & Schuster, 1989.

Apter, David E. *Rethinking Development: Modernization, Dependency, and Postmodern Politics.* Newbury Park, CA: Sage Publications, 1987.

Arlen, Michael J. *Living-Room War.* New York: Viking Press, 1969.

Bailey, George Arthur. "Interpretive Reporting of the Vietnam War by Anchormen." *Journalism Quarterly* 53 (Summer 1976).

———. "Television War: Trends in Network Coverage of Vietnam, 1965–1970." *Journal of Broadcasting* 20:2 (Spring 1976): 149–54.

———. "The Vietnam War According to Chet, David, Walter, Harry, Peter, Bob, Howard and Frank: A Content Analysis of Journalistic Performance by the Network Television Evening News Anchormen, 1965–1970." Ph.D. diss., University of Wisconsin–Madison, 1973.

Baskir, Lawrence M., and William A. Strauss. "The Draft and Who Escaped It." In *Light at the End of the Tunnel: A Vietnam War Anthology*, ed. Andrew J. Rotter, 459–62. New York: St. Martin's Press, 1991.

Baughman, James L. *Henry R. Luce and the Rise of the American News Media*. Boston: Twayne Publishers, 1987.

———. "The Transformation of *Time* Magazine: From Opinion Leader to Supporting Player." *Media Studies Journal* (Fall 1998): 111–18.

Bello, Walden, David Kinley, and Elaine Elinson. *Development Debacle: The World Bank in the Philippines*. San Francisco: Institute for Food and Development Policy, 1982.

Berger, Peter L., Brigitte Berger, and Hansfried Kellner. *The Homeless Mind: Modernization and Consciousness*. New York: Random House, 1973.

Berkowitz, Dan. *Social Meanings of News: A Text Reader*. Thousand Oaks, CA: Sage Publications, 1997.

Berman, Edward H. *The Influence of the Carnegie, Ford, and Rockefeller Foundations on American Foreign Policy: The Ideology of Philanthropy*. Albany: State University of New York Press, 1983.

Berman, Larry. *Lyndon Johnson's War: The Road to Stalemate in Vietnam*. New York: W. W. Norton, 1989.

Bernhard, Nancy E. "Clearer than Truth: Public Affairs Television and the State Department's Domestic Information Campaigns, 1947–1952." *Diplomatic History* 21 (Fall 1997): 545–68.

Bindas, Kenneth J. "The Strains of Commitment: American Periodical Press and South Vietnam, 1955–1960." *Journalism History* 17 (Autumn 1990–Winter 1991): 63–69.

Bird, S. Elizabeth, and Robert W. Dardenne. "Myth, Chronicle, and Story: Explaining the Narrative Qualities of News." In *Media, Myths, and Narratives: Television and the Press*, ed. James W. Carey, 70–71. Newbury Park, CA: Sage Publications, 1988.

Blair, Clay. *The Forgotten War: America in Korea, 1950–1953*. New York: Times Books, 1987.

Bradley, Mark. "An Improbable Opportunity: America and the Democratic Republic of Vietnam's 1947 Initiative." In *The Vietnam War: Vietnamese and American Perspectives,* ed. Jayne S. Werner and Luu Doan Huynh, 15–18. Armonk, NY: M. E. Sharpe, 1993.

Braestrup, Peter. *Big Story: How the American Press and Television Reported and Interpreted the Crisis of Tet 1968 in Vietnam and Washington.* 2nd ed. New Haven, CT: Yale University Press, 1983.

———, ed. *Vietnam as History: Ten Years after the Paris Peace Accords.* Washington, DC: Wilson Center, 1984.

Brasch, Walter M. *Forerunners of Revolution: Muckrakers and the American Social Conscience.* Lanham, MD: University Press of America, 1990.

Bruchey, Stuart. *Enterprise: The Dynamic Economy of a Free People.* Cambridge, MA: Harvard University Press, 1990.

Burns, Edward McNall. *The American Idea of Mission: Concepts of National Purpose and Destiny.* New Brunswick, NJ: Rutgers University Press, 1957.

Buzzanco, Robert. "The American Military's Rationale against the Vietnam War." *Political Science Quarterly* 101:4 (1986): 559–76.

———. *Masters of War: Military Dissent and Politics in the Vietnam Era.* New York: Cambridge University Press, 1996.

Carter, Roy E., Jr. "Newspaper 'Gatekeepers' and the Sources of News." *Public Opinion Quarterly* 22:2 (Summer 1958): 133–44.

Cater, Douglass. *The Fourth Branch of Government.* Boston: Houghton Mifflin, 1959.

Christian, George. *The President Steps Down: A Personal Memoir of the Transfer of Power.* New York: Macmillan, 1970.

Clarke, Jeffrey. "Civil-Military Relations in South Vietnam and the American Advisory Effect." In *The Vietnam War: Vietnamese and American Perspectives,* ed. Jayne S. Werner and Luu Doan Huynh, 188. Armonk, NY: M. E. Sharpe, 1993.

Cohen, Bernard C. *The Press and Foreign Policy.* Princeton, NJ: Princeton University Press, 1963.

Cooper, John Milton, Jr. *Walter Hines Page: The Southerner as American, 1855–1918.* Chapel Hill: University of North Carolina Press, 1977.

Czitrom, Daniel J. *Media and the American Mind: From Morse to McLuhan.* Chapel Hill: University of North Carolina Press, 1982.

DeConde, Alexander. *Ethnicity, Race, and American Foreign Policy: A History.* Boston: Northeastern University Press, 1992.

DeGroot, Gerard J. *A Noble Cause? America and the Vietnam War.* New York: Longman, 2000.

Dewey, John. *The Public and Its Problems.* New York: Henry Holt, 1927.

Dicken-Garcia, Hazel. *Journalistic Standards in Nineteenth-Century America.* Madison: University of Wisconsin Press, 1989.

Donohue, George A., Phillip J. Tichenor, Clarice N. Olien. "A Guard Dog Perspective on the Role of Media." *Journal of Communication* 45 (Spring 1995): 117–19.

Donovan, Hedley. *Right Places, Right Times.* New York: Henry Holt, 1989.

———. *Roosevelt to Reagan: A Reporter's Encounters with Nine Presidents.* New York: Harper & Row, 1985.

Dower, John W. *War without Mercy: Race and Power in the Pacific War.* New York: Pantheon Books, 1986.

Drechsel, Robert. *News Making in the Trial Courts.* New York: Longman, 1983.

Dudden, Arthur Power. *The American Pacific: From the Old China Trade to the Present.* New York: Oxford University Press, 1992.

Duiker, William. "Waging Revolutionary War: The Evolution of Hanoi's Strategy in the South, 1959–1965." In *The Vietnam War: Vietnamese and American Perspectives,* ed. Jayne S. Werner and Luu Doan Huynh, 32–35. Armonk, NY: M. E. Sharpe, 1993.

Elegant, Robert. "How to Lose a War: Reflections of a Foreign Correspondent." *Encounter,* August 1981, pp. 73–86.

Elliott, David W. P. "Hanoi's Strategy in the Second Indochina War." In *The Vietnam War: Vietnamese and American Perspectives,* ed. Jayne S. Werner and Luu Doan Huynh, 69–91. Armonk, NY: M. E. Sharpe, 1993.

Elliott, Osborn. *The World of Oz.* New York: Viking Press, 1980.

Entman, Robert M. "Framing: Toward Clarification of a Fractured Paradigm." *Journal of Communication* 43 (Autumn 1993): 52–53.

Faulkner, Francis Donald. "Bao Chi: The American News Media in Vietnam, 1960–1975." Ph.D. dissertation, University of Massachusetts, 1981.

Fifield, Russell H. *Americans in Southeast Asia: The Roots of Commitment.* New York: Thomas Y. Crowell, 1973.

Fishman, Mark. *Manufacturing the News.* Austin: University of Texas Press, 1980.

Fitzgerald, Frances. *Fire in the Lake: The Vietnamese and the Americans in Vietnam.* New York: Vintage Books, 1972.

Fitzpatrick, Ellen F., ed. *Muckraking: Three Landmark Articles.* Boston: Bedford Books, 1994.

Gallup, George H. *The Gallup Poll: Public Opinion, 1935–1971.* New York: Random House, 1972.

Gamson, William A. "News as Framing." *American Behavioral Scientist* 33 (November–December 1989): 157–58.

Gans, Herbert J. *Deciding What's News: A Study of CBS Evening News, NBC Nightly News, Newsweek and Time.* New York: Vintage Books, 1980.

Gardner, Lloyd C. *Pay Any Price: Lyndon Johnson and the Wars for Vietnam.* Chicago: Ivan R. Dee, 1995.

Gitlin, Todd. *The Whole World Is Watching: Mass Media in the Making and Unmaking of the New Left.* Berkeley and Los Angeles: University of California Press, 1980.

Gottschalk, Jack A. "Consistent with Security: A History of American Military Press Censorship." *Communication and Law* 5 (Summer 1983): 35–52.

Graber, Doris A. "Content and Meaning: What's It All About?" *American Behavioral Scientist* 33 (November–December 1989): 144–60.

Graham, Katherine. *Personal History.* New York: Alfred A. Knopf, 1997.

Greene, Theodore P. *America's Heroes: The Changing Models of Success in American Magazines.* New York: Oxford University Press, 1970.

Grunwald, Henry. *One Man's America: A Journalist's Search for the Heart of His Country.* New York: Doubleday, 1997.

Hallin, Daniel C. "Cartography, Community, and the Cold War." In *Reading the News,* ed. Robert Karl Manoff and Michael Schudson. New York: Pantheon Books, 1986.

———. *The "Uncensored War": The Media and Vietnam.* Berkeley and Los Angeles: University of California Press, 1989.

Hammond, William M. *The Military and the Media, 1962–1968: The U.S. Army in Vietnam.* Washington, DC: Center of Military History, 1988.

———. *The Military and the Media, 1968–1973: The U.S. Army in Vietnam.* Washington, DC: Center of Military History, 1996.

———. *Reporting Vietnam: Media and Military at War.* Lawrence: University Press of Kansas, 1998.

Harrison, James P. "History's Heaviest Bombing." In *The Vietnam War: Vietnamese and American Perspectives,* ed. Jayne S. Werner and Luu Doan Huynh, 130–34. Armonk, NY: M. E. Sharpe, 1993.

Harrison, Selig S. *The Widening Gulf: Asian Nationalism and American Policy.* New York: Free Press, 1978.

Herman, Edward S., and Noam Chomsky. *Manufacturing Consent: The Political Economy of the Mass Media.* New York: Pantheon Books, 1988.

Herr, Michael. *Dispatches.* New York: Avon Books, 1977.

Herring, George C. *America's Longest War: The United States and Vietnam, 1950–1975.* 2nd ed. Philadelphia: Temple University Press, 1979.

———. *LBJ and Vietnam: A Different Kind of War.* Austin: University of Texas Press, 1994.

Herz, Martin F. *The Prestige Press and the Christmas Bombing, 1972: Images and Reality in Vietnam.* Washington, DC: Ethics and Public Policy Center, 1980.

———. *The Vietnam War in Retrospect.* Washington, DC: Georgetown University Press, 1984.

Hess, Gary R. *The United States' Emergence as a Southeast Asian Power, 1940–1950.* New York: Columbia University Press, 1987.

Hess, Stephen. *The Washington Reporters.* Washington, DC: Brookings Institution, 1981.

Higgs, Robert. *The Transformation of the American Economy, 1865–1914: An Essay in Interpretation.* New York: John Wiley & Sons, 1971.

Hilderbrand, Robert C. *Power and the People: Executive Management of Public Opinion in Foreign Affairs, 1897–1921.* Chapel Hill: University of North Carolina Press, 1981.

Hofstadter, Richard. *The Age of Reform.* New York: Vintage Books, 1955.

Hohenberg, John. *Between Two Worlds: Policy, Press, and Public Opinion in Asian-American Relations.* New York: Praeger, 1967.

Hunt, Michael H. *Ideology and U.S. Foreign Policy.* New Haven, CT: Yale University Press, 1983.

———. *Lyndon Johnson's War: America's Cold War Crusade in Vietnam, 1945–1968.* New York: Hill & Wang, 1996.

Isaacs, Norman. "The New Credibility Gap—Readers vs. the Press." *Bulletin of the American Society of Newspaper Editors,* February 1969.

John, Arthur. *The Best Years of the* Century: *Richard Watson Gilder,* Scribner's Monthly *and the* Century Magazine, *1870–1909.* Urbana: University of Illinois Press, 1981.

Joseph, Paul. "Direct and Indirect Effects of the Movement against the Vietnam War." In *The Vietnam War: Vietnamese and American Perspectives,* ed. Jayne S. Werner and Luu Doan Huynh, 170–71. Armonk, NY: M. E. Sharpe, 1993.

Kaestle, Carl F., Helen Damon-Moore, Lawrence C. Stedman, Katherine Tinsley, and William Vance Trollinger, Jr. *Literacy in the United States: Readers and Reading since 1880.* New Haven, CT: Yale University Press, 1991.

Kahin, George McT. *Intervention: How America Became Involved in Vietnam.* New York: Alfred A. Knopf, 1986.

Kaiser, David. *American Tragedy: Kennedy, Johnson, and the Origins of the Vietnam War.* Cambridge, MA: Harvard University Press, 2000.

Karnow, Stanley. *Vietnam: A History.* New York: Penguin Books, 1986.

Katz, Andrew Z. "Public Opinion and Foreign Policy: The Nixon Administration and the Pursuit of Peace." *Presidential Studies Quarterly* 27 (Summer 1997): 496–513.

Kenny, Henry J. *The American Role in Vietnam and East Asia: Between Two Revolutions.* New York: Praeger, 1984.

Kern, Montague, Patricia W. Levering, and Ralph B. Levering. *The Kennedy Crises: The Press, the Presidency, and Foreign Policy.* Chapel Hill: University of North Carolina Press, 1983.

Kernan, Ben. "The Impact on Cambodia of the U.S. Intervention in Vietnam." In *The Vietnam War: Vietnamese and American Perspectives,* ed. Jayne S. Werner and Luu Doan Huynh. Armonk, NY: M. E. Sharpe, 1993.

Kielbowicz, Richard B. "Postal Subsidies for the Press and the Business of Mass Culture, 1880–1920." In *Encyclopedia of American Economic History: Studies of the Principal Movements and Ideas,* ed. Glenn Porter. New York: Scribner, 1980.

Kimball, Jeffrey. *Nixon's Vietnam War.* Lawrence: University Press of Kansas, 1998.

Kinnard, Douglas. *The War Managers.* Hanover, NH: University Press of New England, 1977.

Kissinger, Henry. "In Defense of the Nixon Policy." In *Light at the End of the Tunnel: A Vietnam War Anthology,* ed. Andrew J. Rotter, 221–27. New York: St. Martin's Press, 1991.

Knightley, Phillip. *The First Casualty: From the Crimea to Vietnam, the War Correspondent as Hero, Propagandist, and Myth Maker.* New York: Harcourt Brace Jovanovich, 1975.

Kolko, Gabriel. *Anatomy of a War: Vietnam, the United States, and the Modern Historical Experience.* New York: Pantheon Books, 1985.

Krause, Lawrence B. *U.S. Economic Policy toward the Association of Southeast Asian Nations: Meeting the Japanese Challenge.* Washington, DC: Brookings Institution, 1982.

Krepinevich, Andrew F., Jr. *The Army and Vietnam.* Baltimore: Johns Hopkins University Press, 1986.

LaFeber, Walter. *The New Empire: An Interpretation of American Expansion, 1860–1898.* Ithaca, NY: Cornell University Press, 1963.

Lampard, Eric E. "Urbanization." In *Encyclopedia of American Economic History: Studies of the Principal Movements and Ideas,* ed. Glenn Porter. New York: Scribner, 1980.

Levine, Allen J. *The United States and the Struggle for Southeast Asia, 1945–1975.* New York: Praeger, 1995.

Lewy, Guenter. "The Question of American War Guilt." In *Light at the End of the Tunnel: A Vietnam War Anthology,* ed. Andrew J. Rotter, 357–71. New York: St. Martin's Press, 1991.

Lichty, Lawrence W. "Comments on the Influence of Television on Public Opinion." In *Vietnam as History: Ten Years After the Paris Peace Accords,* ed. Peter Braestrup, 158–59. Washington, DC: Wilson Center, 1984.

——— and Malachi C. Topping, eds. *American Broadcasting: A Source Book on the History of Radio and Television.* New York: Hastings House, 1975.

Lipari, Lisbeth. "Journalistic Authority: Textual Strategies of Legitimation." *Journalism and Mass Communication Quarterly* 73 (Winter 1996): 821–34.

Lippmann, Walter. *Public Opinion.* New York: Harcourt, Brace & Company, 1922.

Luke, Timothy W. *Social Theory and Modernity.* Newbury Park, CA: Sage Publications, 1990.

MacDonald, J. Fred. *Don't Touch that Dial!: Radio Programming in American Life, 1920–1960.* Chicago: Nelson-Hall, 1979.

Maclear, Michael. *The Ten Thousand Day War: Vietnam, 1945–1975.* New York: St. Martin's Press, 1981.

Mandelbaum, Michael. "Vietnam: The Television War." *Daedalus* 3 (Fall 1982): 159–63.

Margo, Robert. "The Labor Market in the Nineteenth Century." National Bureau of Economic Research, *Working Paper Series* 40, August 1992.

McCormick, Thomas J. *America's Half-Century: United States Foreign Policy in the Cold War.* Baltimore: Johns Hopkins University Press, 1989.

———. *China Market: America's Quest for Informal Empire, 1893–1901.* Chicago: Elephant Paperbacks, 1990.

McLeod, Douglas M., and J. K. Hertog. "The Manufacture of Public Opinion by Reporters: Informal Cues for Public Perceptions." *Discourse and Society* 3 (1992): 259–75.

McNeill, William Hardy. *The Pursuit of Power: Technology, Armed Force, and Society since A.D. 1000.* Chicago: University of Chicago Press, 1982.

Merk, Frederick. *Manifest Destiny and Mission in American History: A Reinterpretation.* Westport, CT: Greenwood Press, 1983.

Moeller, Susan D. *Shooting War: Photography and the American Experience of Combat.* New York: Basic Books, 1989.

Mohr, Charles. "Once Again—Did the Press Lose Vietnam?" *Columbia Journalism Review,* November–December 1983, pp. 55–56.

Mott, Frank Luther. *Sketches of Magazines, 1885–1905.* Vol. 4, *A History of American Magazines.* Cambridge, MA: Harvard University Press, 1957.

———. *Sketches of Magazines, 1905–1930.* Vol. 5, *A History of American Magazines.* Cambridge, MA: Harvard University Press, 1968.

Mueller, John E. *War, Presidents and Public Opinion.* New York: John Wiley & Sons, 1973.

Mumford, Lewis. *The Myth of the Machine.* New York: Harcourt, Brace & World, 1967.

Nourie, Alan, and Barbara Nourie. *American Mass-Market Magazines.* New York: Greenwood Press, 1990.

Pach, Chester J., Jr. "The Vietnam War on the Network Nightly News." In *The Sixties: From Memory to History,* ed. David Farber, 90–112. Chapel Hill: University of North Carolina Press, 1994.

Page, Benjamin I., and Robert Y. Shapiro. *The Rational Public: Fifty Years of Trends in Americans' Policy Preferences.* Chicago: University of Chicago Press, 1992.

Pan, Zhongdang, and Gerald M. Kosicki. "Framing Analysis: An Approach to News Discourse." *Political Communication* 10 (1993): 55–65.

Park, Robert E. "News as a Form of Knowledge." In *On Social Control and Collective Behavior: Selected Papers,* ed. Ralph H. Turner. Chicago: University of Chicago Press, 1967.

Patterson, Oscar, III. "An Analysis of Television Coverage of the Vietnam War." *Journal of Broadcasting* 28 (Fall 1984), 401–403.

———. "Television's Living Room War in Print: Vietnam in the News Magazines." *Journalism Quarterly* 61 (Spring 1984): 35–39.

Peck, James. "The Roots of Rhetoric: The Professional Ideology of America's China Watchers." In *America's Asia: Dissenting Essays on Asian-American*

Relations, ed. Edward Friedman and Mark Selden, 50. New York: Pantheon Books, 1971.

The Pentagon Papers: The Defense Department History of United States Decision-making on Vietnam. 5 vols. Senator Gravel edition. Boston: Beacon Press, 1971–1972.

Peterson, Theodore. *Magazines in the Twentieth Century.* Urbana: University of Illinois Press, 1964.

Prochnau, William. *Once upon a Distant War.* New York: Times Books, 1995.

Robinson, John P. "The Audience for National TV News Programs." *Public Opinion Quarterly* 35 (1971): 403–5.

———. "World Affairs Information and Mass Media Exposure." *Journalism Quarterly* 44 (Winter 1966): 217–22.

Roeder, George H., Jr. *The Censored War: American Visual Experience during World War Two.* New Haven, CT: Yale University Press, 1993.

Romano, Carlin. "The Grisly Truth about Bare Facts." In *Reading the News,* ed. Robert Karl Manoff and Michael Schudson. New York: Pantheon Books, 1986.

Rosenberg, Emily S. *Spreading the American Dream: American Economic and Cultural Expansion, 1890–1945.* New York: Hill & Wang, 1982.

Safer, Morley. *Flashbacks: On Returning to Vietnam.* New York: Random House, 1990.

Said, Edward W. *Culture and Imperialism.* New York: Alfred A. Knopf, 1993.

Schiller, Herbert I. *The Mind Managers.* Boston: Beacon Press, 1973.

Schneirov, Matthew. *The Dream of a New Social Order: Popular Magazines in America, 1893–1914.* New York: Columbia University Press, 1994.

Schudson, Michael. *Discovering the News: A Social History of American Newspapers.* New York: Basic Books, 1978.

———. "The Sociology of News Production." In *Social Meanings of News: A Text-Reader,* ed. Dan Berkowitz, 7–21. Thousand Oaks, CA: Sage Publications, 1997.

———. *Watergate in American Memory: How We Remember, Forget, and Reconstruct the Past.* New York: Basic Books, 1992.

Schulzinger, Robert D. *A Time for War: The United States and Vietnam, 1941–1975.* New York: Oxford University Press, 1997.

Selden, Mark. "Okinawa and American Security Imperialism." In *Remaking Asia: Essays on the American Uses of Power,* ed. Mark Selden, 280. New York: Pantheon Books, 1974.

———. "People's War and the Transformation of Peasant Society: China and Vietnam." In *America's Asia: Dissenting Essays on Asian-American Relations,* ed. Edward Friedman and Mark Selden, 372–73. New York: Pantheon Books, 1971.

Shawcross, William. "The Secret Bombing of Cambodia." In *Light at the End of the Tunnel: A Vietnam War Anthology,* ed. Andrew J. Rotter, 212–17. New York: St. Martin's Press, 1991.

Shoemaker, Pamela J., and Stephen D. Reese. *Mediating the Message: Theories of Influence on Mass Media Content.* New York: Longman, 1991.

Sigal, Leon V. *Reporters and Officials: The Organization and Politics of Newsmaking.* Lexington, MA: D. C. Heath, 1973.

———. "Sources Make the News." In *Reading the News,* ed. Robert Karl Manoff and Michael Schudson, 29. New York: Pantheon Books, 1986.

Sigler, David Burns. *Vietnam Battle Chronology: U.S. Army and Marine Corps Combat Operations, 1965–1973.* Jefferson, NC: McFarland, 1992.

Small, Melvin. *Covering Dissent: The Media and the Anti–Vietnam War Movement.* New Brunswick, NJ: Rutgers University Press, 1994.

———. *Johnson, Nixon, and the Doves.* New Brunswick, NJ: Rutgers University Press, 1988.

So, Alvin Y. *Social Change and Development: Modernization, Dependency, and World-System Theories.* Newbury Park, CA: Sage Publications, 1990.

Soloski, John. "News Reporting and Professionalism: Some Constraints on the Reporting of the News." *Media, Culture and Society* 11 (1989): 207–28.

Spector, Ronald H. *After Tet: The Bloodiest Year in Vietnam.* Toronto: Free Press, 1993.

———. "Perception and Reality in America's Military Performance in Vietnam, 1965–1970." In *The Vietnam War: Vietnamese and American Perspectives,* ed. Jayne S. Werner and Luu Doan Huynh, 154–62. Armonk, NY: M. E. Sharpe, 1993.

Stanton, Shelby L. *The Rise and Fall of an American Army: U.S. Ground Forces in Vietnam, 1965–1973.* Novato, CA: Presidio Press, 1985.

Stocking, S. Holly, and Paget H. Gross. *How Do Journalists Think? A Proposal for the Study of Cognitive Bias in Newsmaking.* Bloomington, IN: ERIC Clearinghouse on Reading and Communication Skills, 1989.

Swanberg, W. A. *Luce and His Empire.* New York: Charles Scribner's Sons, 1972.

Tebbel, John. *The American Magazine: A Compact History.* New York: Hawthorn Books, 1969.

——— and Mary Ellen Zuckerman. *The Magazine in America, 1741–1990.* New York: Oxford University Press, 1991.

Tedlow, Richard S. "Advertising and Public Relations." In *Encyclopedia of American Economic History: Studies of the Principal Movements and Ideas,* ed. Glenn Porter. New York: Scribner, 1980.

Thompson, Kenneth W., ed. *The Johnson Presidency.* Vol. 5, *Portraits of American Presidents.* Lanham, MD: University Press of America, 1986.

Tobin, James. *Ernie Pyle's War: America's Eyewitness to World War II.* New York: Free Press, 1997.

Tra, Tran Van. "Tet: The 1968 General Offensive and General Uprising." In *The Vietnam War: Vietnamese and American Perspectives,* ed. Jayne S. Werner and Luu Doan Huynh. Armonk, NY: M. E. Sharpe, 1993.

Trachtenberg, Alan. *The Incorporation of America: Culture and Society in the Gilded Age.* New York: Hill & Wang, 1982.

Tuchman, Gaye. *Making News: A Study in the Construction of Reality.* New York: Free Press, 1978.

Turner, Kathleen J. *Lyndon Johnson's Dual War: Vietnam and the Press.* Chicago: University of Chicago Press, 1985.

United States Bureau of the Census. *Occupational Trends in the United States, 1900–1950.* Washington, DC.

United States Department of Defense. *Combat Casualty Reports, Vietnamese Conflict, 1961–1975.* Washington, DC.

United States Senate Committee on Governmental Affairs. *Pentagon Rules on Media Access to the Persian Gulf War.* Washington, DC: U.S. Government Printing Office, 1991.

Van Dijk, Teun A. *News as Discourse.* Hillsdale, NJ: Lawrence Erlbaum Associates, 1988.

van Zuilen, A. J. *The Life Cycle of Magazines: A Historical Study of the Decline and Fall of the General Interest Mass Audience Magazine in the United States during the Period 1946–1972.* Uithoorn, Netherlands: Graduate Press, 1977.

Vatter, Harold G. *The Drive to Industrial Maturity: The U.S. Economy, 1860–1914.* Westport, CT: Greenwood Press, 1975.

Watts, William. *The United States and Asia: Changing Attitudes and Policies.* Lexington, MA: Lexington Books, 1982.

Weaver, David H., and G. Cleveland Wilhoit. *The American Journalist in the 1990s: U.S. News People at the End of an Era.* Mahwah, NJ: Lawrence Erlbaum Associates, 1996.

Weiss, Carol H. "What America's Leaders Read." *Public Opinion Quarterly* 38 (Spring 1974): 1–23.

Westmoreland, William C. *Report on the War in Vietnam.* Washington, DC: U.S. Government Printing Office, 1969.

———. *A Soldier Reports.* Garden City, NY: Doubleday, 1976.

Willenson, Kim. *The Bad War: An Oral History of the Vietnam War.* New York: New American Library, 1987.

Williams, William Appleman. *The Tragedy of American Diplomacy.* Cleveland, OH: World Publishing, 1959.

Wilson, Christopher. "The Rhetoric of Consumption: Mass-Market Magazines and the Demise of the Gentle Reader, 1880–1920." In *The Culture of Consumption: Critical Essays in American History, 1880–1920,* ed. Richard Wightman Fox and T. J. Jackson Lears. New York: Pantheon, 1983.

Wilson, Harold S. McClure's Magazine *and the Muckrakers.* Princeton, NJ: Princeton University Press, 1970.

Wood, James Playsted. *Magazines in the United States.* New York: Ronald Press, 1956.

Wyatt, Clarence R. "At the Cannon's Mouth: The American Press and the Vietnam War." *Journalism History* 13 (Autumn–Winter 1986): 106–8.

———. *Paper Soldiers: The American Press and the Vietnam War.* New York: W. W. Norton, 1993.

Index

Abrams, Creighton W., 97, 145–47, 193
Aerial bombardment, 129–30; and B-52s, 133; "Christmas" bombing of Hanoi, 131–32; *Time*'s transformation to critic of, 130–31. *See also* Operation Rolling Thunder
Agnew, Spiro T.: on bias in news media, 219
Anson, Robert Sam: on composite sources in *Time* articles, 62–63
Antiwar activists and demonstrators: college teach-ins, 204–5; congressional opponents of war, 204, 211–15; draft evaders and resisters, 209–11; Kent State tragedy and aftermath, 221–22; Moratorium Day, 219–21; newsmagazine portrayals of, 204, 206–9
Ap Bia, Battle of. *See* "Hamburger Hill"
Army of Republic of Vietnam (ARVN), 42, 196–98, 245–49, 252–53; "Vietnamization" of, 50–52, 250–52

Bunker, Ellsworth, 235

Censorship, absence of, 90–92
China, People's Republic of: involvement in Vietnam, 254–55, 261–62, 264; LBJ's concern about, 169
Christian, George E.: on LBJ and the news media, 67, 200–201; on newsmagazines, 201, 206
Civilian casualties, 121, 124, 133–38; and communist terrorism in *Time*, 129, 136; and "moral problems" in *Newsweek*, 135
Cloud, Stanley W.: on reporting process, 59, 60; on role of correspondents, 66; as *Time*'s Saigon bureau chief, 50, 60; Vietnam coverage for *Time*, 111, 235–36, 246; Vietnamization article, 50–52
Clurman, Richard: and Mohr-Fuerbringer dispute, 44–45
Cold War consensus: anticommunist ideology, 18–19; breakup of, 199–200, 217; news media acceptance of, 20
Combat, 76, 82, 87–89, 90, 92–94; results, analysis of, 100–101; sense of purposelessness in coverage of, 101
Cook, William J.: on reporting process, 58, 61–62, 75; on Saigon press corps, 66; Vietnam coverage for *Newsweek*, 78, 82–83, 85–86, 153–54, 161
"Crisis" journalism from Vietnam, 40–41

Diem, Ngo Dinh, 40; news media portrayals of, 41; 1963 greetings to Luce, 45; *Time*'s support of, 41
"Domino theory," 39, 255–56
Donovan, Hedley: change in attitude on Vietnam War, 216, 218; "cheerleader tone" memo, 179–80; discussion of bombing halt, 271–72; doubts about aerial bombardment, 130–31; *Life* editorial on bombing halt, 216; and shift in

Time's attitude on war, 180–81, 215–16; trip to Vietnam, 69

Elliott, Osborn: and newsroom tensions over war, 58, 220; on the situation in Vietnam, 163, 194

Fuerbringer, Otto, 168, 261; dispute with *Time* correspondent Mohr, 43–45; as election observer in Vietnam, 239; management style of, at *Time,* 59–60; meetings with LBJ, 69, 239; told to modify support for war, 179–80
Fulbright, J. William, 212–14

Graham, Katherine, 251
Grunwald, Henry A., 179; management style of, at *Time,* 59–60
Gulf of Tonkin incident, 46–47; *Time* cover story on, 47

Hadden, Briton: co-founding of *Time,* 33; death of, 34
Haldeman, H. R., 221
"Hamburger Hill," 101–3
Herr, Michael, 111
Ho Chi Minh. *See* Minh, Ho Chi
Horrock, Nicholas: reaction to antiwar activity by *Newsweek* staff, 220; on reporting process, 58–60, 62, 65; Vietnam coverage for *Newsweek,* 74, 76, 86, 111–13, 137, 194, 235–36, 244

Johnson, Lyndon B.: approval of Donovan trip to Vietnam, 69; attention to newsmagazines, 15–16; attention to news reports, 67; efforts to influence news media, 69–70, 159–60, 201; meetings with correspondents and editors, 68–69, 178, 189–90, 200–201; monitoring contacts of White House personnel with journalists, 67–68; on news media influence, 201; reaction to *Life* editorial on bombing halt, 215–16; responses by aides to newsmagazine articles, 190–91. *See also* "Propaganda"/public-relations campaign of President Johnson

Journalists in Vietnam: accreditation and privileges of, 84–85; relationship with military, 85

Kennedy, Robert F., 214–15
Korean War: censorship policy, 91; comparisons to Vietnam War, 169–71, 176–77. *See also* "Stalemate" theme
Ky, Nguyen Cao, 235, 238–39, 241

Luce, Henry R.: anticommunist attitude of, 20; co-founding of *Time,* 33–34; editorial philosophy of, 35–36; lifelong interest in China, 34; support for Vietnam War, 34

Magazines: modern, development of, 25–31; origins of news commentary, 31–33; readership demographics, 37
Magnuson, Ed: on authority of editors, 60, 168; on editing and writing procedures at *Time,* 53, 59, 70; Gulf of Tonkin cover story, 47; Saigon press corps article, 44
McManus, Jason: on editing and reporting process at *Time,* 55–56, 60–61, 70–71; at luncheon with Donovan to discuss support for bombing pause, 271–72; on *Time*'s transformation concerning the war, 180
McNamara, Robert S., 118, 164–65, 181; on Operation Rolling Thunder, 128
Minh, Ho Chi, 256–57, 258–61, 264
Modernity theory (modernization), 22–24, 225
Mohr, Charles: dispute with *Time* editors, 43–45; resignation from *Time,* 45
My Lai massacre, 106–7

Newsmagazine correspondents: competition among, 86; procedures and routines, 52–54, 57–58, 60, 63–65; relationships with military in Vietnam, 64, 85–86; relationships with peers in Vietnam, 65–66; role of, 66; status of, 16, 86–87; traveling in Vietnam, 83–85
Newsmagazines: appeal of news analysis, 229–30; categories of articles on Vietnam

War, 76, 82, 227, 266; comparison with newspapers, 2; competition among, 6–8, 10, 36–37, 72–73, 218–19, 272–73; competition with television, 75–76; correspondents in Vietnam, 76–77; "directed synthesis" process, 53; distribution patterns, 17; editing and reporting process, 52–53, 55–60, 70–72; frequency of articles on Vietnam War, 77–78, 100–101; importance of international news, 229–30; journalistic style, 10–12, 25, 35, 61–62; length of Vietnam War articles, 56–57; origins of news commentary, 31–33; readership demographics, 15; role in American news media, 2–3, 5, 10; status of, 16–17; unidentified and anonymous sources, 61–63

Newsweek: antiwar activity by news personnel, 220; circulation during Vietnam War, 12–13; on civilian casualties and "moral problems," 135; cover stories on Vietnam War, 9; descriptions of enemy, 265; founding of, 34; "Last Chance" essay furor, 242–43; "More of the Same Won't Do" essay, 192, 217; news-content categories, 14; news-to-advertising ratio, 13; perspective on war, 8–9; political viewpoint, 6–7; purchase by *Washington Post,* 36; "Their Lions—Our Rabbits" furor, 250–51; war coverage assessed, 48–49, 274–78

Ngo Dinh Diem. *See* Diem, Ngo Dinh
Nguyen Cao Ky. *See* Ky, Nguyen Cao
Nguyen Van Thieu. *See* Thieu, Nguyen Van
Nixon, Richard M.: attention to newsmagazines, 16; attention to news reports, 67; criticisms of, 221–23; criticized for resuming aerial bombardment, 131; efforts to influence newsmagazines, 69, 200–201

Operation Maximum Candor, 46
Operation Rolling Thunder, 122–26, 129; doubts about effectiveness of, 127

People's Army. *See* Vietcong and People's Army

Pines, Burton Y.: reporting process, 60, 63, 65; on Saigon press corps, 66; Vietnam coverage for *Time,* 85–86, 101, 161

"Propaganda"/public-relations campaign of President Johnson: backlash from, 188–89; creation of, 159, 181–82; details of, 183–84, 200; effects of, 184–86

Rauch, Rudolph, III: reporting process, 59, 63, 75; on role of correspondents, 66; Vietnam coverage for *Time,* 82–83, 234, 237, 240, 246, 252–53

Reedy, George, 17; on LBJ and news media, 67; on LBJ's reaction to news reports, 189, 201

Rostow, Walt W., 23, 169, 251, 255; on newsmagazines, 67, 159; on news media, 182, 189; on Operation Rolling Thunder, 127; and "propaganda" campaign, 159, 178, 181–83, 200; "propaganda" campaign effects, 182–83; on public opinion, 217; rebuttal of *U.S. News & World Report* article, 190–91; on Saigon press corps, 66; on "stalemate" theme, 177–78, 181; withholding CIA report, 184

Salisbury, Harrison, 128–29
Schell, Jonathan: "Village of Ben Suc" article in *New Yorker,* 135
Soviet Union: involvement in Vietnam, 251, 261–62, 264; LBJ's concern about, 169
"Stalemate" theme, 159, 176–77, 179–82; in *New York Times,* 177

Television news: characteristics of war reporting, 3; and myths about Vietnam coverage, 1–2
Tet offensive, 186, 187–88, 191–92; Johnson administration responses to, 189–91
Thieu, Nguyen Van, 235, 239
Time: on African American soldiers, 95–96; anticommunist attitude of, 20; circulation during Vietnam War, 12–13; "comments-and-corrections" review, 59–60;

cover stories on Vietnam War, 9; descriptions of enemy, 265; founding of, 33–34; on globalism, 21; Gulf of Tonkin cover story, 47; journalistic style criticized, 11, 35–36; Mohr-Fuerbringer dispute, 43–45; news-content categories, 14; news-to-advertising ratio, 14; perception of bias among readers, 12; perspective on war, 8–9, 216–18; political viewpoint of, 6–8; Republican Party alignment, 8; "right war, right time" essay, 6; on Saigon press corps, 44–45; transformation to critic of war, 129–31, 136, 222–23; Vietcong spy in Saigon bureau, 257–58; war coverage assessed, 48–49, 274–78

U.S. government policy on Vietnam, 37–42; aid to Vietnam, 233–34; efforts to influence news coverage, 46; military intervention, 47; nation-building, 232–33

U.S. military and news media, relationship of, 42–43, 46, 85–86, 90–91

U.S. military personnel: attitude toward and relationship with Vietnamese, 103–5; combat heroism and valor, 78–81, 87, 94–95, 99; commanders and officers, 97–98; discipline problems, 108–10, 111, 112, 113–14; drug abuse, 110, 111, 112–13; misconduct, 98–99, 105–6; morale problems, 107–11; professionalism of, 97–98; racial and ethnic identities, 94–96; racial tension, 110, 111, 112, 114–15

U.S. military strategy and tactics: confidence in, 162, 166–67, 171; criticism and skepticism of, 120–21, 138–43, 145–46, 158–59, 162, 171–74; defoliants, 152–54; devices and weaponry, 151–52; factional disputes, 118–19, 128, 139–40, 164–66; firepower effects, 120, 132, 134; "free-fire" zones and resettlement, 134–35; helicopters, 147–51; progress assessments, 166–74; technology, 120, 154

U.S. News & World Report: circulation during Vietnam War, 13; descriptions of enemy, 265–66; founding of, 34–35; merger of *U.S. News* and *World Report,* 35; news categories, 14; news-to-advertising ratio, 14; perspective on war, 8–9; political viewpoint, 6–7; post-Tet article on failure of strategy, 190–91; war coverage assessed, 48–49, 274–78

Vietcong and People's Army, 258, 263–64, 266–69; Hué massacre, 268–69; newsmagazine descriptions of, 265–66

Vietnam, Democratic Republic of (northern Vietnam): government, 261–62, 264; society, 258–59

Vietnam, Republic of (southern Vietnam): Buddhist rebellions, 241–42; government, 235, 237–38; modernization effort, 225; nation-building, 23; society, 225, 230, 234–35, 238, 239–41, 244; "Their Lions—Our Rabbits" furor, 250–51. *See also* Army of Republic of Vietnam (ARVN)

Wallace, James N.: reporting process, 60; Vietnam coverage for *U.S. News & World Report,* 82–83, 137, 144, 161, 235, 236, 268

Westmoreland, William C., 79, 96–97, 144–46, 247; as *Time* Man of the Year, 97

Zorthian, Barry, 46, 62